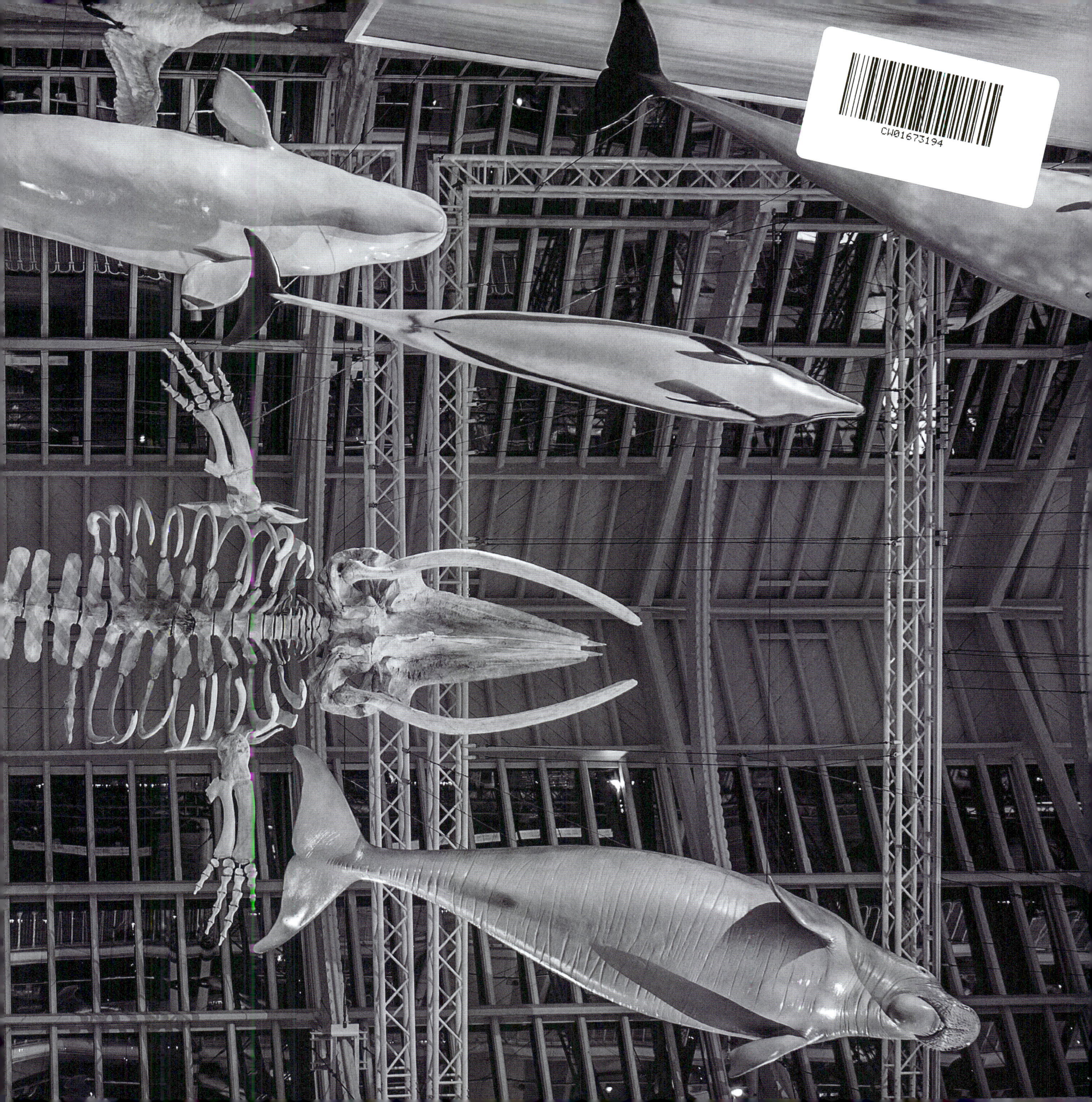

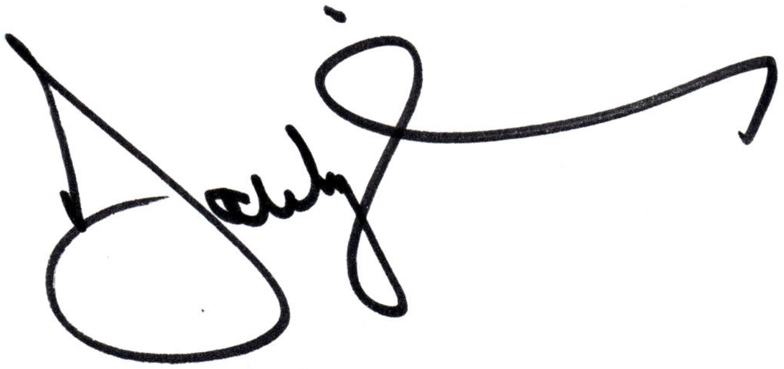

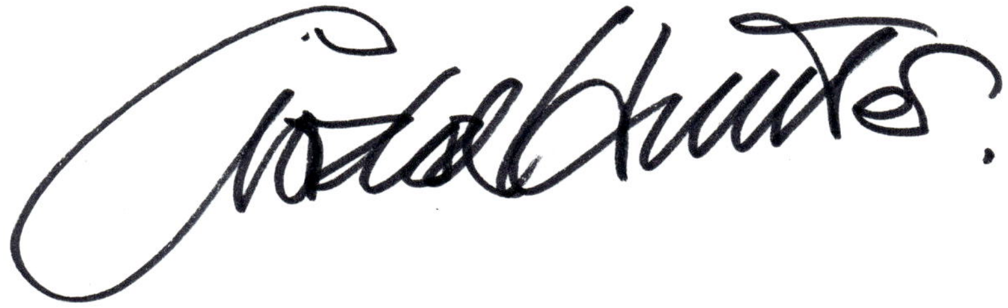

EDINBURGH REVISITED

GORDON HUNTER & DON LEDINGHAM

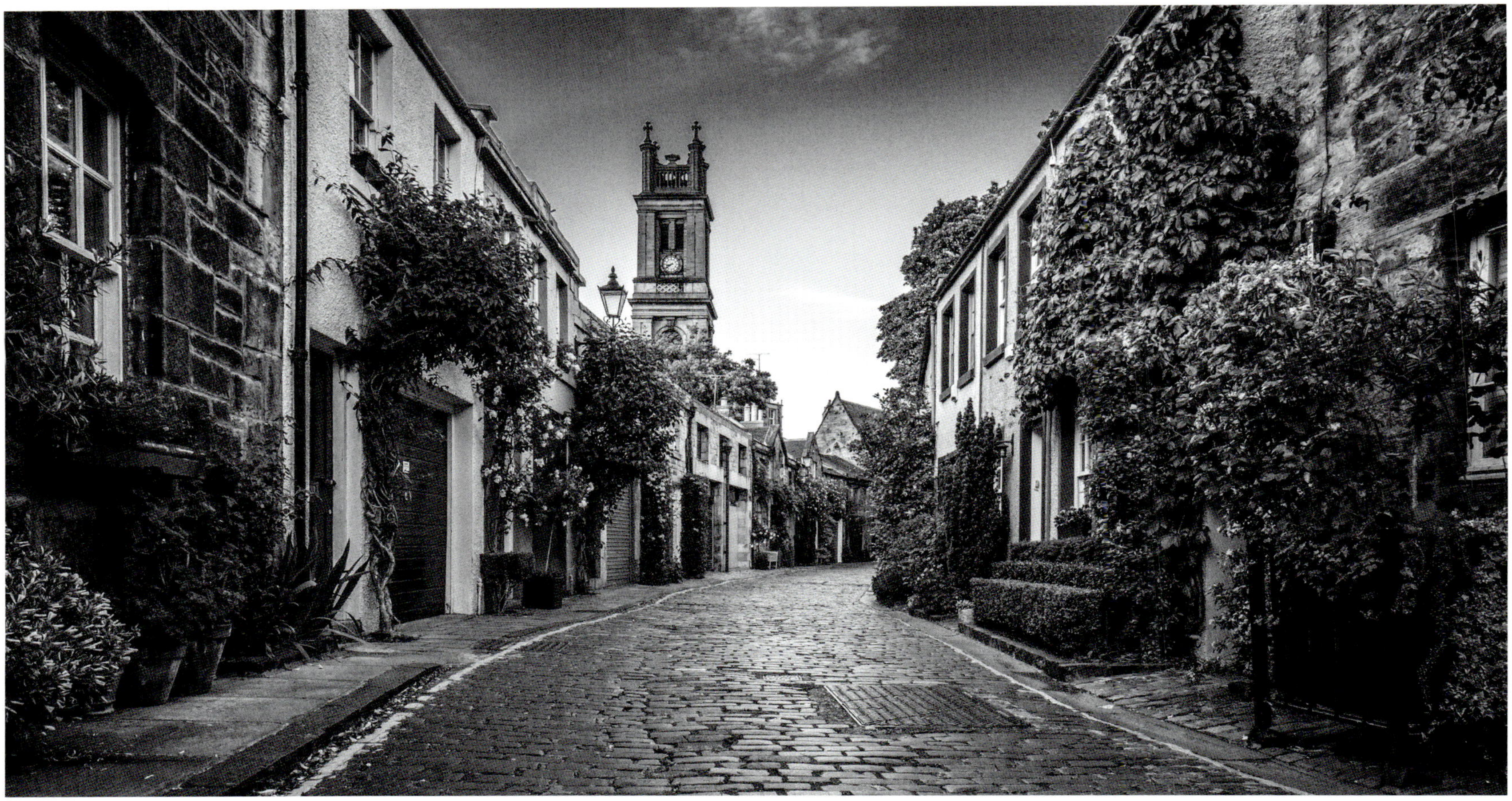

Editor: John Smail
Designer: Hayley Hunter – Hillside Creative www.hillsidecreative.co.uk
Produced by Hunter-Ledingham.

Published by Hunter-Ledingham, Headshaw, Ashkirk, Selkirk, TD7 4NT, Scotland.
First published in Scotland, October 2019

ISBN: 978-1-5272-4150-3

Printed and bound in Italy by Printer Trento SRL.

More information on Edinburgh Revisited can be found at: www.edinburghrevisited.co.uk

Picture-Poem prints can be purchased on the website.

SPONSORS

A huge thank you goes out to a number of Edinburgh-based businesses that provided financial and moral support to the *Edinburgh Revisited* project. These included:

BAILLIE GIFFORD
Investment managers

SHEPHERD+ WEDDERBURN

AMA Homes
When Quality Matters

THE BALMORAL
EDINBURGH
A ROCCO FORTE HOTEL

ASHKIRK

CEANNAS™
MEANS LEADERSHIP

CHARITIES WE ARE SUPPORTING

500 miles

REGISTERED NUMBER: SC038205

www.500miles.co.uk

leuchie HOUSE
NATIONAL RESPITE CENTRE

REGISTERED NUMBER: SC042249

www.leuchiehouse.org.uk

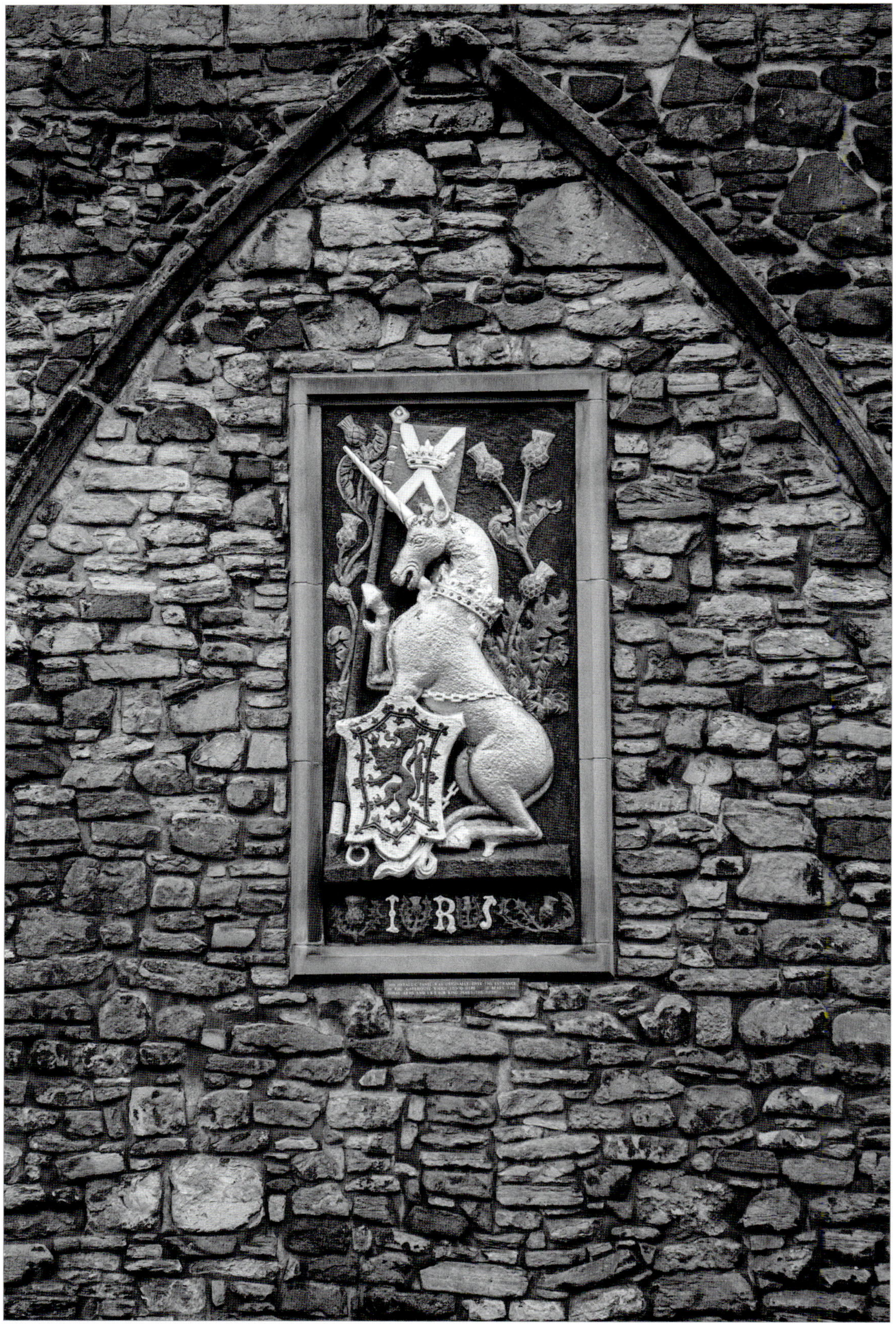
I R S

BUCKINGHAM PALACE

Edinburgh is a place that you can never tire of visiting. This book, *Edinburgh Revisited,* should prompt anyone - whether they be a resident, a visitor, or those who have not returned for many years - to reflect on what a wonderful city this is, and to take another look with a fresh pair of eyes at a city that has so much to offer.

The proceeds from the book will be divided between two Scottish based charities. Leuchie House, where I am Patron, supports people with MS, stroke patients, or those living with a number of other neurological conditions, and provides essential breaks for them and their carers. The second charity is "500 Miles", which works to develop and deliver prosthetic and orthotic services in Malawi and Zambia and in Zanzibar.

I hope this book inspires a new love of the city in its readers.

Anne

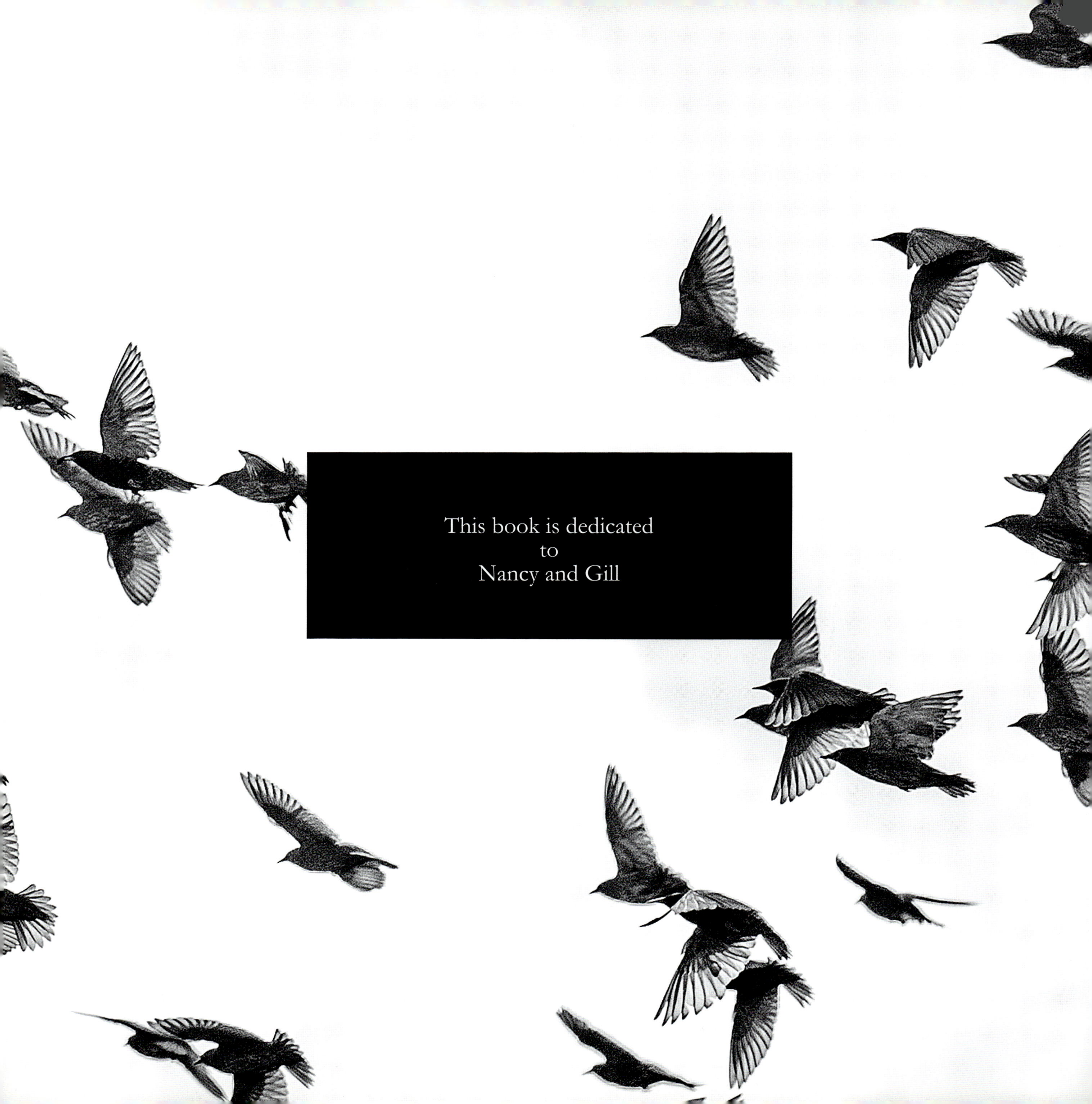

This book is dedicated
to
Nancy and Gill

CONTENTS

FOREWORD BY ALEXANDER McCALL SMITH 9
INTRODUCTION 12

EDINBURGH REVISITED

Hinterland 13
The Balmoral Clock 15
The Surgeon's Knife 17
Friendship 19
Contribution by Lady Anne Smith 21
McEwan Hall 23
Waves Against The Wind 25
Scott Monument 27
Salisbury Crags 29
Contribution by Jason Connery 31
A City's Crown 33
Flowershop 35
Portobello Bather 37
Looking East 39
Contribution by Sir Angus Deaton 41
The Royal Society of Edinburgh 43
The Forth Bridge 45
The Bank 47
Royal Mile Pharmacy 49
Contribution by Alistair Moffat 51
The 'Bloody' Fringe 53
The Scotsman Building 55
Holyrood Garden Party 57
Ramsay Garden Cat 59
Contribution by Jack Lowden 61
Sunshine On Leith 63
Blue Planet 65
A Child's Hand 67
Princes Street Conversations 69
Contribution by Lord David Steel 71
Scottish Parliament 73
The Flying Scotsman 75
Return From Singapore 77
Gravity 79
Contribution by Ian Rankin 81
Edinburgh's Monumental Night Out 83
19 Bellevue Place 85
High Tide 87
Unexpected Moment 89
Contribution by Olivia Giles 91
Stockbridge Lovers 93
Portrait Of A President 95
The Old Royal High School 97
Duddingston Skater 99
Contribution by Glyn Satterley 101
One O'Clock Gun 103
The Unfinished Monument 105
Edinburgh Castle Guardians 107
Afternoon Tea At The Balmoral 109
Contribution by Gavin Hastings 111
Murrayfield Dreams 113
Waverley Station Pigeons 115
A Marching Band 117
Poems in a High Walled Garden 119

BORDERS INHERITANCE 122

Luck 123
The Cow And The Photographer 125
Tweed Mist 127
The Clipping 129
December Milking 131
A Farmer's Hands 133
Freedom 135
Last Of The Blackies 137
Leaderfoot Lady 139
Contours 141
The Starling Symphony 143
Langshaw Echoes 145

SCOTTISH INHERITANCE 148

Swilcan Bridge 149
Abandoned Boat 151

BEHIND THE PICTURE-POEMS 153
BIOGRAPHIES 165
BEHIND THE PHOTOGRAPHS 167

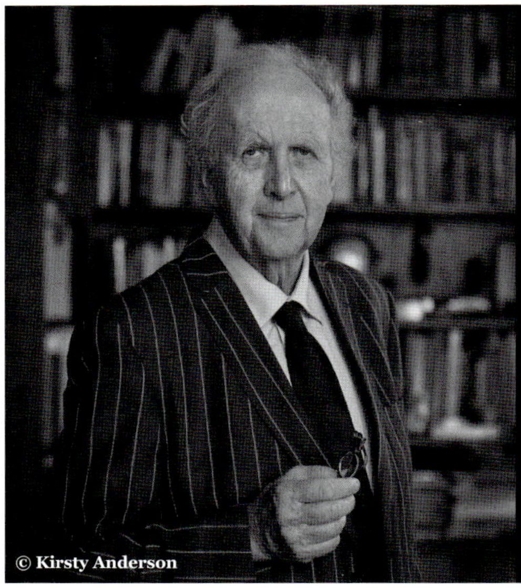
© Kirsty Anderson

ALEXANDER McCALL SMITH CBE

Author; and Professor Emeritus of Medical Law, University of Edinburgh

Alexander McCall Smith is a Scottish author whose internationally best-selling books have been translated into over 40 languages throughout the world. He has written and contributed to more than 100 books, including specialist academic titles, short story collections, and children's books.

He is best known for *The No. 1 Ladies' Detective Agency* series, set in Botswana, which has sold over 20 million copies in the English language alone. His *44 Scotland Street* series, first published in "The Scotsman" newspaper, is now the longest-running serial novel in the world. Alexander's works include the Edinburgh-based *Isabel Dalhousie* novels, the *von Igelfeld* novels, and the *Corduroy Mansions* series. The first of his Swedish-based *Ulf Varg* novels has been published under the title of *The Department of Sensitive Crimes*.

Alexander has written a number of stand-alone novels, including *My Italian Bulldozer*, *Fatty O'Leary's Dinner Party*, *Trains and Lovers*, and *The Second Worst Restaurant in France*. He has also authored many non-fiction titles, such as *A Work of Beauty: Alexander McCall Smith's Edinburgh* and *What W. H. Auden Can Do For You*.

The recipient of numerous awards for his writing, including the Bollinger Everyman Wodehouse Prize for Comic Fiction, he received a CBE for services to literature in 2007. In 2011 he was honoured by the President of Botswana for services through literature to the country, and in 2017 he was the recipient in New York of the National Arts Club Annual Medal of Honour for achievement in literature.

FOREWORD

Artistic partnerships are tricky things. Sometimes they work seamlessly, and result in the creation of works of art that would have been much the less had they not been the work of two minds. On other occasions, they have the mark of the committee upon them, and lack the vision that may come from a single world view. This extraordinary collection of poetry and photographs falls firmly into the former category – it works, and it works very well. This is a collection where two visions have come together and sparked off against each other. The result is a journey informed by two entirely complementary and harmonious guides.

Gordon Hunter and Don Ledingham, photographer and poet, have chosen Edinburgh as their subject. That is a happy choice, because it is abundantly clear from every image and every line in this book that these two love this city. What they have done is to set out a tribute that captures the character of one of the world's great cities – a city that has inspired generations of artists, writers, and musicians. Edinburgh is not a brash, in-your-face city – it is a reticent place, a subtle place.

Its charms are not always revealed at first glance, but become apparent only when you stop and look, and then look again. Yes, there is a theatrical grandeur to it; yes, there is a heart-stopping skyline; yes, there is a mantle of history that touches virtually every part of the city; but there is also something much quieter, much more elusive and intriguing. There are the small closes, the narrow wynds, the tucked-away gardens and green places. There are the rooftops to which you do not give a second glance until you suddenly realise that they are topped with stone thistles, or strange domestic turrets. Then there is the uniform greyness of stone that suddenly reveals itself as honey-coloured or pink in a certain light. There are the historical references, not immediately apparent to the visitor, but poignant, or tragic, or simply astonishing once one has learned the story.

Gordon Hunter's evocative photographs capture the city perfectly. His eye has selected public things and private things – a famous building, perhaps, and then a woman sitting in a garden, or children playing. There is the imposing façade of The Scotsman building, expressing all the civic pride and intellectual confidence of the city, and then there is a sideways view of a very ordinary street. Sometimes the photographs show scenes that are deserted; on other occasions, there are ordinary people going about their daily business. In both cases, we feel that we are there, with the photographer, privileged observers of how the city really is.

A good black-and-white photograph can be powerfully evocative – how much more so when it is accompanied by words that point out to us some important aspect of the image. Don Ledingham's poems all address a theme suggested by the photograph. They may be specific in their bearing on the subject of the image, or they might allude to a theme that the image suggests. So it is that the poet turns to the subject of friendship when he contemplates that famous statue of Greyfriars Bobby. Without the poem, the photograph is simply a photograph of a statue of a dog; with the poem, the photograph becomes a paean to friendship. Similarly, a photograph of the famously incorrect Balmoral clock becomes more than a photograph of a well-known clock – it triggers thoughts on time, and how time moulds the way we live our lives.

Those who live in a city will usually have a whole host of personal associations around particular streets and buildings in the city. They will remember meeting a friend in such-and-such a street; they will remember being caught in the rain in another; they will remember being sad one day in a café; they will remember being in love in a public garden or a bar, or anywhere really. Cities are like that, and Edinburgh seems particularly evocative of such memories. This should not surprise us: it is a romantic city, a city of poets – and photographers. Its fragile beauty, its feminine character, its sheer delightfulness are not easy qualities to capture. In this collection, words and image succeed in doing just that – creating a striking record of the love affair that so many of us have with this city. This book is a love letter – but not a private one: it is a love letter in which we all might share.

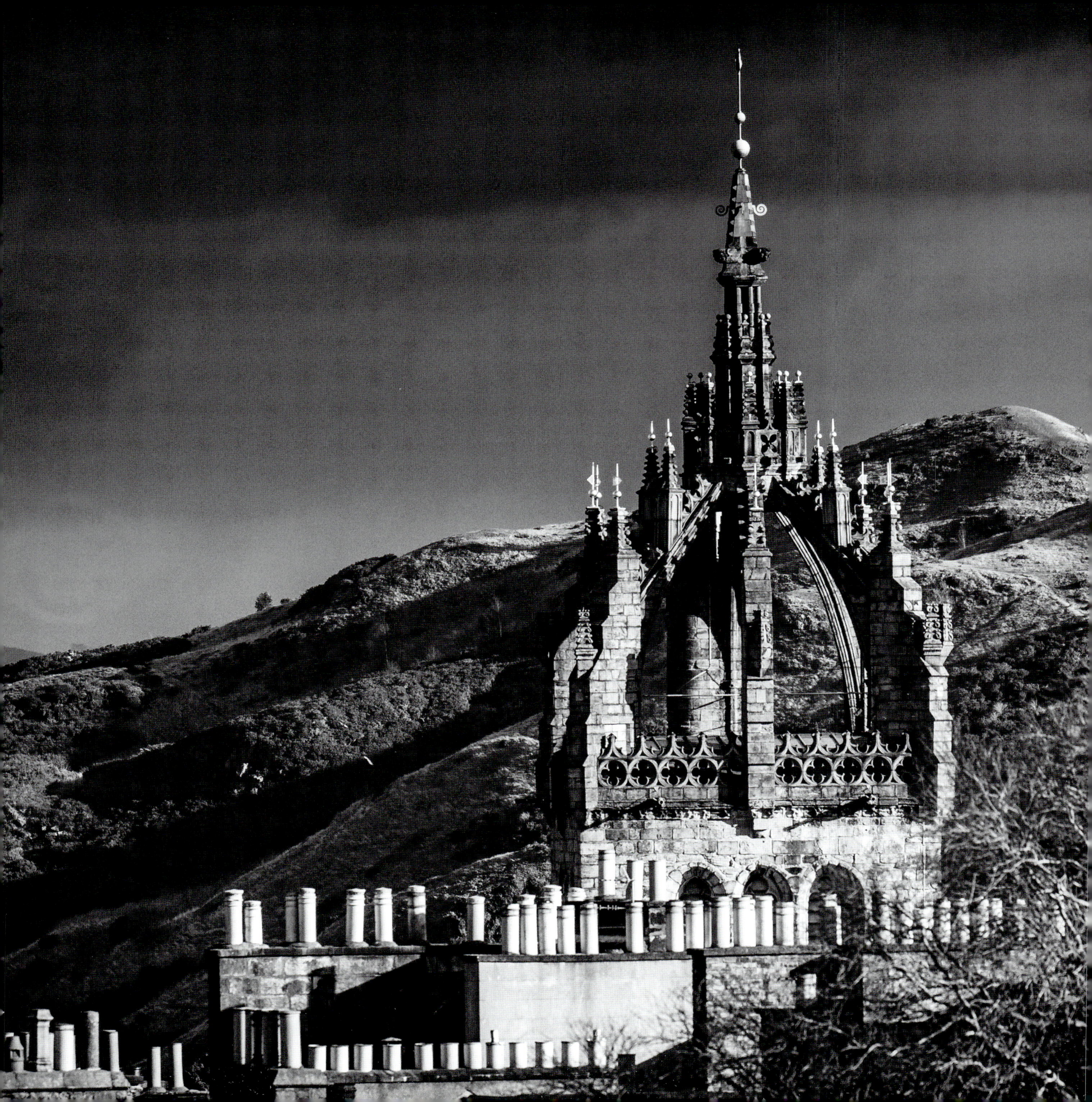

EDINBURGH REVISITED

INTRODUCTION

If you live in Edinburgh, have lived in Edinburgh or have visited Edinburgh, then you will be familiar with many of this remarkable city's iconic sights and buildings.

Edinburgh Revisited picks out many of these traditional, some might say clichéd views, putting a twist on them both in terms of the photographs and the accompanying poems.

The book also includes contributions from a number of well-known Scots with strong connections to the city who have lived, studied or worked in Edinburgh. Each gives a unique perspective on Auld Reekie.

Gordon Hunter and Don Ledingham grew up together having both attended the same school in Edinburgh, before leaving to make their respective homes in the Scottish Borders. Don played rugby for Gala and Gordon for Selkirk. They both represented the senior South side. Gordon was a member of the 1984 Scottish Rugby Grand Slam team, and Don wasn't.

Over the past 30 years they have established reputations in their respective fields of photography and poetry. In 2000 they first exhibited a collection of Picture-Poems entitled 'Borders Inheritance'. The collection - capturing the changing landscape of Scottish agricultural life - was exhibited throughout Scotland, helping to raise significant funds for charity and culminating in an invitation to exhibit in the Scottish Writers Museum in Edinburgh.

A selection of the Picture-Poems from 'Borders Inheritance' is included in this book as a reference to the work Gordon and Don were undertaking at the turn of the millennium. *Edinburgh Revisited* builds upon that experience and features many of the places Gordon and Don grew up beside.

They hope you enjoy the collection, and trust it will provide readers with an alternative insight into the city that will add to their pleasure of this incredible place.

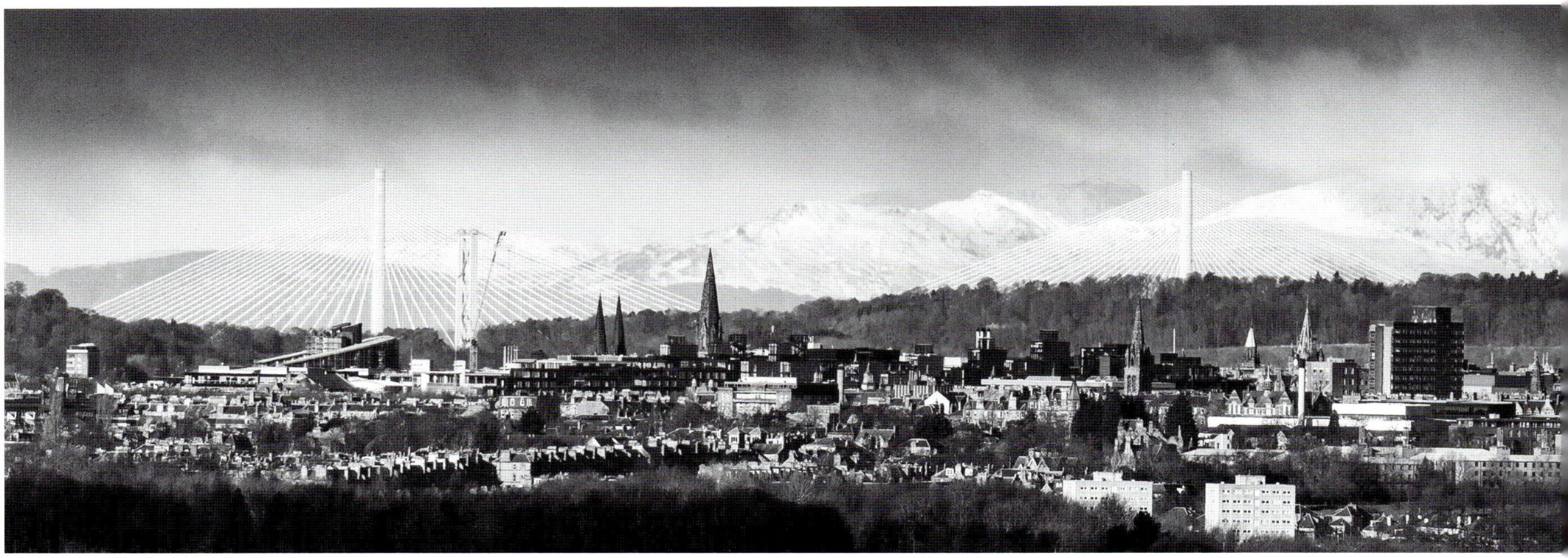

HINTERLAND

Beyond the city's limits,
Beyond our narrow field of view,
Beyond the castles and the spires,
Beyond the ancient and the new;

It dominates the distance,
In a place we seldom understand,
Yet in the catchment of our minds,
Lies our shadowed hinterland;

It looms on our horizon,
Yet just keeping out of sight,
It guides our every step,
And every moment of our night;

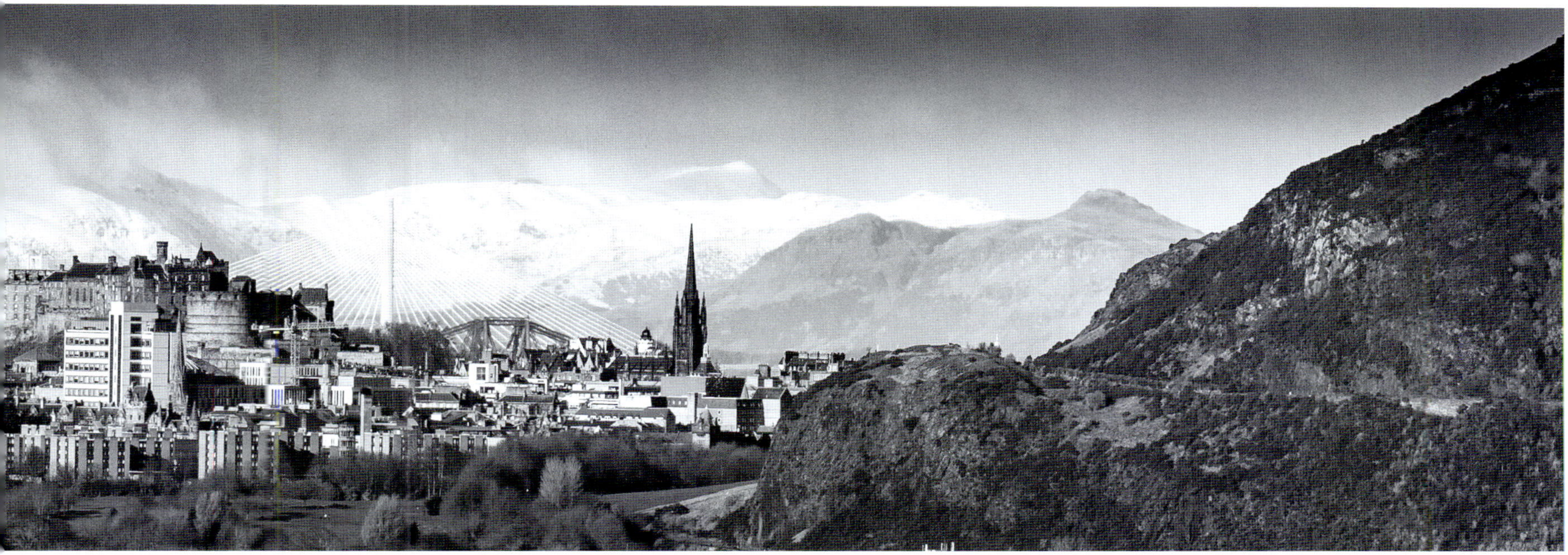

And in that uncharted landscape,
There lies our hidden source,
Where rise our mighty rivers,
That carve their knowing course;

And from our phantom roots,
That others neither know nor see,
Which guide and shape our present,
And who we are to be;

So catch those transitory glimpses,
Of our unrecovered past,
Those unoccupied recollections,
That never seem to last;

Beyond our city's limits,
Beyond our outstretched hand,
Beyond our castles and our spires,
Lies our forgotten hinterland.

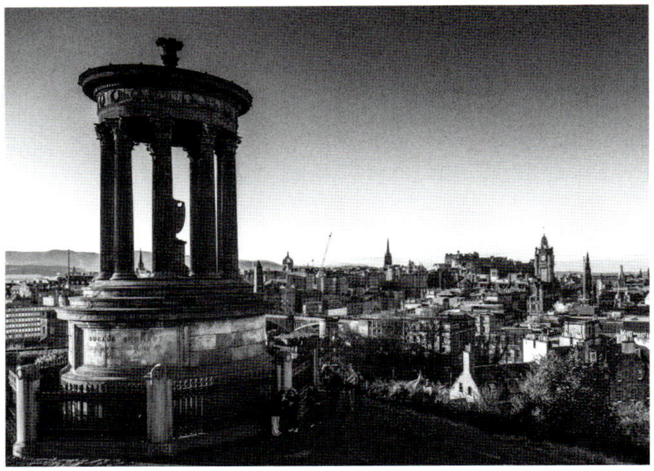

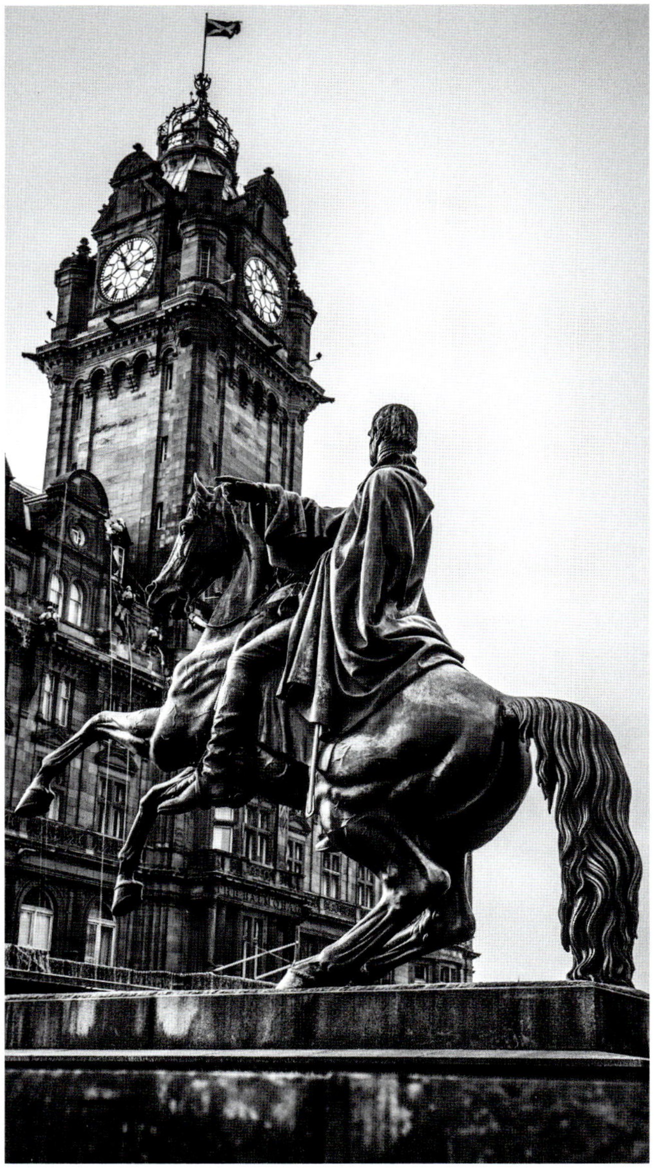

THE BALMORAL CLOCK

Edinburgh's time machine
Runs three minutes fast,
Reaching forwards
Into unknown time, and
Experiencing a future
Before we get there,
Saving us anxiety
By building a buffer
Between the then,
And the now;
I always
Used to wonder,
If something
Happened in
Those three
Short minutes,
Could we get
That time
Again?
Erasing our
Mistakes,
As if they
Hadn't really
Happened;
Perhaps,
We should all wind
Our watches forward,
And live,
Perpetually,
In three minutes
Of grace.

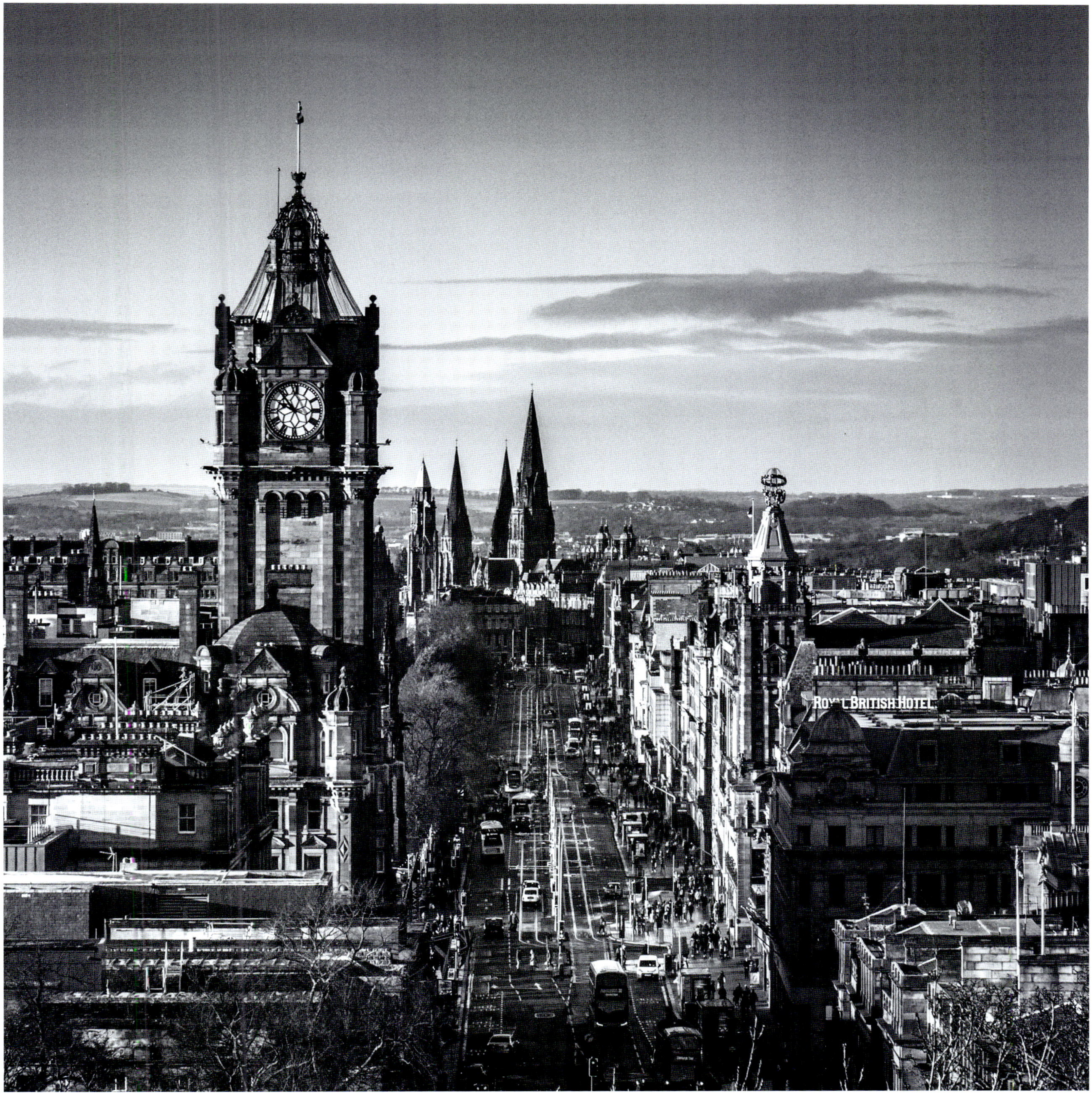
BRITISH HOTEL

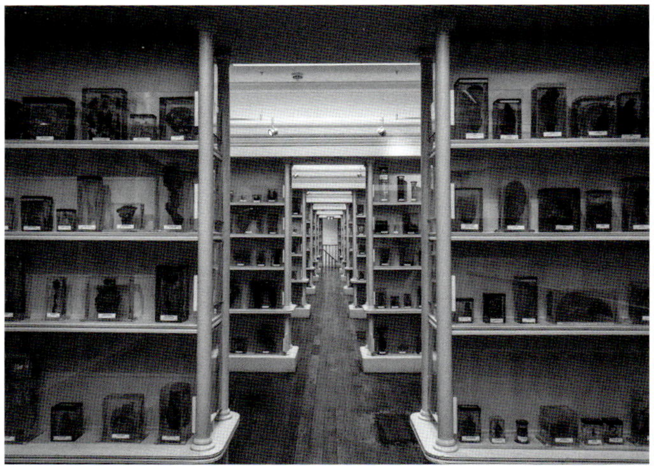

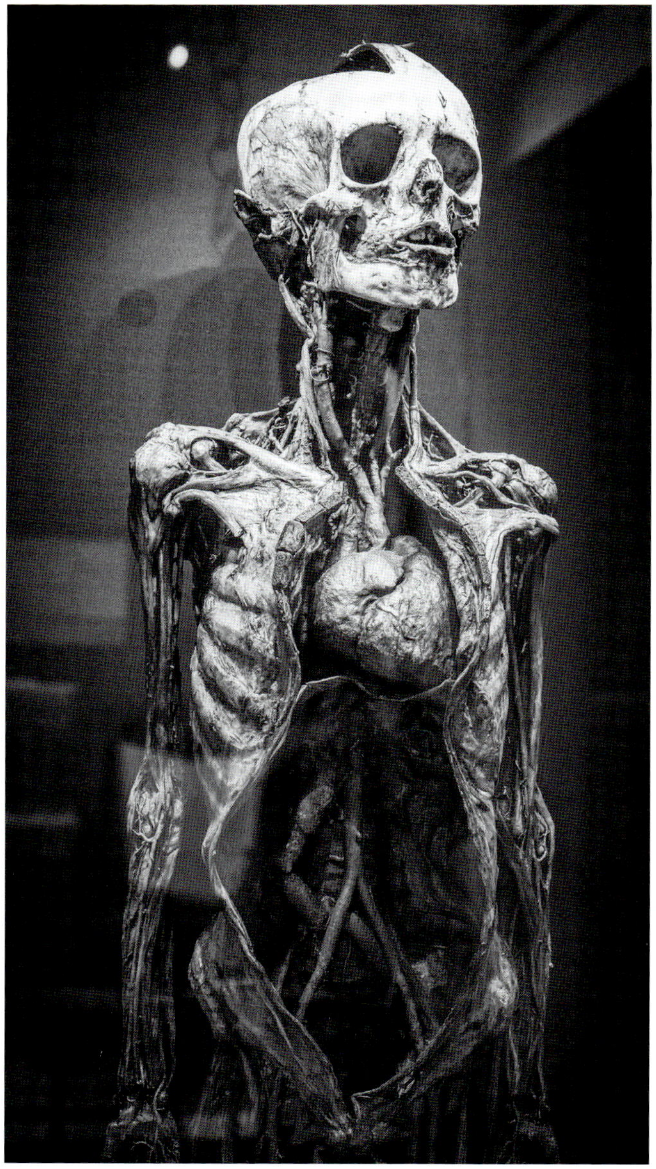

THE SURGEON'S KNIFE

See a moment's pause
Before the cut,
The breaking of the seal
To breach the world
Beneath our rind,
Our shield, our sheath,
Exposing ourselves,
Giving ourselves,
With ultimate trust,
To expert hands,
Which effortlessly enter
In bold restraint,
With singular blends
Of hand and eye,
Of mind and soul,
Of fortitude and will,
Depositing their learning,
Their book years,
Apprenticed years,
Leaving something
Of their lineage,
The barber and the screams,
The emptied graves,
The chaos of the field,
Wisdom upon wisdom,
All lead to here,
A haven from a septic world;
And, lost in perfect concentration,
They finish and retreat,
Through whence they came,
Reluctantly returning,
To an ordinary life.

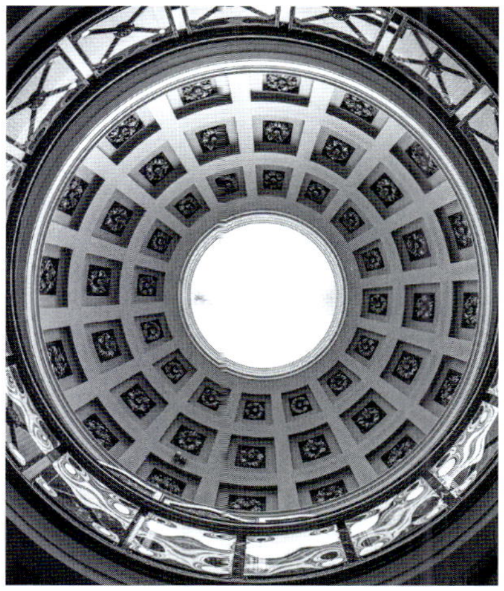

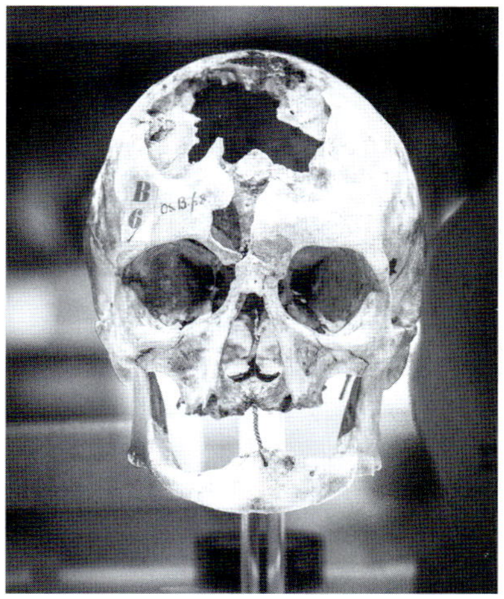

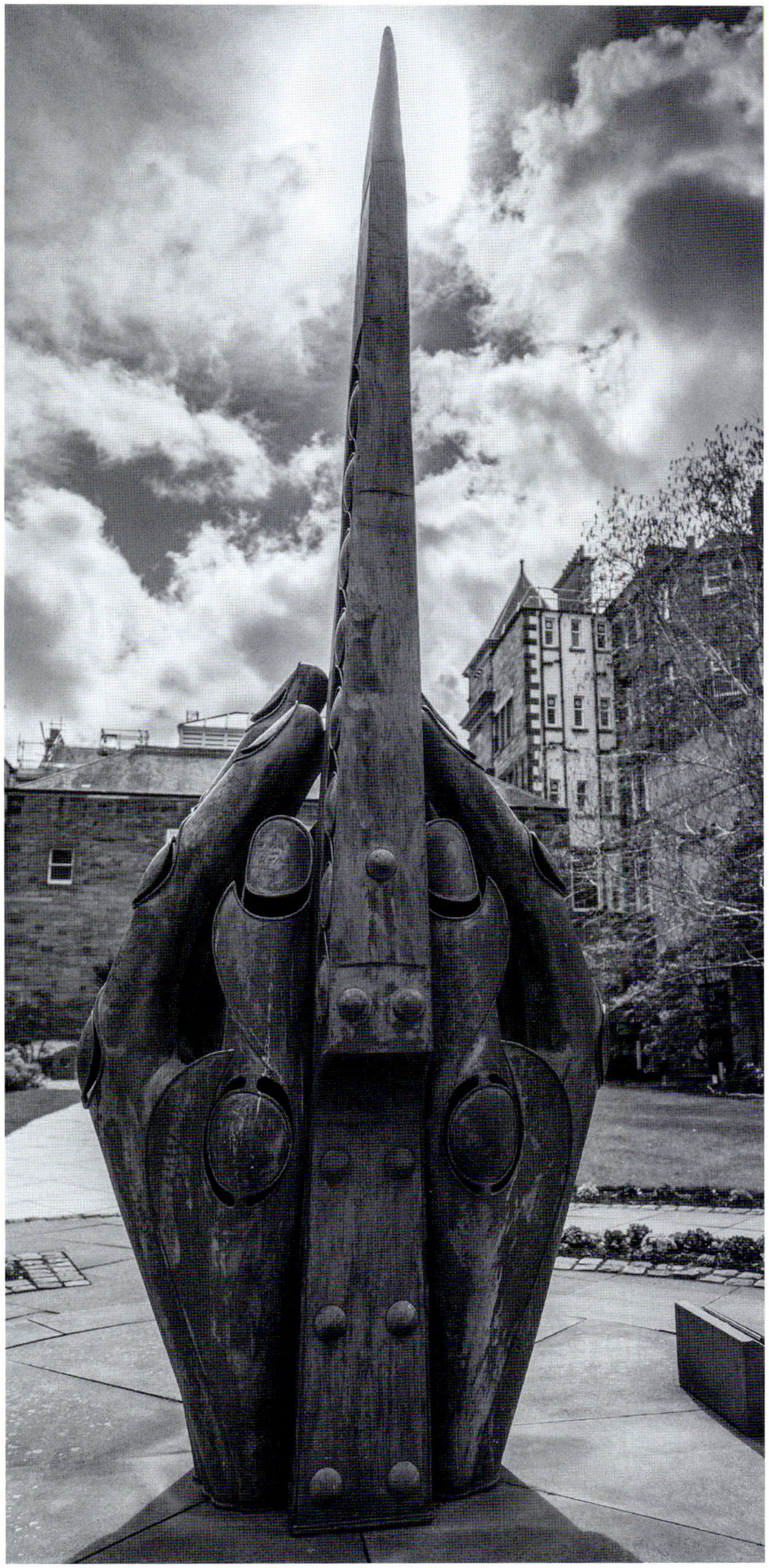

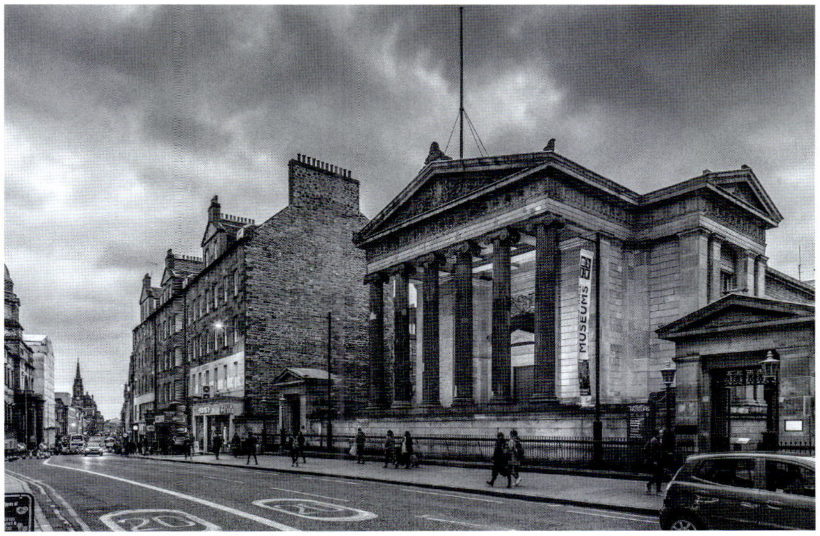
MUSEUMS

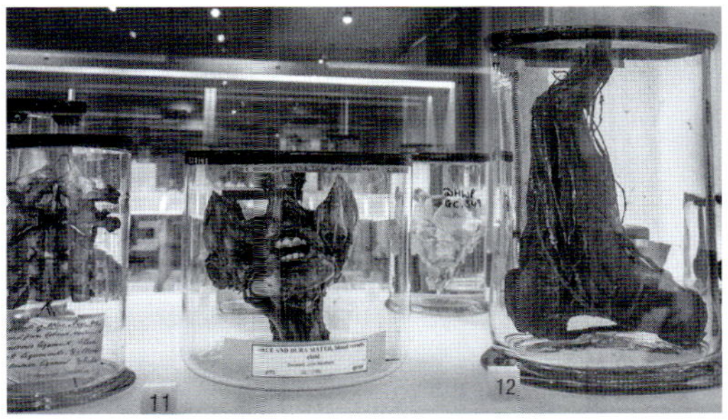
11
12

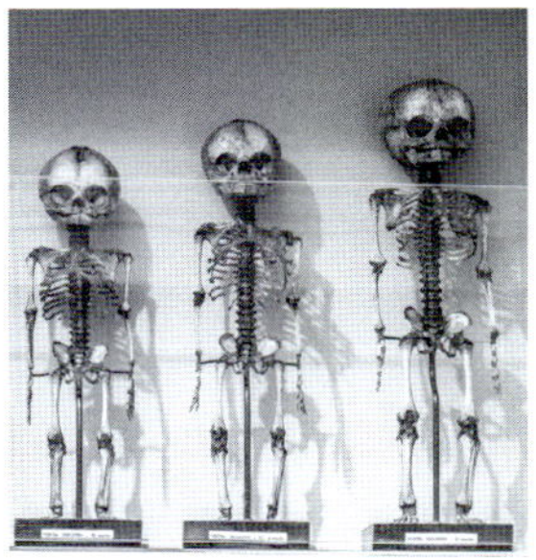

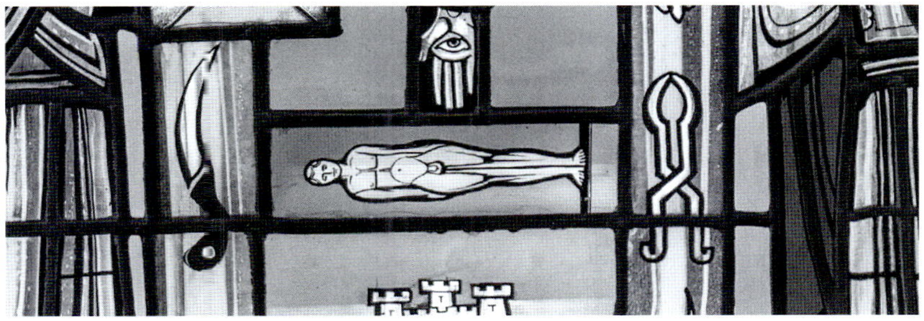

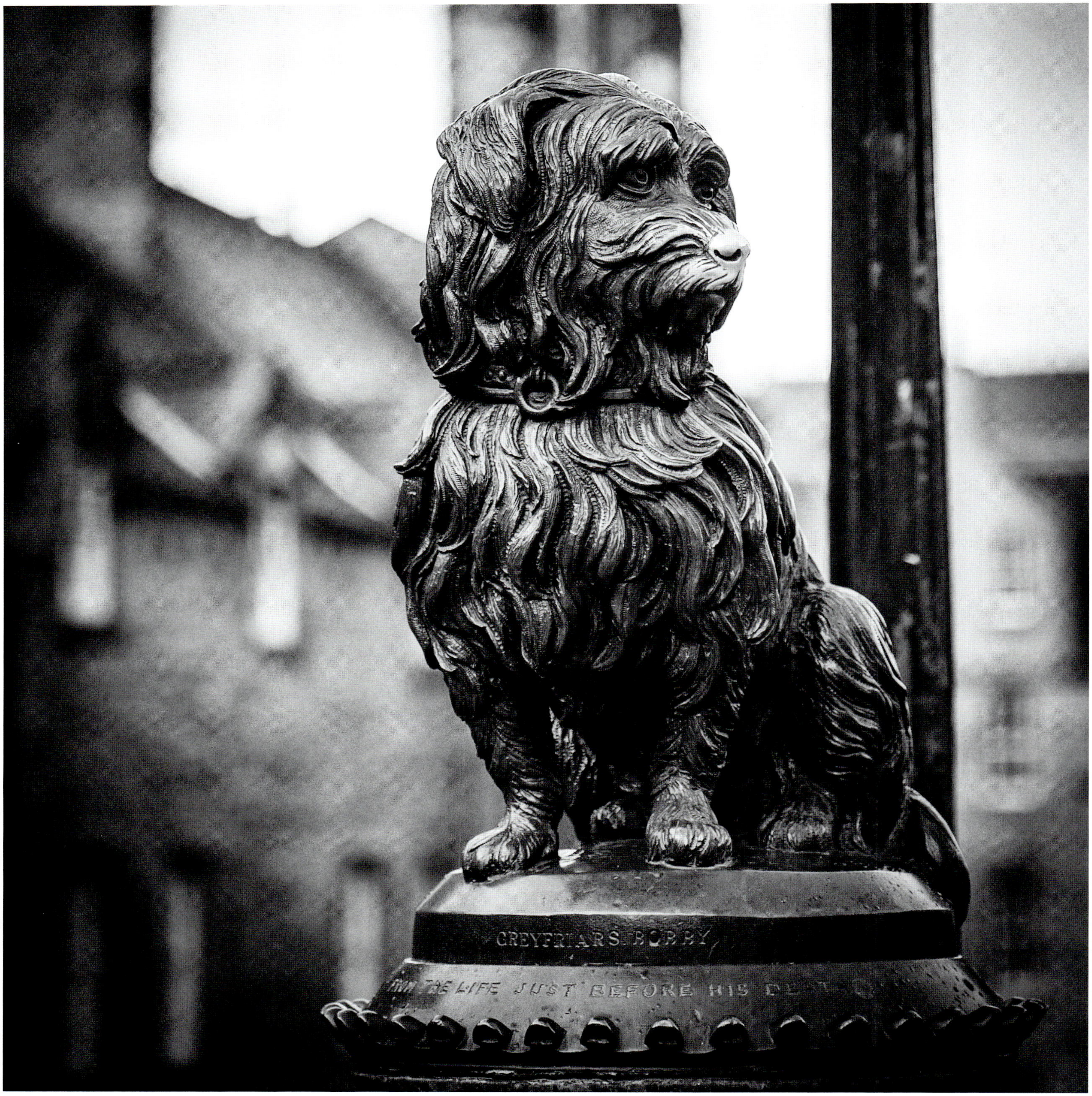
GREYFRIARS BOBBY
THE LIFE JUST BEFORE HIS

FRIENDSHIP

Throughout our lives,
True friends emerge
In short supply,
Amongst the
Temporary travellers
Who share our path,
In fleeting fellowship,
Then disappear from view,
Without a backwards glance;
For friendship sows a seed,
A bond that grows,
A tie, that absence cannot break,
Becoming something in itself,
A cherished object, locked away,
That places no conditions on its gift,
Nor hastening to judge;
For friendship sees our better side,
Behind the drawn curtains
Of our public lives,
To share in our success,
Or take our arm,
In moments of self-doubt,
Or bear the blows on our behalf,
In an unspoken pact,
That holds a mirror to ourselves,
And asks the question,
In which our deep
Discomfort lies:
Do we behave,
As would our lifetime's
Friend?
And asks again:
Do we behave,
As would our lifetime's
Friend?

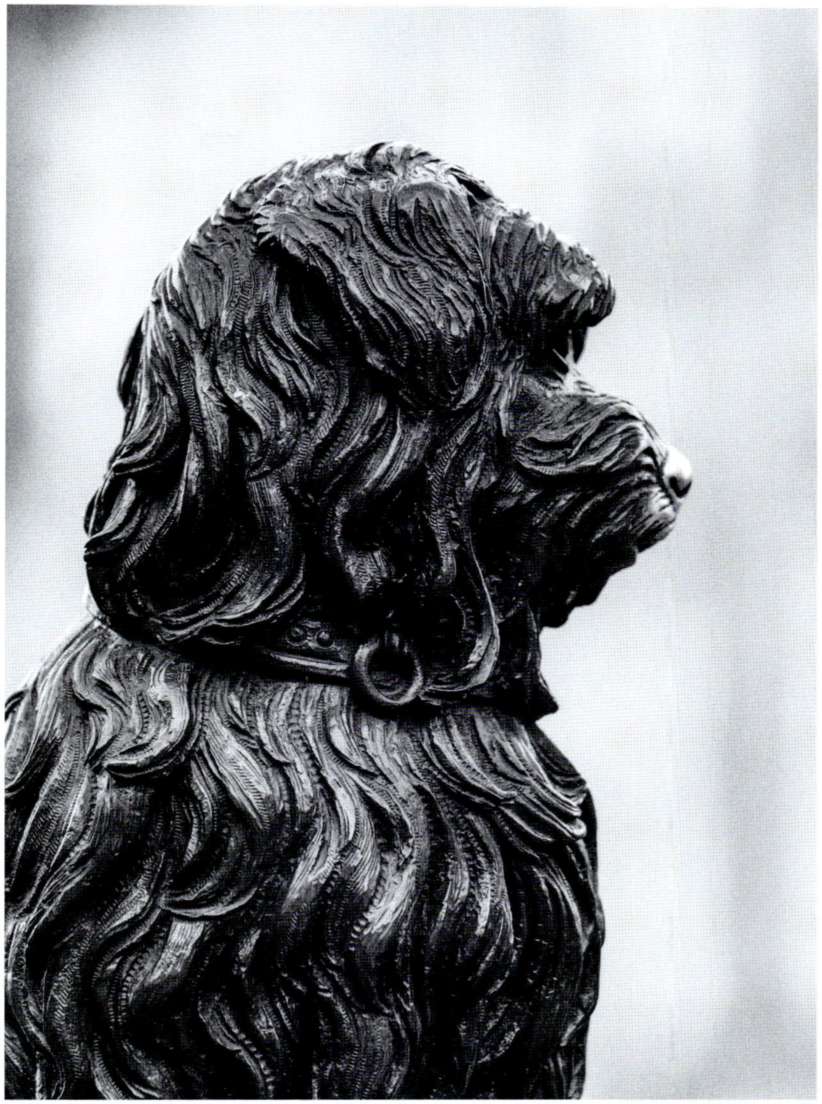

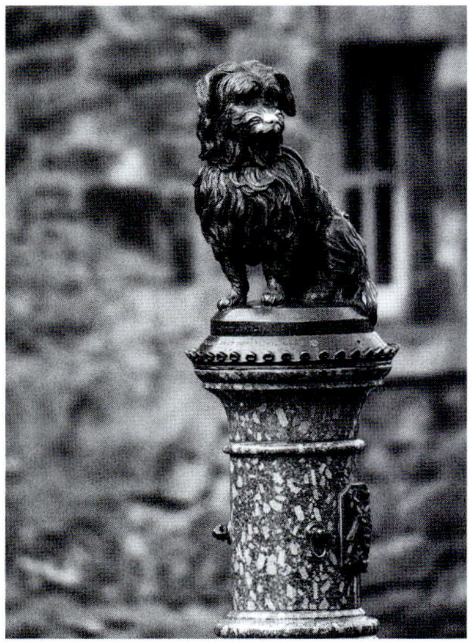

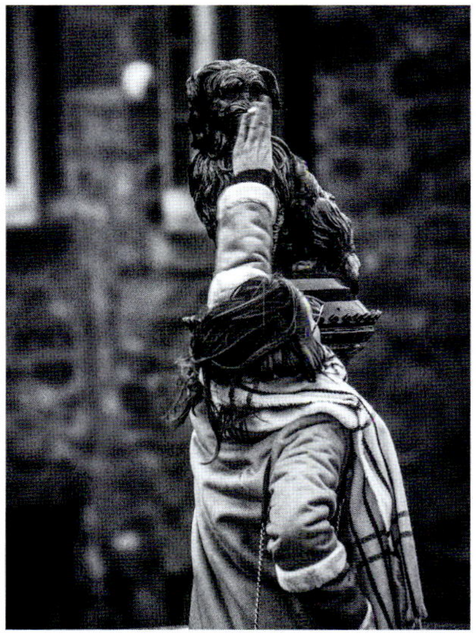

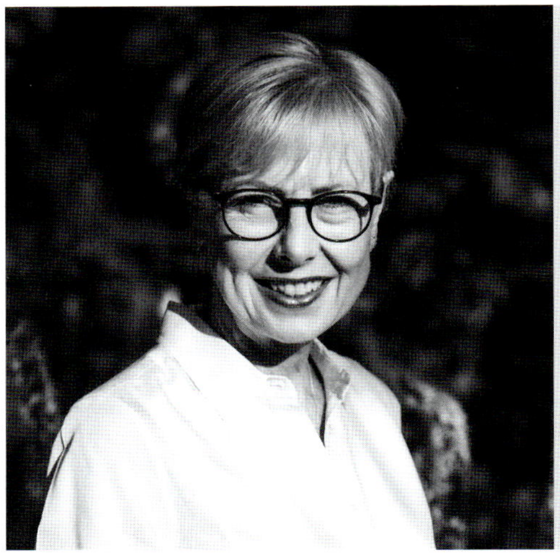

LADY ANNE SMITH

Lady Smith studied at Edinburgh University, graduating with LLB (Hons) in 1977. She served a solicitor's apprenticeship with Shepherd & Wedderburn WS where she met her husband, David Smith, then a partner of the firm. She was admitted to the Faculty of Advocates, as one its very few female members, in 1980. She took silk (became a Queen's Counsel) in 1993, and was appointed to the bench of the Court of Session in 2001, becoming the third woman to join the College of Justice in Scotland.
Lady Smith is also the President of Scottish Tribunals and currently chairs the Scottish Child Abuse Inquiry.

In 1997 she caused a stir by being the first woman to appear before the Court of Session wearing trousers, not as a fashion statement, but in an effort to keep warm. The central issue in the litigation, which was whether or not the parents of a child born after a failed sterilisation should be entitled to damages was, she has always maintained, far more interesting than her trousers.
When not working, Lady Smith pursues her love of the outdoors, of her garden, of music, of precious time with her family and of the company of the many good friends that life in Edinburgh has engendered.

I didn't know that one of the many joys of marriage would be the forging of a quite separate, deep and intimate relationship. Forty years ago I completed my solicitor's training at Shepherd & Wedderburn WS in Charlotte Square, and crossed the great divide from the New Town to begin life as a wife on the south side of Edinburgh, initially in the Grange and then in Morningside. So it was that I was courted and quite easily seduced by all that the Meadows and Bruntsfield Links had to offer, particularly as a place to walk, watch, reason and reflect.

We were first introduced when I was a student; it was, in the 1970s, a place where we didn't dare walk after dark. But from my first tentative days of 'devilling' at the Faculty of Advocates to my present days of judicial life, it became and remains my regular walk across to the Court of Session in Parliament House, behind St Giles Cathedral, in darkness and in daylight.

It was my walking route to the ante-natal clinic at the Simpson Memorial Maternity Pavilion, it was a place to take the children, their bikes, their tennis racquets and their golf clubs, it was and is a place to think about the challenges of the working day - of what's to come and what has been - and as I absorb all its sights and sounds and scents, whether of student barbecues, or children walking to school, or exuberant dogs, or trees withstanding a gale, to regain a sense of proportion when work - these days as a judge - seems overwhelming.

The Meadows (formerly the windswept Borough Loch) and Bruntsfield Links (formerly the Burgh Muir) cover over 90 acres of rustling green space, presided over by the bulbous mounds of Arthur's Seat. The Burgh Muir was a gift from King David I in 1143, in gratitude for being saved from a fierce stag when out hunting there; by the early 18th century, "The Gowf" (golf) took precedence over much of it. Sir Thomas Hope was responsible for the project that began the draining of the Burgh Loch and, by 1743, the establishment of wide, tree-lined walks. By the 19th century sport abounded and, to this day, cricket, tennis, rounders, Frisbee, running and cycling (to name but a few) are all absorbed, whilst still leaving ample space for those who just want to stride and stroll and sit between the many species of awe-inspiring trees, ranging from elm to whitebeam to birch. We owe so much to those two men, and to those councillors who had the vision to ensure that this very special place has remained open, airy, and free of buildings, giving citizens and visitors alike room to breathe.

WALKING IN AN EDINBURGH LIFE
by
- Lady Anne Smith -

Walk with me.
Walk where muir and windswept loch,
The gifts of a King,
Were bettered in hope, embraced in delight,
And loved into rebirth.

Walk with me.
Walk where my stratified memories
Lie deep in the earth
Suffusing prunus, ash and elm
In a clear white beam.

Walk with the young lawyer
Growing and learning
From minds as well ordered
As the gridded town and the astragals
In Charlotte Square.

Walk with me.
Walk where I have walked as advocate,
As Counsel of Her Majesty,
As mother, wife and judge,
In gratitude for my meadow-sweetened life

Walk with me.
Walk where rising reason
Carved his triumph
With the ease of the curve
On the dome of the McEwan Hall.

Walk with me.
Walk where shining morning faces,
Tartan pleats and Lowry-like cyclists
Glide past,
Caught shimmering in long autumn sunbeams.

Walk with me.
Walk with me in duty.
Walk with me in joy.
Walk with me in gladness.

Embrace with me this place, this city that tests you –
Now, harshly biting, wetly hurling her worst.
Now a bladed wind,
Now dark gloom, hiding her summer-honeyed stone.
But then a pause, a fresh light, a warm apology,
And beauty unrivalled.
She will love you if you let her.

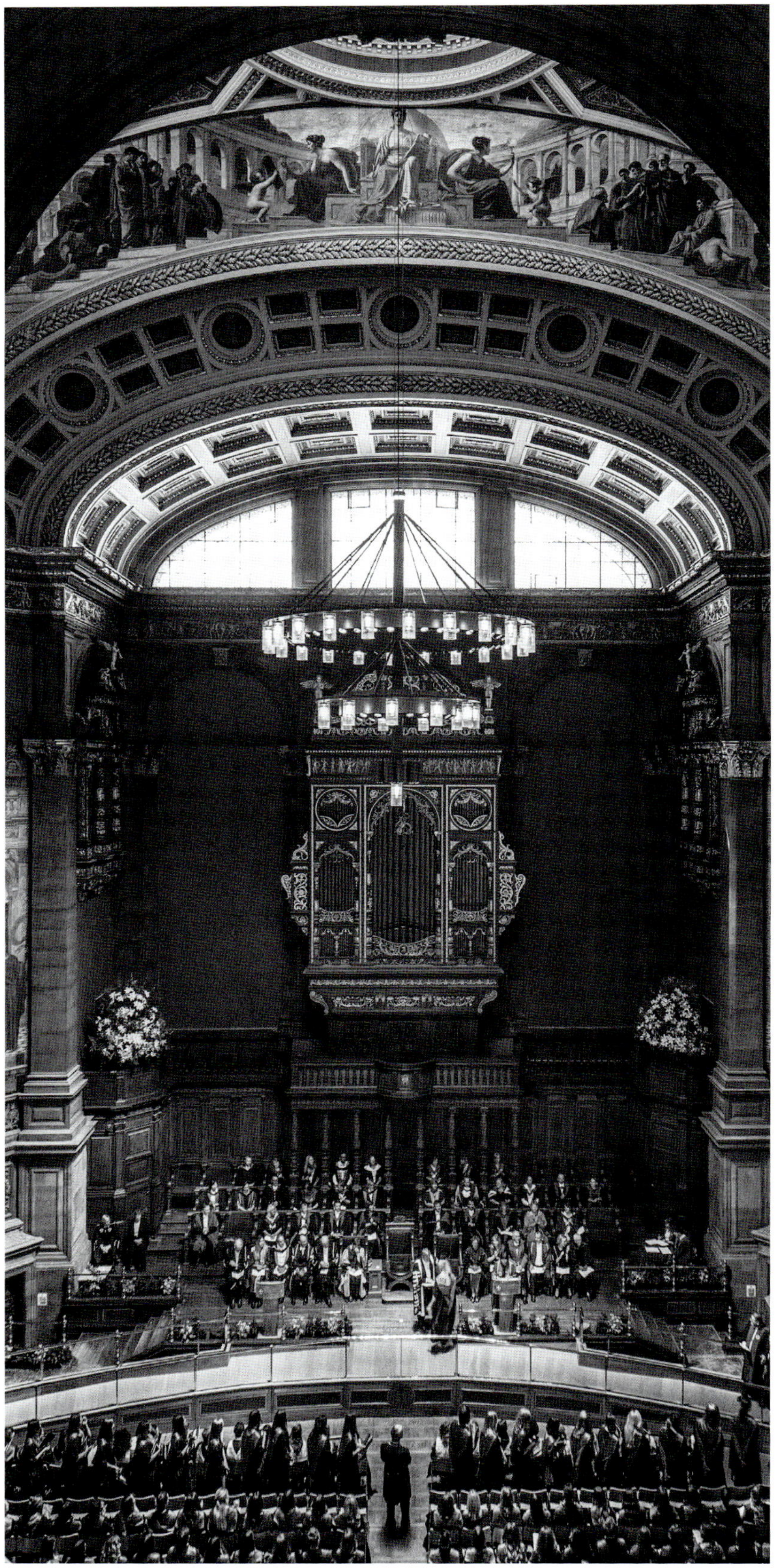

McEWAN HALL

Step into this palace of remembrance,
This silent witness to success,
This legacy from a forgotten house,
And hear your name pronounced,
Then step across the venerable stage,
Pause, precisely, at the designated spot,
Bow gently down before the gods,
To feel the bonnet touch your head,
And in that instant, letters,
Now attach your name,
And so the ceremony repeats,
New minted graduates take their seats,
Their studied years,
Captured and compressed,
Within a parchment scroll;
Now,
Conceive the congregated learning,
Sitting side-by-side,
Throughout the years,
Who sat in your chair?
What were their dreams?
What were their fears?
Give them a name,
Give them a life;
For this is your obligation,
Not to the unknown future,
But to the unbroken
Past.

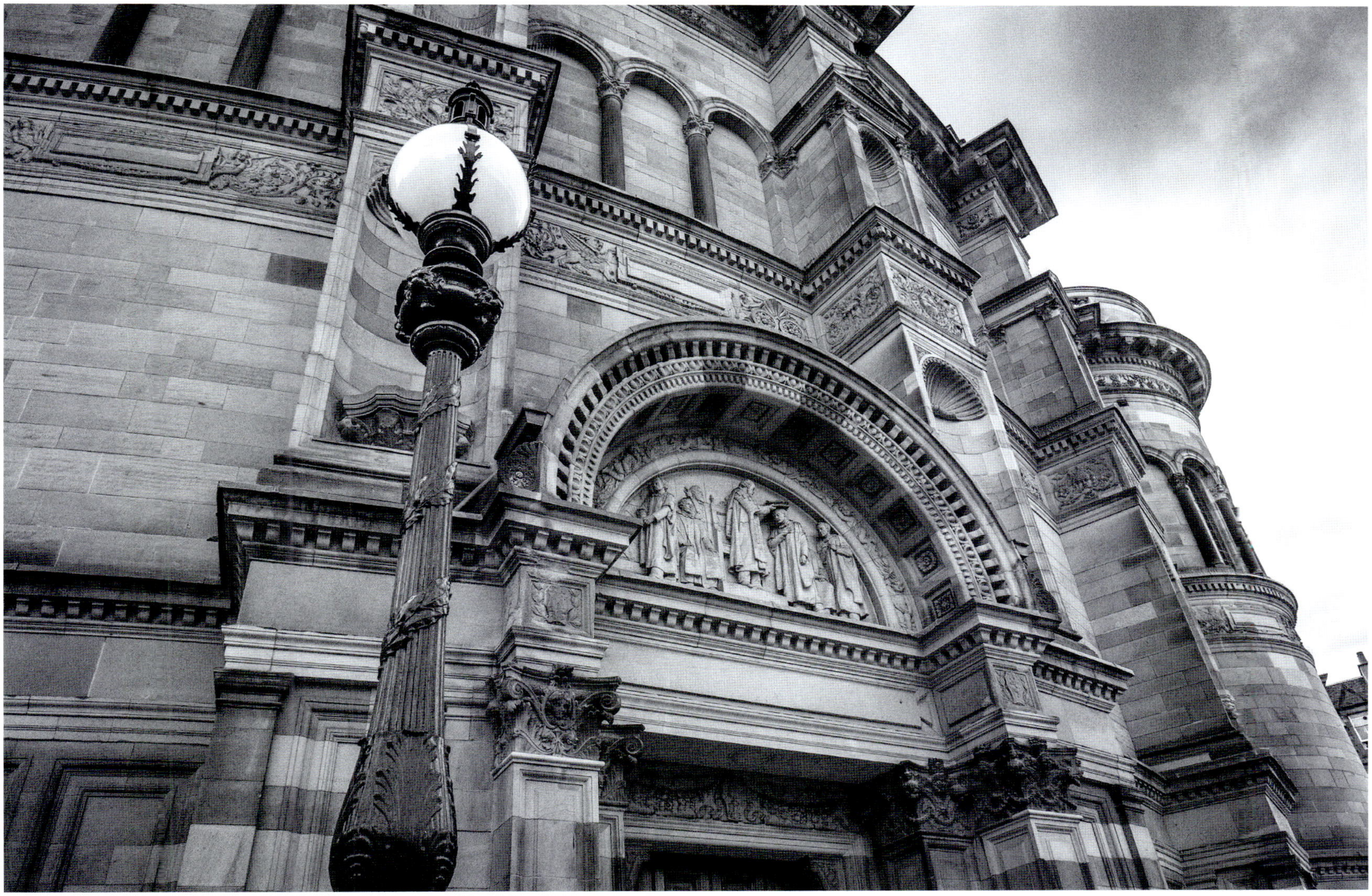

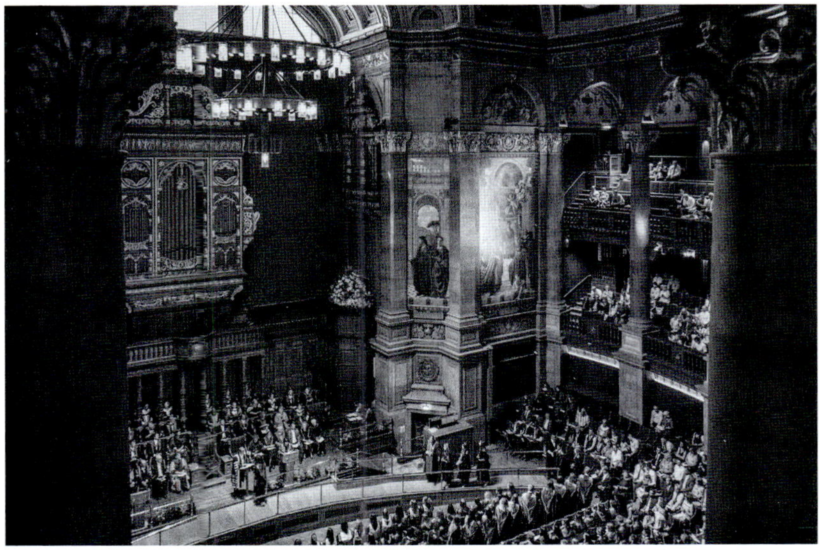

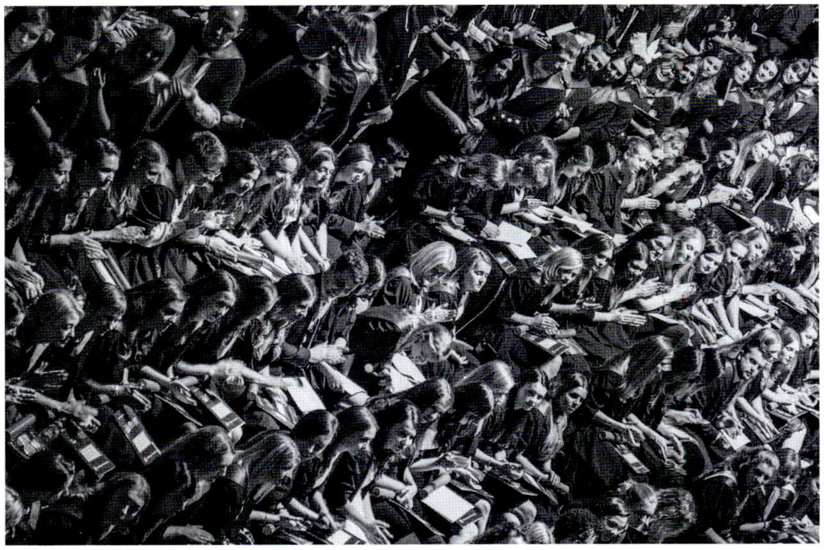

WAVES AGAINST THE WIND

We are waves against the wind
And have two ways to reach the shore
By keeping low we hide behind,
The crashing waves that lead the blind;

But those who dare to rise and fight
And lead the charge in selfless flight
Can bear their chests against the storm
Their silver manes give god-like form;

They shout and roar their battle cry
Whilst lifting up their pennants high
Of danger they need take no heed
And live their lives at reckless speed;

On reaching shallows stand their height
Before they drop their heads mid-flight
And crash and die and live no more,
Amidst those of us who slide ashore.

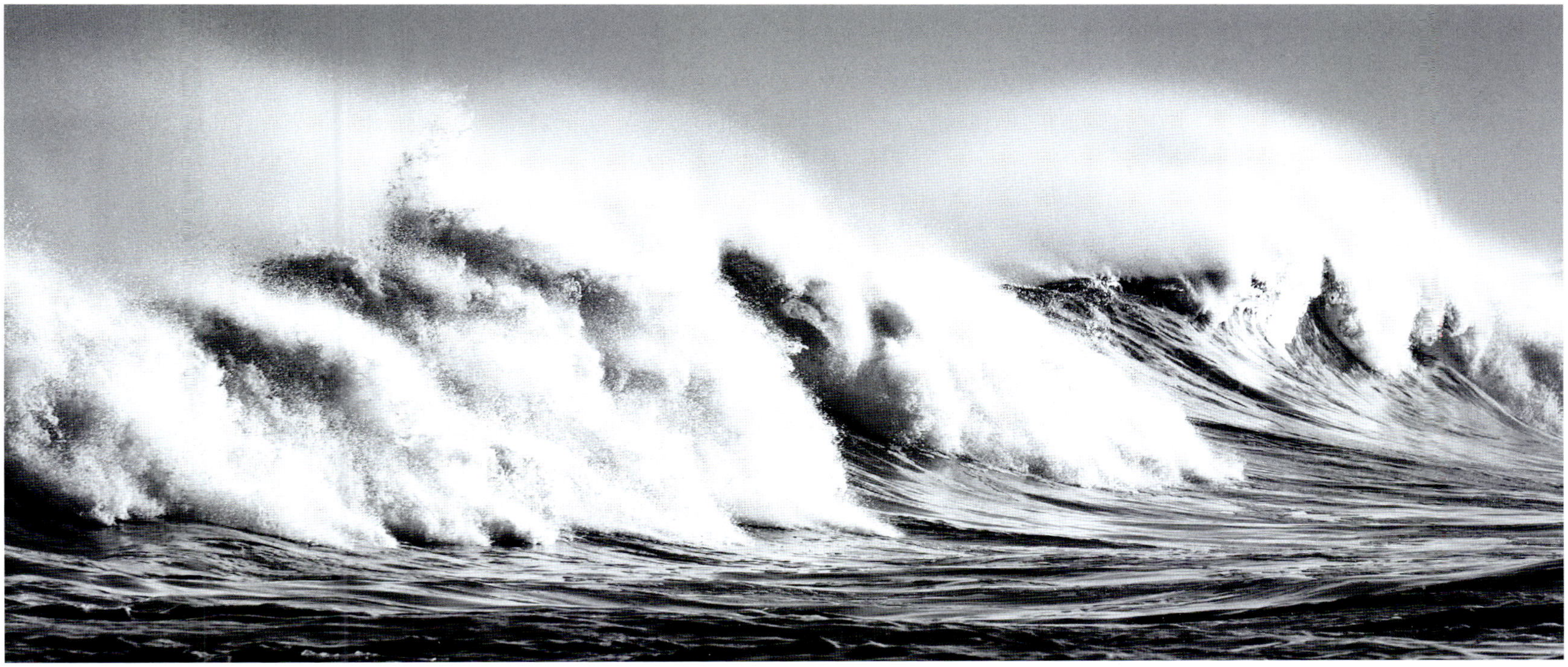

SCOTT MONUMENT

I
Am a
Gothic
Rocket,
Readying
For launch,
Fuelled by
Imagination,
With a single
Astronaut, He
Is tired of his
Legend, he is
Weary of his
Crown, And so
We schemed
Together to
Escape this
Melancholy town,
The countdown it
Has started, 5, 4, 3, 2, 1,
And before anyone has
Noticed we are reaching for
The sun, the tourists run for
Cover, their cameras scatter
On the ground, as we gradually
Lift off in a cacophony of sound,
The young they stare in wonder, as
We lift up to the sky, for no one can
Believe, that such a monument can fly,
With my buttresses as boosters, and my
Spire as my cone, we break free from gravity,
And soon we are alone, who knows when we'll
Return, as we pass beyond the moon, but we have
Tasted freedom, and I know it won't be soon, for I
Am a Gothic rocket, we are driven by his dreams, as
We stretch beyond the stars, which pass in ceaseless
Streams, beyond the Milky Way towards the edge of
Time, as the man at the controls, selects a boundless line,
So if in years ahead, you come upon our empty site, look
Up towards the heavens, and imagine never-ending flight.

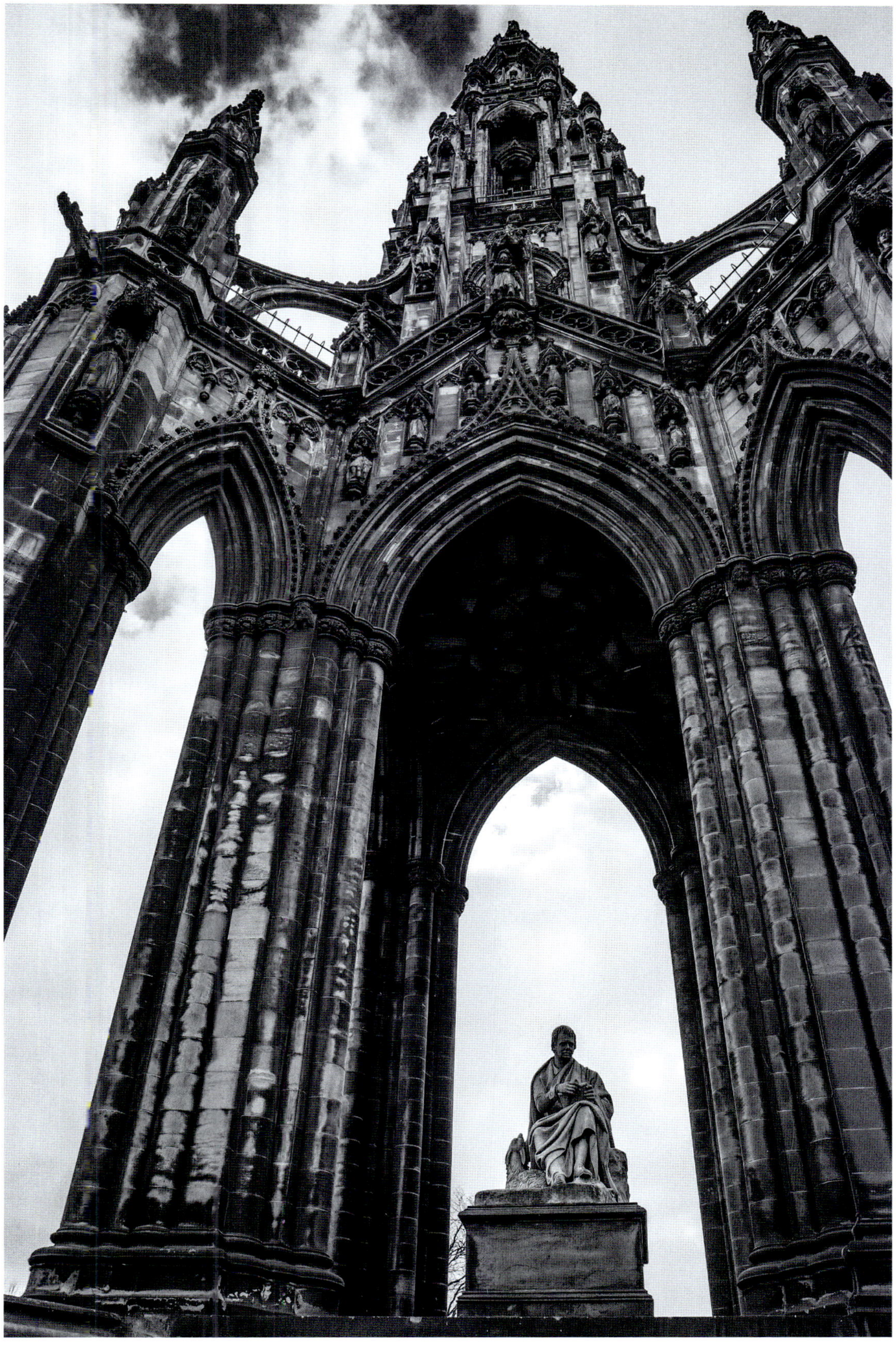

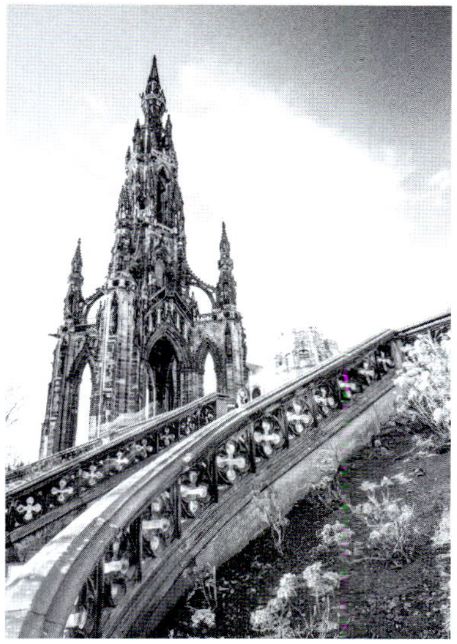

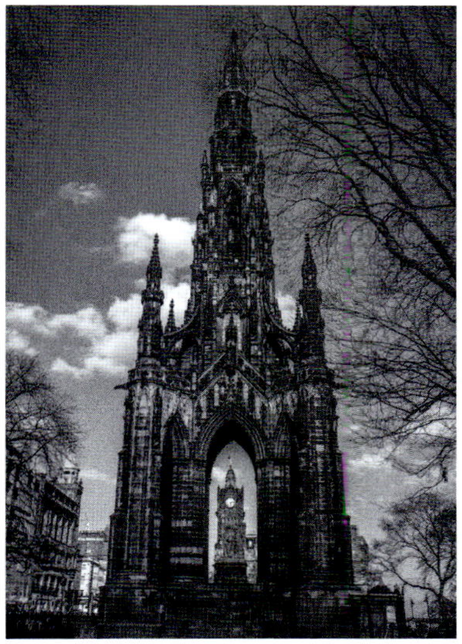

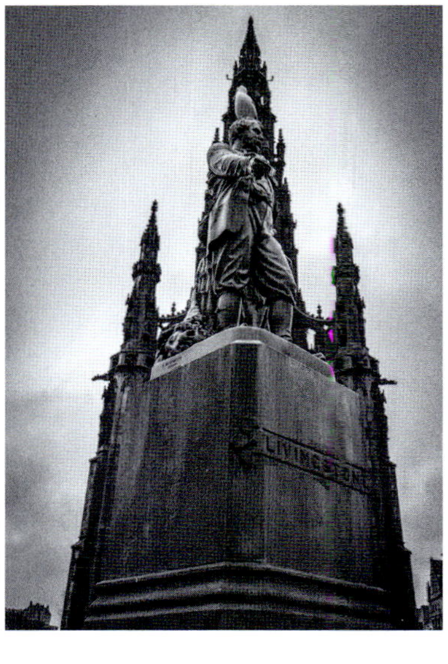

SALISBURY CRAGS

The terracotta curtain
Collects the evening sun
By hanging the cliff-face,
In the air,
Tipping back upon itself
Like a broken flagstone,
Cantilevered,
Against the
Momentary city,
Angling back,
Effortlessly,
Towards the sky,
Revealing the ground
Beneath our feet,
The hard rock,
Floating in space,
The Dolerite layers
The Basalt columns,
Aligned with
Slide-rule perfection
By nature's Eye,
A seamless
Counterweight, to
The random geometry
Of Edinburgh's
Sloping silhouette.

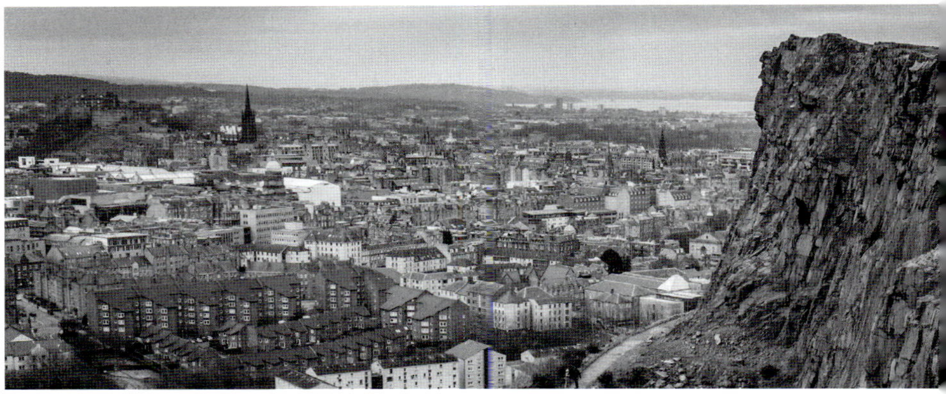

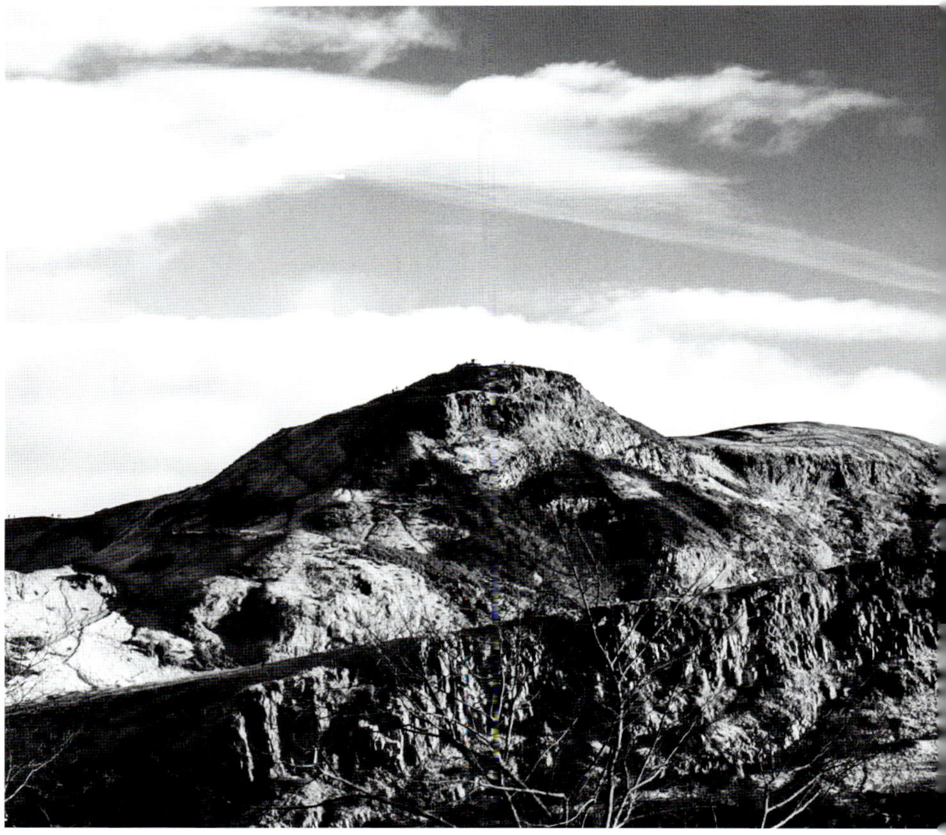

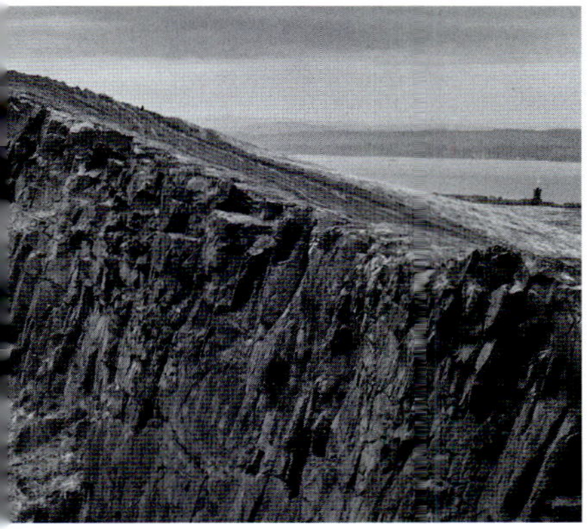

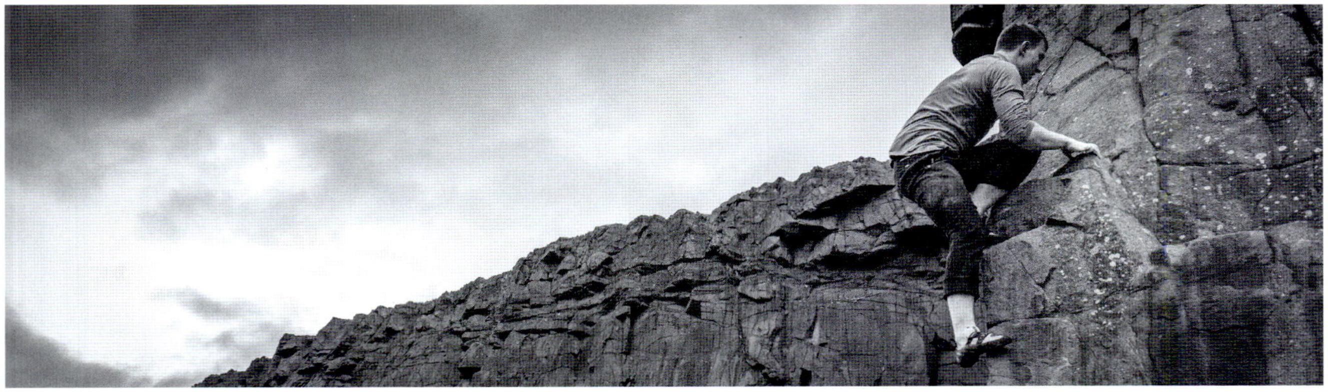

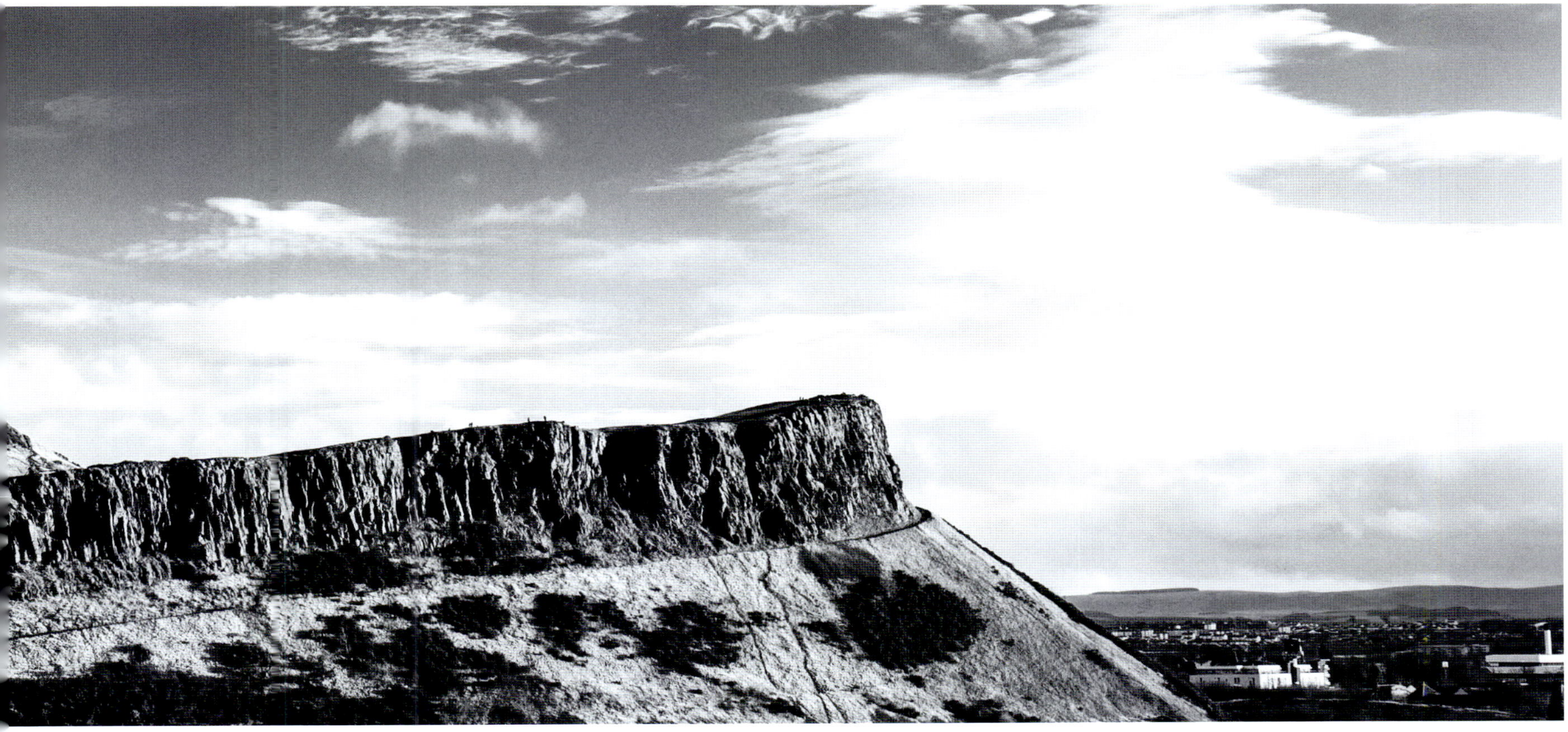

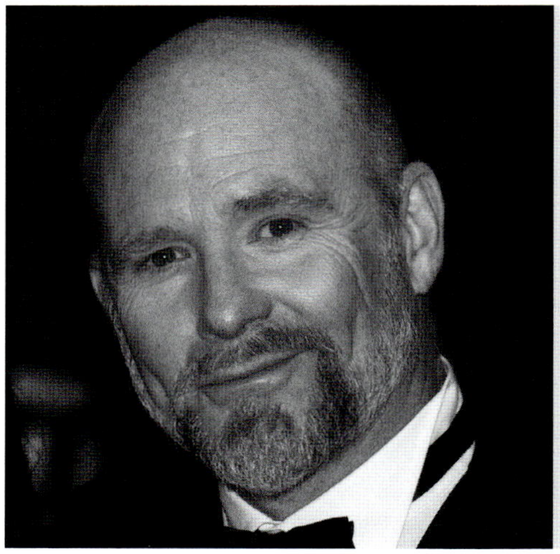

JASON CONNERY

After leaving school, Jason Connery auditioned and was accepted into the Bristol Old Vic Drama School. One year later he joined the Perth Repertory Company in Scotland. His big break came in 1985 when he took over the role of Robin Hood in the highly popular UK television series *Robin of Sherwood* (1985). He has since had starring roles in over 80 feature films, television movies and series.

In 2008, Connery started "Short Mondays", where on the first Monday of every month filmmakers could come and show their films and have a Q & A session afterwards. He threw himself into making short films, all leading toward directing his first feature, *Pandemic* (which he also produced), in 2008/2009. He went on to direct and produce *The Devil's Tom*b, *Area 51* and *The Philly Kid*, released through Warner Brothers in May, 2012.

In 2015 he shot *Tommy's Honour* in Scotland. The film opened the Edinburgh International Film Festival in 2016, winning the Scottish BAFTA for best film later in the year (www.tommyshonour.com).

Connery has a number of other projects in development and will start principal photography on *Tortilla* in the Canaries at the beginning of September, 2019. He has also been touring the United States teaching an intense weekend acting class, starting with the basics and working towards an on-camera monologue and specifically selected scenes for each individual.

I have been lucky enough in my career to travel all over the world. I have lived in some incredible cities - London, Paris, New York, Marbella, Los Angeles - but the constant in my life has always been Scotland. I was educated here, started my professional career here and have kept a wee cottage in the Borders for over 25 years. There is something about the countryside, with its undulating hills opening into yellow gorse-strewn valleys and its patchwork of multi-coloured fields, that makes my heart sing.

I have just moved back from Los Angeles to Edinburgh. I've visited the city many times, but now find myself living and working here in its centre. The cityscape is extraordinary. Everything is walkable, in fact you can experience hundreds of years of architectural history within the space of a short walk.

The pinnacle at the centre is of course Edinburgh Castle. It's as if the castle grew out of the earth and rose up on a wave of lava, the change from earth to castle wall almost imperceptible. It sits overlooking the city, strong and impregnable, yet somehow protective and reassuring. Like the city, the castle has had many different additions - St Margaret's Chapel is from the 12th century, the Grand Hall alongside it from the 16th century.

Looking down the Royal Mile, where every building is steeped in history, to the Old Town with its medieval lanes and alleyways and on to St Giles Cathedral, dating back to 1124. It's a joy to discover. Every day my partner Fiona and I travel to new areas ogling the different views - not just the buildings, but the spectacular landscape of Arthur's Seat and Holyrood Park with its verdant grassy banks dotted with wild flowers. It runs close to the centre of the city, now and again peeking above the myriad of chimney pots - city and countryside side by side in harmony.

We usually end up at the Grassmarket, a beautiful market square dating back to the Middle Ages, featuring pedestrian-friendly cafes and shops. There you'll find the White Hart Inn, where I'm told Robbie Burns once wrote poetry. The place rings with history and has the added bonus of Mary's Milk Bar serving the best ice cream in the world, a sheer delight not to be missed.

In some ways it isn't fair to compare Edinburgh to a city like Los Angeles, but having lived there for 22 years, I am struck by how little signage there is in Edinburgh. There are many beautiful homes in LA's residential areas, with an array of influencers - Cape Cod, Mediterranean, Tuscan and Craftsman to name a few. However, in the commercial areas every space is filled with bill boards, advertisements and neon signs. In fact LA is as much a literary experience as an architectural one, with writing everywhere.

In Edinburgh the space is clear because its buildings are the focal point, claiming their surroundings for all to see. In fact buildings such as The Balmoral, Jenners, The Scotsman, The Caledonian and many more have a single title over their door, nothing more. It lends itself to calming the eye and uncluttering the mind.

This leads me to Gordon Hunter and Don Ledingham, two people who have known each other their whole lives. Two people who obviously have enormous talent and a true desire to express their love, in different ways, for the city of Edinburgh. The beautiful photographs by Gordon and the exquisite poems by Don capture the essence of Edinburgh. It is such a pleasure for me to contribute in some way, and to describe what it has been for me to discover Edinburgh as my new home.

This beautiful book can travel across the globe and be admired and viewed anywhere in the world. If you are reading this piece, you own the book. So here it is. Enjoy.

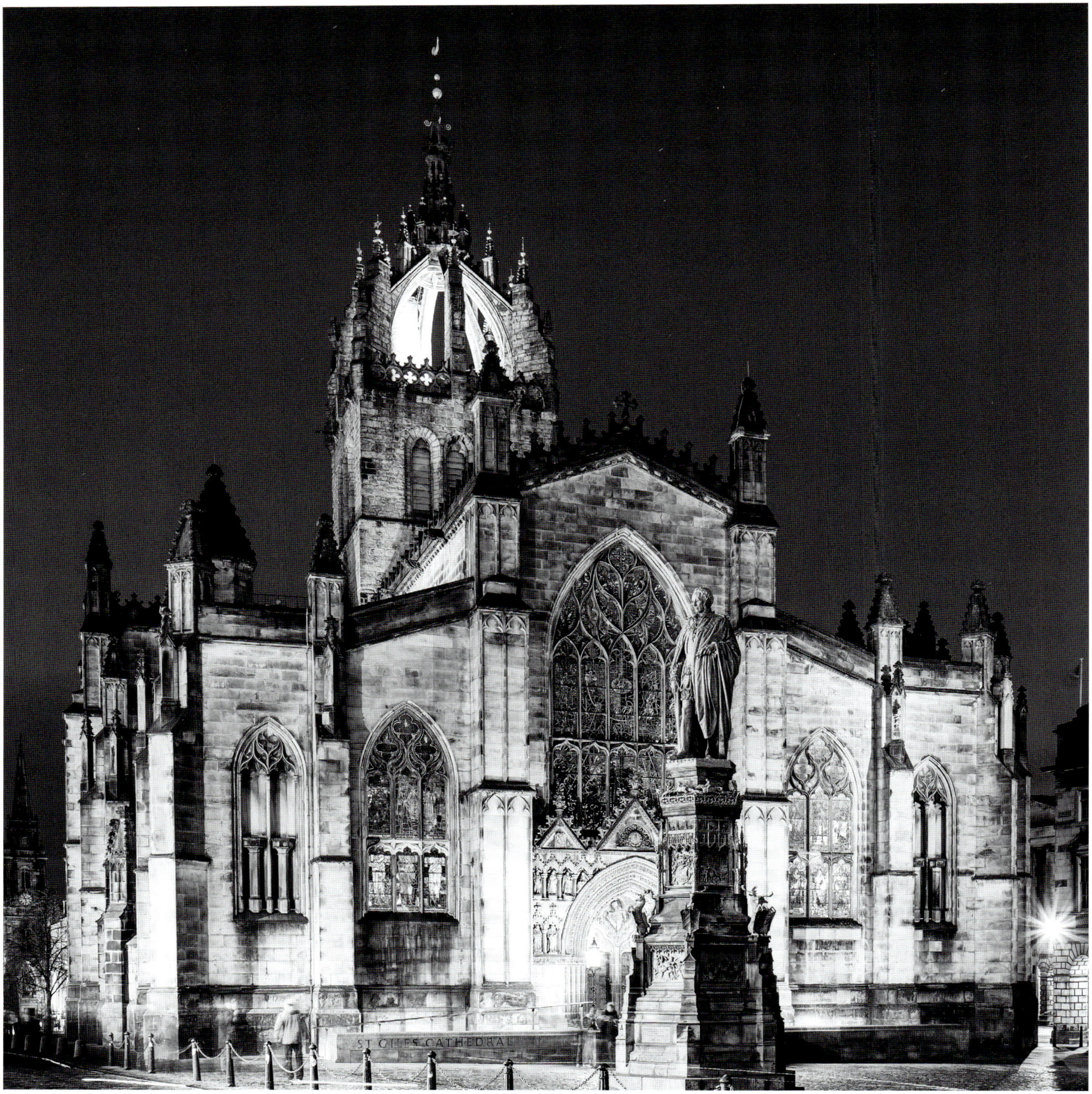
ST GILES CATHEDRAL

A CITY'S CROWN

This Queen of cities
Wears a jewel-encrusted crown;
While others reach towards the sky
And raise a multitude of hands
To claim attention and respect,
Elbowing their neighbours,
Shouting their names,
The Gherkins and the Shards,
With mirrored glass,
And ever-changing shapes;
This Kirk, this High Kirk,
Keeps its nerve, unwavering,
Confident in itself,
No need to shout
Above the crowd,
Precisely set upon the
Monumental Tower,
Its floating arches,
Welcoming the light,
See the morning garnets flash,
The amethysts at sunset,
The iridescent pearling light
Of flat Edinburgh afternoons;
Resolute, it holds its place,
Self-assured and grounded;
A People's Crown,
After all.

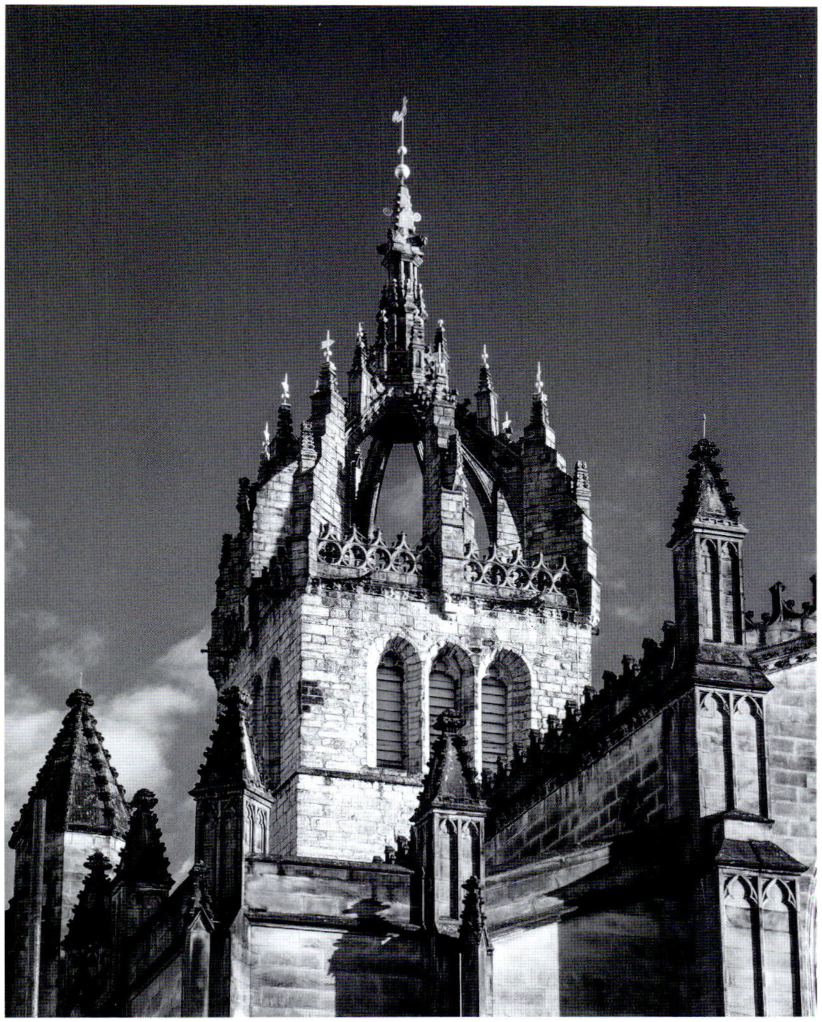

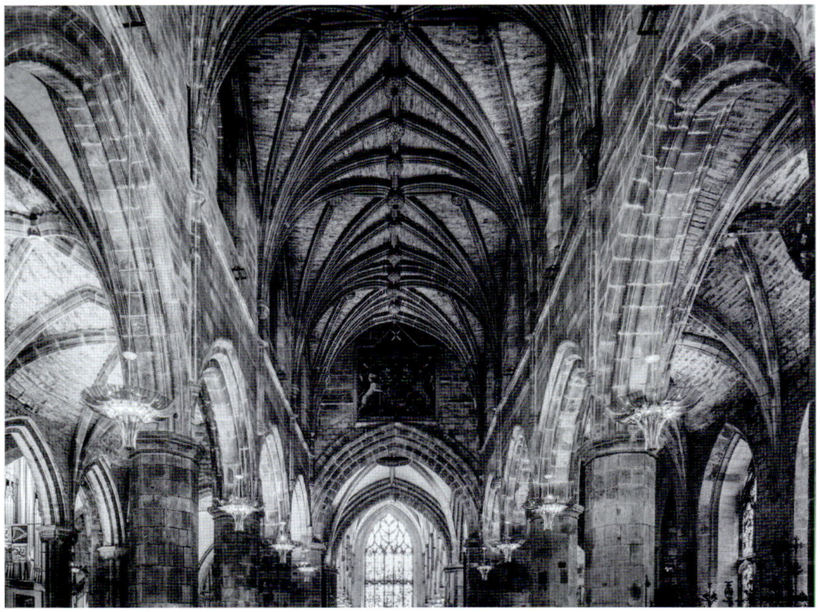

FLOWERSHOP

The ladies in the shop
Would cut the flowers
On the diagonal,
To extend their lives,
Readying them to mark
Our journey's way,
Unboxed,
Unbound,
Unbundled,
The green smell of stem
Permeating the cold dampness,
Overpowering
The mix of scents,
Engineered wreaths,
Bouquets,
Wired into
Ornate displays,
Or tied in
Simple bunches;
While all the while
The lily
Waited its turn,
Its heavy breath
Tolling its bell,
Ready to occupy
Every room.

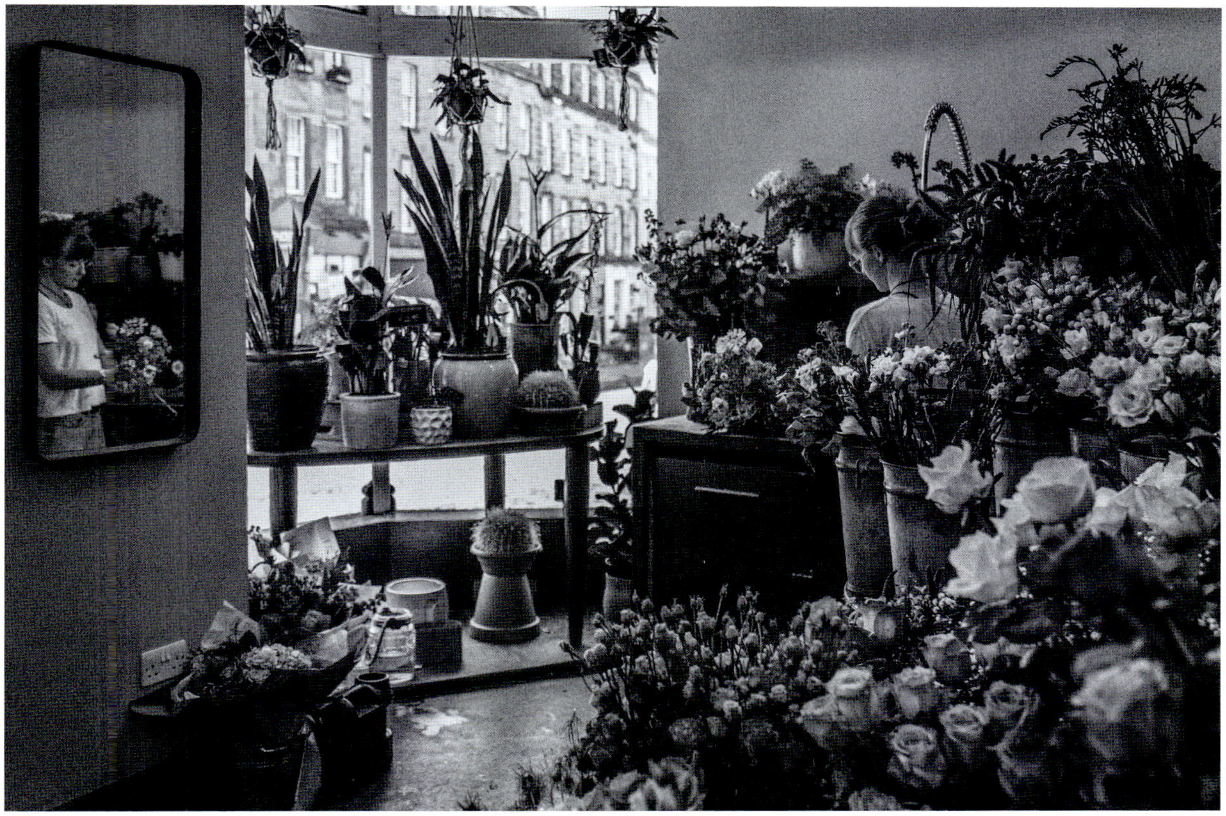

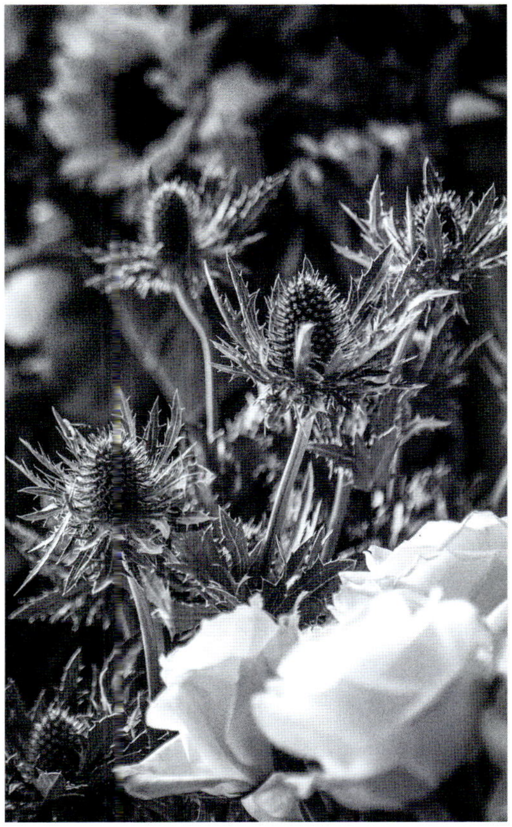

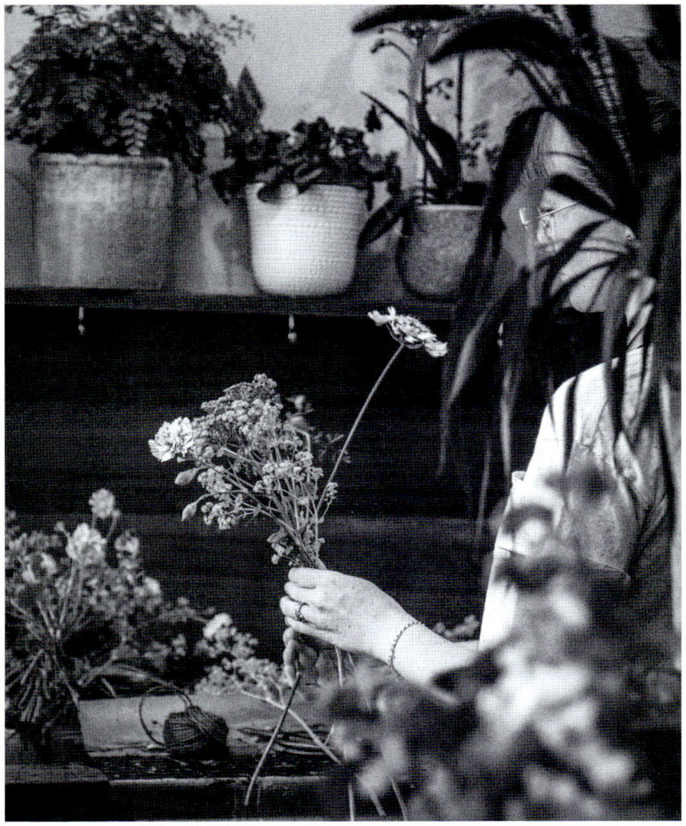

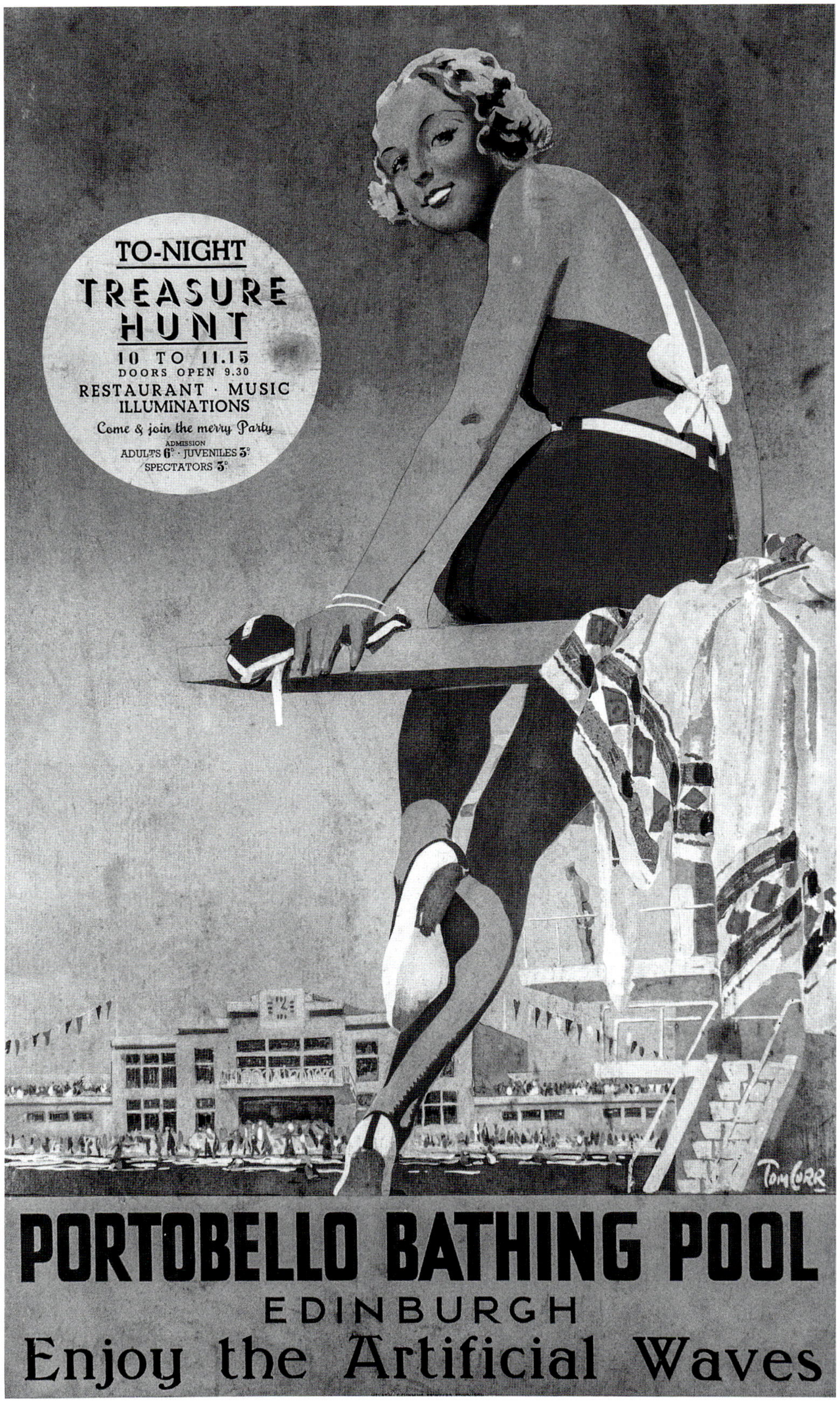
TO-NIGHT
TREASURE HUNT
10 TO 11.15
DOORS OPEN 9.30
RESTAURANT · MUSIC
ILLUMINATIONS
Come & join the merry Party
ADMISSION
ADULTS 6D · JUVENILES 3D
SPECTATORS 3D
TOM CURR
PORTOBELLO BATHING POOL
EDINBURGH
Enjoy the Artificial Waves

PORTOBELLO BATHER

The LNER Poster looked out at me
From behind the dirty glass,
"Enjoy the artificial waves"
You beckoned, invitingly,
But I remember the reality,
The great lumps of freezing water
Rolling up the from the depths,
Forcing us onto our tip-toes,
Our stick-like arms held aloft, and
Capturing our breath;
The artist has elevated you, icon like,
Immaculately posed upon your diving board
Forever looking down over your shoulder
Against a pitch perfect sky;
Your 1930's finger wave curls,
Your porcelain ankles,
And Ivory skin,
A Madonna in red,
With a Benediction smile;
Portobello misses you,
Your promises of promise,
All gone now,
Quietly slipped into the sea
When no one was watching,
Save for the 'Baths',
Still there in their Victorian splendour,
In soft, red, sandstone,
With its enormous smokestack,
Redundant now, yet preserved,
Much like the town,
Looking for a future,
But unable to let go of its past
"Enjoy the artificial waves"
You proclaimed.

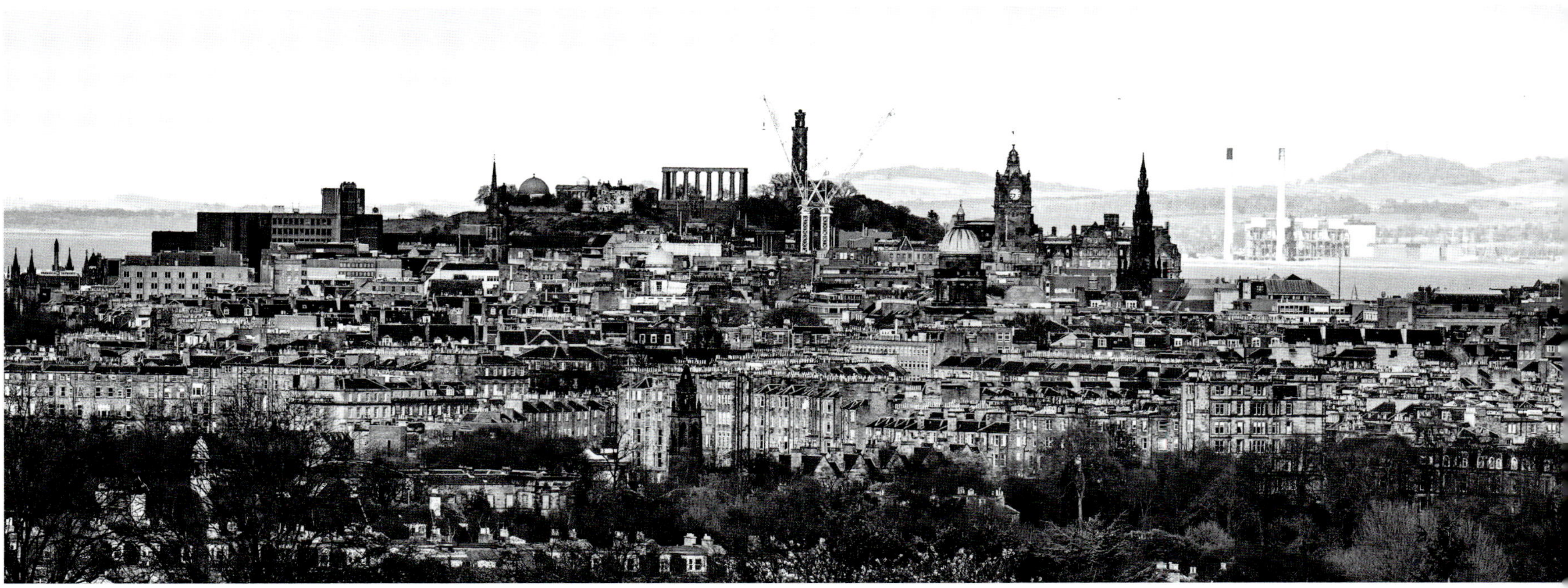

LOOKING EAST

Looking East,
The twin towers grew,
Perpendicular
To a green horizon,
Rising up from the shore
To hold their place,

Straightening,
Together yet apart,
A concrete embrace,
Winding themselves
Into our memories
Coiling a spring,

Taking a space
On recall's shelf,
As the black coal
Lifted from the ground
Beneath their feet
Fed the perpetual fire

Spiralling their plumes
Towards the heavens,
Fifty years of
Smoke signals,
Signalling
Their end.

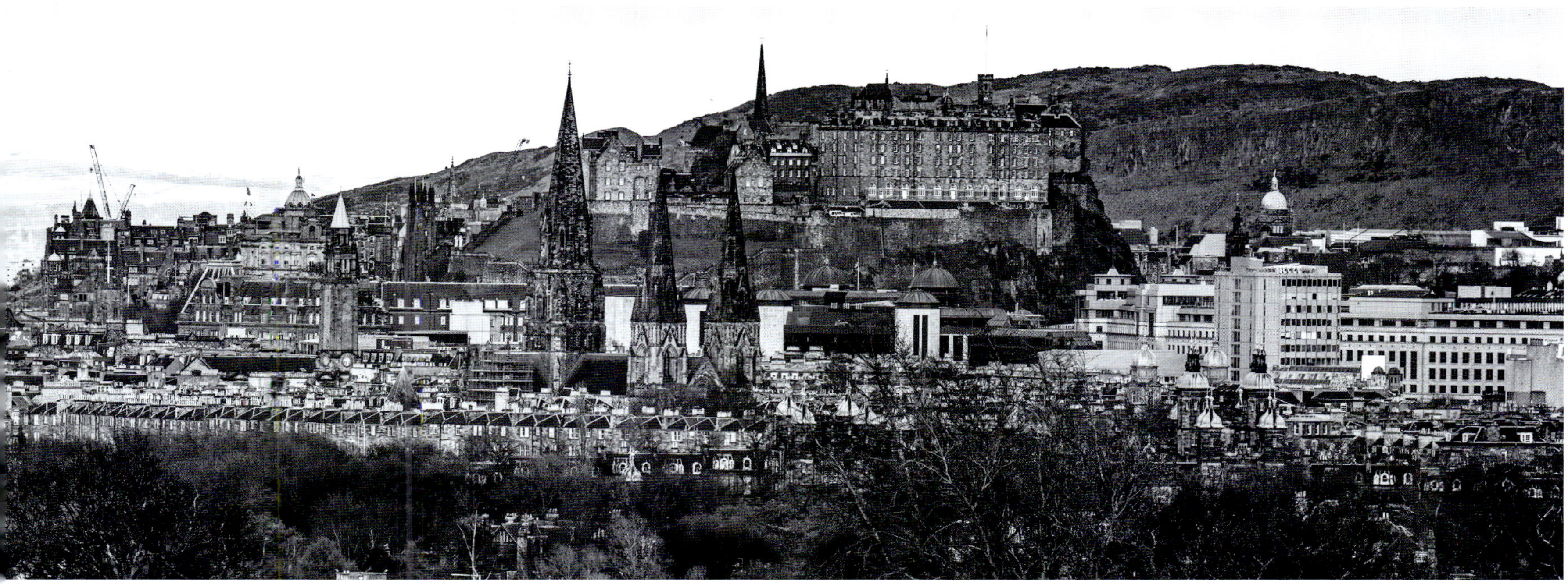

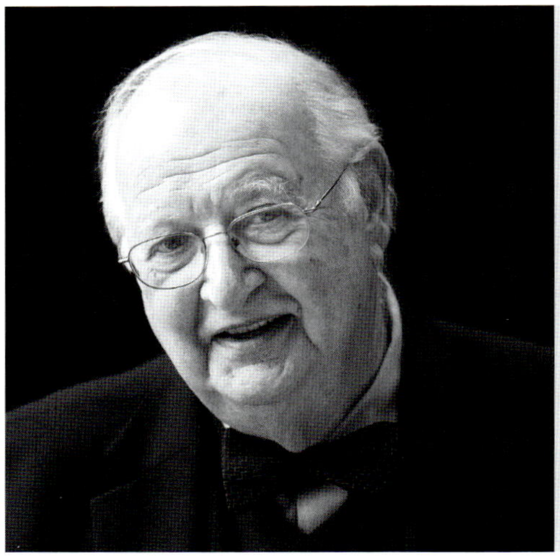

SIR ANGUS DEATON

Sir Angus Deaton, who was born in Edinburgh, is Senior Scholar and Professor Emeritus at Princeton University, and Presidential Professor of Economics at the University of Southern California. He is the author of *The Great Escape: health, wealth, and the origins of inequality* and, with Anne Case, the forthcoming *Deaths of despair and the future of capitalism*.

His interests span domestic and international issues and include health, happiness, development, poverty, inequality, and how to best collect and interpret evidence for policy. He is a member of the National Academy of Sciences and the American Philosophical Society, a Fellow of the British Academy, and an Honorary Fellow of the Royal Society of Edinburgh. He is a Past-President of the American Economic Association. His BA, MA, and PhD are from Cambridge University, and he holds several honorary doctorates from universities in Europe and the US.

In 2015, he received the Sveriges Riksbank Prize in Economic Sciences in Memory of Alfred Nobel "for his analysis of consumption, poverty, and welfare." He was made a Knight Bachelor in the Queen's Birthday Honours List in 2016.

I was born in Edinburgh at the very end of the Second World War. We lived on the Meadows, still given over to allotments. The One O'Clock gun split my day: 'you be home for your dinner before the gun!' Melville Drive had trams that we rode to all parts of the city, to Granton Harbour, to the zoo in Corstorphine, and to the Botanic Gardens.

Greyfriars Bobby and the (then) Chamber Street Museum were an easy walk, as was the children's library on George IV Bridge, a home from home. So was a griddle scone shop near the university; that it was a university I did not know for many years. A more frequent task was to "do the messages" on Argyle Place, where there was a barber shop, a bagpipe maker, a newsagent and, on Sciennes Road, a fishmonger and a butcher.

My Edinburgh is a city of education and of enlightenment. My father had little education as a child, was invalided out of the army with tuberculosis, and worked for Blyth and Blyth on George Street while going to night school at Heriot-Watt. He cared about education, and paid the modest fees to send me to James Gillespie's Boys' School, then opposite John Rebus' flat on Marchmont. We were taught that we lived in the 'Athens of the North', and learned much about Edinburgh's rich history of science and medicine. Yet the greats of economics, David Hume and Adam Smith, were not prominent; indeed, much more recently, when I was admitted to the Royal Society of Edinburgh, and told of its greats, Hume and Smith were mentioned only in passing. The statue of Smith, near St Giles, was erected only in 2008.

The ideas of Smith and Hume came to America through John Witherspoon, a successful minister in Paisley, who became the sixth President of Princeton University in 1768. He had a revelation that the Kingdom of Heaven would come, not in Scotland, but in America, where he set about building it - his church, on Witherspoon and Nassau Streets, is still a centre of life in Princeton. Witherspoon was a teacher and politician, and a Founding Father of the new republic. Another Founder, Ben Franklin - he of the kite and the lightning conductor - made two pilgrimages to Edinburgh to meet Smith and Hume. He stayed with Hume in St David's Street (the name is a contemporary joke about Hume's suspected atheism). Franklin founded the American Philosophical Society for Useful Knowledge in Philadelphia in 1743, and was the first foreigner elected to the Royal Society of Edinburgh in 1783. Both societies, unlike the Royal Society in London, have retained their breadth, and celebrate their writers, statesmen, and philosophers (and economists), along with their physicians and scientists.

'Useful knowledge' is what I was brought up on in Edinburgh. The idea is at the heart of the Scottish Enlightenment, of the Industrial Revolution, and of the prosperity that we all enjoy today.

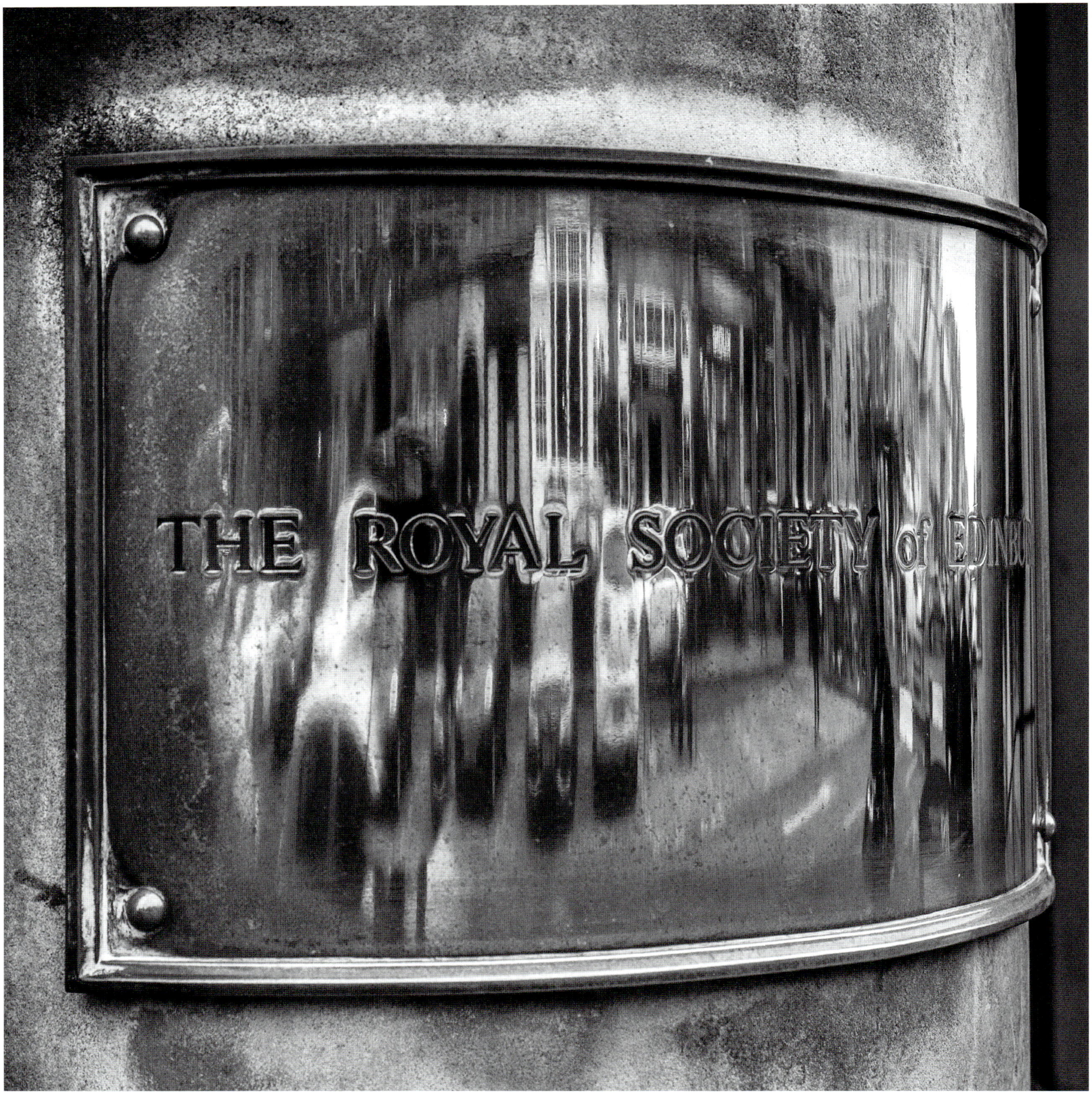
THE ROYAL SOCIETY of EDINB

THE ROYAL SOCIETY OF EDINBURGH

We learn to walk,
One step following another,
And so we see this
As the way to reach
Our destinations,
In straight lines
From here to there,
Following our compass,
Connecting the dots,
In logical linearity,
Yet in our heart of hearts
We know the folly
Of straight lines,
For successful journeys
Rarely follow
Well-trodden routes,
Instead remember
The unintentioned arrival
At that special place,
Which opens out in front of us,
Surprising us with our luck,
So break free from
The tyranny of rational roads,
Of safety's small-minded steps,
And jump instead,
From stone to stone,
Leap chasms,
Navigate the swamps,
Swim the rapids,
Take a chance
By closing your eyes
And following that eye,
Which lurks,
Deep within your mind.

THE FORTH BRIDGE

His eye travelled as the crow flies
Stretching from one shore to the next
Fusing the gap within his mind
Short-circuiting the distances
By reaching out his arms
And gifting us the time;
Insatiable, we stuff our pockets
Hoarding it, storing it
Shaping it, shaving it
Squeezing three days into one
Stockpiling the seconds
Higher and higher;
And yet it always wins
By yielding us no interest
And never being cashed

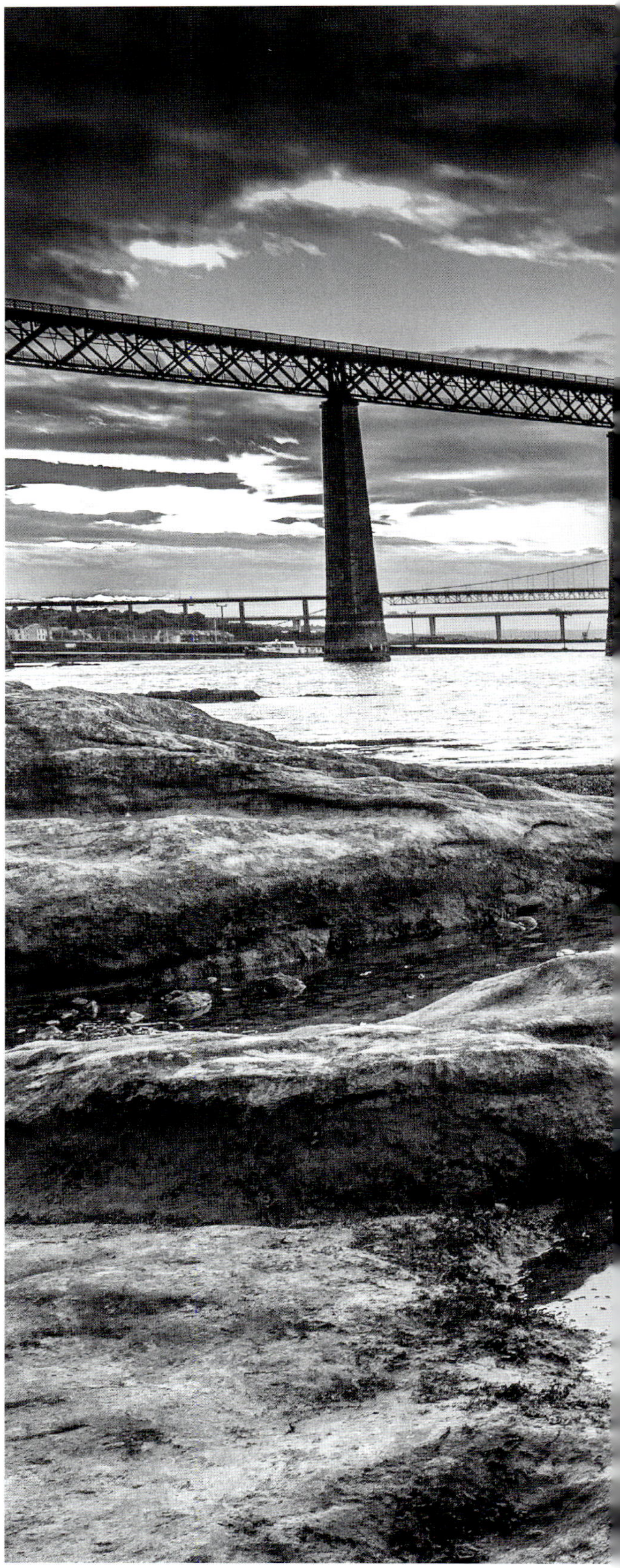

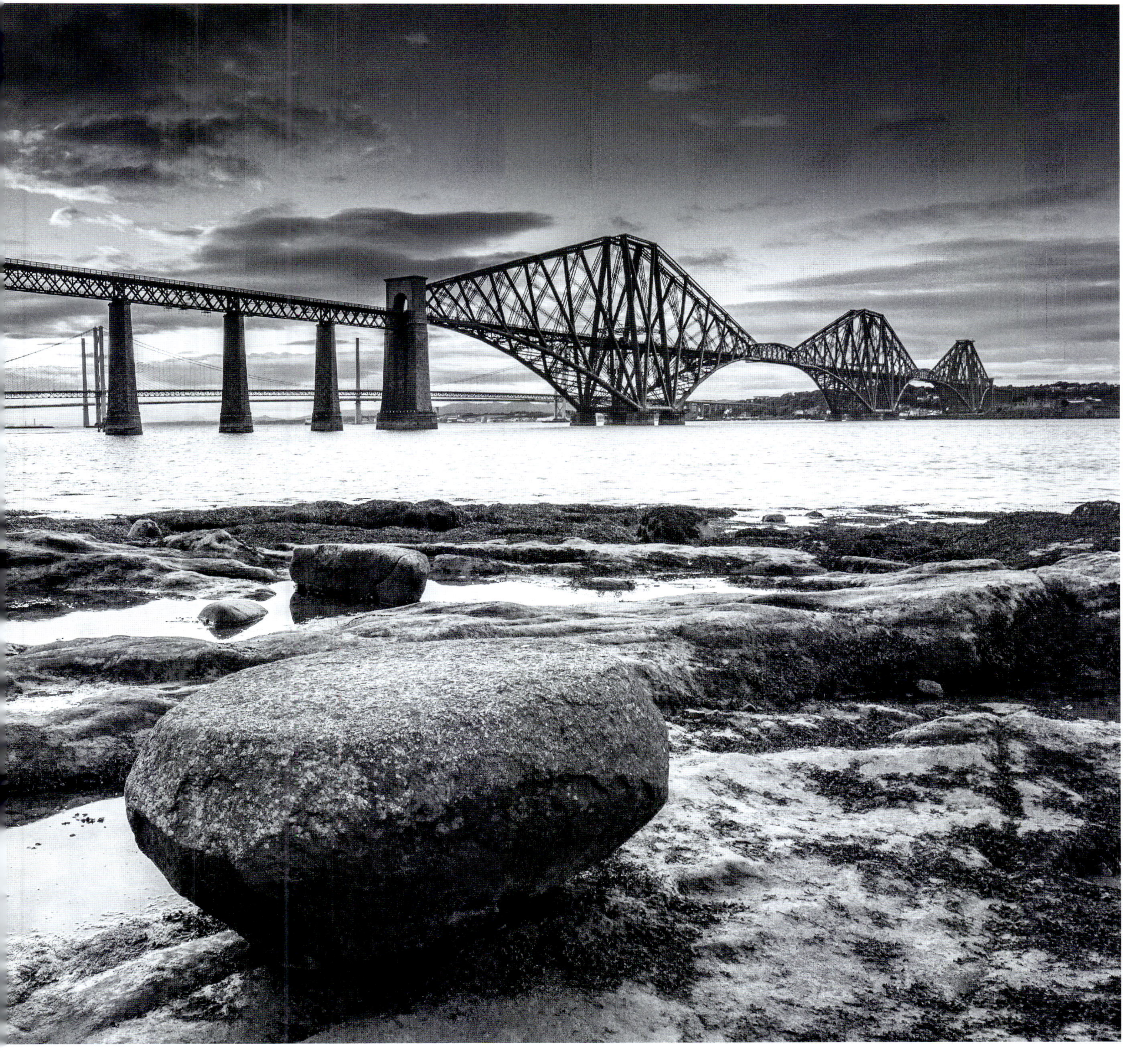

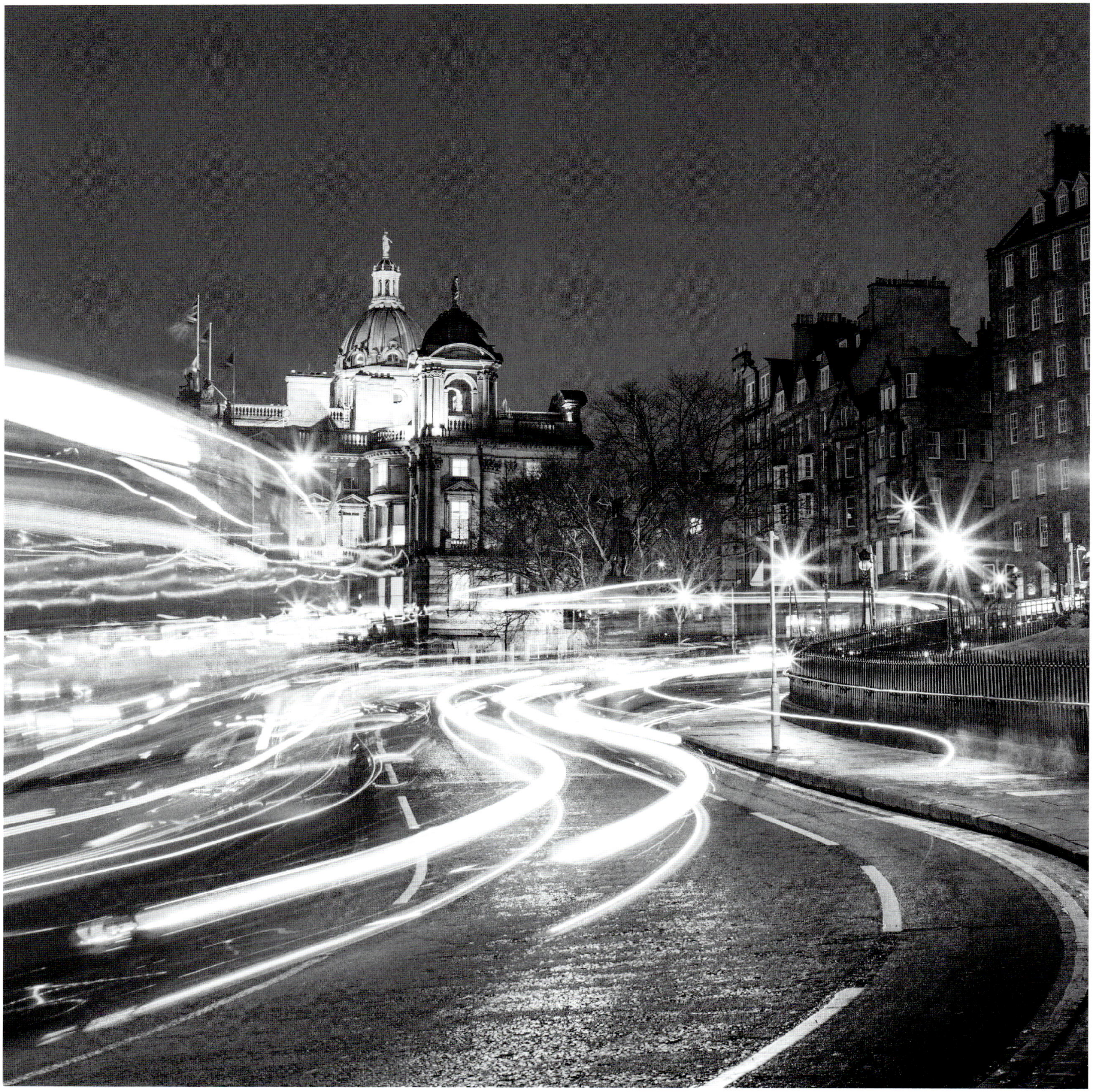

THE BANK

"I promise to pay
The bearer on demand"
Is signed beneath
With sloping hand,
And on this vow
We place our trust,
Not because we can
But because we must;
For in exchange
Of goods or labour,
We treat the stranger
As our neighbour,
And on such
A promissory bill,
We come to judge
They bear no ill,
And so, upon,
These good intentions,
We build a set
Of new conventions,
Of loans and transfers
Accounts and debts,
The system builds
On gives and gets,
So, watch these
Notes of promise grow,
To make return,
On what they owe,
And place your faith
In trusted hands,
The rock on which
This very building
Stands.

ROYAL MILE PHARMACY

Pharmacy is such a proper word,
A proper word for a proper place,
Tucked away down the Royal Mile,
With a mortar and pestle above the door,
In line of sight of the apothecary;
And just before nine they begin to gather,
The agitated, the shuffling, the desperate,
The stick-thin, and the loud,
Comrades-in-arms awaiting their turn,
But the door remains closed,
And minutes stop here, while seconds elongate ,
Stretching into infinity,
Now, for the only instant in their day
Does time take on a presence,
Take on a value in their lives,
These men, for whom routine
Long departed, their scaffolding unbolted,
The building blocks of time removed,
That measurer of life,
Beyond the dimension of the diary;
Yet now, in these extended minutes,
Time stands still - an act of unwilling
Mindfulness where reality intrudes,
And just when it seemed the hour would
Never strike - the door yields,
And in they flood, escaping seconds later
Clutching their day ahead,
Or, having sipped the green nectar,
Look forwards to a timeless day,
And all the while I sit across the street,
Nursing an Americano with hot milk,
Readying myself for my 9.15 meeting
How fragile the line between one world
And the next?

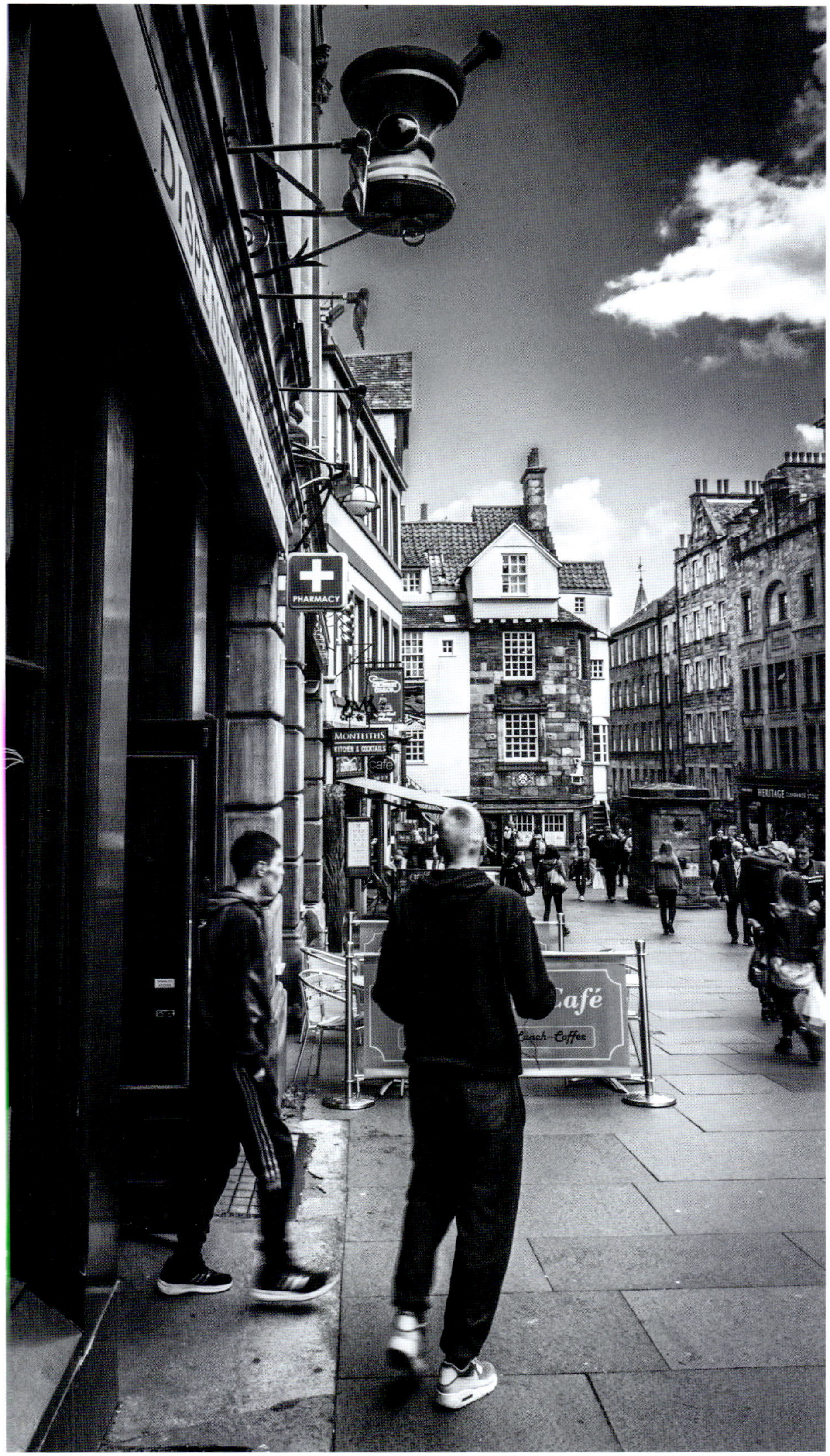
PHARMACY
MONTEITHS
KITCHEN & COCKTAILS
Café
Lunch-Coffee
HERITAGE

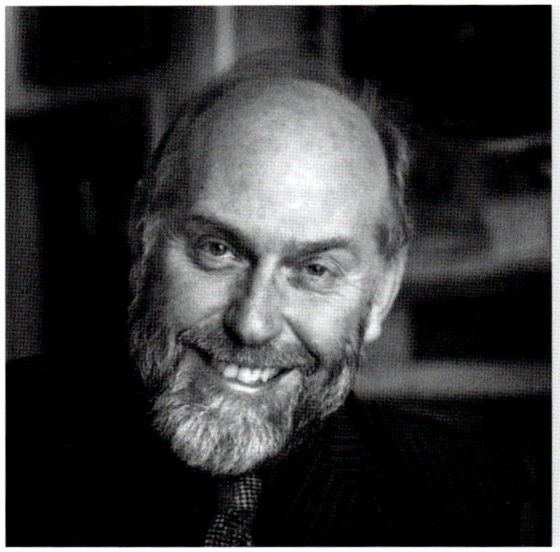

ALISTAIR MOFFAT

Born and raised in Kelso, in the Scottish Borders, Alistair Moffat has often left the place in body, but never in spirit. He attended the universities of St Andrews, Edinburgh and London, and also received some tough education on the rugby fields of the Borders.

In 1976 Alistair took over the running of the Edinburgh Festival Fringe. Over the next six years, under his watch, it grew into the world's largest and most dynamic arts festival.

Moffat then moved to Scottish Television and rose through the ranks to become its director of programmes. On the way he made several award-winning documentaries, before taking over the running of the children's schedule on ITV. After a period as chairman of Scottish Television, he returned to the Borders to live and work. He founded the Borders Book Festival, staged in Melrose each June, and the event has grown to become one of the UK's most popular and successful literary gatherings.

A prolific and respected author, Alistair's books include *Kelsae*, *The Borders*, *The Reivers*, *The Sea Kingdoms*, *The Wall* and *Tuscany*.

In 1972, for reasons lost to memory, I started an arts festival in Kelso, my home town. The closing act in the Tait Hall was Genesis. In between my booking them and their appearance, they had become successful but still did the gig. Their finale, accompanied by indoor fireworks, appalled the hall manager. "I'll need to speak to your faither," she growled between gritted teeth. In the dressing room afterwards I negotiated a price discounted for cash with Phil Collins. "OK, but none of that Scottish money!" The reality was that I didn't have £600 on me, and had to persuade the manager of the TSB to open the safe on a Sunday night.

All of which, and much else, persuaded me to apply for the job of running the Edinburgh Festival Fringe in 1975. At the interview, lovely Andrew Cruickshank, the distinguished actor who was chairman, said he had been very impressed by the reviews for the Kelso Festival. When I told him that I had written them myself, he roared with laughter.

Monday, January 5, was my first day in the Fringe office in the Royal Mile Centre, a set of function suites and bars in the High Street where the Fringe Club was held. In the depths of a very cold winter, the pipes in the toilets above the office had burst over the Hogmanay weekend, and I opened the door to discover the floor covered in raw sewage. I knew I would have to deal with shit in this job, but it arrived early.

For the first four months, there was only me on the payroll, something that seemed just daft for a festival on such a scale. And so I set about making the Fringe bigger, better and more professionally run. Assembling a superb team (two of whom ran the Edinburgh International Book Festival and another did the Fringe), we began to innovate. We had no structured idea of what to do, we just did the next thing we could think of, too young to know how badly wrong it could go. We started Fringe Sunday, closed the High Street for the first time, invented the Perrier Awards for Comedy, attracted high value sponsors and created the first of the 'super-venues'. The Fringe grew from 143 performing groups in 1975 to 494 when I left in 1981, making it the largest arts festival in the world.

Those six Festival Fringes I did were the best job I ever had. The Fringe Club had a licence until 2am, because performers who finished late needed somewhere to eat and drink. In those days the pubs closed at 10pm. Everybody wanted to get into the club. I once welcomed Princess Margaret and she held my hand during our conversation, drinking in the atmosphere. Our bouncers were two huge men who worked at Bilston Glen Colliery and they greeted the Queen's sister with: "Good evening, your worship." Sean Connery's brother, Neil, looked like him and he managed to get in without a membership card. When he turned up again, the Bilston Glen men were wise to the ruse and refused entry. The problem was that it really was Sean Connery that time. Luckily I spotted this and ushered the great actor up to the bars. The former Labour leader, John Smith, performed at the cabaret, singing a Gaelic song after Rowan Atkinson had finished his set. It was an unforgettable time.

What we helped create was something unique. There are several festivals around the world like the official Edinburgh Festival, with orchestral concerts and suchlike, but nothing on the scale and diversity of the Fringe. It converts Edinburgh into a cultural wonderland, exciting, jammed with people, full of possibility. When I go each year, I love to walk around the streets, with a permanent smile on my face.

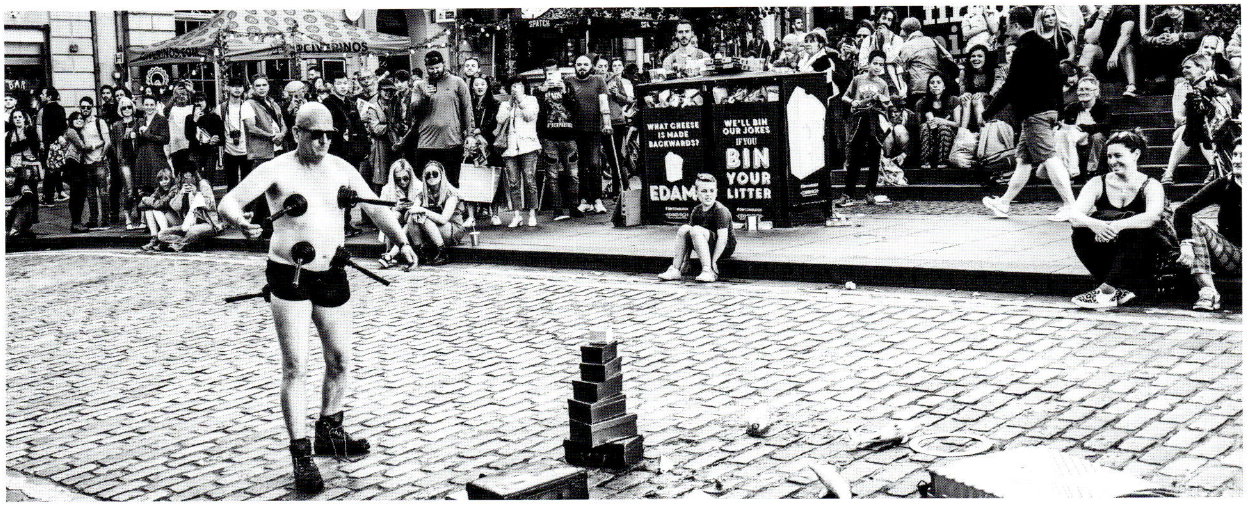
WHAT CHEESE IS MADE BACKWARDS?
EDAM
WE'LL BIN OUR JOKES IF YOU BIN YOUR LITTER
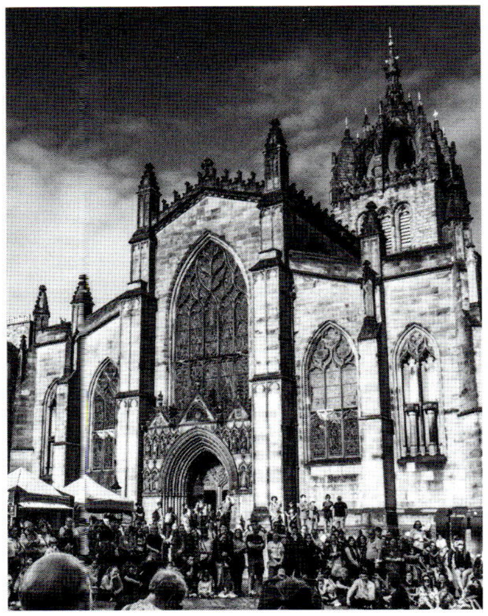
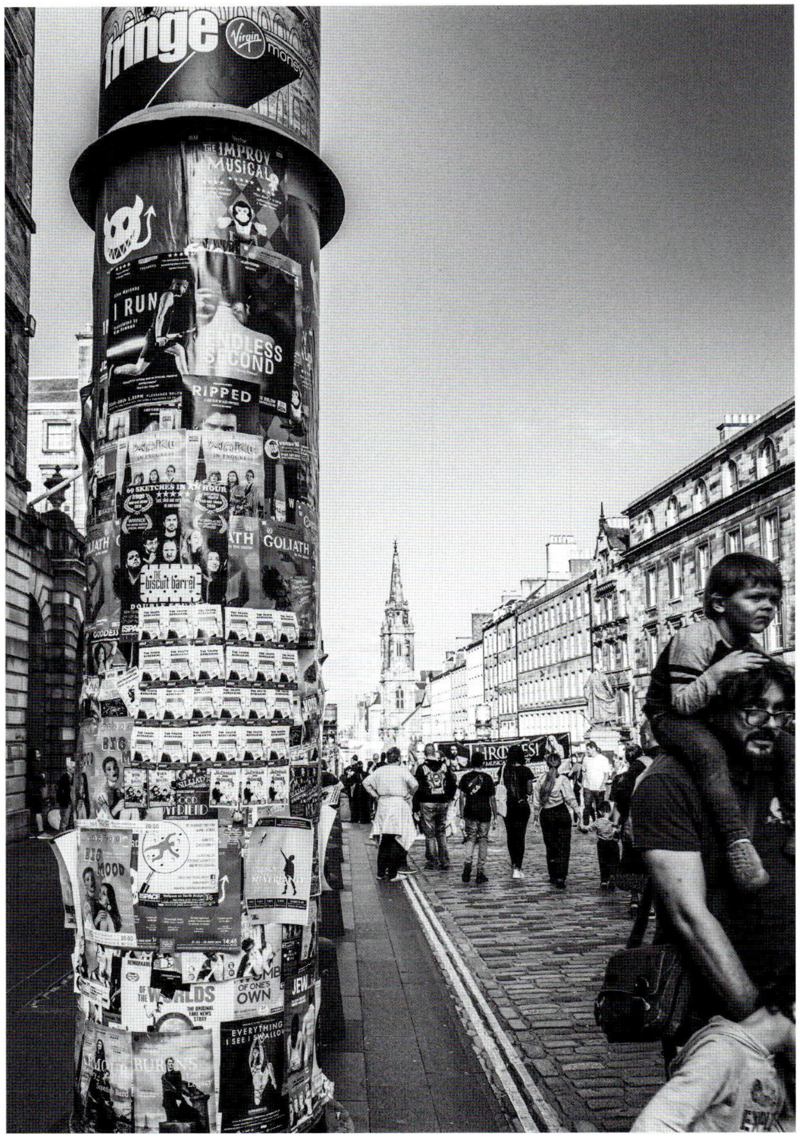
fringe
Virgin money
I RUN
ENDLESS SECOND
RIPPED
GOLIATH
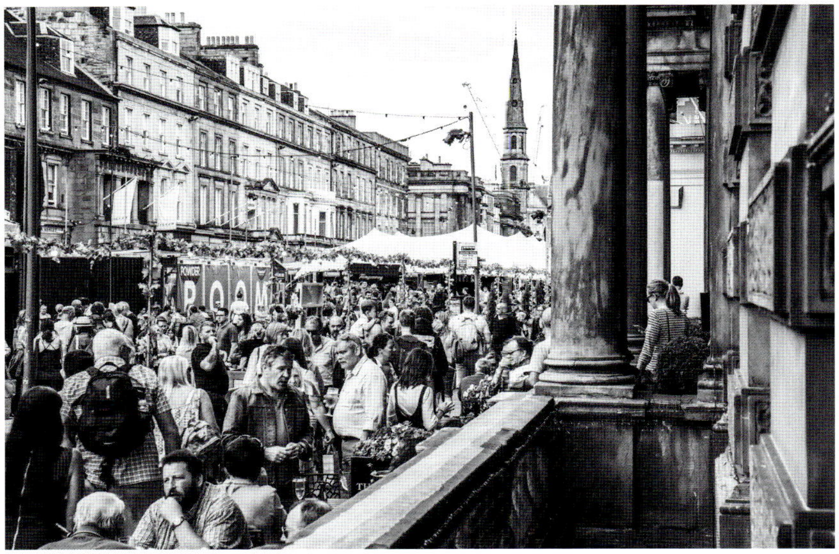
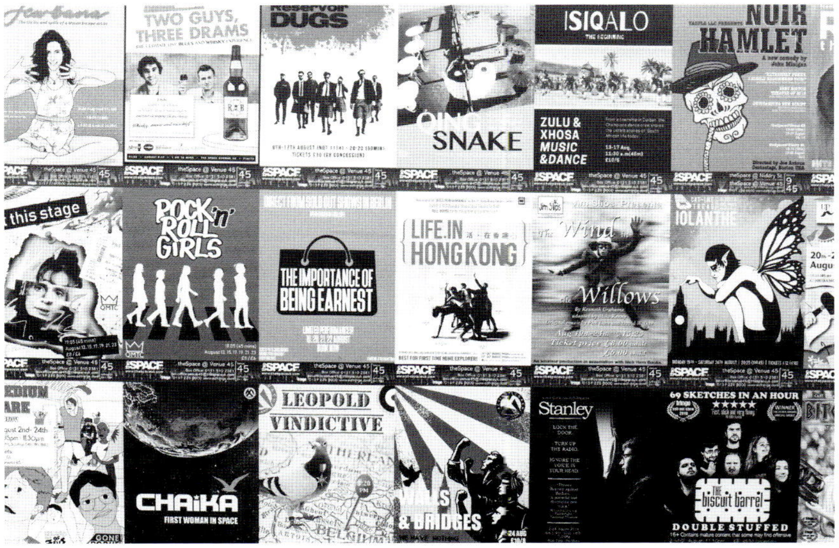
TWO GUYS, THREE DRAMS
ISIQALO
NOIR HAMLET
SNAKE
ZULU & XHOSA MUSIC & DANCE
this stage
ROCK 'n' ROLL GIRLS
THE IMPORTANCE OF BEING EARNEST
LIFE.IN HONGKONG
IOLANTHE
LEOPOLD VINDICTIVE
CHAiKA
FIRST WOMAN IN SPACE
WALLS & BRIDGES
Stanley
69 SKETCHES IN AN HOUR
DOUBLE STUFFED

THE 'BLOODY' FRINGE

Pushed to one side,
We see the city
Slide from out our hands,
In annual separation;
The wandering audience
On their migration,
Like Serengeti wildebeest,
Driven on by instinct,
Following, following
The stars, while
The big cats lie,
Waiting idly under trees,
Before picking off the weak;
Overhead the vultures glide,
Lifting on the August air
Until they dive
To pick on the dried bones
Of anxious comedians;
"Who are you for?"
The hyena asks,
But still they come
The acrobats and clowns
The students and the brave,
Throwing themselves
Against the wall of hope;
"Leave us be", we cry,
And all too soon it does,
Departing suddenly,
With an embrace,
A fleeing lover's farewell;
A Kiss - adieu;
Until next year.

THE SCOTSMAN BUILDING

Stand outside the building, when no one is watching,
And place your hand against the stone,
To feel its gentle thrum, or, late at night, listen
Carefully to hear the oiled presses roll;
For this was a heavy industry where ships were built,
Leviathan carriers of the truth,
That launched across the world to a daily deadline;
Deep into the morning dark the lorries rolled,
The trains departed carrying the news,
And behind them the words soaked into the walls,
The ink saturating through the floors,
The men and women starting every day afresh,
Setting out to build another craft,
Feeding the never-ending beast;
And round and round the circle went,
Until, one day, the deadline missed,
The news departed, shape shifting,
Leaving behind its anachronistic past;
But join me and place a hand upon the stone,
Feel the gentle thrum from deep within its soul,
For this is a building,
That will forever keep its
Word.

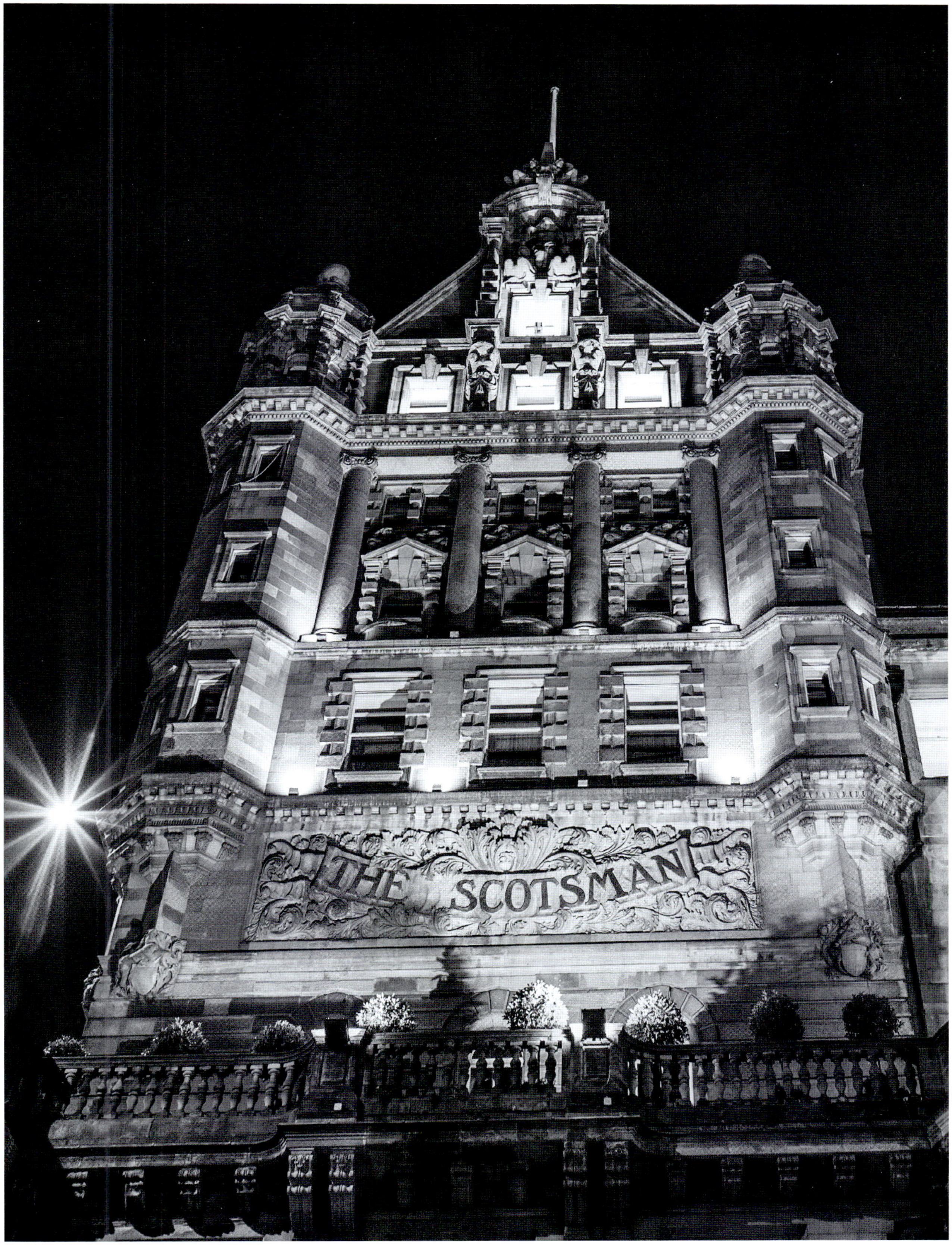
THE SCOTSMAN

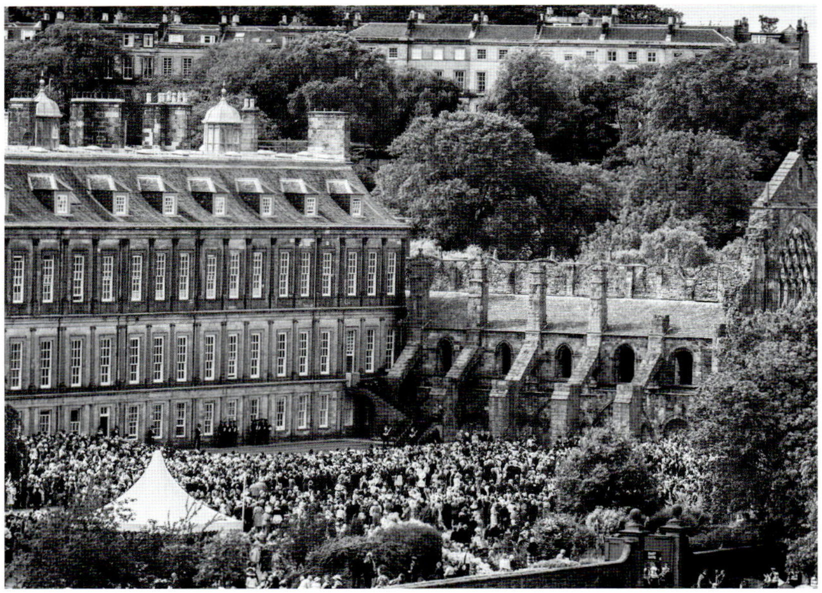

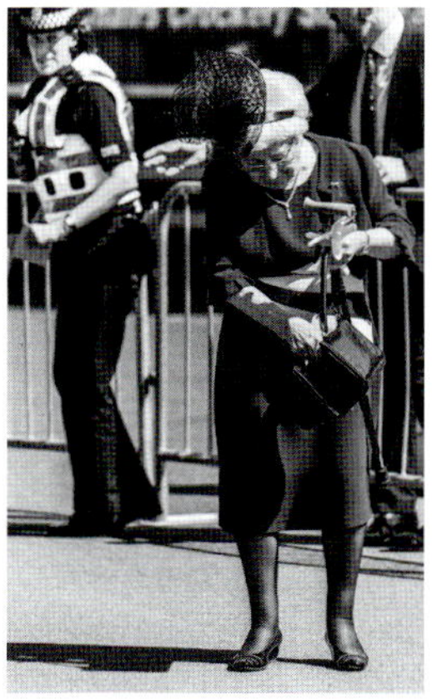

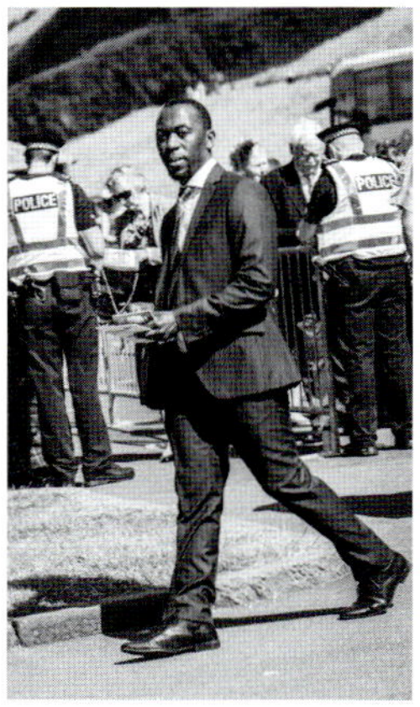

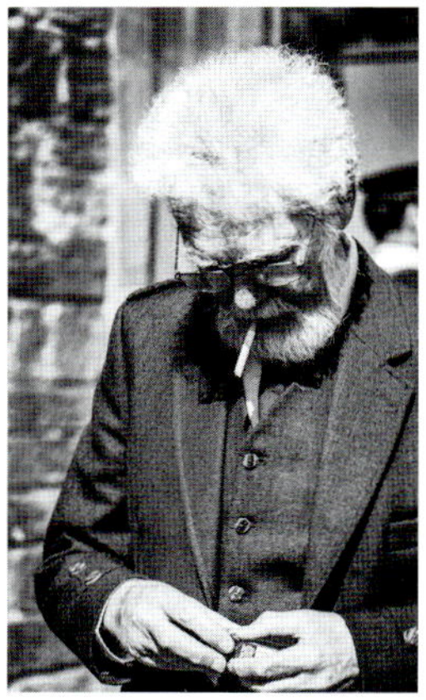

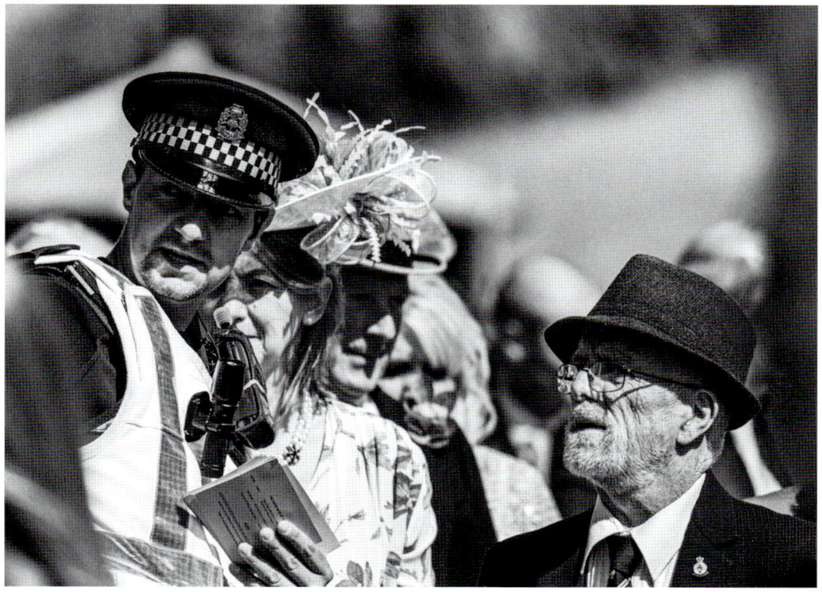

HOLYROOD GARDEN PARTY

They wait,
In the undiscriminating queue,
Each clutching
A sovereign's invitation,
On a white embossed
And weighty card,
That has, that very morning,
Been ceremoniously removed
From its honoured place,
To call them here,
The uncomfortably suited,
And the morning suited,
The unfascinating fascinators,
The wide brims and the pillboxes,
The medals and the braid,
The high street combinations,
The designer labels,
The Highland dress
And Buddhist robes,
The clashing of the colours,
The tightness of the shoes,
The privileged by birth,
And those who work the earth,
The provost and the cook,
The postman and the duke,
Each offers up their name,
And passes through
The watchful royal gates,
To walk, gratefully,
For a single afternoon,
Upon forbidden
Grass.

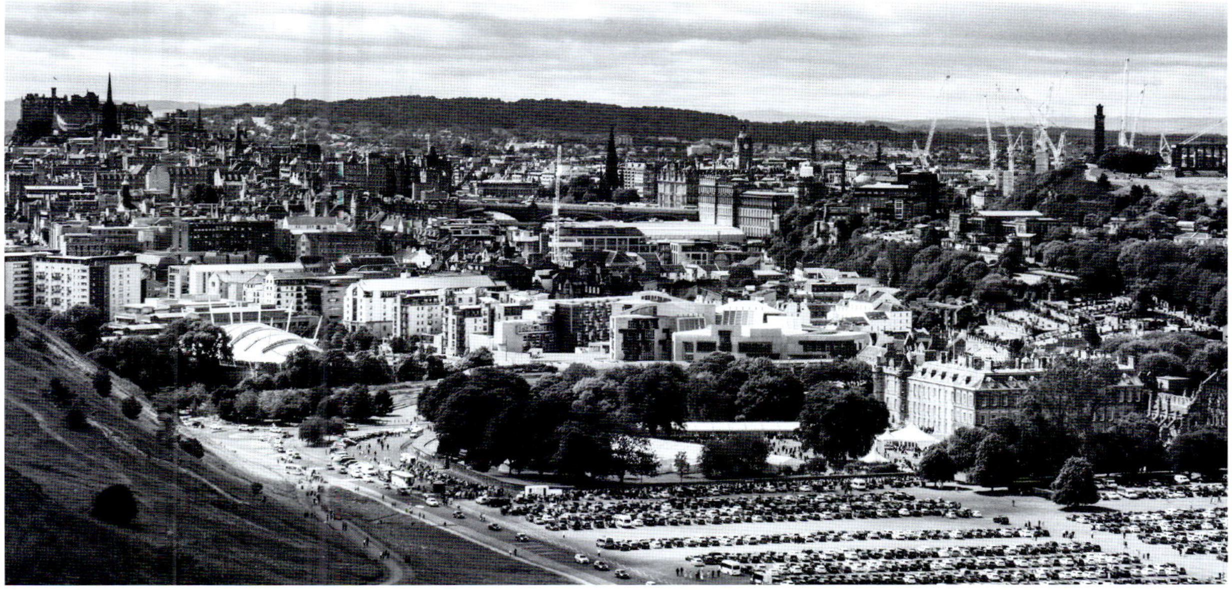
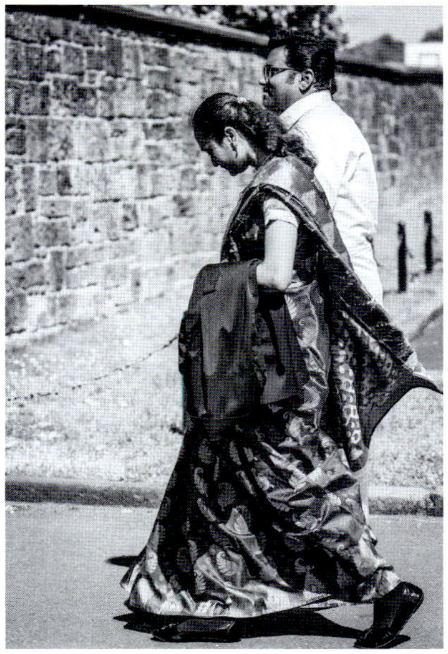
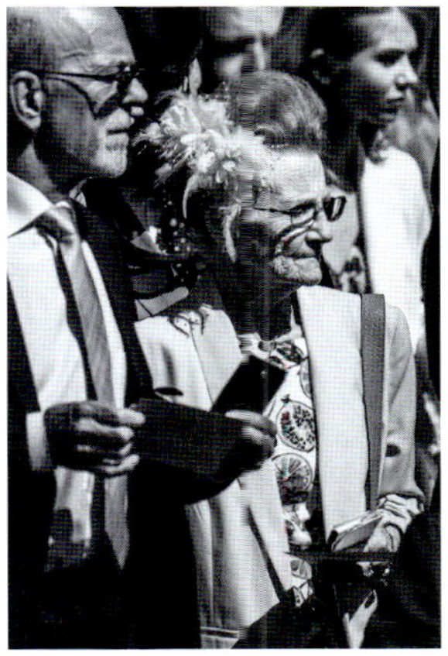
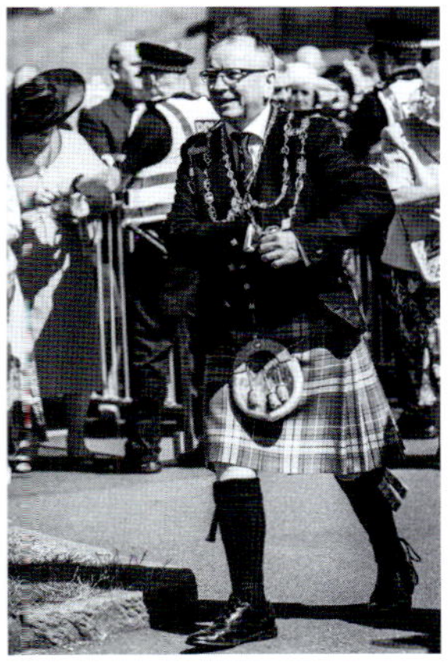
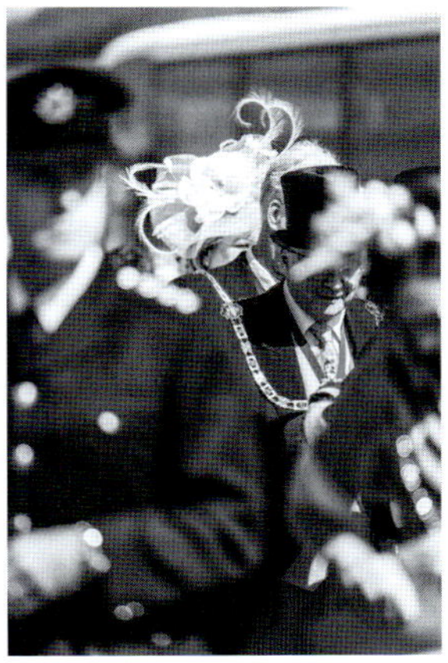
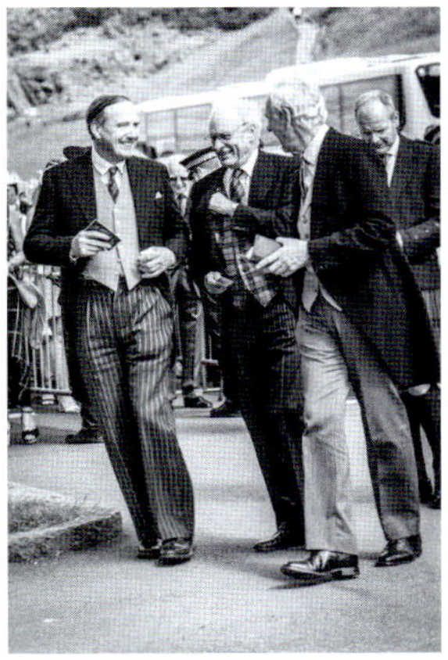
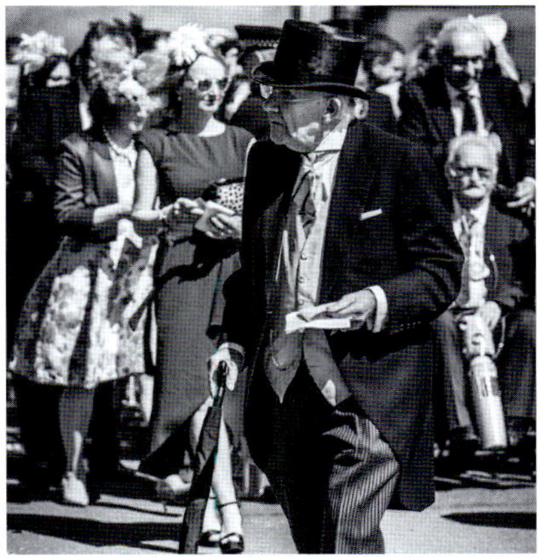
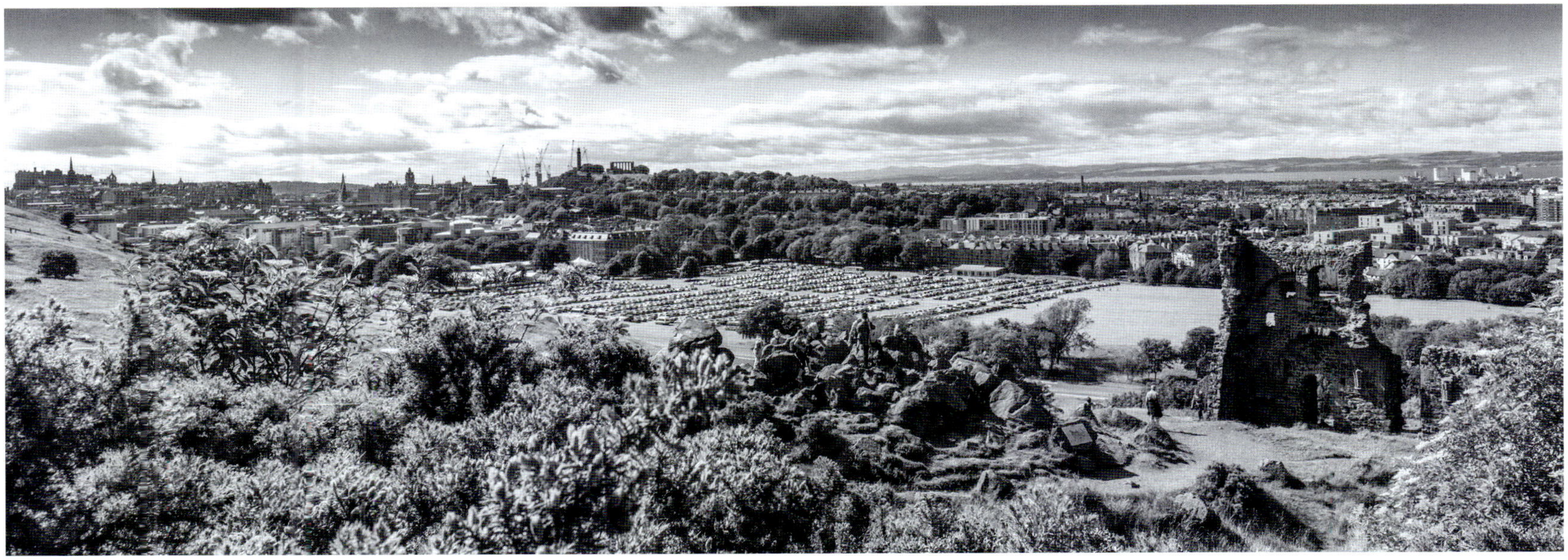

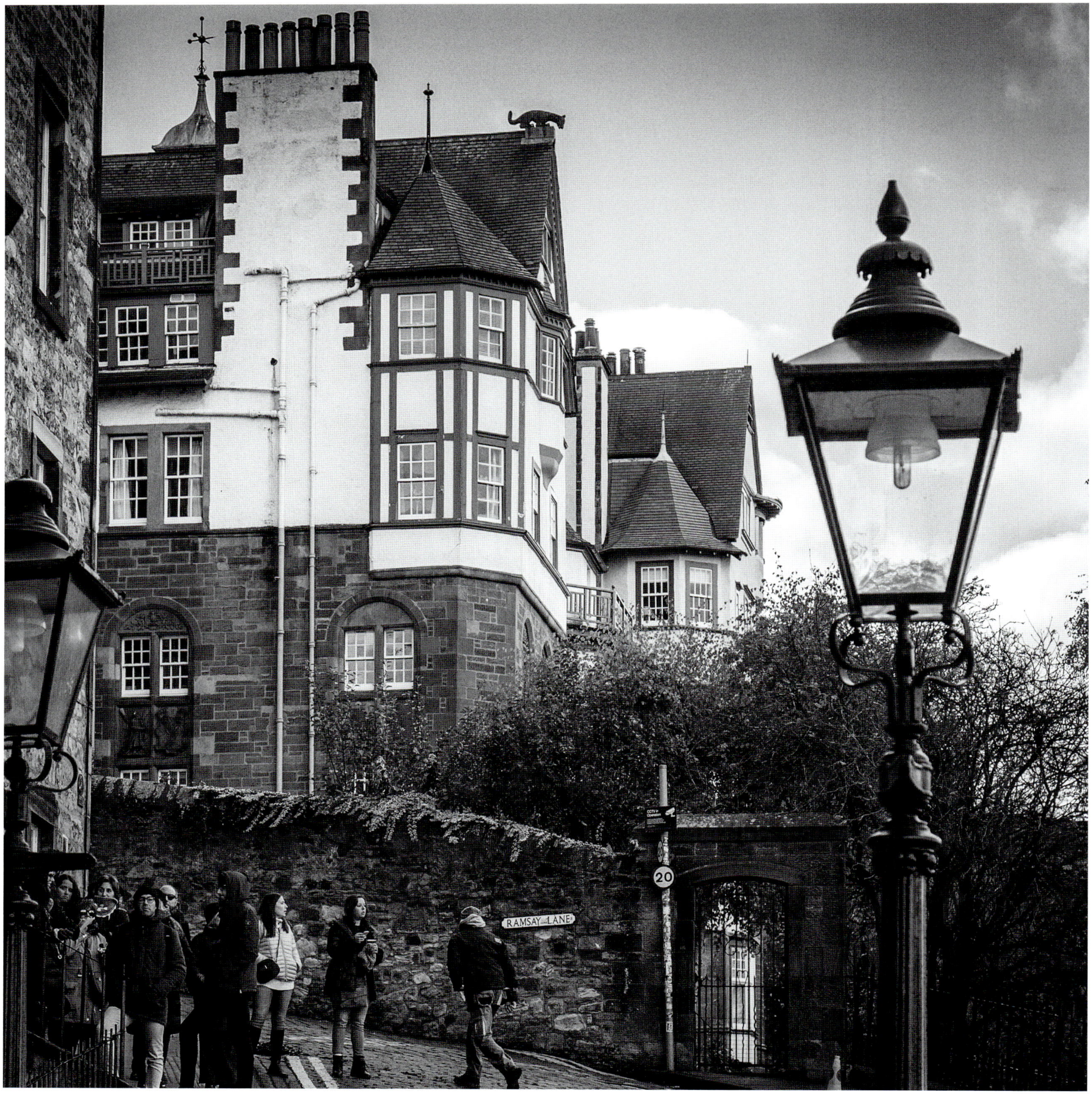
20
RAMSAY LANE

RAMSAY GARDEN CAT

The City,
Continues, unawares,
Beneath the crouching form,
Whose devil's wings
And dragon's horns,
Were lost to scouring
Edinburgh winds;
Transformed,
A silhouette appears,
Arching its spine
In perpetual coil,
And readying to launch
To everlasting space;
I watch it, certain
Of the leap,
But no, it waits,
With all the patience
Of a hunting cat,
Toying with us,
Its unsuspecting,
Prey.

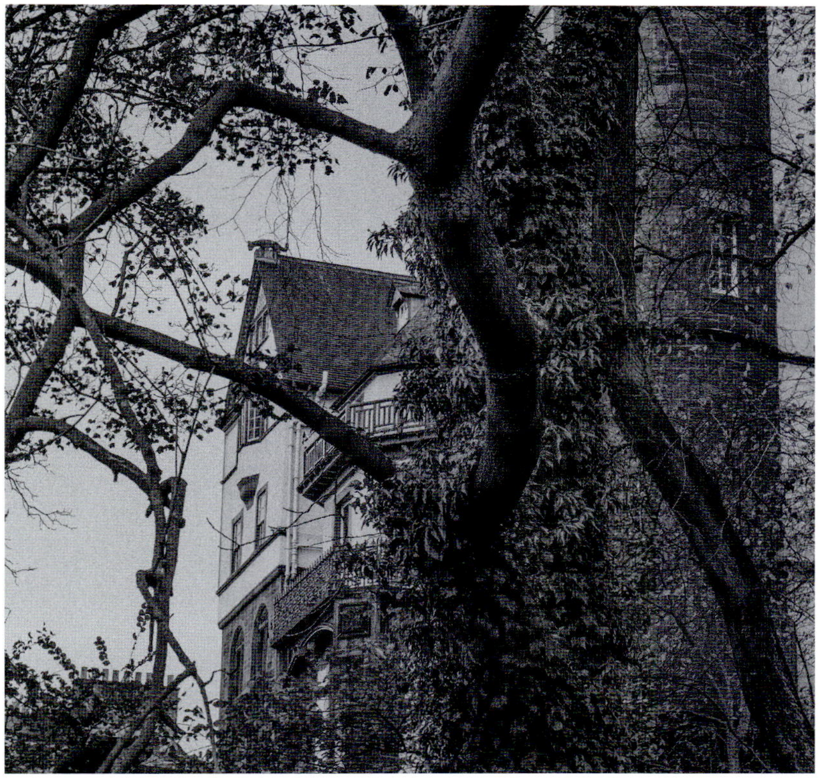

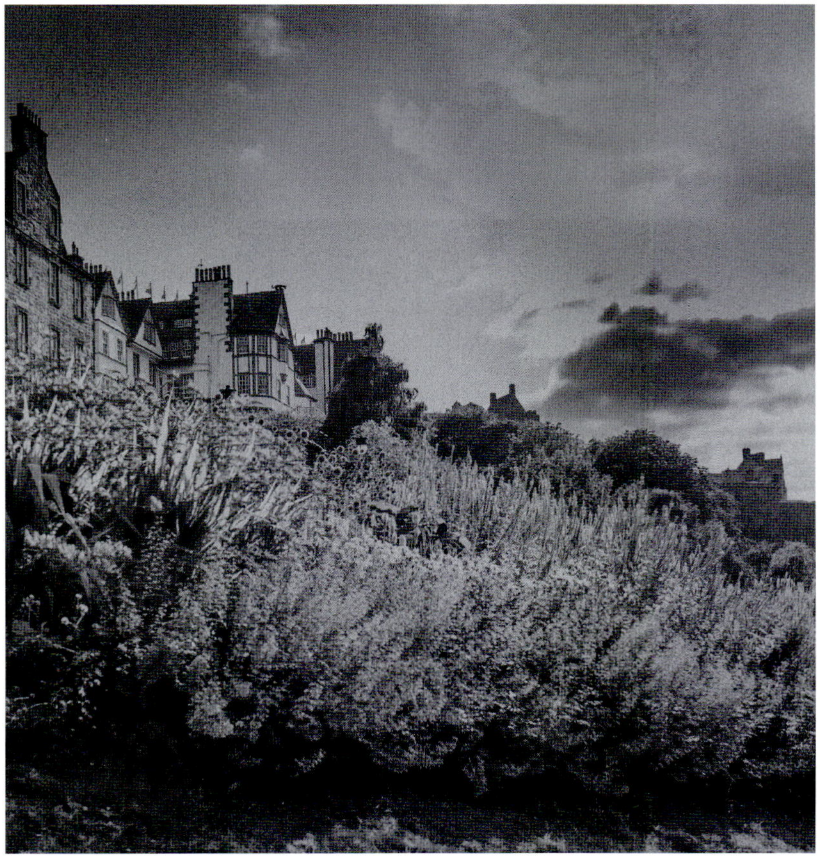

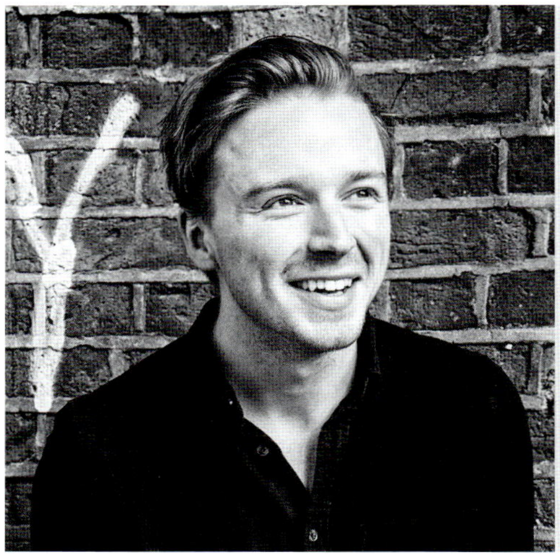

JACK LOWDEN

Jack trained at the Royal Conservatoire of Scotland and began his acting career with the National Theatre of Scotland in *Black Watch*. Jack is best known for his work in TV, *The Long Song*, *War & Peace*, and for his film roles in *Fighting with My Family*, *Mary Queen of Scots*, *Dunkirk*, *England Is Mine*, *Tommy's Honour* and *Calibre* (for which he won the 2018 British Academy Scotland Award for Best Film Actor). Jack has also won an Olivier Award for Best Supporting Actor for Richard Eyre's West End revival of *Ghosts*.

I've always been obsessed with history, particularly Scottish history, and that's why I love Edinburgh. It's a beautiful, craggy-faced old storyteller, but being able to live in the same place where Bonnie Prince Charlie sauntered, where Lord Darnley was blown up and strangled, or where Charles I played golf (shout out to Leith Links there), is why it is such a special place to me.

And its bravery. I love the idea of people years ago standing on the banks of the Firth of Forth and thinking 'Fife's actually no' that far like', and then building something as extraordinary as the Forth Bridge, or a different bunch of folk hundreds of years before that looking at the dormant volcano looming over their roofs and saying: 'Aye Stuart, put the castle up there.'

It's a city that's always had a quiet, winking confidence and self-assurance that I guess comes with being just that little bit better looking. It's also the home of inventors and thinkers, and that much-needed restlessness - that keeps it pushy and probing - hasn't left the city since the days of Hume and Smith. Like building the madly unique and bold Scottish Parliament right over the road from Holyrood Palace. It's always made me think of a rebellious teenager, dyeing her hair green, piercing her nose and then standing in front of her antiquated granny saying: 'I'll wear what I want, Gran!'

It's just the best place to live, and these beautiful photographs and poems perfectly sum up the Auld Toon with all the answers.

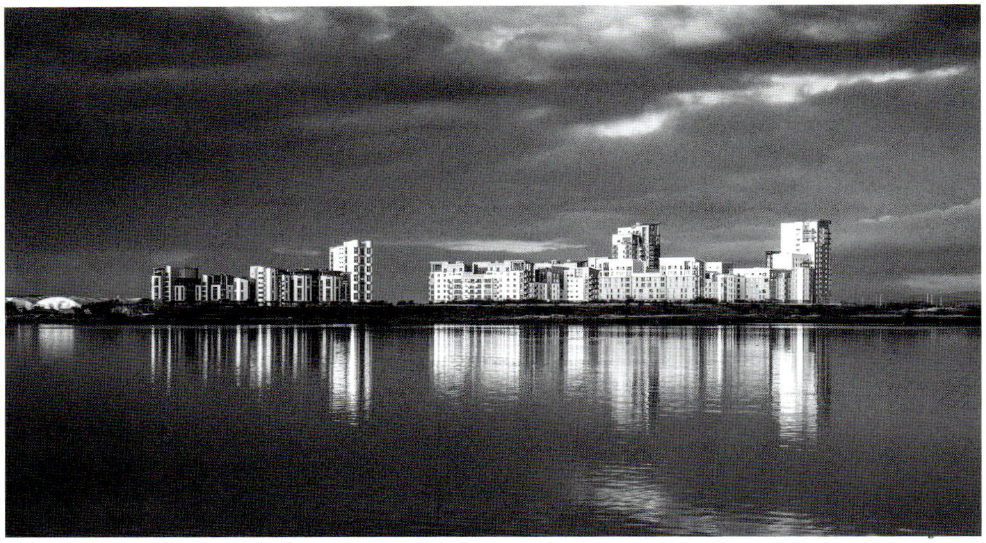

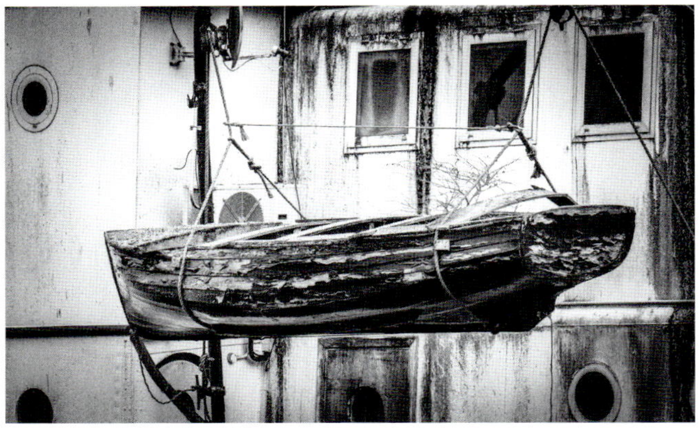

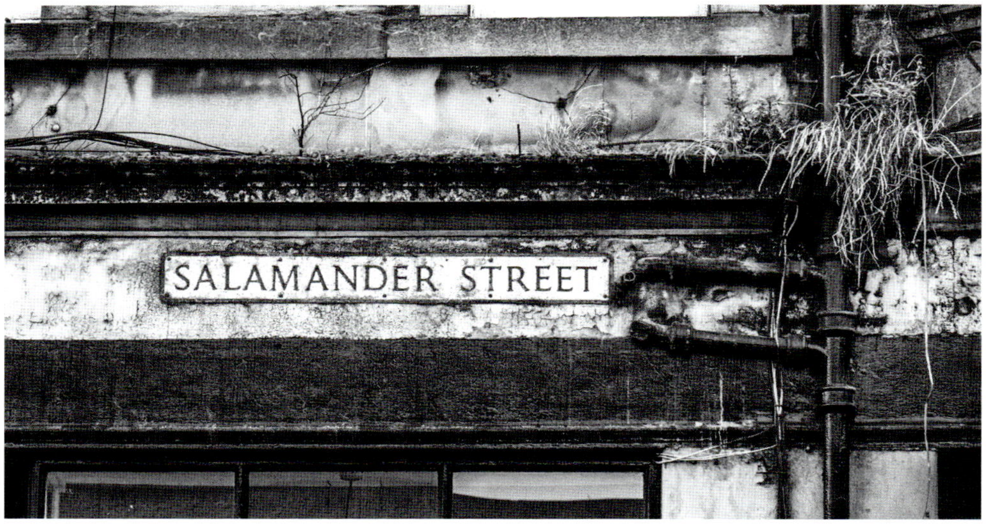
SALAMANDER STREET

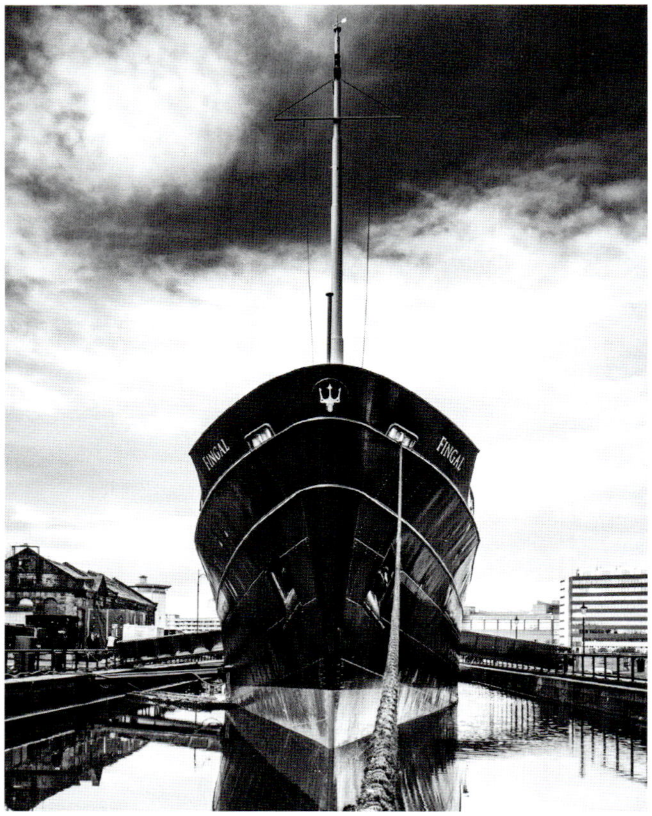

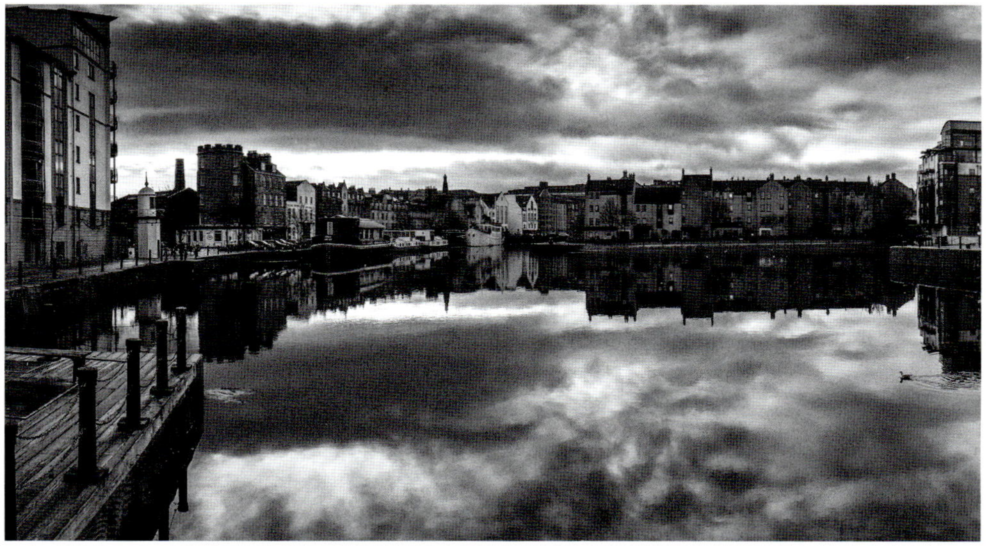

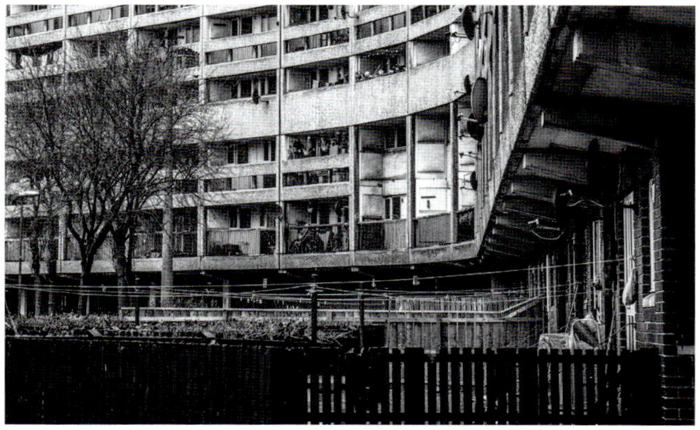

SUNSHINE ON LEITH

Where once the whalers left for Arctic seas,
Their death points sharpened by a razoring wind,
Where herring boats swarmed like angered bees,
Their silvered catch disgorged upon the quays,
The entrails of their 'ever-lasting' grounds;
Observe, the shadowed vessels, almost hiding,
Readied for their deviled route,
Emptying the Dark Continent,
To the cane plantations for an eternity of grind,
And returning innocently to port,
Laden with their sweet burden,
Icing the futures of genteel Edinburgh generations;
Watch as barreled Bordeaux roll across the cobbles,
Mixing with the scent of highland malt,
Smell the sweet Speysides, and the island peats,
See the oysters lying in omnipresent piles,
Feeding for common man;
Hear the boat-building and the machine,
The steel and the steam, the sound of a revolution,
The thrusting blackening smokestacks;
Then silence, as all depart, the seas run dry,
The builders shift across the globe,
Trade squeezed into Goliathan craft;
Touch the underbelly of a deceptive city,
The women of the street,
The salamanders of the night,
The flashing blades and knuckled fights,
The 'spotting trains', and brown sugar
Of a different kind,
They too, pushed aside,
Gentrification squeezing all before it,
The Banana Flats, the Royal Yacht,
The cruise ships emptying
Another human trade,
But still the river runs;
Persevere they proclaim,
And so it shall,
The sun will always,
Shine on Leith.

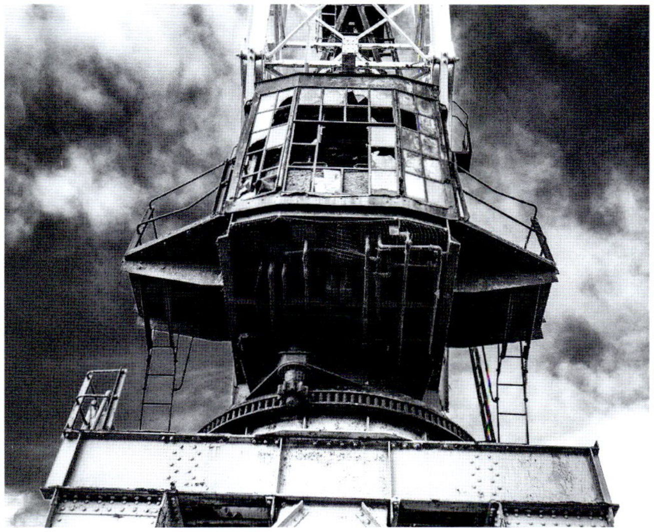

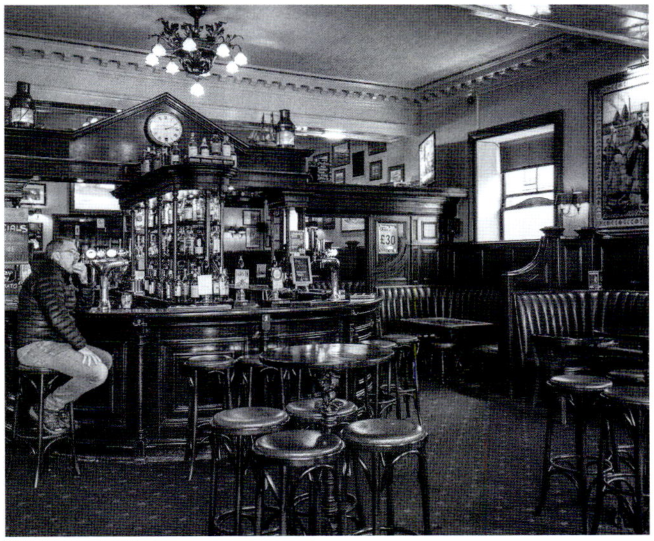

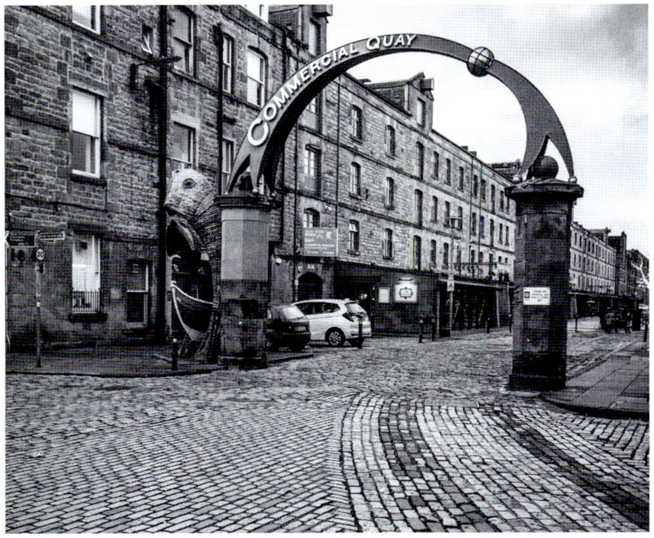

BLUE PLANET

We went to the National Museum
To wait in a winding queue
To see a piece of moon rock,
It was grey and disappointing,
And unimpressed, I spent
The rest of my time wandering,
Lost under the Blue Whale,
Trying to take in its scale,
This traveller of the globe,
Reduced to a skeleton,
Swimming above my head,
One of 10 million objects,
But only the top
Of the pyramid on show,
The rest stored carefully
Under dustsheets,
Embodying our world,
Yet when I think back
To the astronaut,
And his small step for man,
Picking up that piece of rock,
He could block out the
Whole of the blue earth,
With only the top
Of his
Thumb.

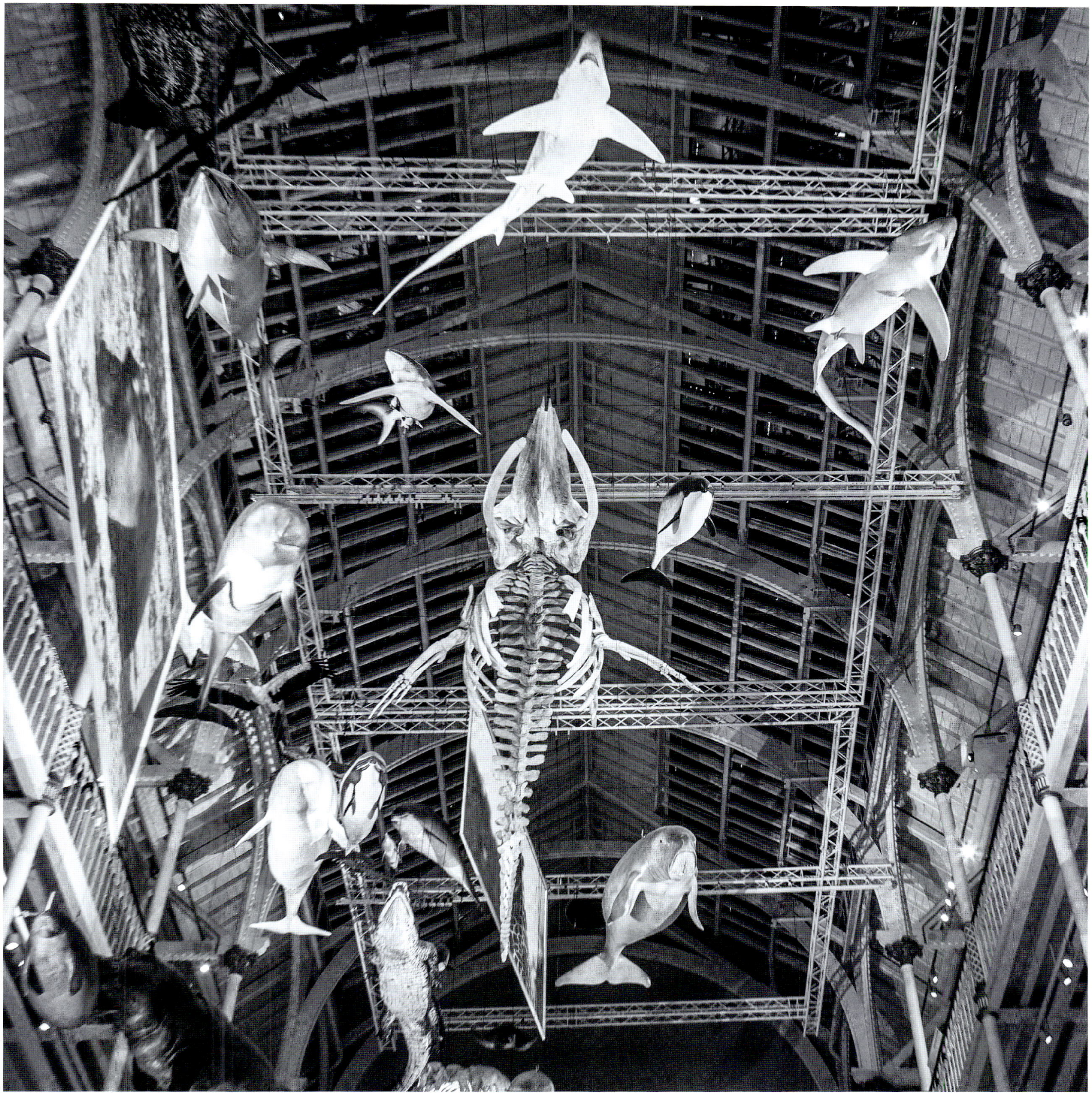

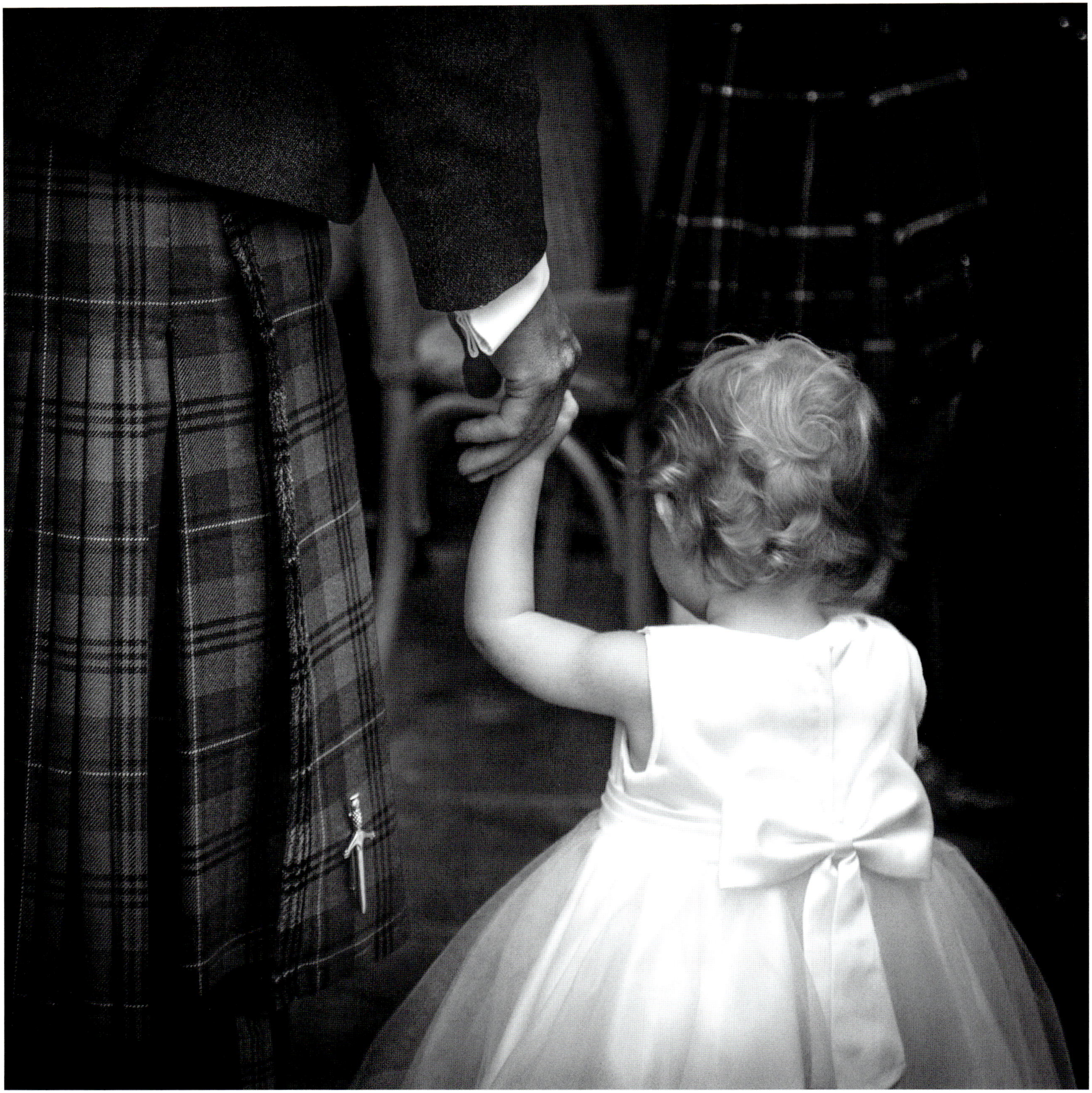

A CHILD'S HAND

Take your child by the hand
And hold the future there;
Keep them upright if you can
Release them if you dare.

PRINCES STREET CONVERSATIONS

A river of conversations
Snatched in the passing
Tumble downstream
In a wall of broken sound,
Eavesdropped from other worlds,
The private and banal,
The intimate and profane,
The guttural grunts,
The over-engineered sentences,
Of Morningside ladies,
The voices of the continents,
The language of the streets,
Shouting and whispering,
Gossiping,
Loving and hating,
Promising,
Pleading,
Lying and trusting,
But passing by,
They fade together,
To a single passage,
Eventually,
Emptying out,
To that place
We dare not
Care to
Mention.

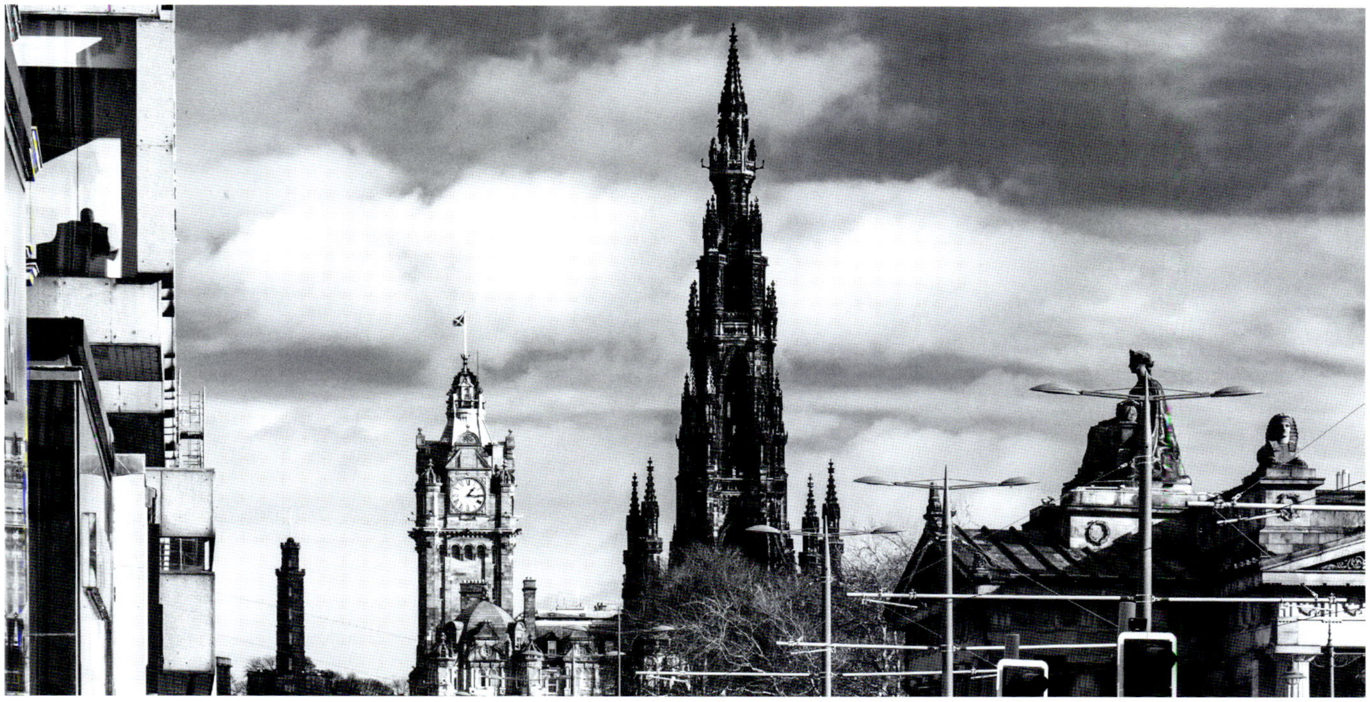

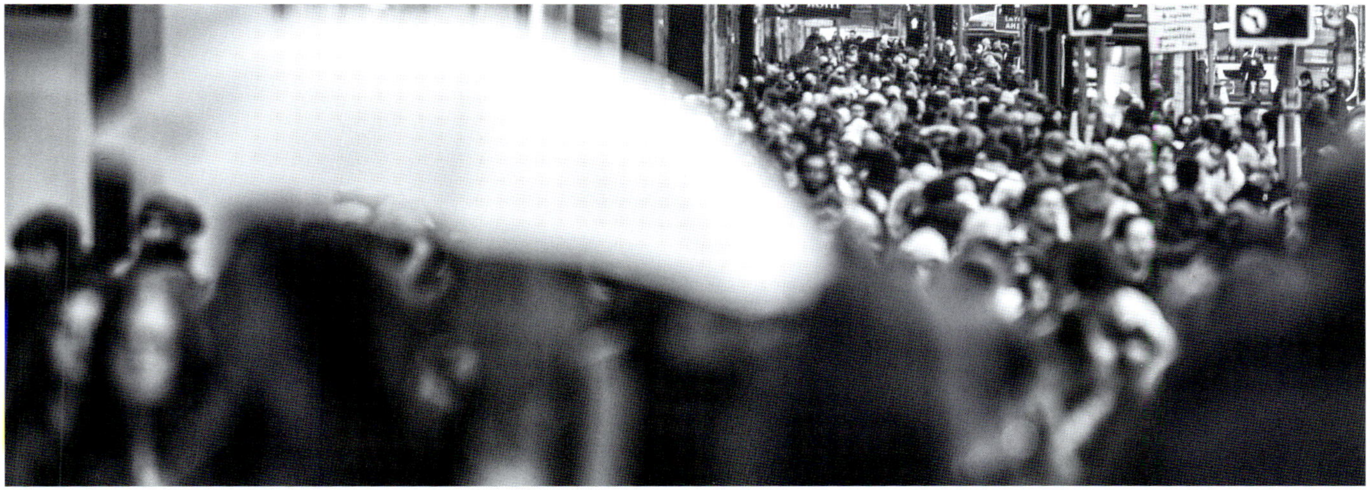

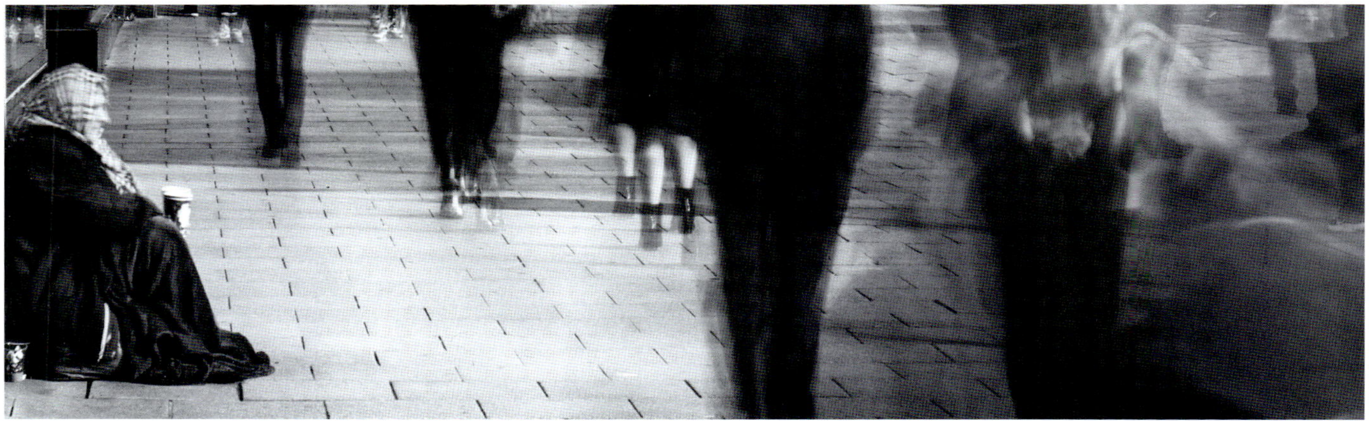

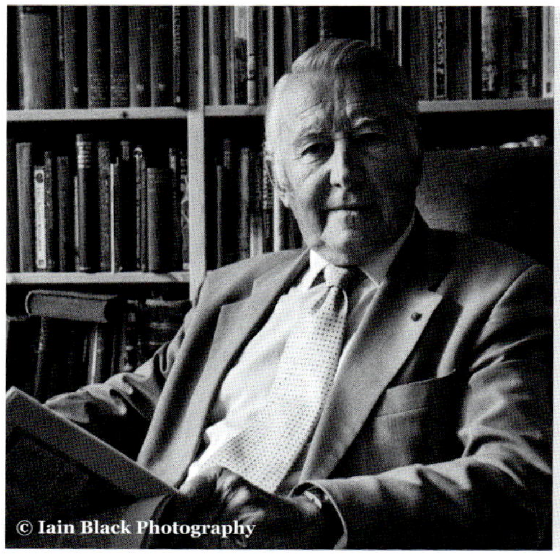

LORD DAVID STEEL

David Steel, Baron Steel of Aikwood, KT, KBE, PC, began his political career in the Liberal Party, serving first as MP for Roxburgh, Selkirk and Peebles (1965-1983), then as MP for Tweeddale, Ettrick & Lauderdale (1983-1997). He rose to become the Liberal Party's final leader (1976-1988). His tenure spanned the duration of the alliance with the Social Democratic Party, which began in 1981 and concluded with the formation of the Liberal Democrats in 1988.

Lord Steel served as the Liberal Democrat Member of the Scottish Parliament (MSP) for Lothians from 1999 to 2003, and was elected as the Scottish Parliament's first Presiding Officer on May 12, 1999. He stepped down as an MSP prior to the 2003 election, but remained as Presiding Officer until he had overseen the election of his successor, George Reid. Since 1997 he has been a member of the House of Lords as a life peer.

Lord Steel was born in Kirkcaldy, Fife, the son of a Church of Scotland minister (also called David Steel) who would later serve as Moderator of the General Assembly of the Church of Scotland. Brought up in Scotland and Kenya, he was educated at Dumbarton Academy, James Gillespie's Boys' School, the Prince of Wales School in Nairobi, and George Watson's College. He graduated from the University of Edinburgh with an MA in 1960 and a law degree in 1962. He later served as the university's Rector from 1982-1985.

During his time as an MP at Westminster, Lord Steel was responsible for introducing, as a Private Member's Bill, the Abortion Act 1967. A fierce critic of apartheid, he served as President of the British Anti-Apartheid Movement (1966-1970), and is currently President of the All-Party Parliamentary Group on Africa, holding the same position with the All-Party Parliamentary Group on Taiwan.

As somebody who went to school and university in Edinburgh, and first set up married home there before moving to the Borders, I have never lost my love of the city. I recall celebrating VE day in 1945 by riding round the Marchmont circle, aged seven, on the top of a tram car.

But in 1999 I half-returned to the city when elected to the new Scottish Parliament in the Lothians, and was subsequently elected by its members as its first Presiding Officer. My wife found a wholly unsuitable flat opposite our temporary back door at the Assembly Hall, and soon afterwards we bought a small flat at St Leonard's to use during the week. As Presiding Officer I chaired the Parliament's Corporate Body, which comprised one member from each political party. Our most difficult task was overseeing the construction of our new parliament building.

First Minister Donald Dewar and I used to meet over dinner once a month, without officials, to review how the Parliament was working. The new building was our most difficult topic. At one such meeting Donald said to me that "we mustn't play pass the parcel with this project", to which I responded: "But you have already played it – you chose the site, the architect and the contractor, and then landed it on my plate".

The problem was that the Blair government's White Paper on devolution had included an estimate of £40M for a new building, but that was never the projected cost of what Dewar had chosen. Moreover it was not big enough. Over dinner with me one evening, architect Enric Miralles drew on a paper napkin what became the new dramatic garden lobby - with 'upturned boat' skylights - which gave us the necessary extra space. Restoring Queensberry House became the most expensive part of the new parliament, since it was in a much poorer state than first reported.

Despite the premature deaths of both Donald Dewar and Enric Miralles, we have added to Edinburgh a most outstanding and popularly visited building whose interior – especially the committee rooms – is acclaimed internationally.

Yet one person who still regards the building as controversial is the Duke of Edinburgh, who claimed he had planted a tree in the garden of Holyrood Palace to plug the viewing gap of "Steel's Parliament". When I heard about this I tackled him, saying the view was surely better than that of the old dirty disused brewery that had previously been on the site. With a twinkle in his eye he responded to me in one word – "marginally".

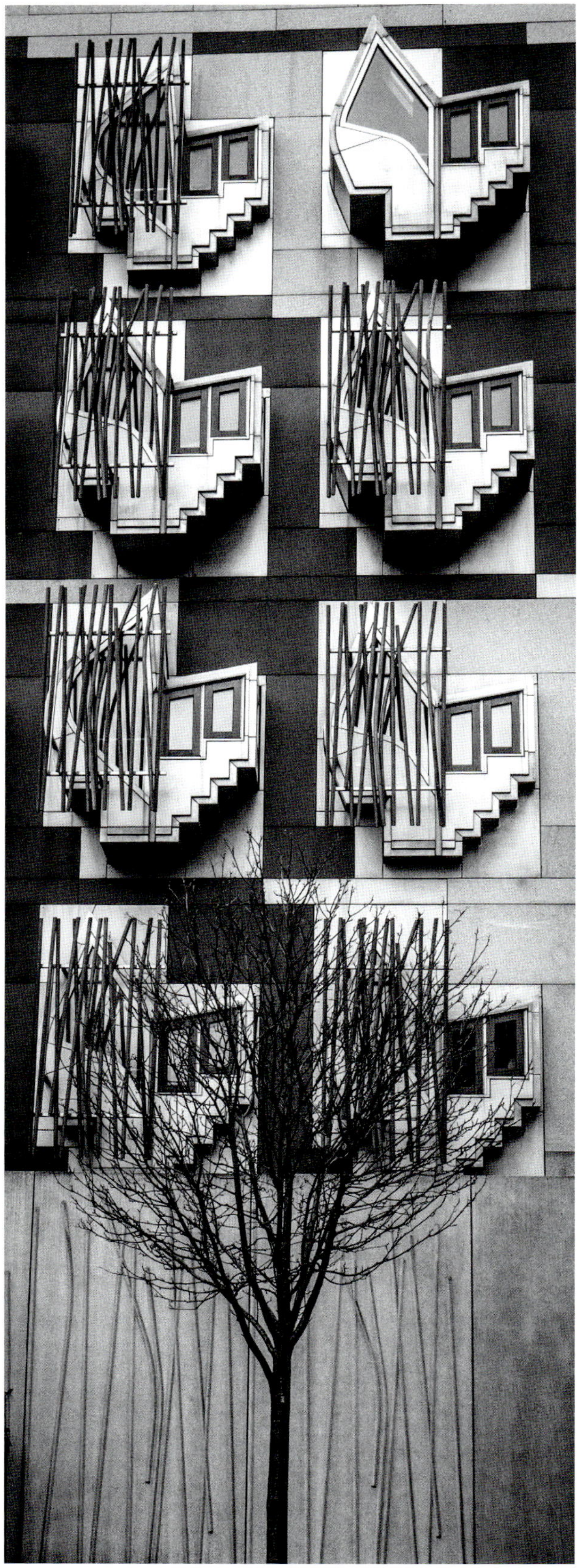

SCOTTISH PARLIAMENT

The Spaniard upturned the boats,
Heaving them over with his imagination,
Manhandling them with elegant precision,
To capsize our narrow expectations,
Of function, and of form;
Then wandering through the brightness
Of his mind, probing for a place,
Between the people and the land,
He conjured this uncommon space,
Shaping it with sculpted beams
To vault the weighty Scottish sky,
And channel its inclining light
Across repeating echoes,
Across the granite and the oak,
Across the concrete and the steel,
Each surface holding his attention,
Disturbing his sleep,
Until his wakened dreams took shape,
Beyond confinement, escaping
The formality of dullness,
The chains of common sense,
To look in upon our land,
To see what we cannot,
Telling our story;
For this is more than just a building,
It is a poem for a nation,
Beyond the finite grasp of humankind,
Abstracting the geometry of thought,
It challenges us to think
Far beyond those who judge
With an accountant's eye;
For this is a place of liberty,
Of wisdom of the mind,
So treat it with respect,
For we are all,
Including him,
But passers
By.

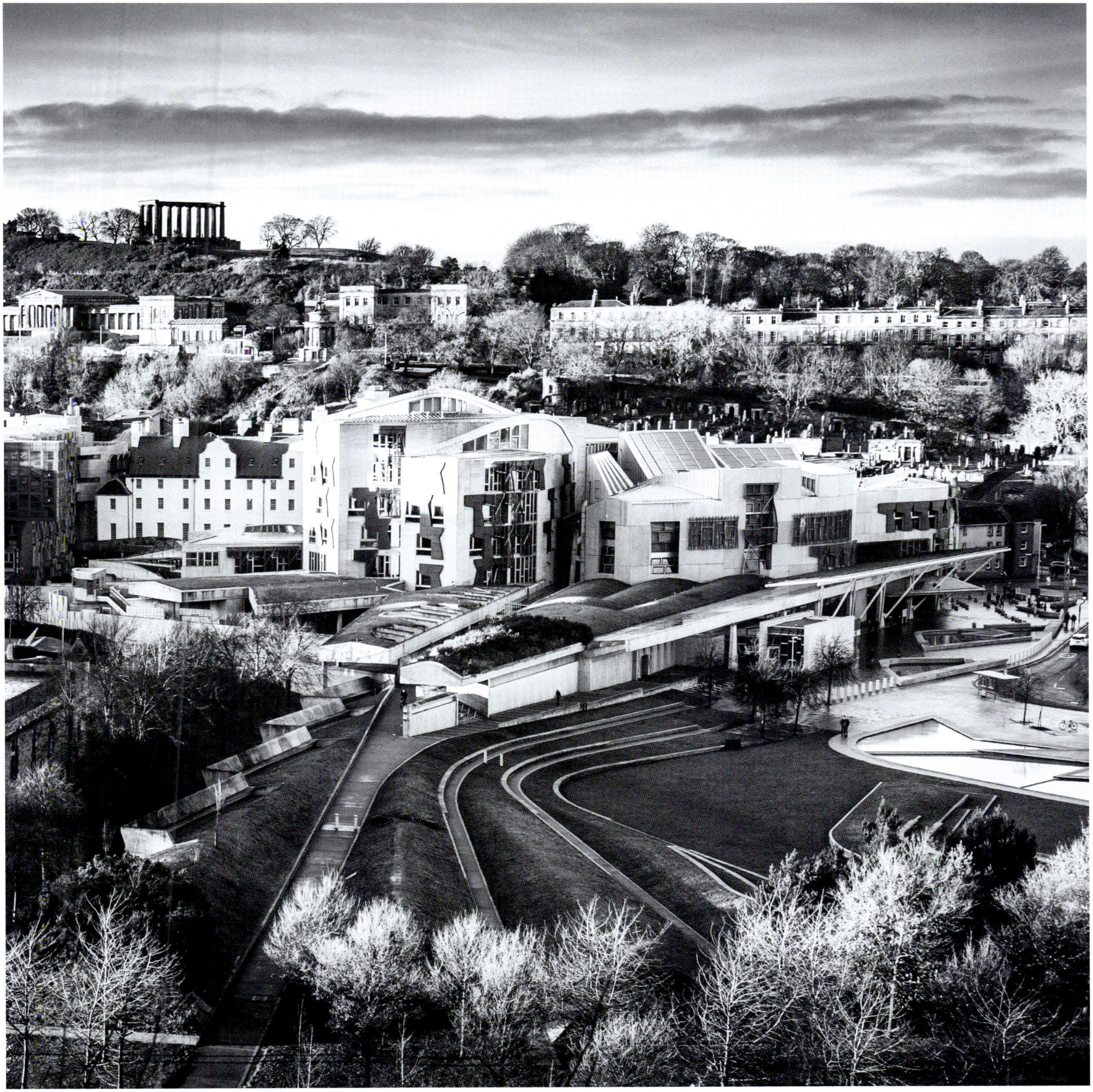

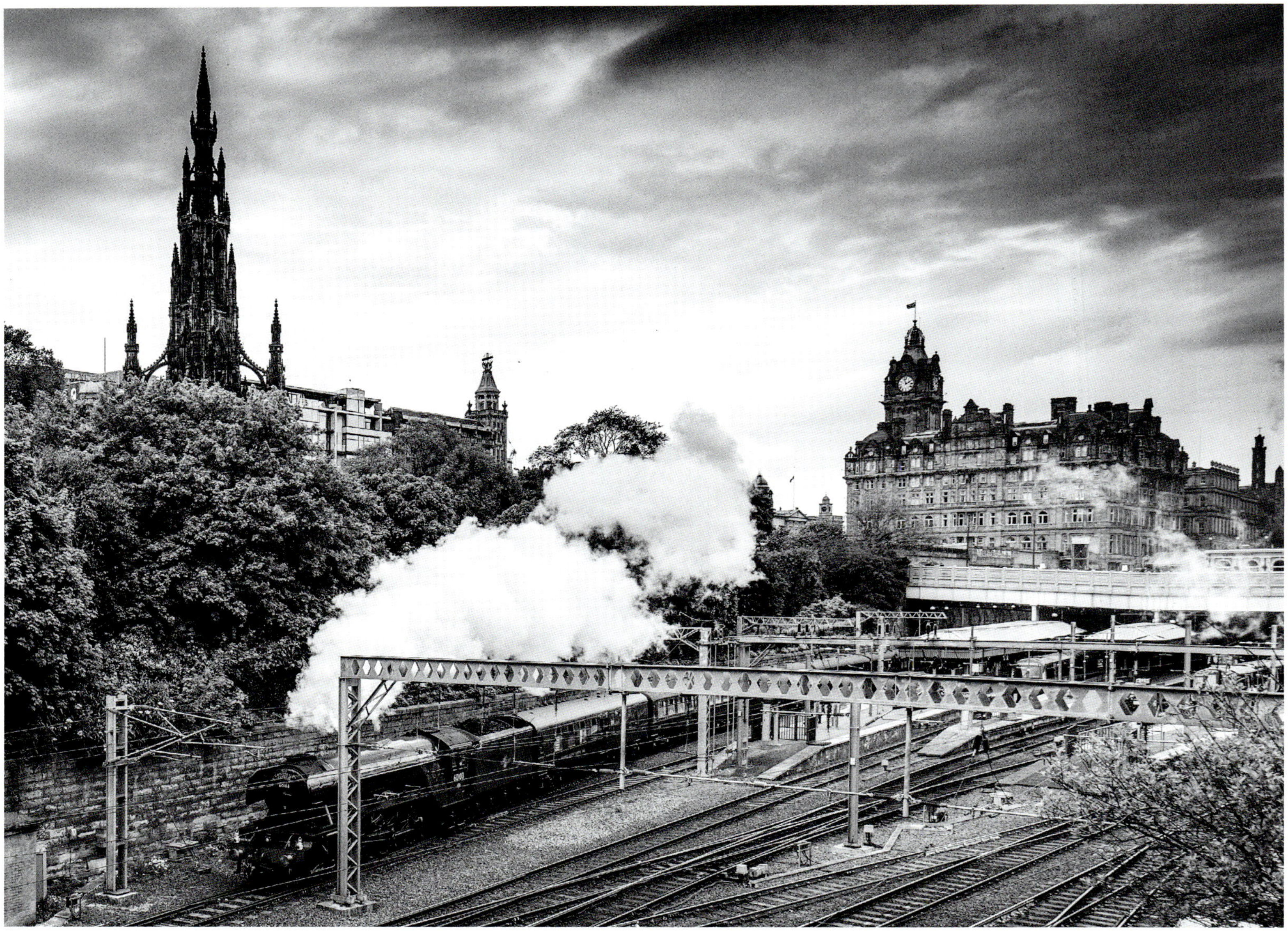

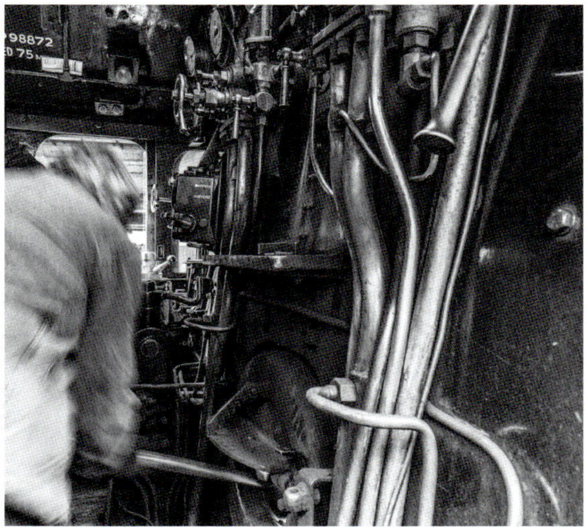

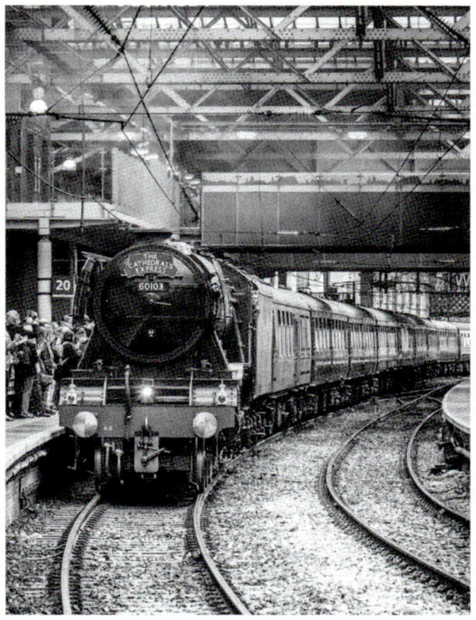

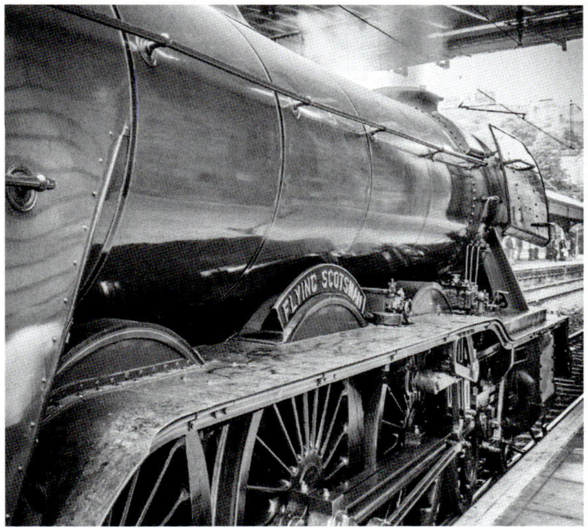

THE FLYING SCOTSMAN

Standing in a row
Outside Waverley Station,
Fingers pushed through the wire.
Duffel coats and gloves,
Socks round ankles.
Black,
Everything black.
Pot-bellied trains
Spitting steam
Pushing and pulling
Hissing,
Fighting?
Fighting against the tide.
All come to a standstill
As the Flying Scotsman
Flashes under the bridge
And disappears from view
But not from sight.

RETURN FROM SINGAPORE

I took my granny,
In her wheelchair,
To the Royal Botanic Gardens,
She sat in the chair,
And I rode behind her,
As we careered
Around the paths,
Shouting and screaming,
Screaming and shouting,
Leaving families
In our wake,
Until we got
To the glasshouse,
Where the heat and humidity,
Triggered an untold tale,
Taking her back to 1942,
The Beradin Rubber Estates
With the Japanese at the door,
And escaping to Singapore,
Where, waiting on the quay,
With two precious tickets
For the last boat home,
My grandfather
Saw a solitary friend, and,
Without a moment's thought,
Offered her his freedom,
And here, in the wet, wet, heat,
Of the glasshouse,
My granny cast a single tear,
And every year,
I return to this place,
Feeling the sweat
Gathering on my back,
And I share that moment,
With them both,
Long gone, but forever
Here.

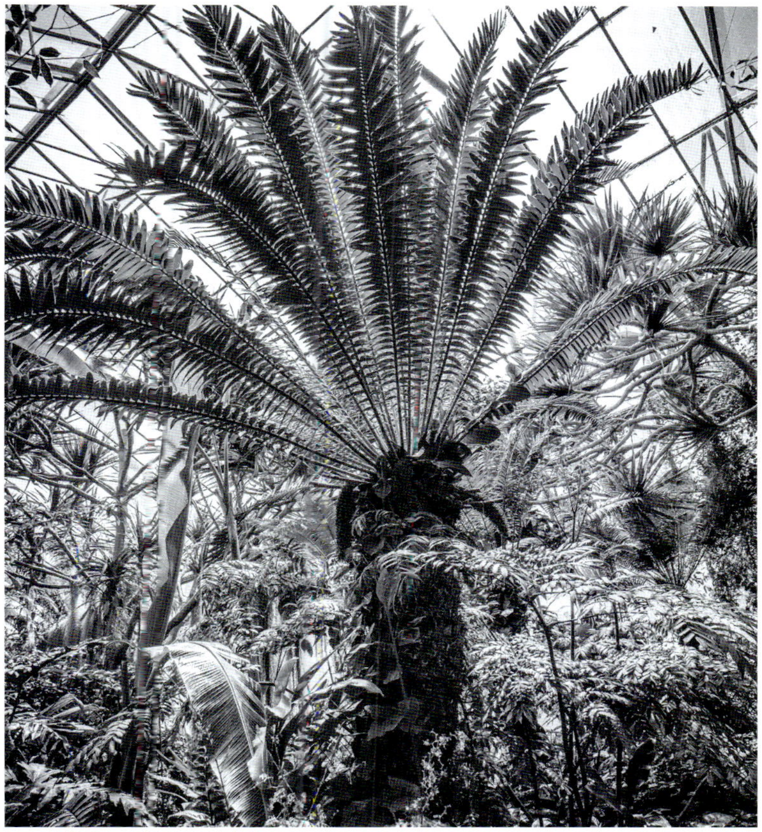
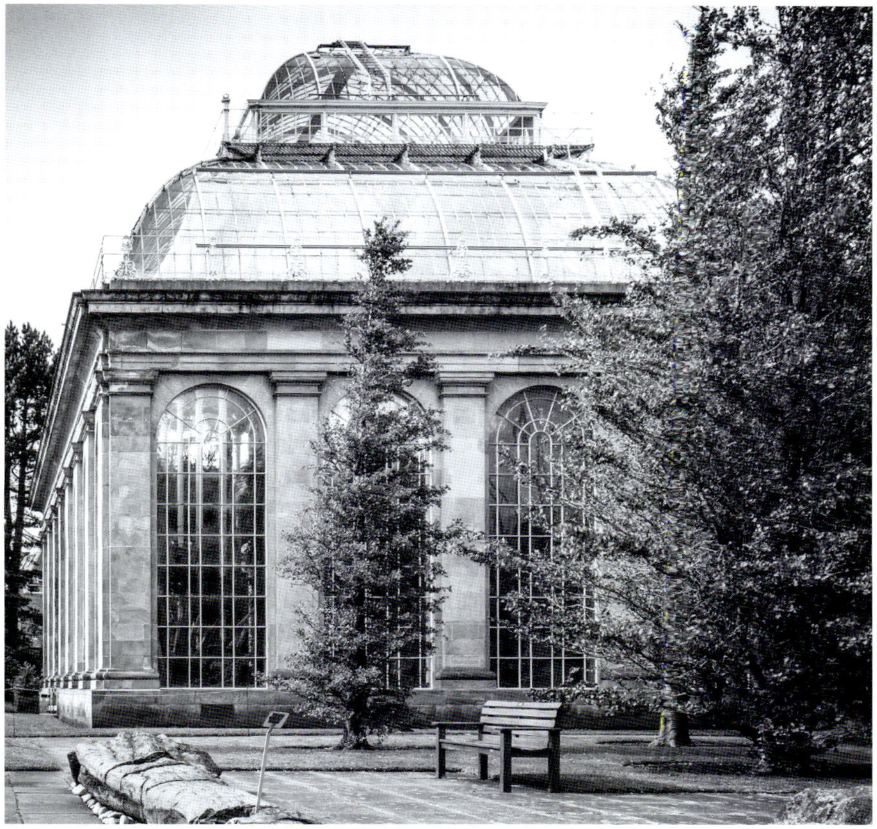
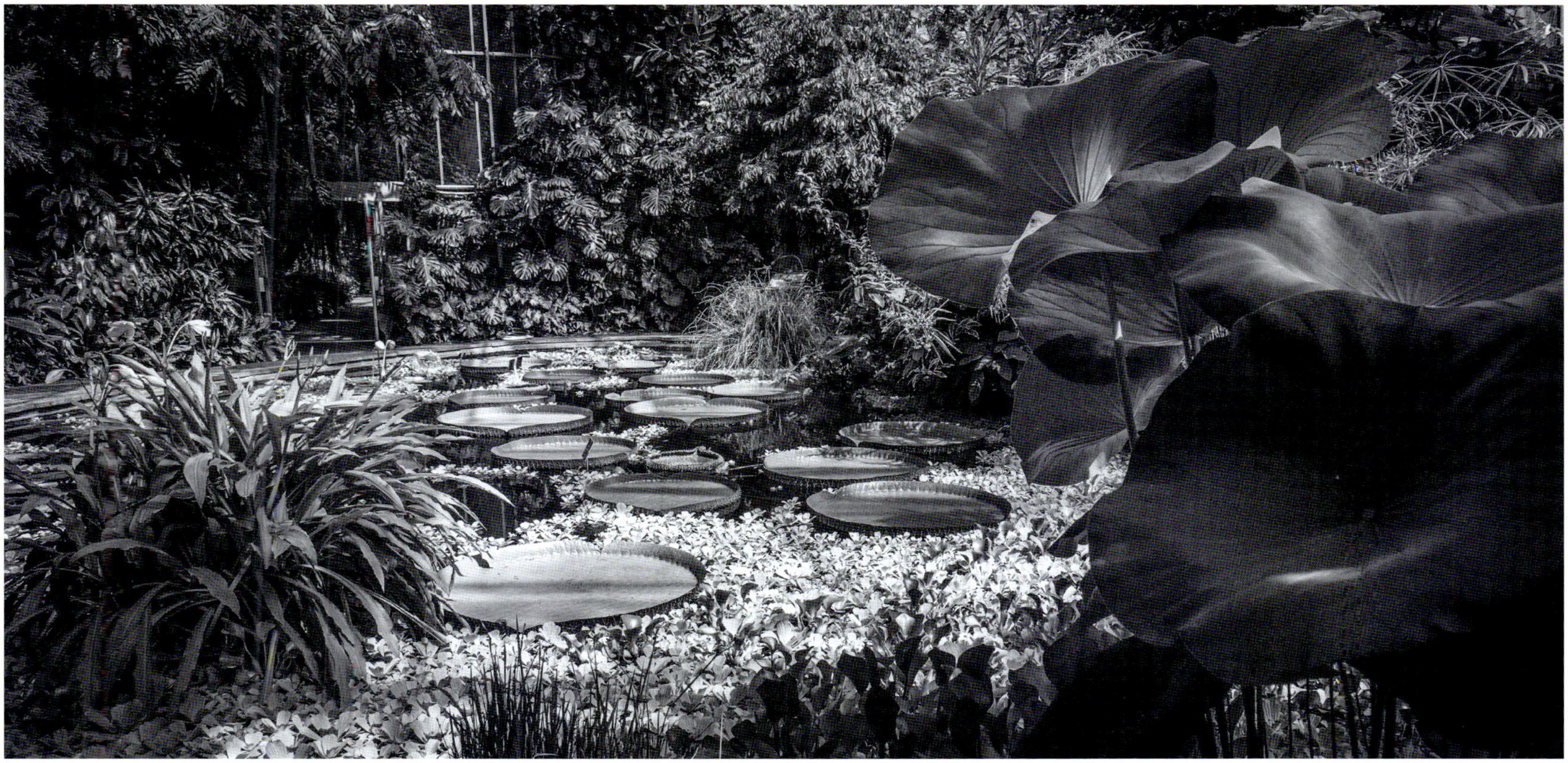

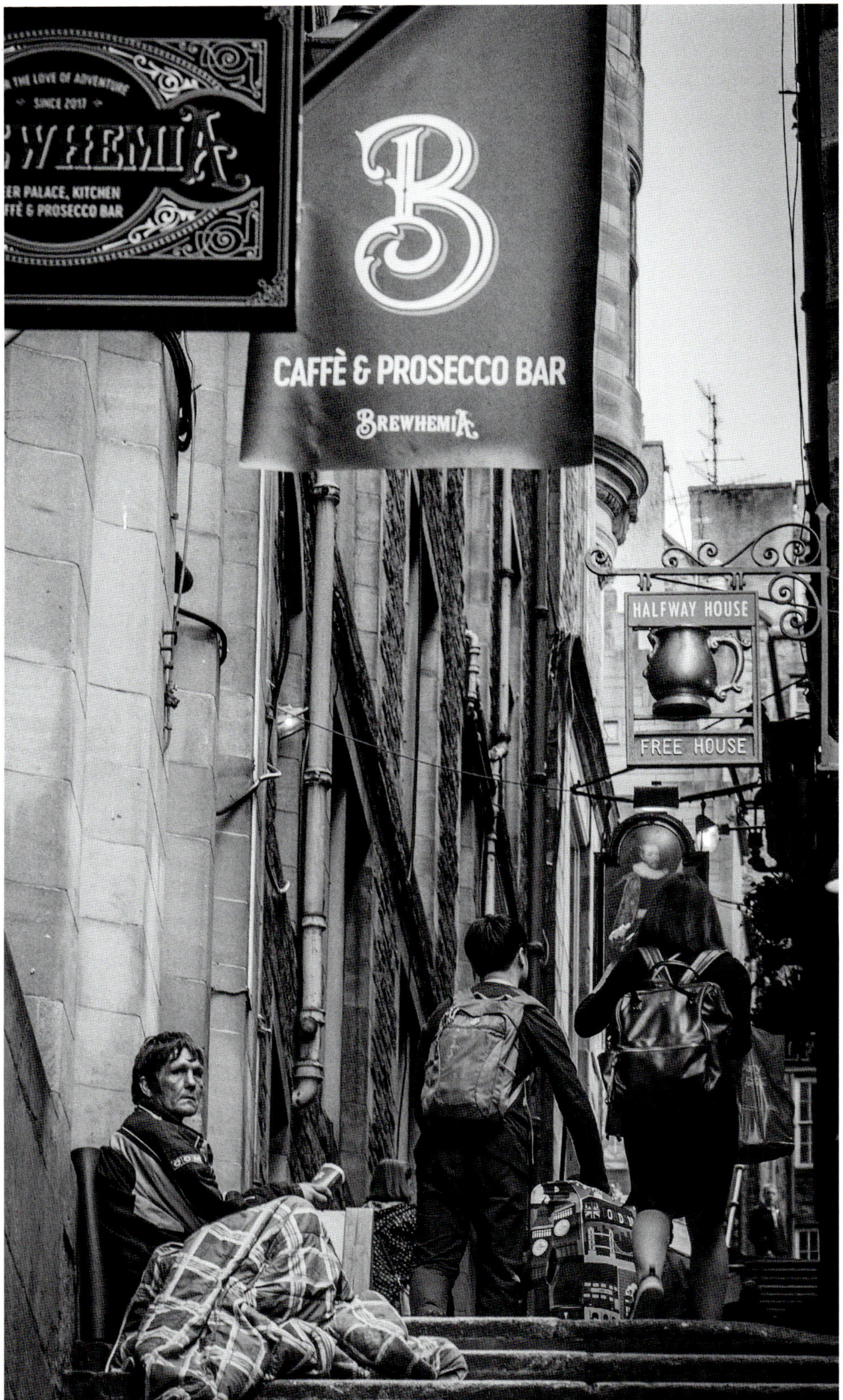
SINCE 2017
B
CAFFÈ & PROSECCO BAR
BREWHEMIA
HALFWAY HOUSE
FREE HOUSE

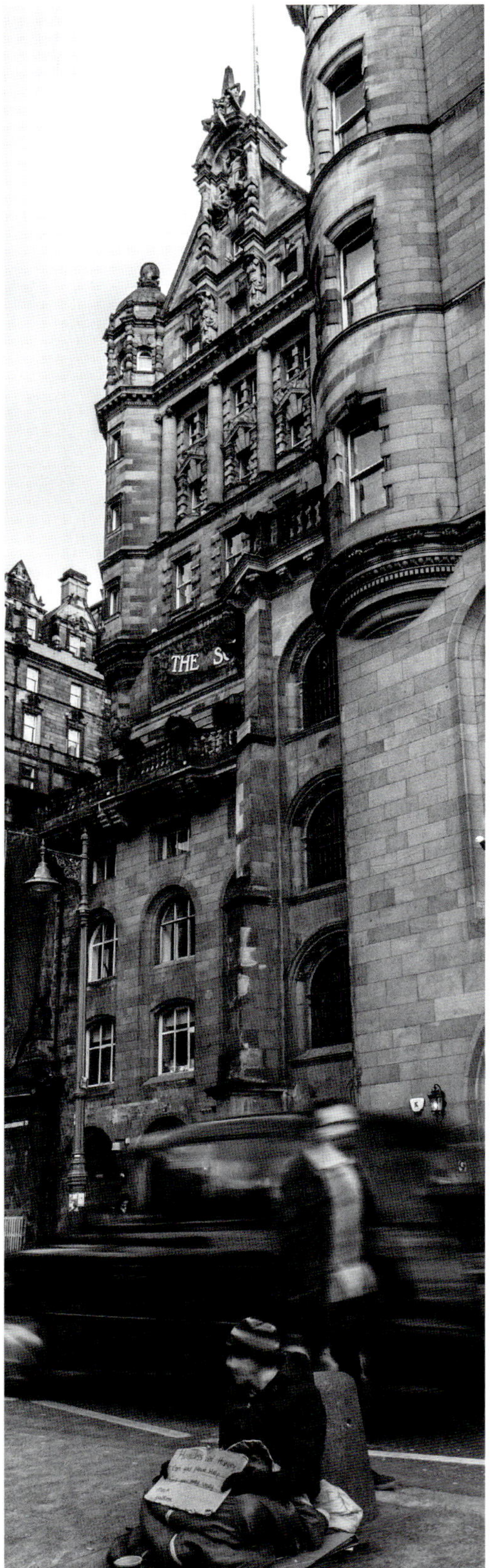

GRAVITY

Living in a world
Four feet below our heads,
The flat bodies melt
Into the wet pavement,
Gradually absorbed
By the cold, damp stone,
Which reaches up, unseen,
And drags them down,
Drawing them into
The unforgiving earth,
Digesting them, slowly,
One piece at a time;
Exhumed, they shamble
The unforgiving streets,
But the pavement has
A gravity all of its own,
A force that pulls
Upon their souls,
Their fallen bodies
Lying at our feet,
In a world
Four feet
Below our
Heads.

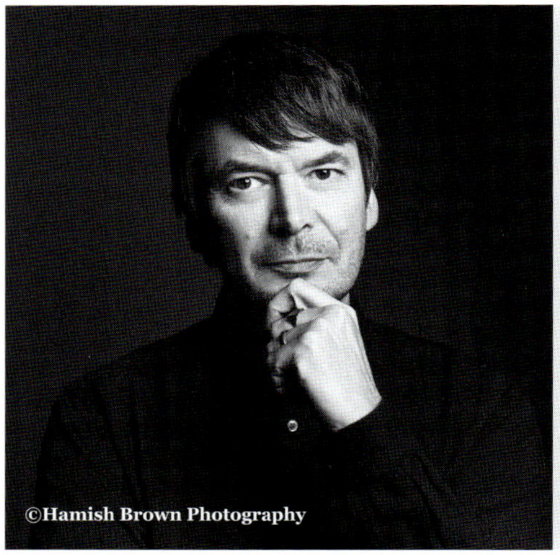

IAN RANKIN

Ian Rankin is the author of over 30 novels, 22 of which feature Inspector Rebus.
He lives in Edinburgh and is probably busy writing another book.

I arrived in Edinburgh in the October of 1978 to start university, having grown up in the Fife mining village of Bowhill. As a child, visits south of the Forth had been few and far between, so the city seemed strange and maze-like. I would walk its streets, trying to make sense of the place. At that time I was writing poetry in my spare hours and minutes, but I couldn't pin Edinburgh down in lyric form. The city required long-form prose.

Enter Detective John Rebus. As a cop, he had access to each and every layer of Auld Reekie, from its seediest corners to its elegant mansions. I decided he would live on the same street as me in Marchmont (an unusual location for a copper, I only later learned) and work in a real-life police station – St Leonard's to begin with, and latterly Gayfield Square. He would have reason to visit the mortuary in the Cowgate, and frequent smoke-filled bars where his snitches waited, eager to pass on the latest 'word on the street' for the price of a pint or a dram.

When off duty, Rebus gravitated – as I did – to the Oxford Bar. Why 'the Ox'? Because to me it was emblematic of 'secret' Edinburgh – the city the tourist seldom saw. It was central (a two-minute walk from Princes Street) but tucked away, and a fascinating cross-section of Edinburgh types drank there, including lawyers, politicians and, yes, police officers. It was a place where Rebus could unwind, a place where he could feel safe.

My first Rebus novel, *Knots and Crosses*, was heavily influenced by Robert Louis Stevenson's *Doctor Jekyll and Mr Hyde*. Stevenson had been influenced by the true story of William Brodie, gentleman by day, scoundrel by night. Muriel Spark borrowed Brodie for her brilliant novel *The Prime of Miss Jean Brodie* (Miss Brodie tells us she is descended from William Brodie, but neglects to add that he was a thief who was eventually hanged for his crimes). Jean Brodie is a complex character – we are never sure to what extent she is the hero or the villain of the story. Maybe she is both, as can also be said for Henry Jekyll. My passion for these books convinced me that the Edinburgh of the 1980s was still very much a Jekyll and Hyde city, cultured and elegant on the surface, but if you dared to scratch its surface you might reveal something uglier and more dangerous. The city even seemed to me to be structured in a Jekyll and Hyde fashion, the New Town planned and rational, the Old Town more chaotic and feral. It is a city of enlightenment which has also played host to serial killers, body snatchers and at least one notable act of cannibalism, and in centuries past it didn't take much to rouse its largely douce denizens to riot through its streets.

Stevenson described it memorably as a 'precipitous city', and a short walk takes us from the giddy heights of Castle Rock to the canyon-like Cowgate, reminding me always that I live in a place of staggering wealth but also grinding poverty. In some cities this might not be noticeable, but Edinburgh exists in fairly strict confines, circumferenced by water and hills. Yet still it manages to be like Doctor Who's Tardis, larger on the inside than its physical dimensions would suggest, which is why I've yet to grow weary of it. It continues to sustain me creatively, bringing me new stories in abundance. I thank Edinburgh for that.

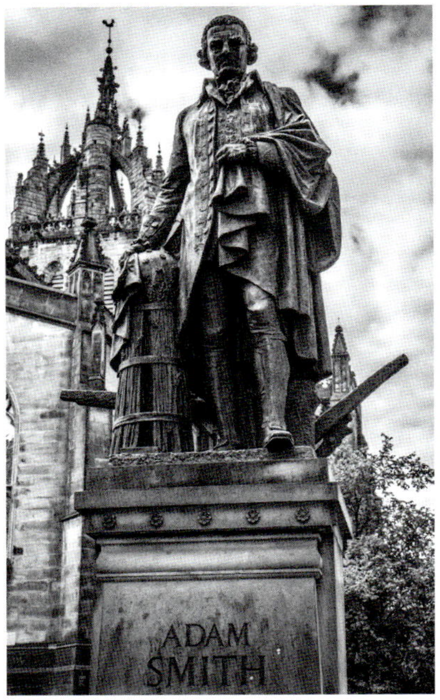

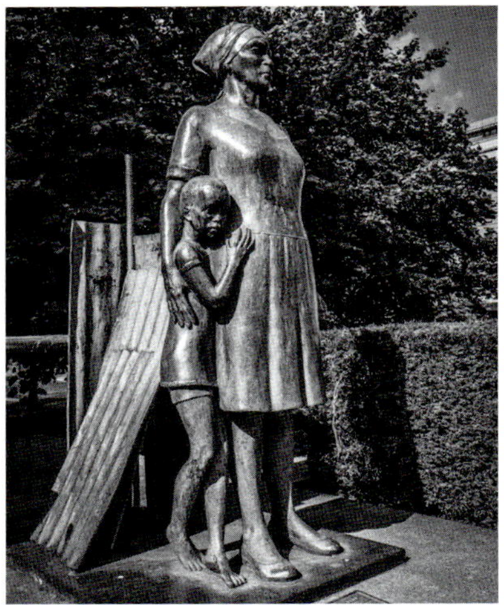

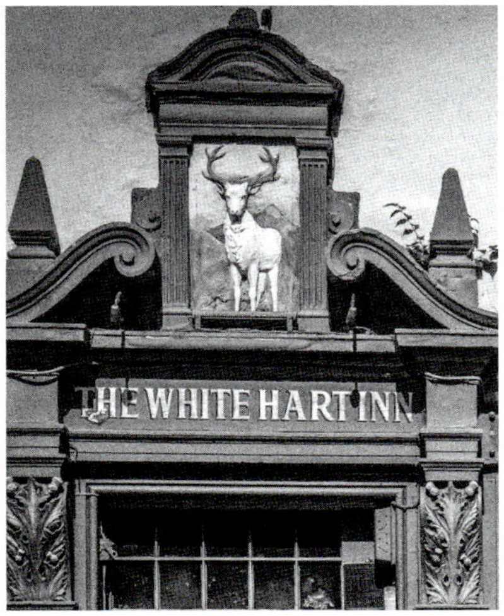

EDINBURGH'S MONUMENTAL NIGHT OUT

Every year, on winter's shortest day, in dead of night,
Edinburgh's statues stir, readying themselves,
For their annual expedition, their annual jamboree,
Livingstone, the great explorer, leads the way,
Then Wellington, the Iron Duke, descends his horse,
Holmes wraps his cape around himself against the cold, then
Hume, the giant, climbs stiffly from his plinth,
While Fergusson and Burns, arm-in-arm, reunite in reverie,
Then the artists and the scientists,
Then the kings and dukes and earls,
Then the doctors and the dreamers walk,
Then churchmen, and the men of law,
The men of war, and the men of peace,
From all around the city, each man takes his rightful place,
Making his way towards the Old Town's White Hart Inn,
To argue, talk and sing and play, for an evening's resurrection,
To join the throbbing throng, in a fleeting reconnection,
To pass the foaming ale amongst themselves,
All rivalries forgot, in joyful merriment,
While Smith, controls the purse, an economist to the end,
And Knox sits in his corner, nursing a hidden gin,
Yet still the party livens with stories, songs and rhymes,
The drams pour as if no thought of closing time,
As Burns takes the floor and holds the eye,
And then, in the midst of the swagger and the boast,
The door opens, and two women, uninvited, enter,
The Queen, the Widow of Windsor,
And an unnamed black woman and her child,
The men – all fifty-three of them,
These symbols of excellence,
Chastened into silence,
Bow their heads,
In awkward,
Shame.

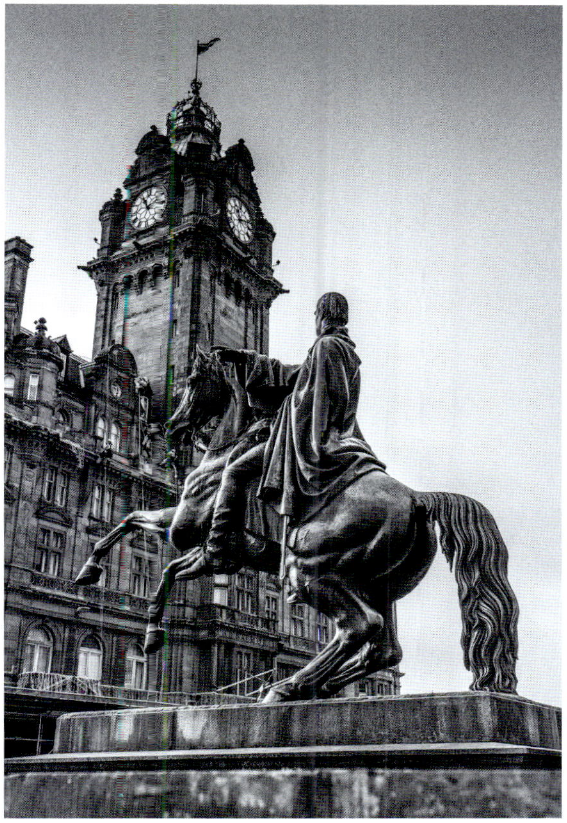

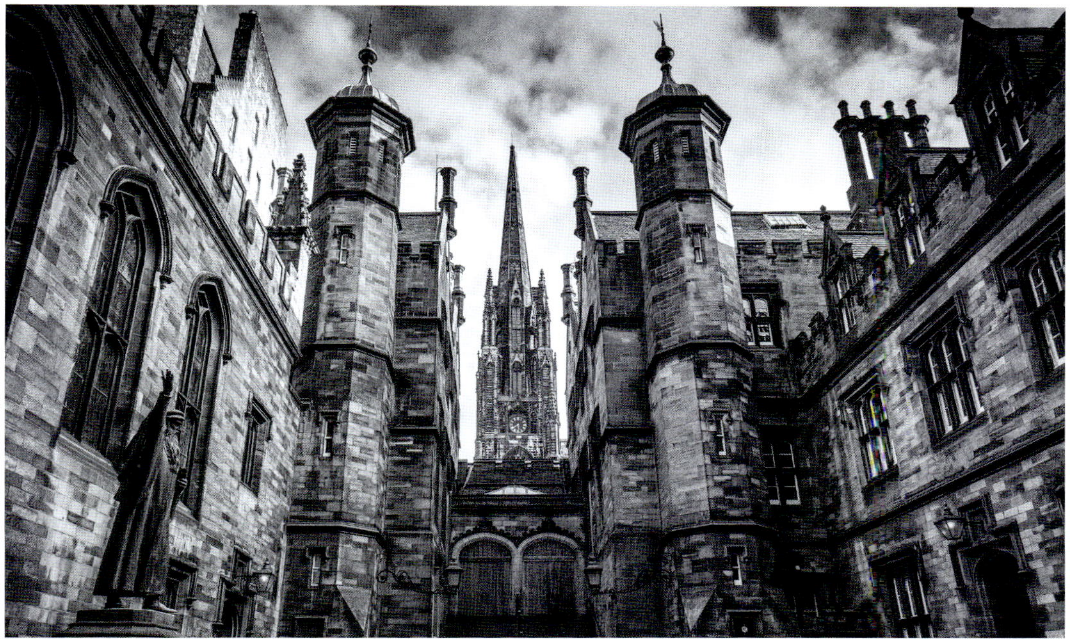

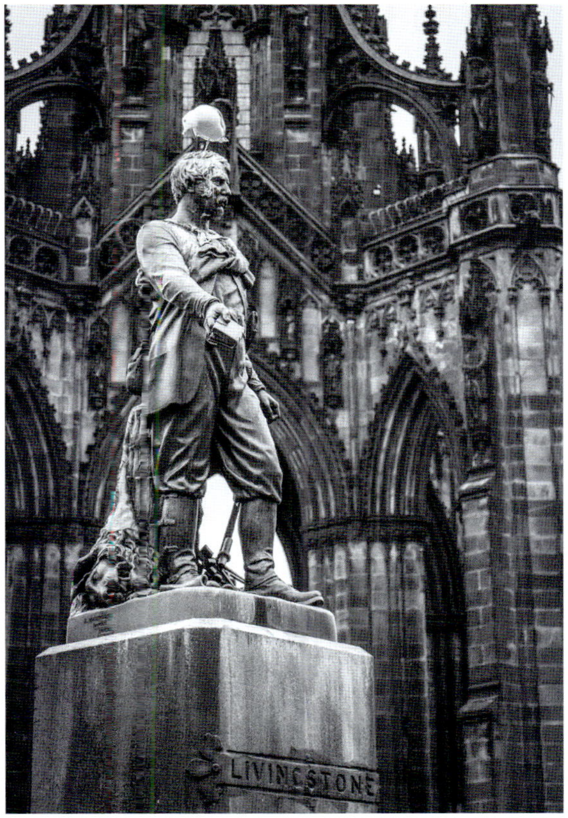

LIVINGSTONE

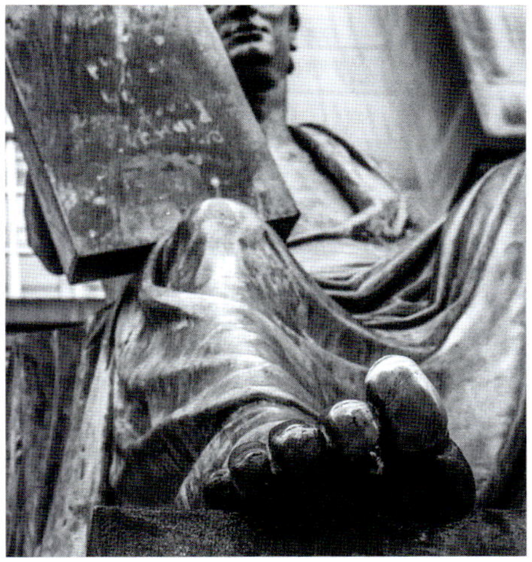

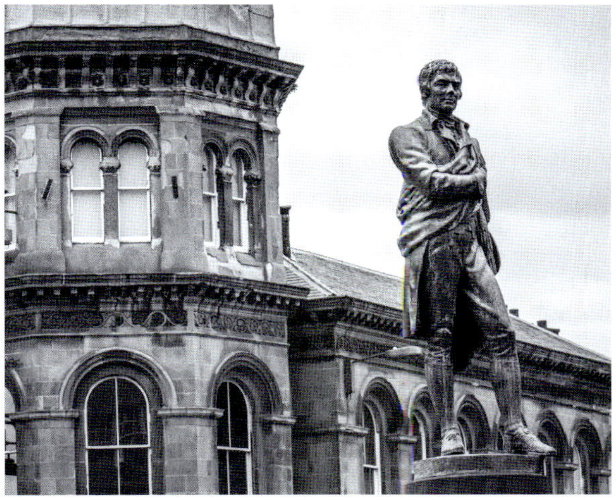

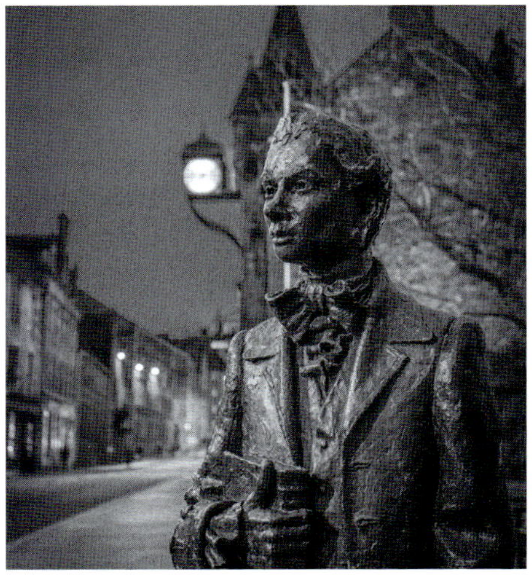

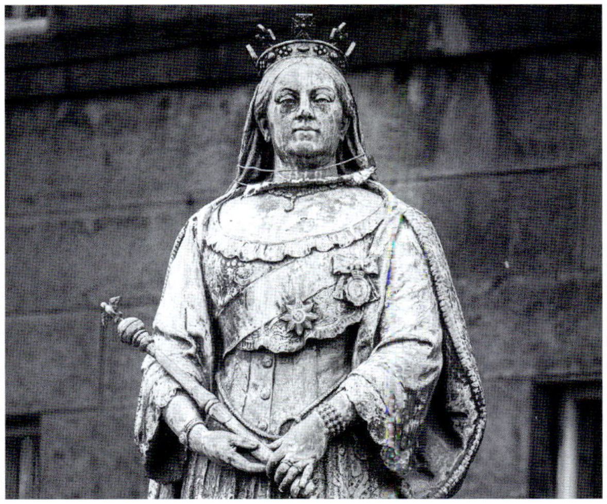

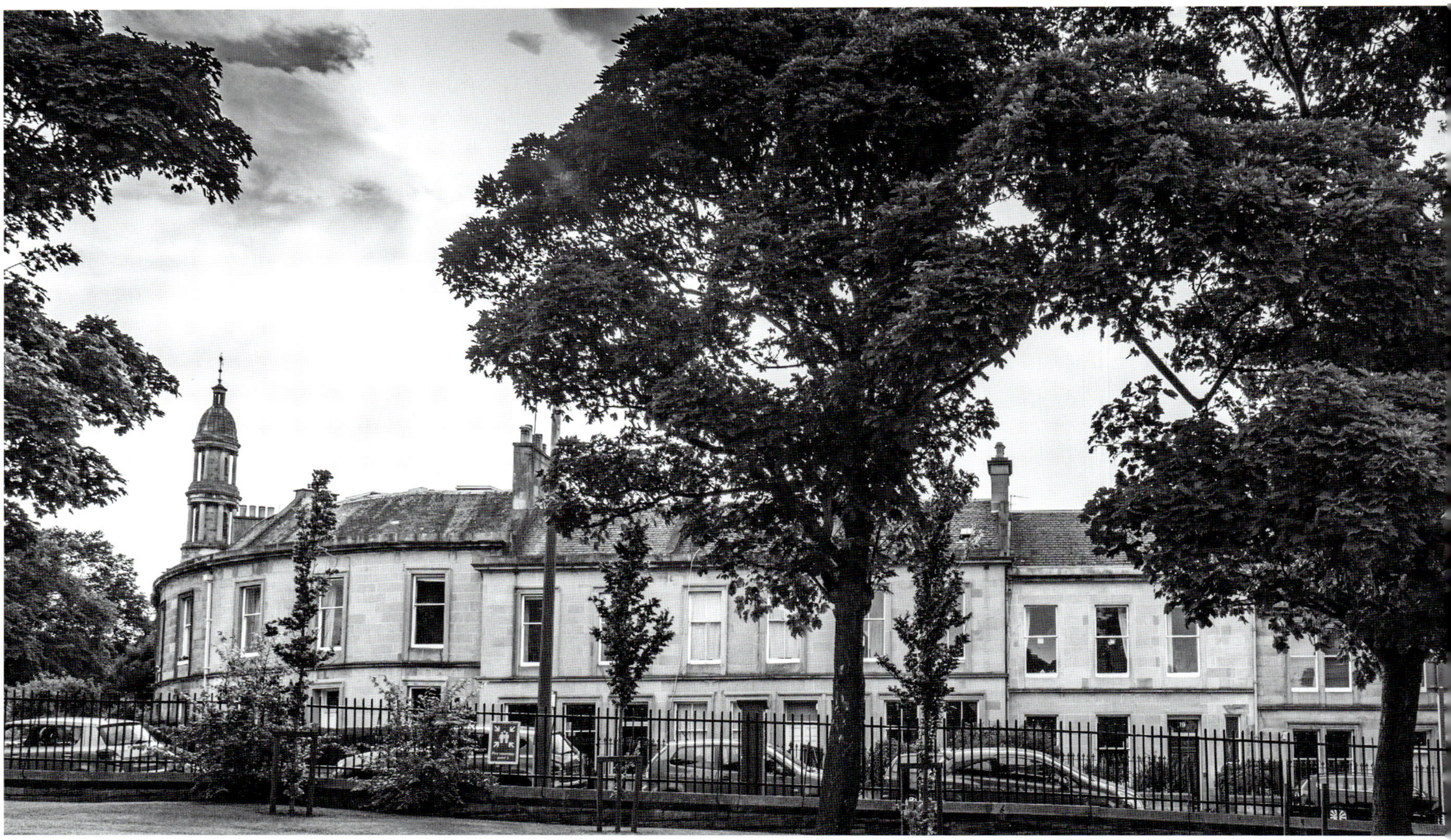

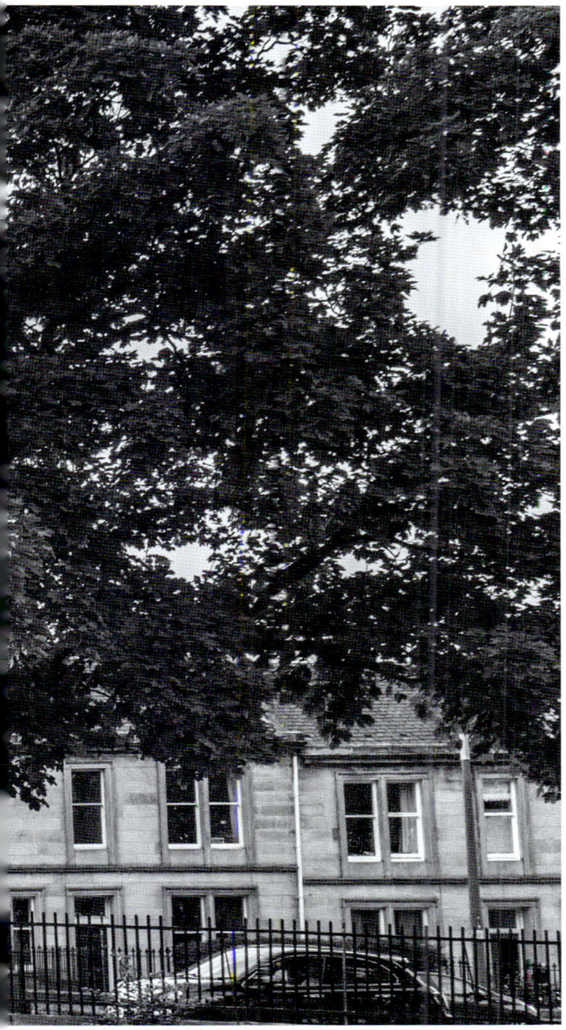

19 BELLEVUE PLACE

We occupied the same space
This morning,
Outside 19 Bellevue Place,
You leaving for school,
A full family behind,
And me, walking to work;
And here we meet,
Bumping into each other,
Forty years apart,
That boy, and this man;
I recognise you,
You catch my eye,
A fleeting recognition,
And there it is,
We are, and were, the same,
Time travelling;
Enjoy yourself,
I whisper.

HIGH TIDE

Release a flight of children's' feet,
Upon a page of virgin sand.
And watch them tumble, run and leap,
And trace their freedom on borrowed land.
Too busy building memories,
To notice froth-tipped fingertips,
Drawing them towards their edge,
Or kissing stones with Judas lips.
Names are dragged beneath the surface,
Ramparts stormed and footprints sifted.
The blue cloth wipes across the slate,
And serves each one an equal fate.
Reclaiming ground without elation,
High to low............a generation.

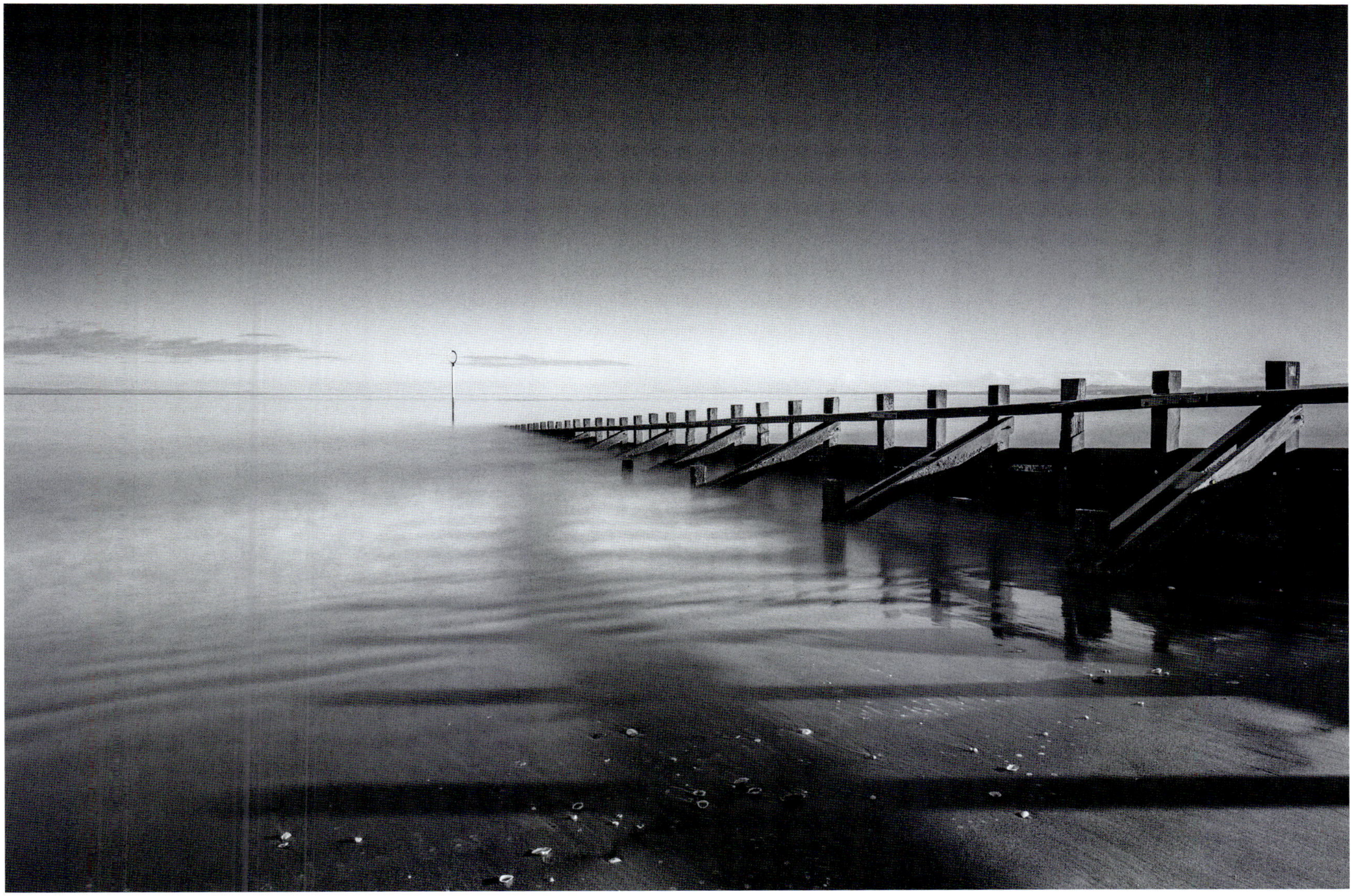

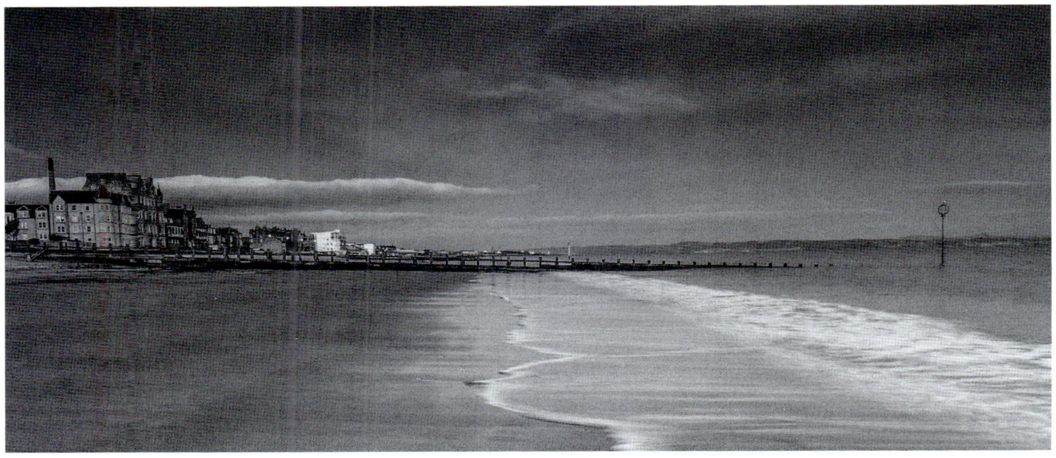

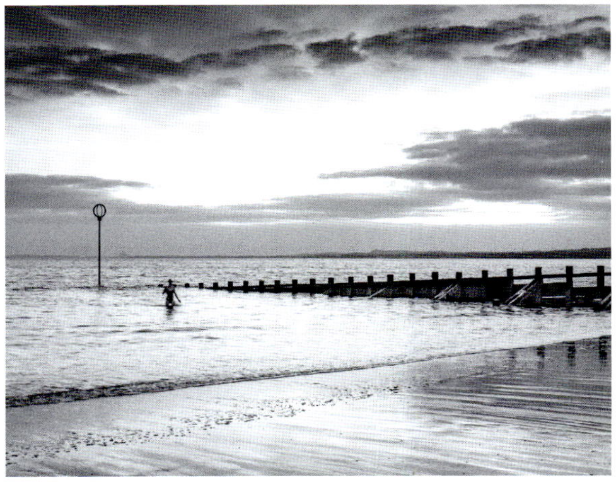

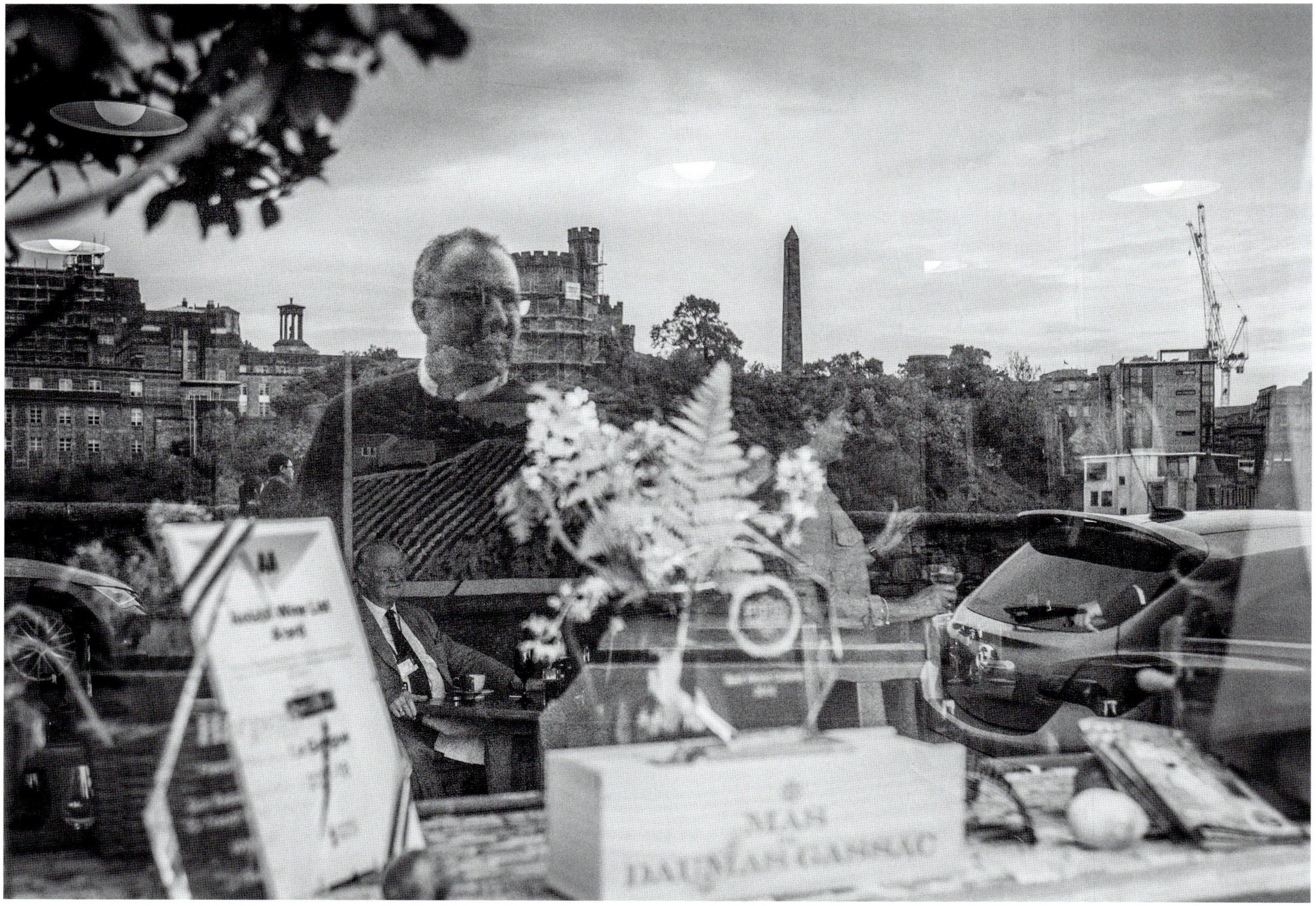
MAS

UNEXPECTED MOMENT

Through my own reflection
I saw you standing there
An unexpected moment
I couldn't help but stare
For in those fleeting seconds
I saw not a mother or a wife
Not a partner nor a lover
But the heartbeat of my life

I loved that simple moment
And have locked it in my mind
A treasure to be cherished
With others of its kind
Just to see you out of context
To escape from background noise
To be free from daily clutter
To see your smile and your poise.

So why does such a moment
Give rise to such a shock
Is it just that very closeness
Which can build a mental block?
Or has it more to do with living
Just keeping everything on track
The frantic bustle for survival
Makes it a problem stepping back?

So let me step inside that window
And take you by the hand
Let me catch that unexpected moment
And block the falling sand
And in those captured seconds
Hold not a mother or a wife
A partner nor a lover
But the heartbeat of my life

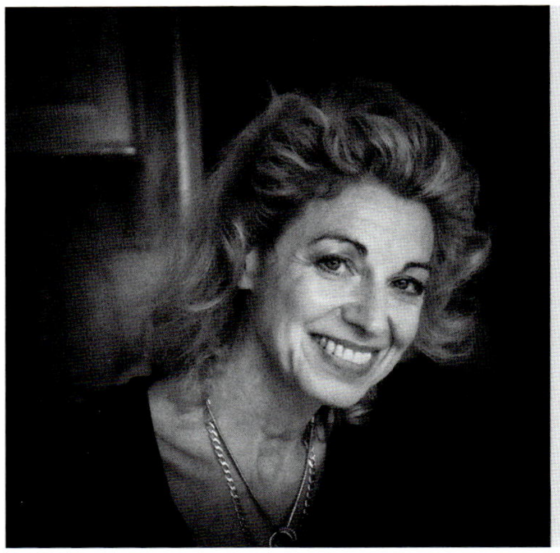

OLIVIA GILES

Olivia Giles graduated in law from Glasgow University, and until 2002 was a commercial property partner with Scottish law firm Maclay Murray & Spens. That year she contracted the blood poisoning form of meningitis, as a result of which both of her lower legs and both of her lower arms had to be amputated. After months of rehabilitation she made a full recovery and is fully mobile on prosthetic legs.

In 2007 Olivia founded the charity, '500 miles', which helps disabled people in Malawi and Zambia who have lost limbs (or the use of limbs) to enjoy maximum mobility and body function by helping them get access to artificial limbs and limbs supports. Olivia has run and fund-raised for the charity since its inception. She was awarded an OBE in 2010 and the Robert Burns Humanitarian Award in 2015 for her charitable work.

My first memories of Edinburgh are of day trips with my family to the Fringe and to the waxworks, although I don't remember any of the shows or exhibits. Instead, what I remember is the monochrome palette of the New Town where we must have parked - the cool, dark grey flagstones and flat-fronted buildings, the black iron railings, globes of light from the white street lamps suspended in pale mist, and hard white ice cream in a tea room on the High Street. It seemed to be a magical place of secrets and treats.

Less than 15 years later I was living and working there - in the grey buildings of Charlotte Square, Clarendon Crescent and York Place, but also on the southside in Leamington Terrace, Viewforth and Bruntsfield Links. I walked everywhere – to work, as a barmaid and as a lawyer, and at the weekends up Arthur's Seat and all the way to Granton and Portobello. It's one of the things I still love about Edinburgh, it's a walkable city where main thoroughfares can be narrow cobbled alleys, broad elegant streets or paths through gardens. The compact nature of the city also means you're unlikely to walk the length of George Street without meeting someone you know!

Of course, since I lost my lower legs I can't walk as much as I used to, but Edinburgh offers plenty of sedentary pleasures. The two weeks of the Edinburgh International Book Festival in Charlotte Square are my favourite two weeks of the year in the city. I'm sure that's partly because it evokes memories of those childhood holidays, but it's also because the huge variety of the programme and the accessibility of so many renowned authors alongside potential new finds gives it all the excitement of a grown-up sweetie shop - and all with a sense of stealing a look behind the curtain.

The sweet tooth of my childhood hasn't deserted me and I always enjoy sampling Edinburgh's many elaborate, modern and delicious afternoon teas served in beautiful salons, as well as the fact there are apparently 57 coffee shops in Bruntsfield and Morningside where I now live - many of which I know well!

I love the Scottish Parliament building, the Canny Man's, and The Proclaimers' Leith in the sunshine. However, I think a little part of my soul will always be around the green and blossom-laden grounds at Astley Ainsley Hospital where, with the help of its local rehabilitation staff, I learned to walk again ... even if not quite 500 miles!

If I could suggest one major improvement for Edinburgh, it would be to establish a pick-up/drop-off point within walking distance of Waverley and Haymarket Stations where it is not actually illegal or plain dangerous to stop. That would be nice, and not just for me!

Edinburgh Revisited is a wonderfully evocative depiction of the city in words and pictures which would, in any event, have a place on our book shelves, but I am especially thrilled and honoured that my charity, '500 miles', is one of the two beneficiaries of Gordon's and Don's talent, energy and kindness, alongside Leuchie House.

STOCKBRIDGE LOVERS

Lifting over George Street
With the Castle to your back,
See Fife on the horizon
Silhouetted all in black;
Pass Thistle Street,
And Queen Street,
Then Gardens left and right,
Then wonder at the lawyers' row
That stretches out of sight;
The cut stone and the palace fronts,
The lampposts and the rails,
Where each townhouse is a landmark,
With their chronicle of tales;
But there is no time to linger,
The journey is half-done,
As the black and shining cobbles
Each pulsate against the sun;
Turn down Royal Circus,
Two halves, a perfect whole,
A symmetrical precision
That animates the soul;
Then pass the beckoning curve,
Of Royal Circus Lane,
With its carriage homes and flagstones,
That imprint upon the brain;
While the gentle slope will lead you,
Inexorably down,
Towards the running water,
Which boundaries the town;
To stand above the river,
Which stretches to the sea
And build a recollection
That will forever
Set you free.

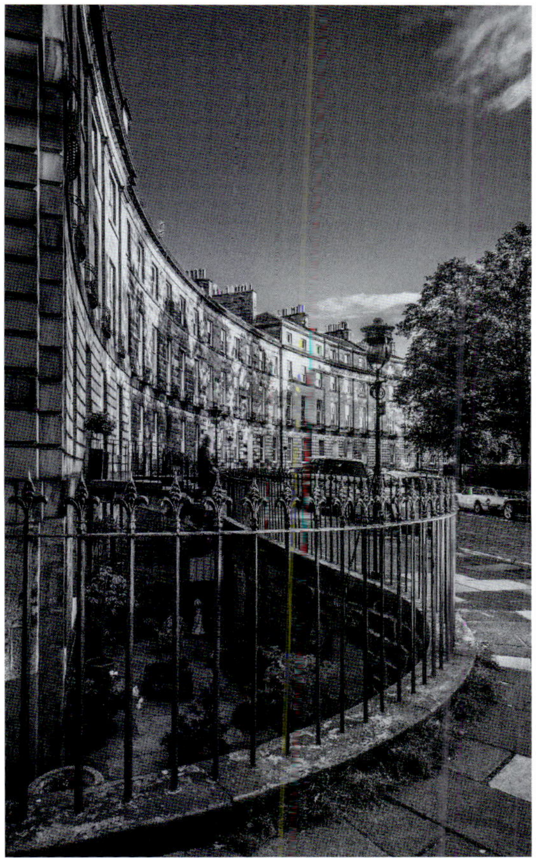

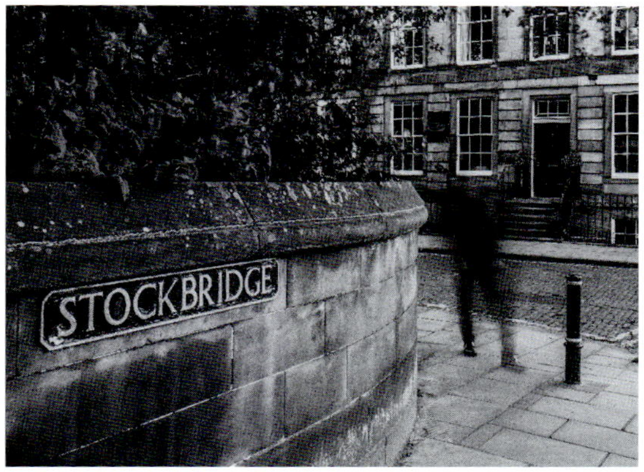
STOCKBRIDGE

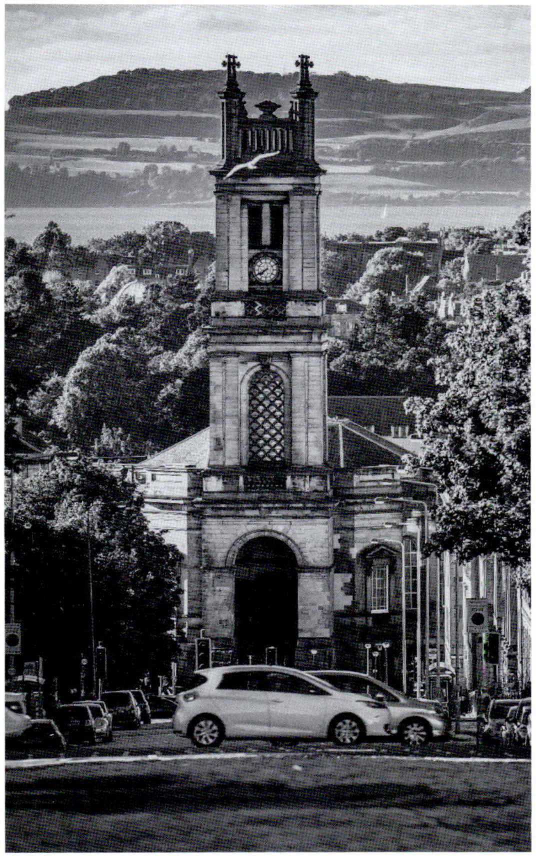

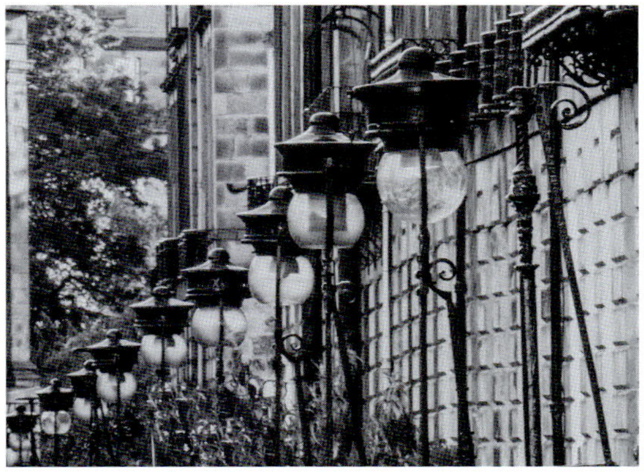

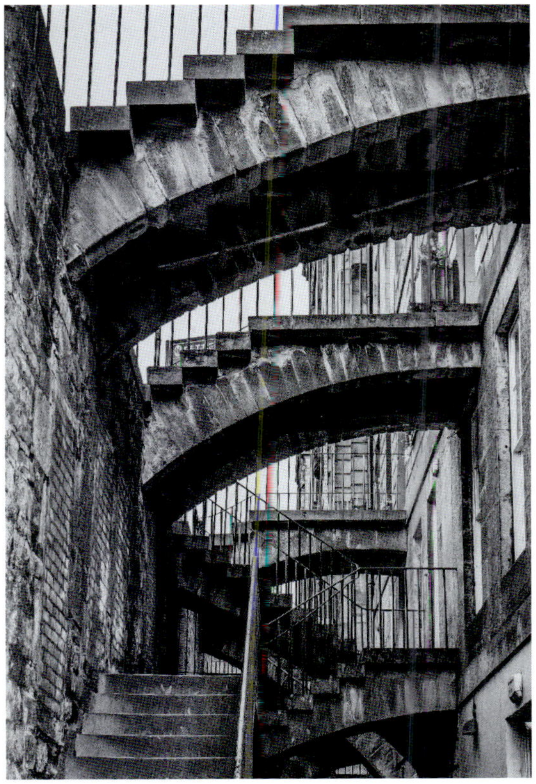

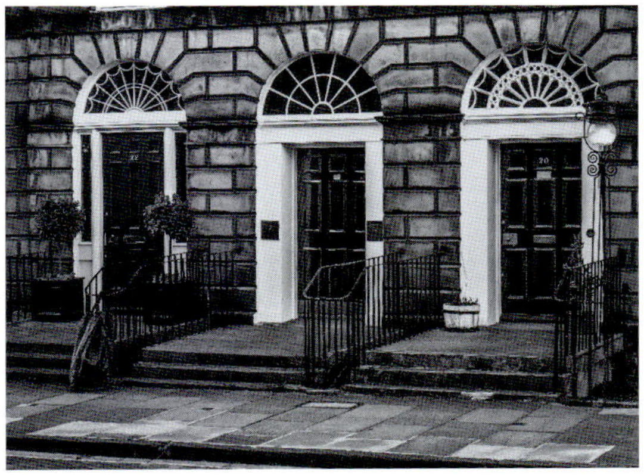

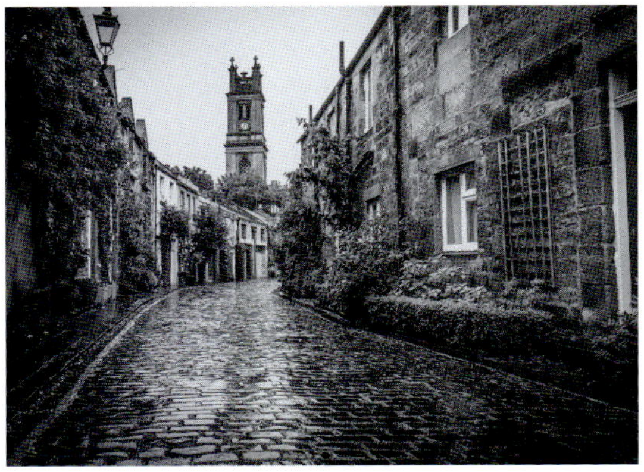

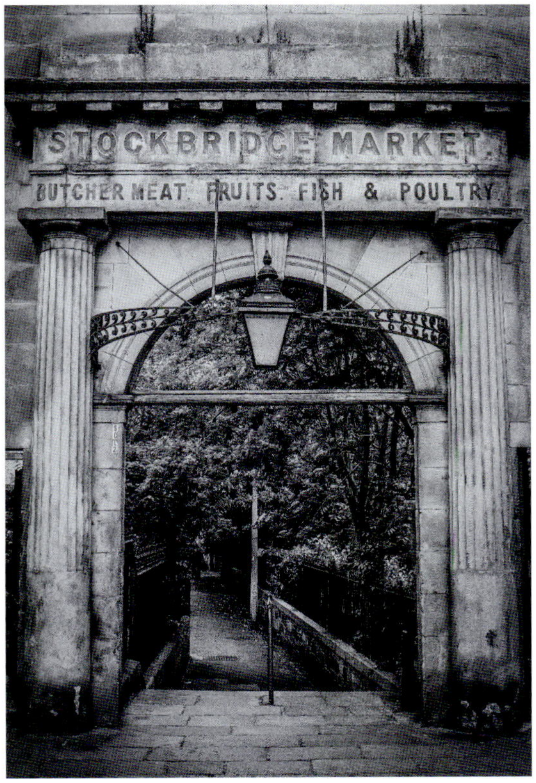
STOCKBRIDGE MARKET
BUTCHER MEAT FRUITS FISH & POULTRY

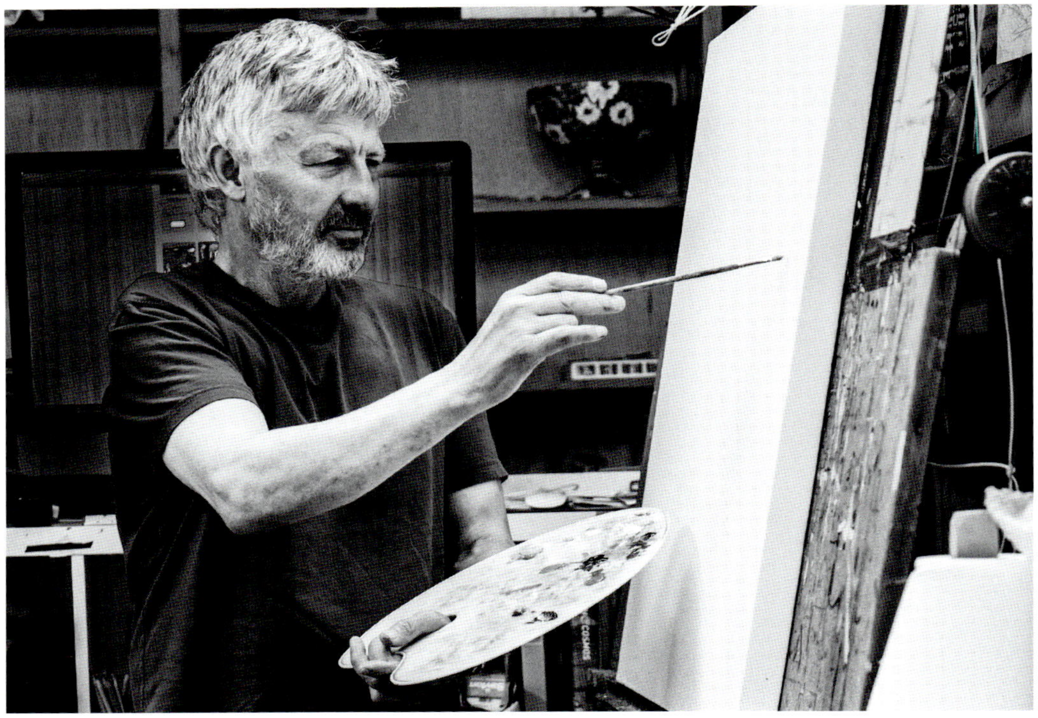

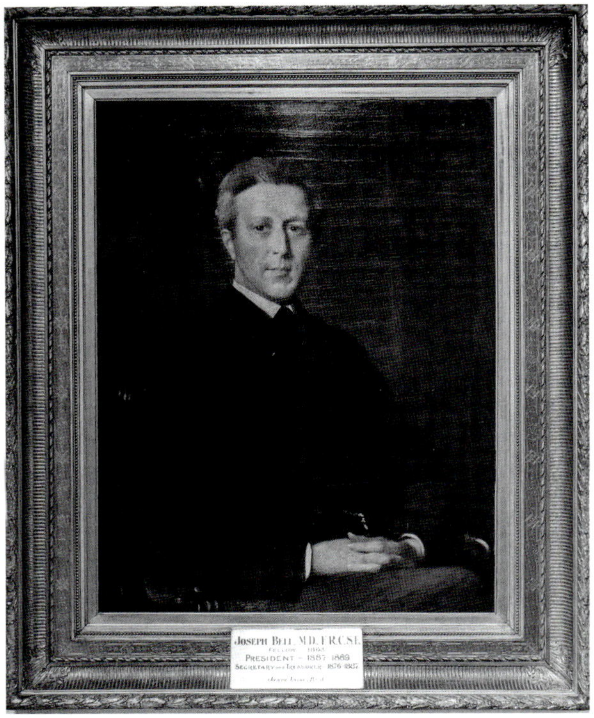
JOSEPH BELL M.D. F.R.C.S.E.
PRESIDENT – 1887 1889

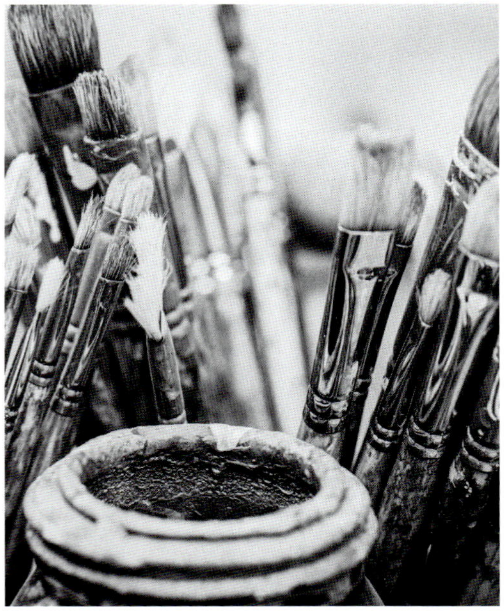

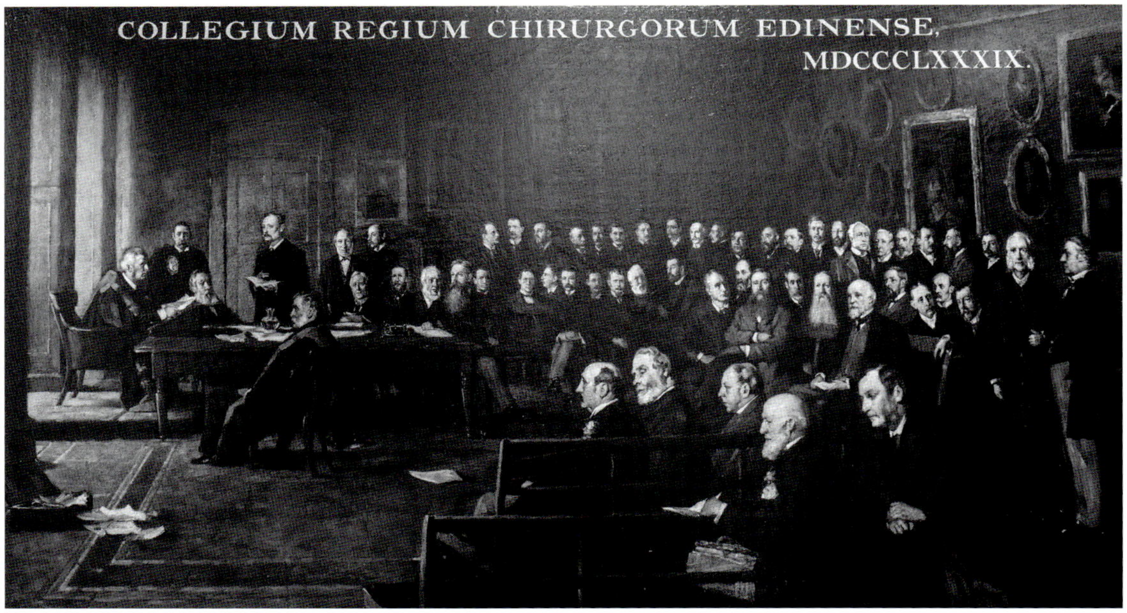
COLLEGIUM REGIUM CHIRURGORUM EDINENSE,
MDCCCLXXXIX.

PORTRAIT OF A PRESIDENT

The palette holds the painting of the man,
Amongst the pressed and vibrant swirling oils,
Where waits the surgeon in his robes and chain,
Who travelled to this very moment
Through a lifetime's journey of achievement;
For this is a step to immortality,
An instant's recognition than never wanes;
And so, for once, the surgeon sits,
A passive object of the artist's gaze,
Who took a separate path
To stand before him, brush in hand,
The two conjoined professions,
Of eyes and minds and hands,
The white canvas, indifferent
To its destiny, absorbs the marks,
The brush becomes the knife,
The knife becomes the brush,
The shaping of the form,
The record of the man,
Emerging from the flat dimension;
The surgeon relocates,
Escaping from the unreliability of flesh,
A recreation of a hand that sees,
His being flowing through the artist's eyes;
Unveiled it takes its place upon the wall,
A marker for his generation,
A peg placed in the ground,
To slip gently down the corridor,
Through the advancing years.

THE OLD ROYAL HIGH SCHOOL

"Vivas Schola Regia"
Or so the school song went,
"Sicut arx in colle sita"
'Like a citadel placed on a hill'
Watching over its city,
But empty now,
Empty for fifty years,
Boys long departed,
Old men now;
And with each departing soul
The memories are reabsorbed,
Into the Athenian walls,
The pillars and the place,
Until, one day,
The last breath slips away,
And, in that final moment,
If you listen very carefully,
You will hear it whisper,
"The school is dead"
Long live the school,
Vivas Schola Regia

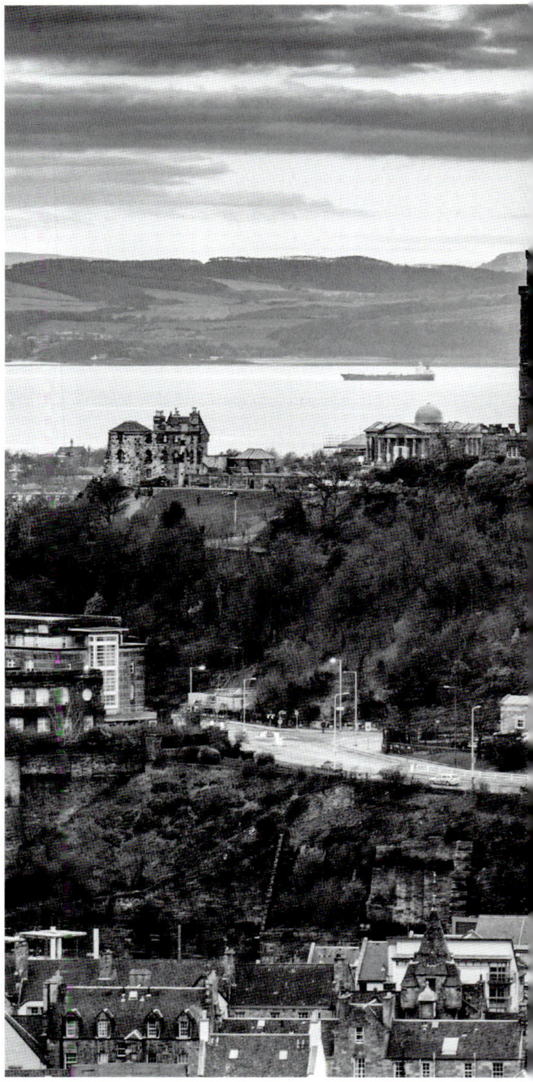

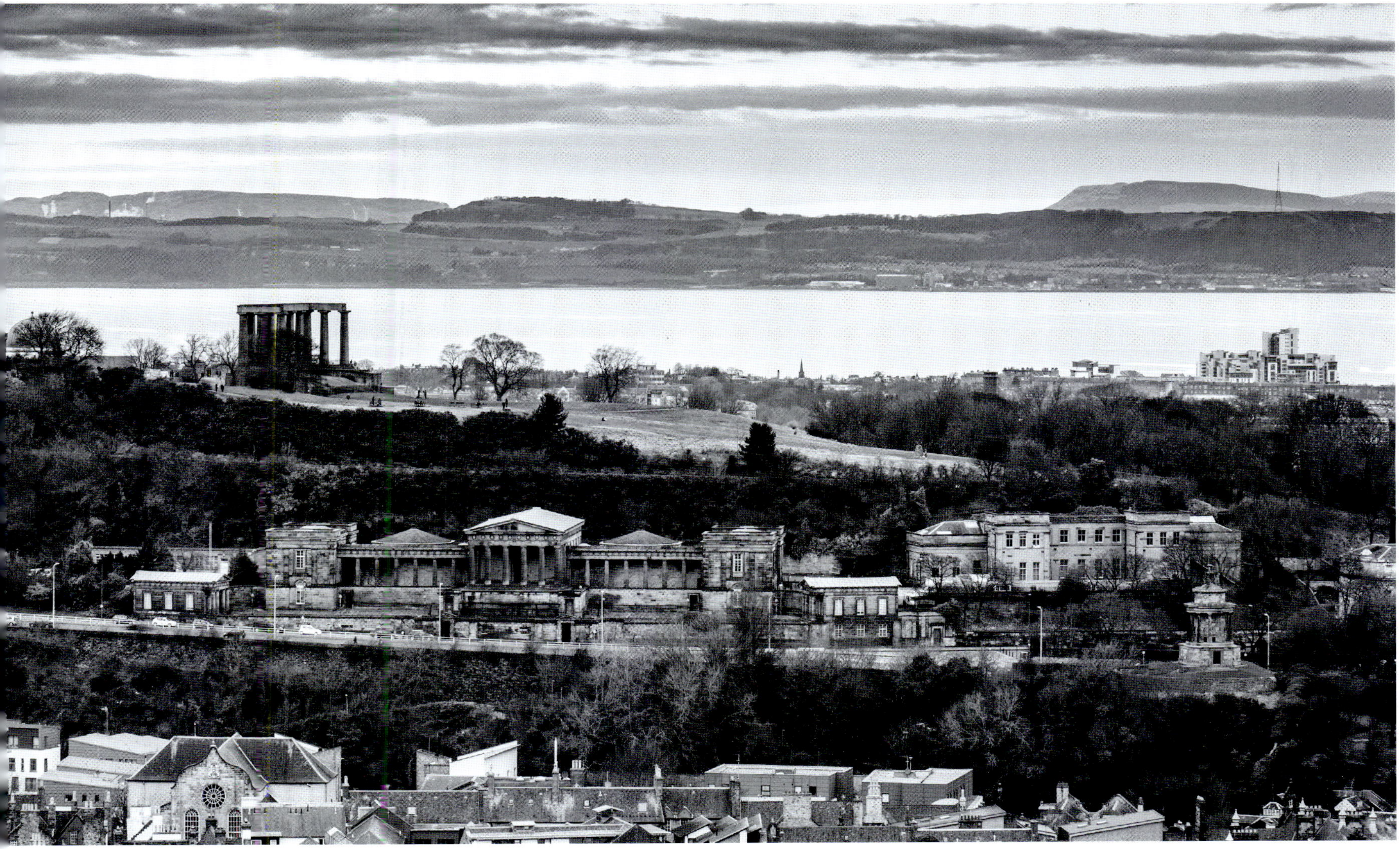

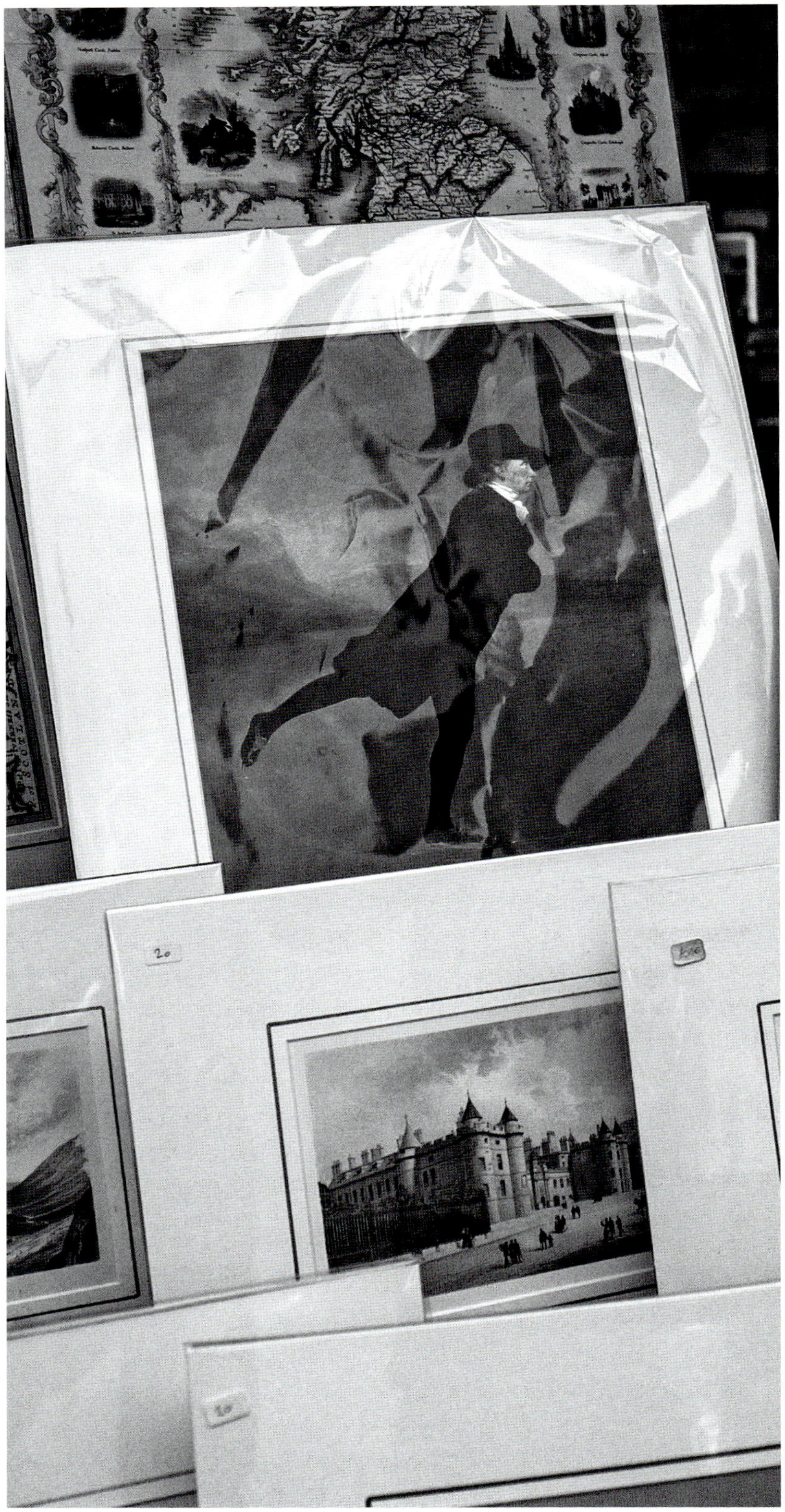

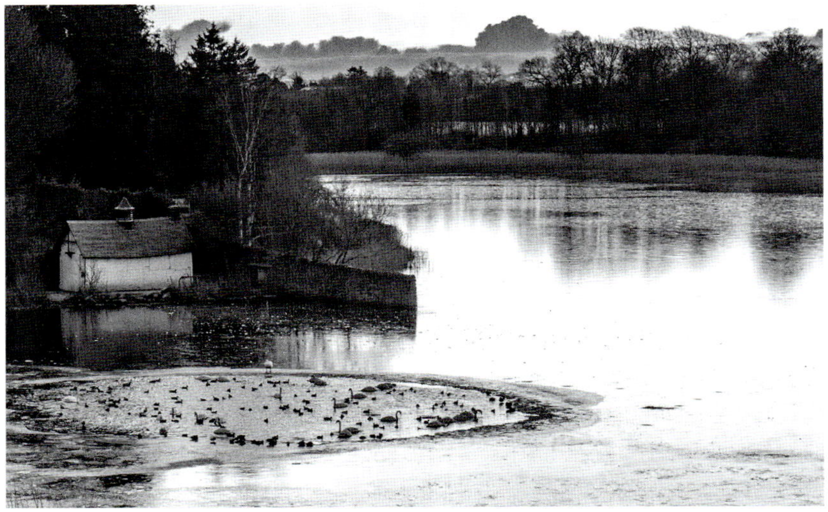

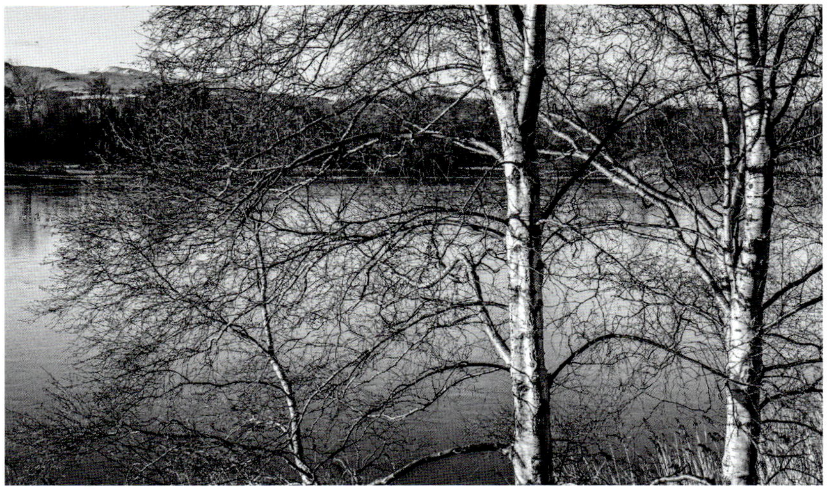

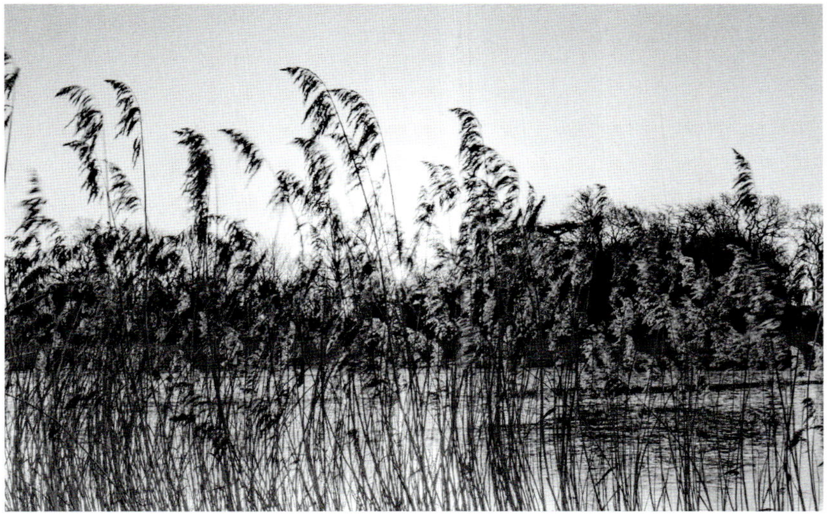

DUDDINGSTON SKATER

Raeburn trapped him,
The skating reverend,
Reducing him to an instant,
His leisurely turn transformed
Into immortality;
Forget whatever else
He might have done,
He stays with us,
Upright, gliding forgetfully
Towards his end,
Long gone now,
But outliving all,
Long beyond
Our stare.

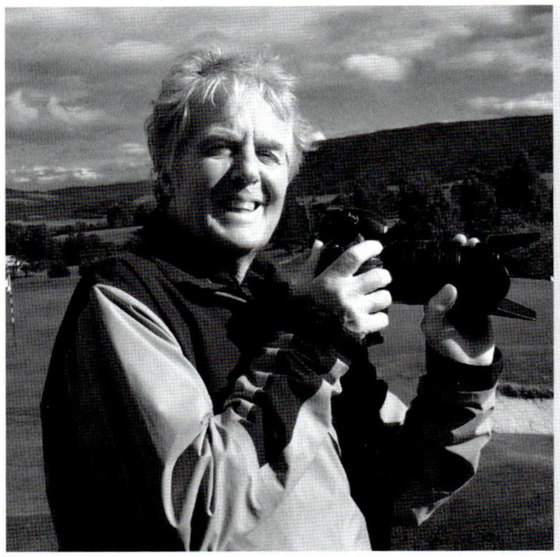

GLYN SATTERLEY

Although born and brought up in Kent, Scotland has been Glyn's adopted home for the last 35 years, initially living in Edinburgh and then in East Lothian. He is best known for his books on Highland sporting estates, and for his black and white, evocative and sometimes quirky images of Scottish golf, landscape and the people who inhabit it.

A project to photograph Caithness and Sutherland, funded by the then Highlands and Islands Development Board, introduced Glyn to the Highlands, resulting in his first book, *Life in Caithness and Sutherland*. Glyn was bowled over by the people he met there and the beauty, bleakness and changing light of the landscape. He considers the two years spent commuting there from Kent by caravanette as his photographic apprenticeship - a welcome release after finishing a Fine Art degree in painting. His unique style developed through this period.

A successful career as an editorial freelance followed, working throughout the UK and abroad, but his on-going love affair with the Scottish Highlands continues. He still documents estate life - stalking, shooting and fishing - and some of his most memorable photographs have resulted from this work, when the light is right, or a figure within his frame works its magic.

Glyn's work has been exhibited widely and can be found in private collections, Scotland's National Collection, Strathclyde and St Andrews University Collections and the Martin Parr Foundation Collection.

His books include *Life in Caithness and Sutherland*, *Trustlands*, *The Scottish Golf Book*, *The Scottish Fishing Book*, *The Scottish Whisky Book*, *The Highland Game* and *Going to the Hill*.
[See: www.glynsatterley.com]

My relationship with Edinburgh began in 1981, with my first Scottish photographic exhibition at the Edinburgh Fringe. It was held in the Highland Tolbooth Kirk at the top of the Royal Mile, now known as The Hub. There I met my wife Andrea, who had just finished two years of documentary photography at Newport and moved back to the city to start freelancing. She was surprised that, '...an Englishman had managed to take such emotive images of Caithness and Sutherland'! We got chatting... Coincidentally photographer John Charity, at that time a senior lecturer at Newport, walked into my exhibition the next day. He became our best man and remains a lifelong friend.

Photographically my heart was, and still is, in the Highlands and Islands. Most of my personal work has been produced there. Life in the 'remote' corners of Scotland in those days was quiet and wonderfully unspoilt, just like its landscape, and I have been drawn to it all my life. In the early '80s, like 'Scotland's Far North', the Festival Fringe was just starting to be discovered by visitors from south of the border. No-one could have anticipated the worldwide artistic honeypot it has become today.

I've had a fondness for Edinburgh ever since, and we lived in Dalkeith Road for several years before making our home in East Lothian. I loved the scale of the place: being able to run from our flat round Arthur's Seat and back (via a swim in the Commonwealth Pool); skittles and a pint in the Sheep's Heid at Duddingston. I loved dawn and dusk in the city: the early morning street cleaners, hosing down Princes Street statues; water cascading down the National Gallery steps; the evening glow on Salisbury Crags, or Dean Village or the Forth Bridge. I also enjoyed the many assignments I had in and around the city. Most memorable was the sad retiral of the milk horses and their drivers, who had been such a feature of the city's early morning life. I was also privileged to have been able to meet and photograph many 'well-kent' Scots there, including John McGrath, Norman MacCaig, Stan Wood the fossil hunter, Alexander McCall Smith, Ian Banks, The Proclaimers and sculptor Ronald Rae.

Coincidence also introduced me to my close friend Gordon Hunter. I needed a picture of 'a fisherman on a boat in a loch having a dram' for Field magazine. Someone suggested Gordon might be the man to try, so one day I met him down at Headshaw Farm, where he kindly set me up with a loch, a boat, a fisherman and a dram. Afterwards we got chatting... He was dabbling in photography, and was keen to have a longer chat and a few sessions learning how to print in our wet darkroom. Little did I know he would become the fine photographer he is today, who along with Don Ledingham has managed to weave together so beautifully, in words and pictures, the magic of this city.

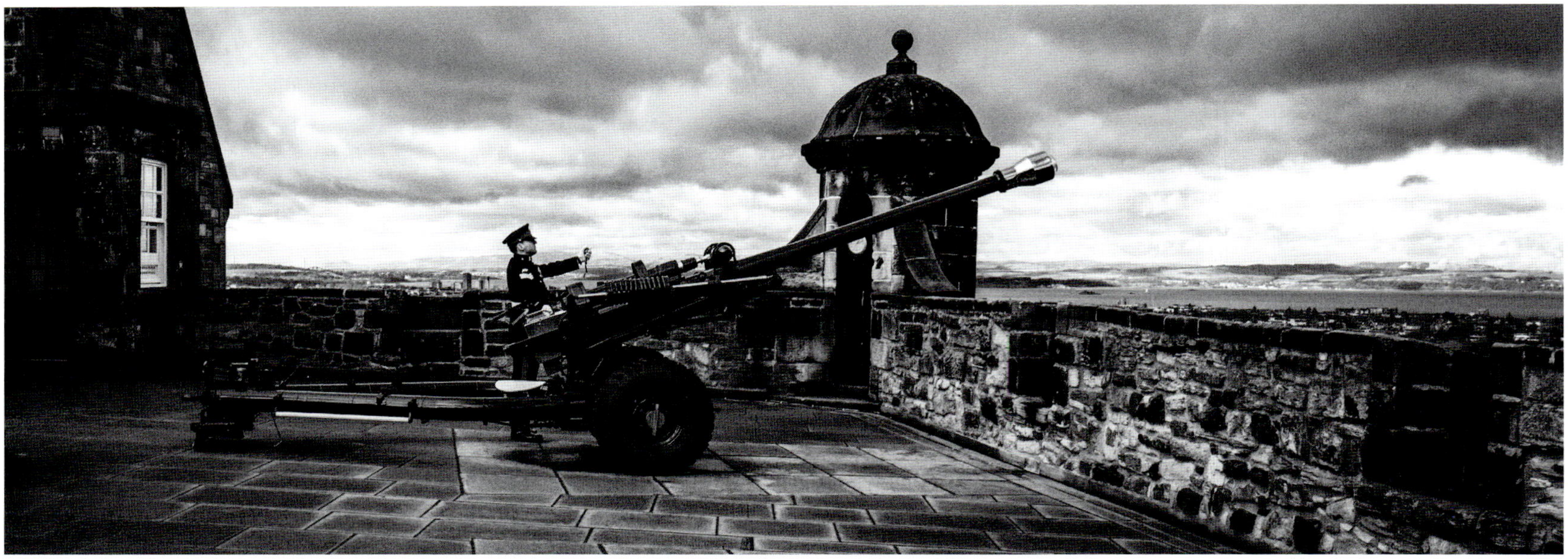

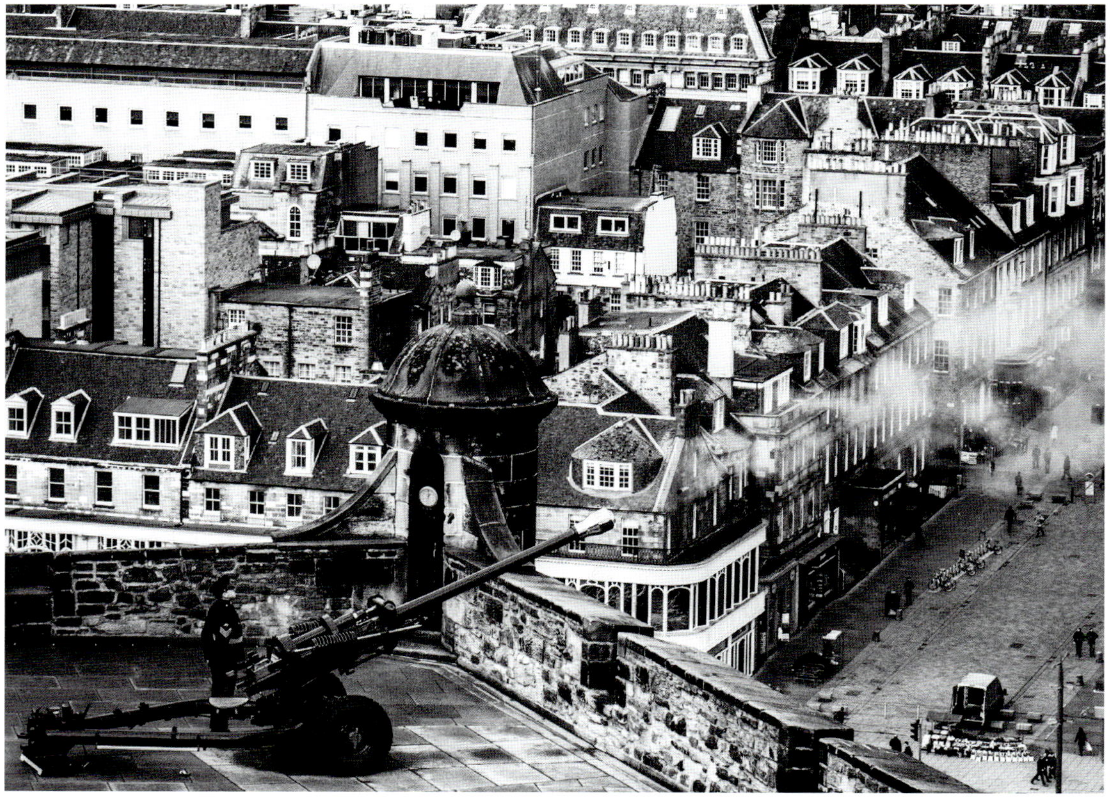

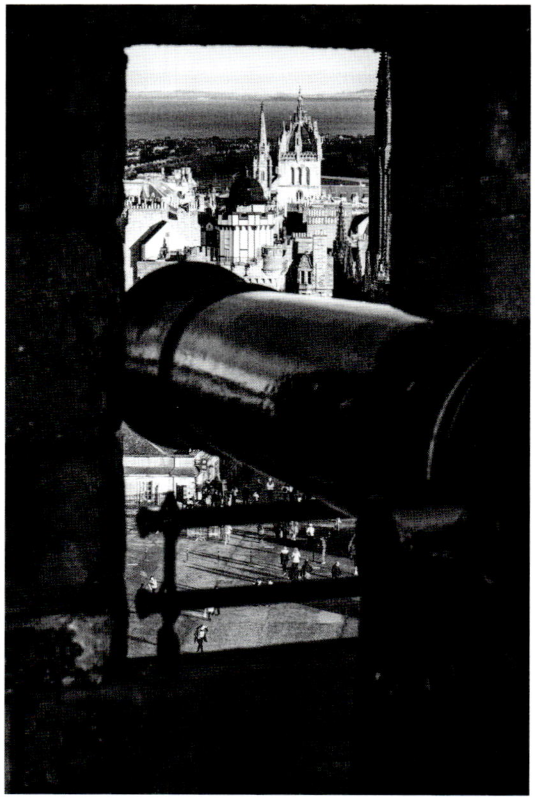

ONE O'CLOCK GUN

In those
Disappearing seconds
Before the hour,
A weapon lies,
Prepared and primed,
And aimed upon
The uncertainty of time;
Down below,
Defenceless masses,
Trudging through
The business of their day,
Dig into their
Oblivious positions;
As a timepiece
Gives the order to discharge,
And the city echoes,
To the monstrous
Anger of the gun,
Dispatching
Unprotected bodies to the air;
"Advance"
The unforgiving clock commands,
Occupy the hours
Beyond this point,
Never tread this time again,
Until tomorrow,
When in those
Disappearing seconds
Before the hour,
The weapon will
Fire once again
A battle of attrition,
From which
No victory
Comes.

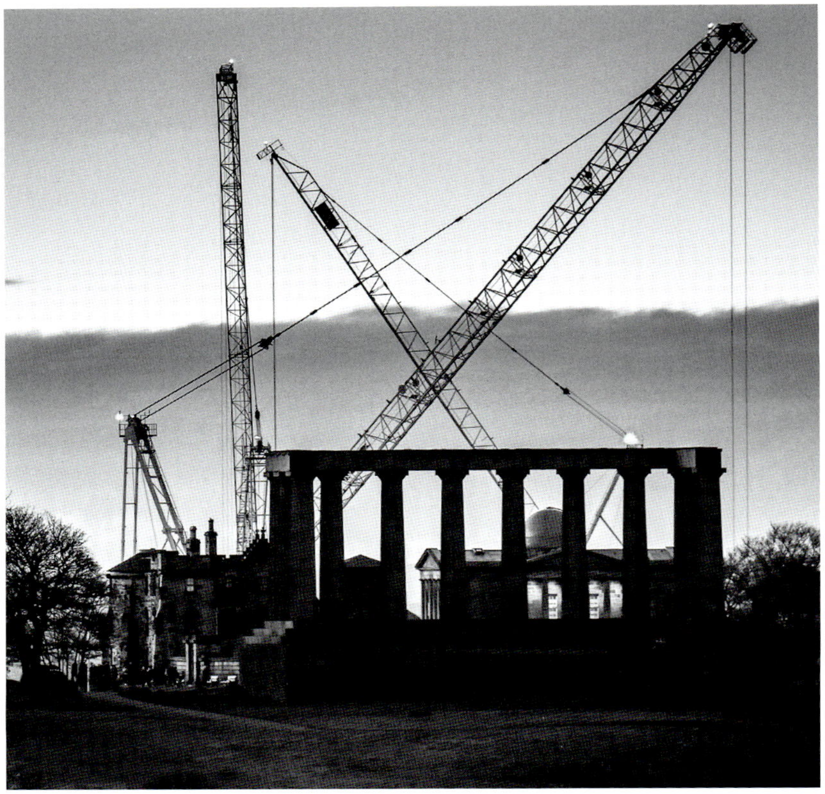

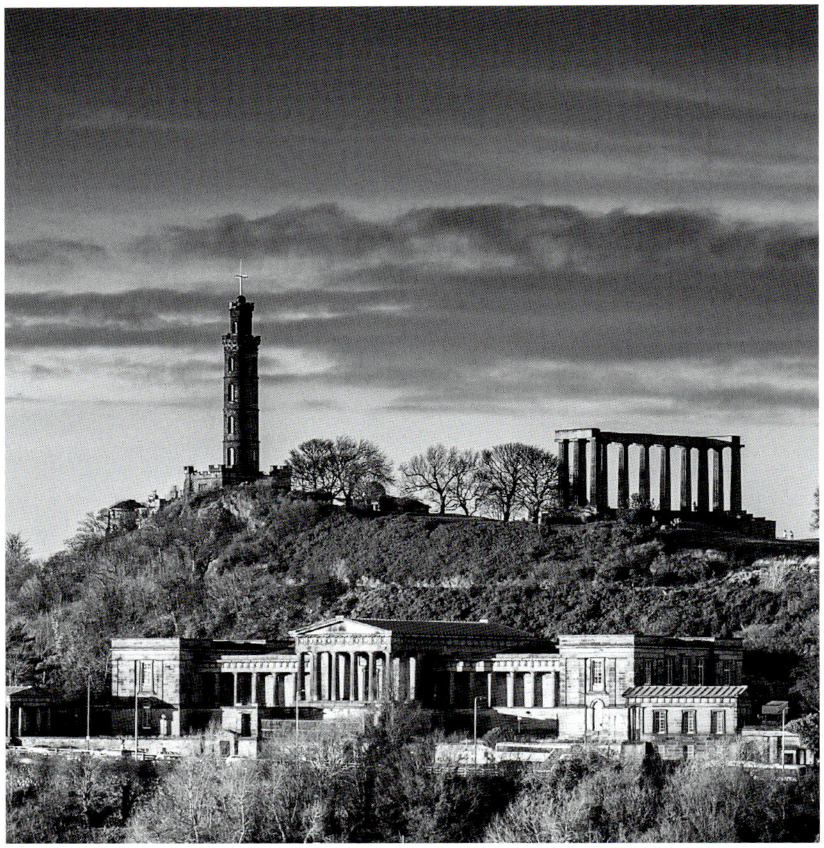

THE UNFINISHED MONUMENT

I've grown up with you
Admiring you from afar,
The backdrop to a city,
Watching over us,
From every angle,
Squeezing yourself,
Each hour of the day,
Into a thousand
Thoughtless images,
The anonymous stranger,
Standing in the back row,
The nameless face,
The disremembered relative,
Locked away upon your hill,
Yet perfect in,
Your imperfection;
Be patient with our folly,
Forgive our tedious disdain,
For none of us,
Who wander carelessly,
In ignorant superiority,
Have any greater claim,
To be complete.

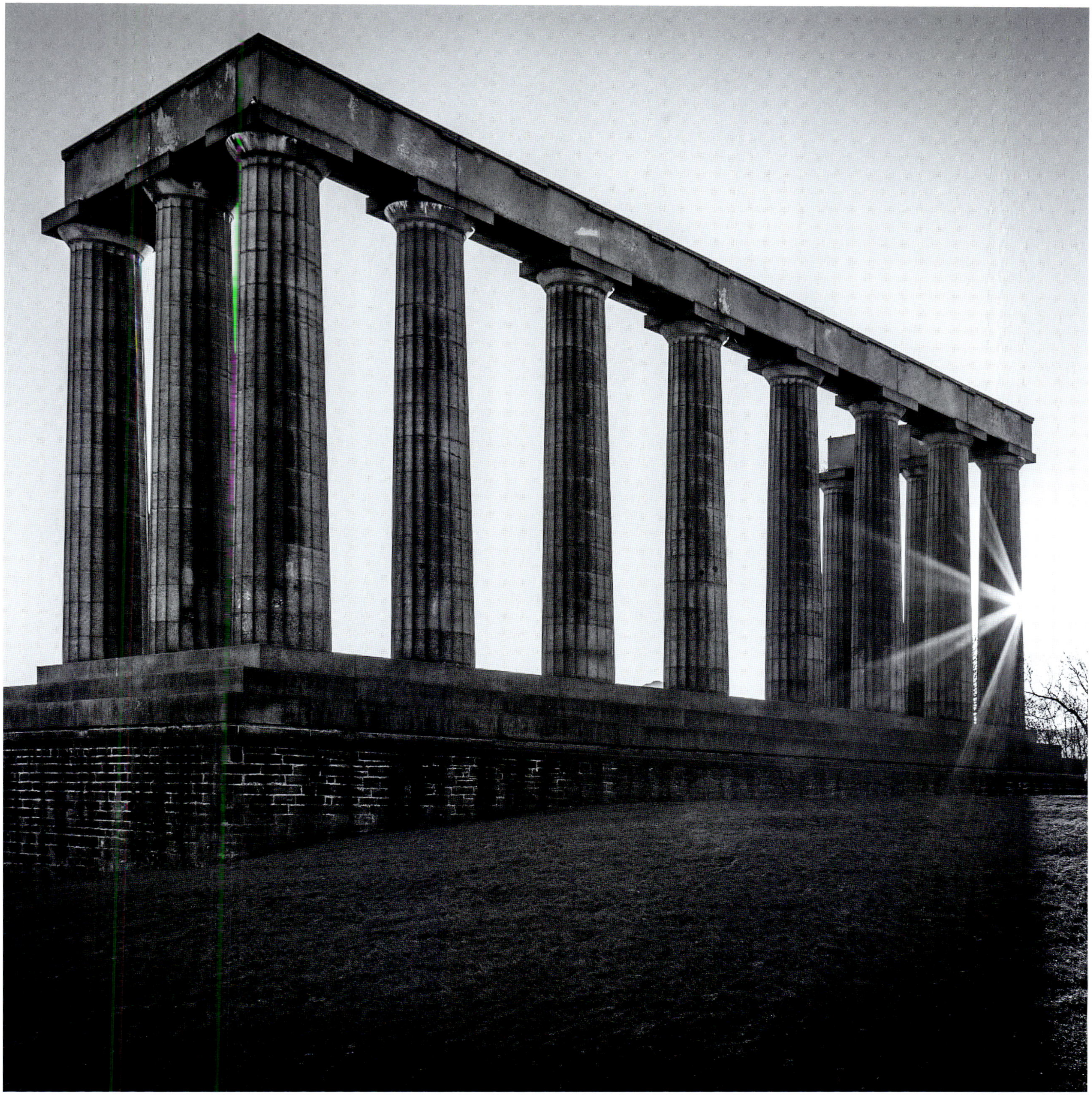

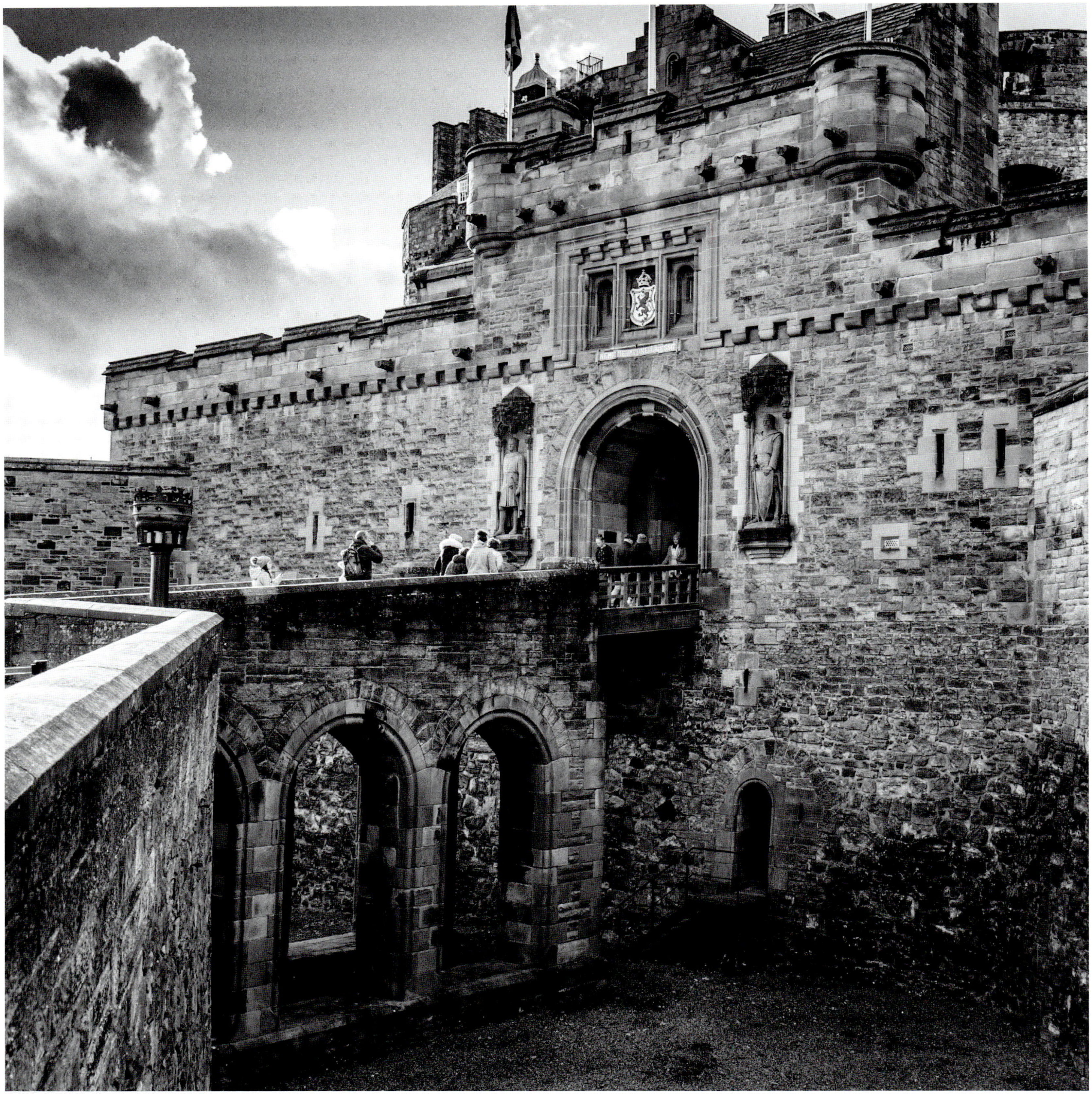

EDINBURGH CASTLE GUARDIANS

Sir William Wallace:
"I got up this morning.
I like to get up in the morning;
It gives me the rest of the day to myself."
King Robert the Bruce:
"I was out walking the other evening.
This fellow stopped me,
And asked if that was the moon up there in the sky.
I told him that I had no idea as I was a stranger here myself."
William Wallace:
"No Bad.
Bobby, is it possible to mistake
Schizophrenia for telepathy?
I hear you ask?"
Robert the Bruce:
"Like it.
There's a new slimming course just out
Where they remove all your bones.
Not only do you weigh less,
But you also look so much more relaxed."
Wlliam:
"Brilliant.
I admit to spending a fortune in my time on women,
Drink and gambling.
The rest I squandered."
Robert:
"Ha ha.
I saw this tourist last week.
He was dressed as a cowboy.
Wi' a broon paper hat, paper waistcoat and paper troosers.
He was wanted for rustling."
Wullie:
"Oh Bobby that's a gid yin.
I'm no a fan of the new pound coin,
But then again,
I hate change."
Bobby:
"Aye weel Wullie,
You and I won't be gawn anywhere soon,
So we micht as weel
Enjoy oorsels!"

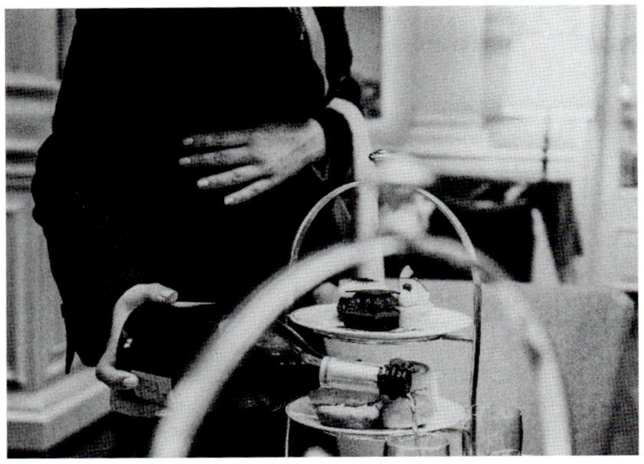

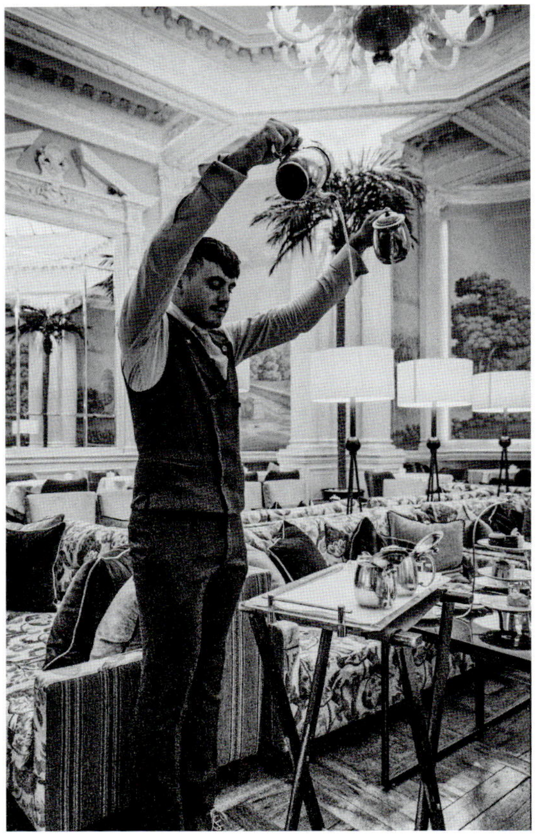

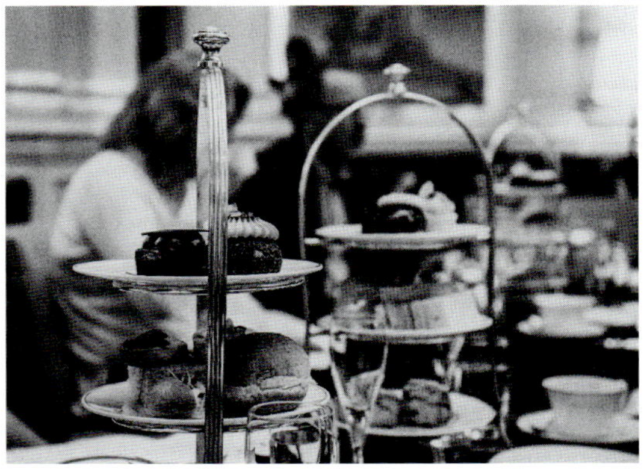

AFTERNOON TEA AT THE BALMORAL

Elegance,
Plays softly on the ear,
And easy on the eye,
Deceiving us
With a simplicity,
That belies the truth;
The practised polished hand,
The effortless endeavour,
Distilled, and then refined,
Where less is more;
And here,
On a wet and windy,
Edinburgh afternoon,
We escape,
To an exotic place,
A world of infusions,
From Darjeeling,
And Nepal,
To a land
Above the clouds;
The art of ceremony,
The easy grace,
The dignity of service,
The ritual of restraint,
The spinning stops,
Albeit for an instant,
In long-to-be
Remembered,
Sumptuous,
Scottish,
Splendour.

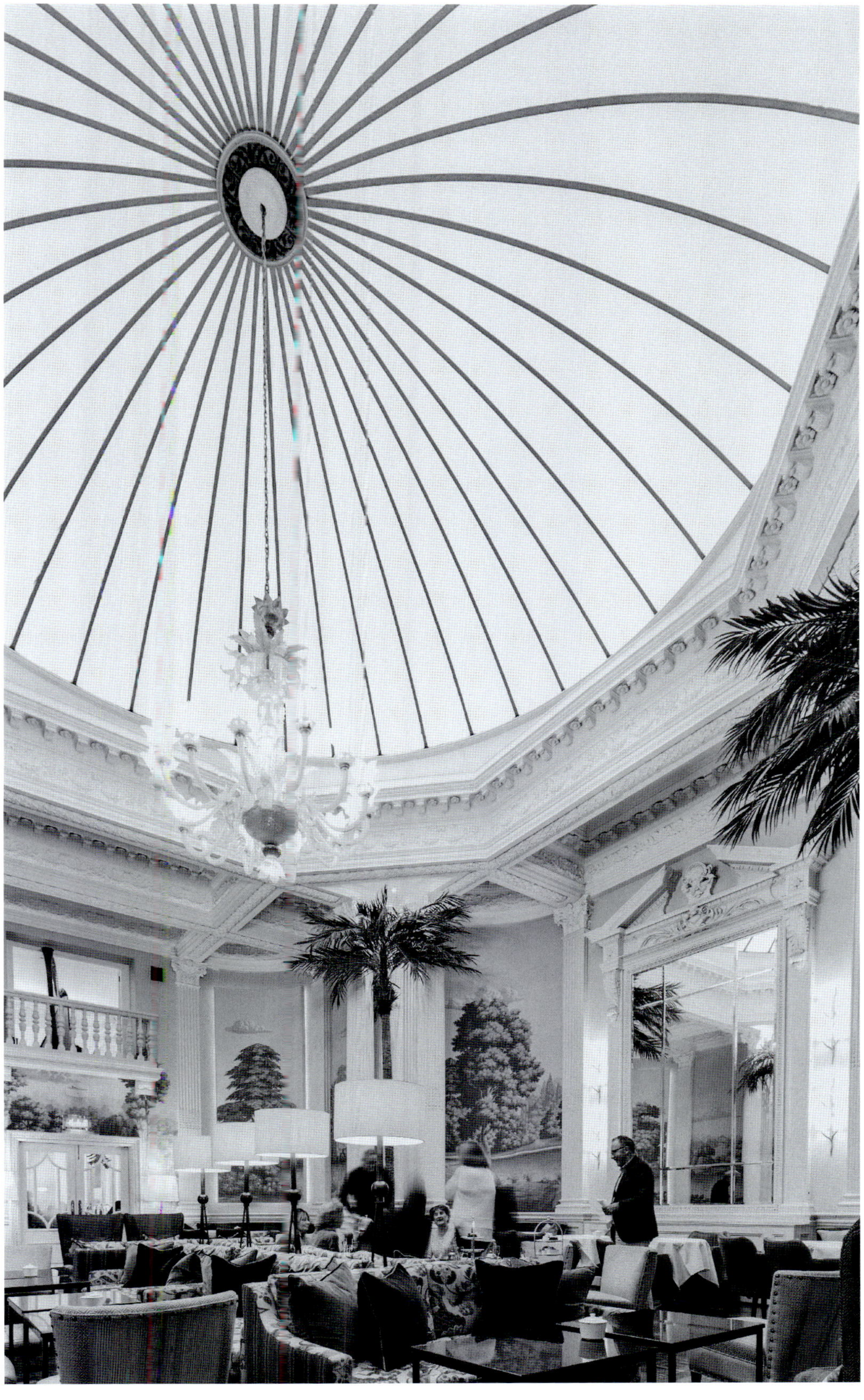

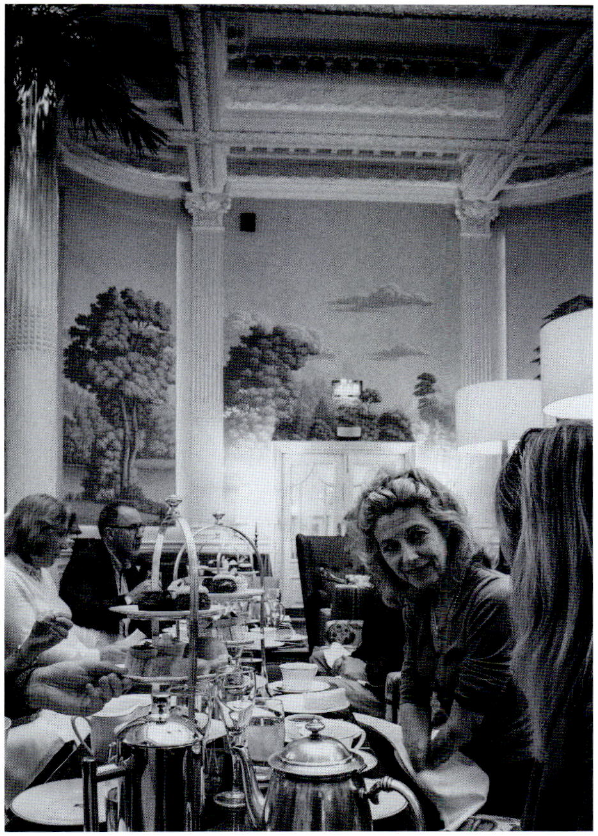

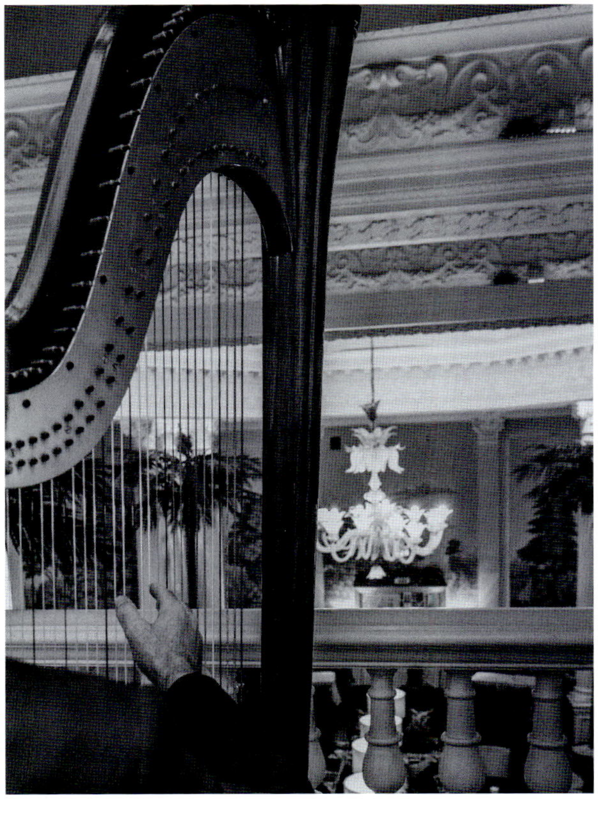

EDINBURGH REVISITED

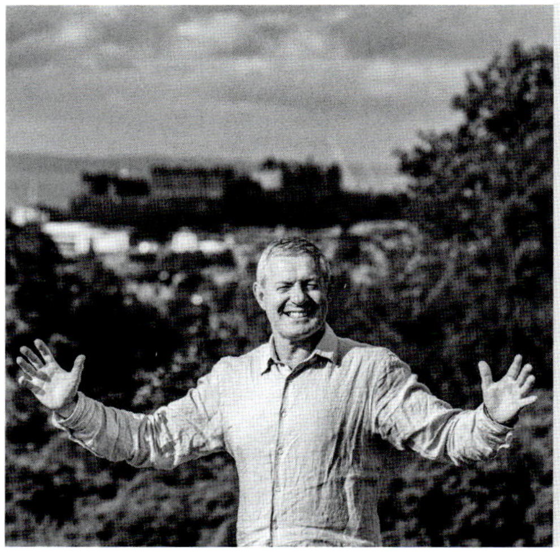

GAVIN HASTINGS

Gavin Hastings, OBE, is widely regarded as one of Scottish rugby's best-ever players, winning 61 caps for his country, 20 as captain. Equally revered on the global rugby stage, he twice toured with the British & Irish Lions - to Australia in 1989, and then as captain on the 1993 Lions' tour to New Zealand. Gavin was inducted into the International Rugby Hall of Fame in 2003, and into the World Rugby Hall of Fame in 2013. As well as winning two Blues while at Cambridge University, he played club rugby for Watsonians and London Scottish, also turning out for the Barbarians and the Co-optimists. Born in Edinburgh, he was educated at George Watson's College, Paisley College of Technology (now the University of the West of Scotland) and Magdalene College, Cambridge, graduating in 1986 with a BA in land economy.

When I was captaining the Scotland rugby team I used Edinburgh Castle as an image for how I wanted to play. In my role as full-back – playing behind everyone as the last line of defence - it helped me to think of myself as that huge block of granite with its impenetrable walls as the foundation of the team.

As one of four brothers growing up in Edinburgh – inevitably with a ball in my hands or at my feet – I grew to love this city. We used to go family walks up on the Braid Hills and I would look out over the city and see the Castle, the city silhouette and onto the Firth of Forth. Saturday afternoons were taken up watching games at Myreside and then throughout the year we would play whatever sport was on the telly; Wimbledon tennis, Open Championship golf, cricket from Lord's and then rugby from Murrayfield. Who would have guessed that just a few years later I would be running out onto that famous pitch?

As my rugby career progressed I moved away to London, but as is so often the case, it was a woman who brought me back home. I'd met Diane in 1990 during our Grand Slam season, before she went off travelling around the world. I said to her that by the time she came home I would be back in Edinburgh and so it turned out just like that and we have been together ever since.

I've come to realise that rugby is just but a moment in your life – nothing I've done since I retired in 1995 has made me a better player, apart from the passing of time!

Of course, if truth be told, my true passion is golf. Living in Edinburgh there are so many wonderful courses in the city and just down the coast too. I'm fortunate to be a member at Gullane, Muirfield and the R&A at St Andrews – how many other places in the world could I step out of my front door and be within striking distance of such amazing and world famous courses?

Memories of my playing days are still vivid and I'm fortunate to have so many friends from around the world as a consequence of my rugby career. I love nothing more than showing them around my city. It's sometimes only when you introduce others to Edinburgh that you realise just what a great city it is and what it means to you.

Starting off at Inverleith Park – with its magnificent view of the Castle – and heading south towards the trendy area of Stockbridge, then the majesty of the New Town and its cobbled streets and squares as it rises up to Princes Street and on up the Mound to the Royal Mile. It never ceases to bring me pleasure just to walk in the city – and especially with friends.

Playing rugby for Scotland and in the old Five Nations was all about being part of a community. You belonged to something bigger than yourself. I think that's something that people miss when they talk about Edinburgh. It's not just a place to visit. It holds you and connects you to something more than just being a nice place to live.

Edinburgh is part of me, and perhaps in a small way, I'm part of it.

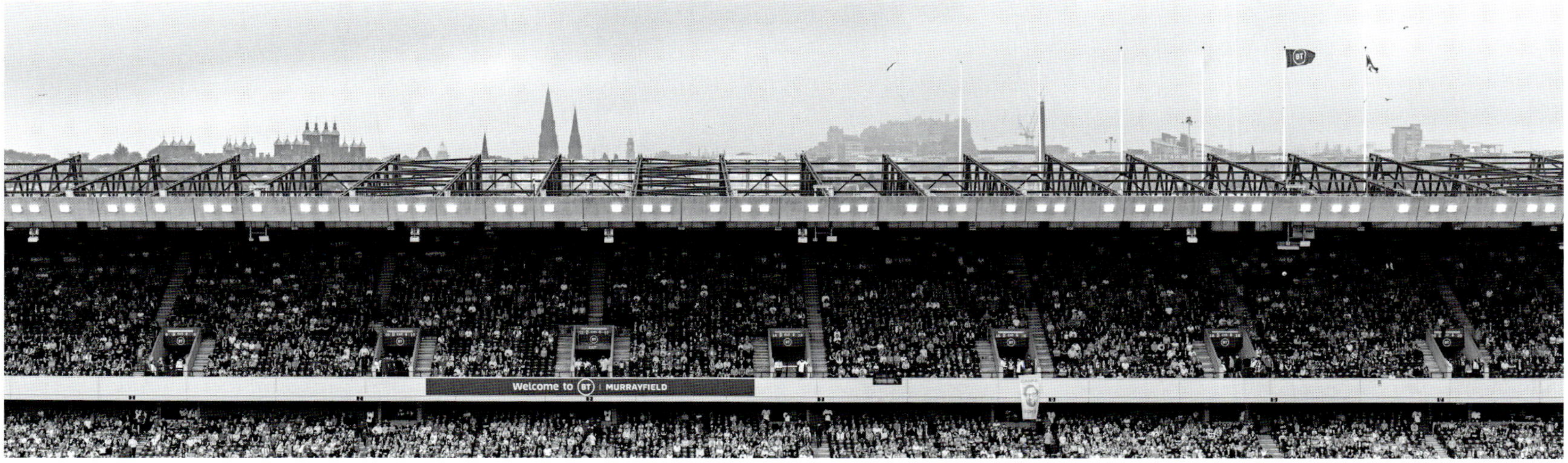
Welcome to BT | MURRAYFIELD

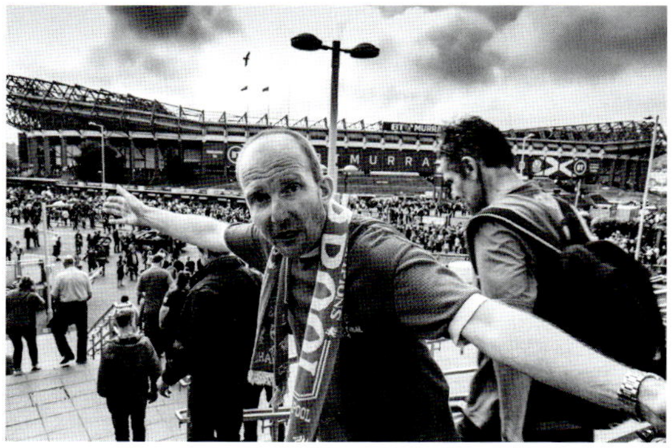

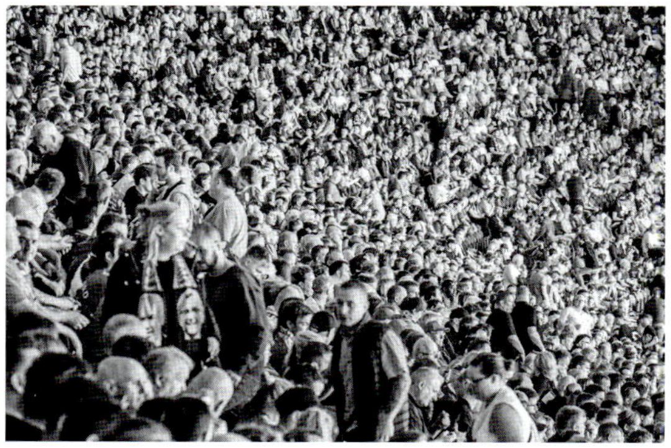

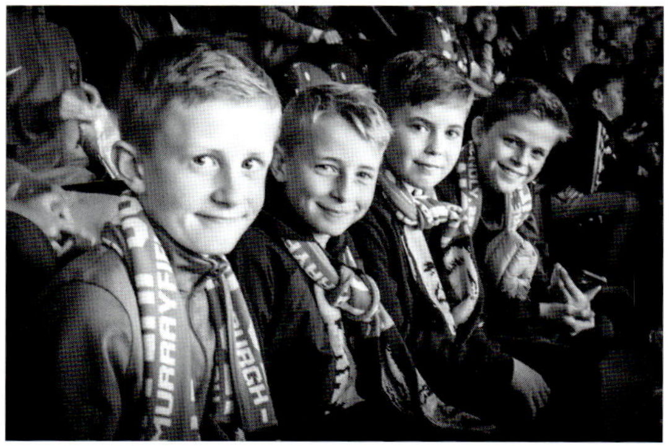

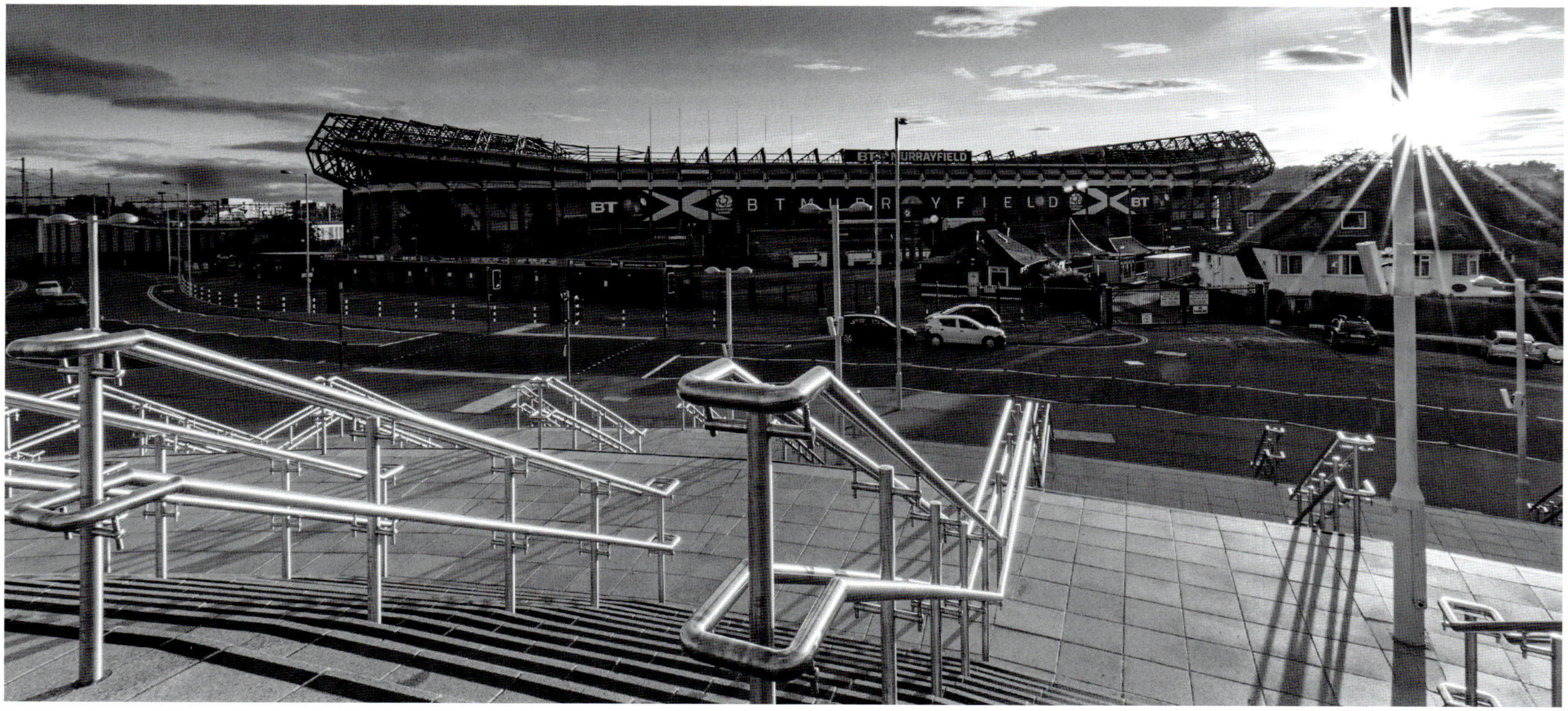
BT MURRAYFIELD

MURRAYFIELD DREAMS

We can all escape to places deep within our minds
Where memories are sharpened by the years,
Where essence is distilled and unadulterated
And where movements slow and grow in grace;
This piece of ground,
This simple field of gloried pasture,
Where each square foot
Holds moments from the past,
For those who are here today,
For those who are long forgotten,
And those we have never known;
For this is a canvas,
Capturing an instant,
Which we can conjure up,
Throughout our lives,
The spontaneous and inspired,
The artistry of skill,
Replayed at will;
So, all those who follow
In their footsteps,
Tread gently on this ground,
For you tread upon
Our dreams.

WAVERLEY STATION PIGEONS

With echoes of
King's Cross,
Ladybank,
And Cardenden
Hanging in the air,
Two boys make statues
At a pigeon,
Which stands its ground,
Staring back,
Tilting its head;
They throw another shape,
It tilts again,
Before it turns,
And claps itself
Into the travellers' vaulted space;
A moment of childhood,
Departing, without even an
Announcement.

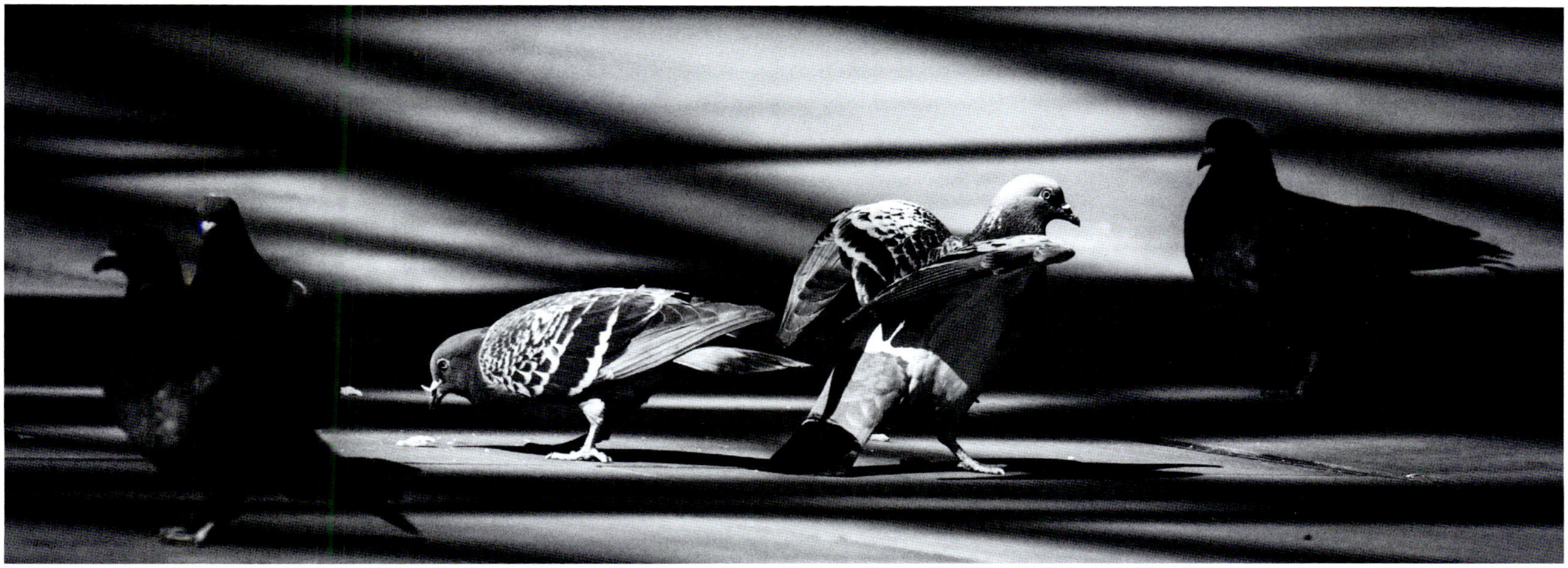

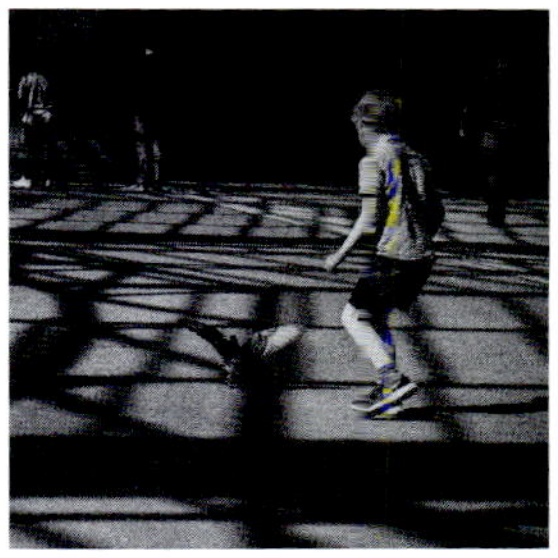

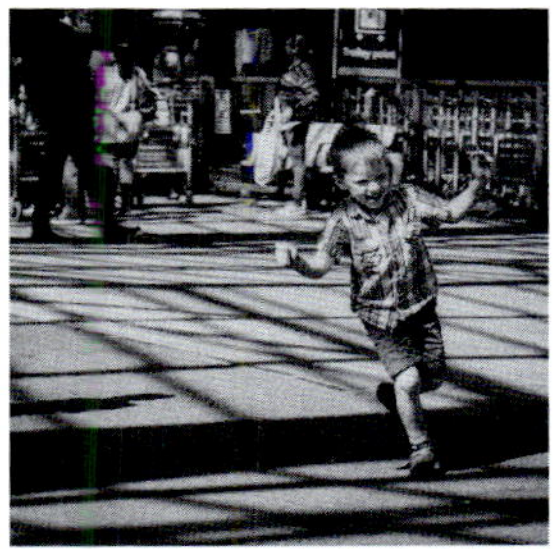

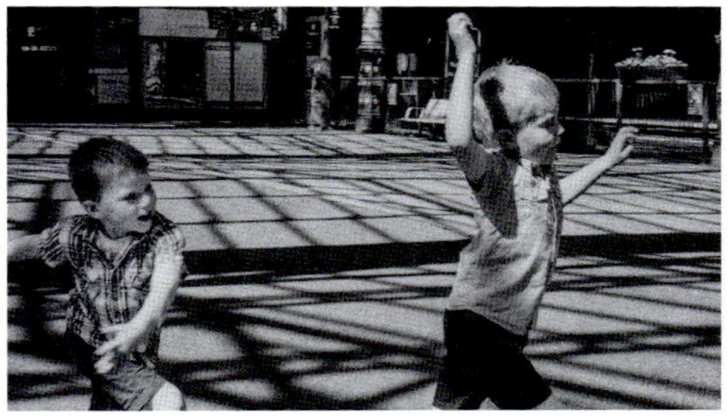

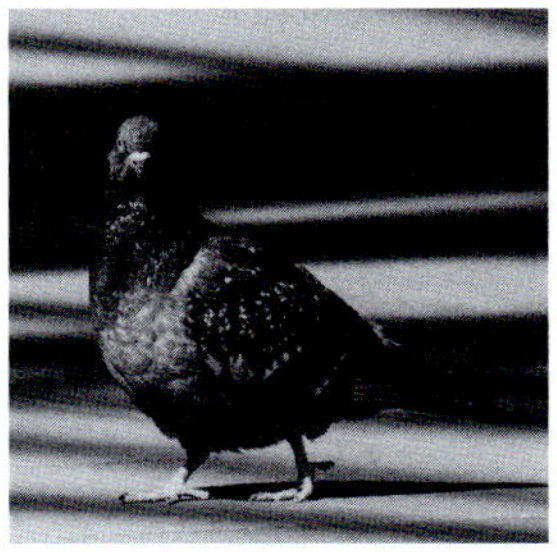

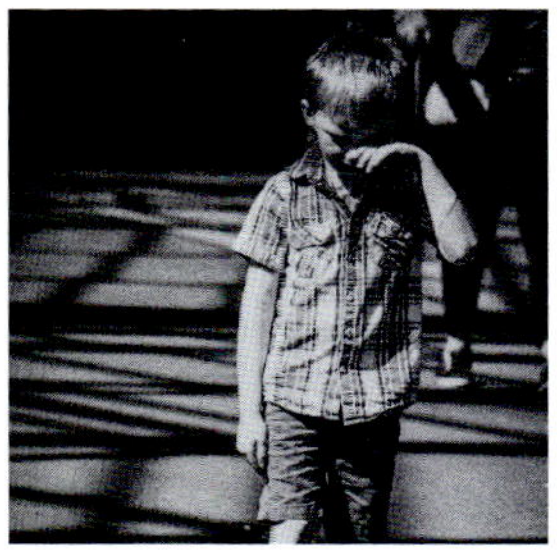

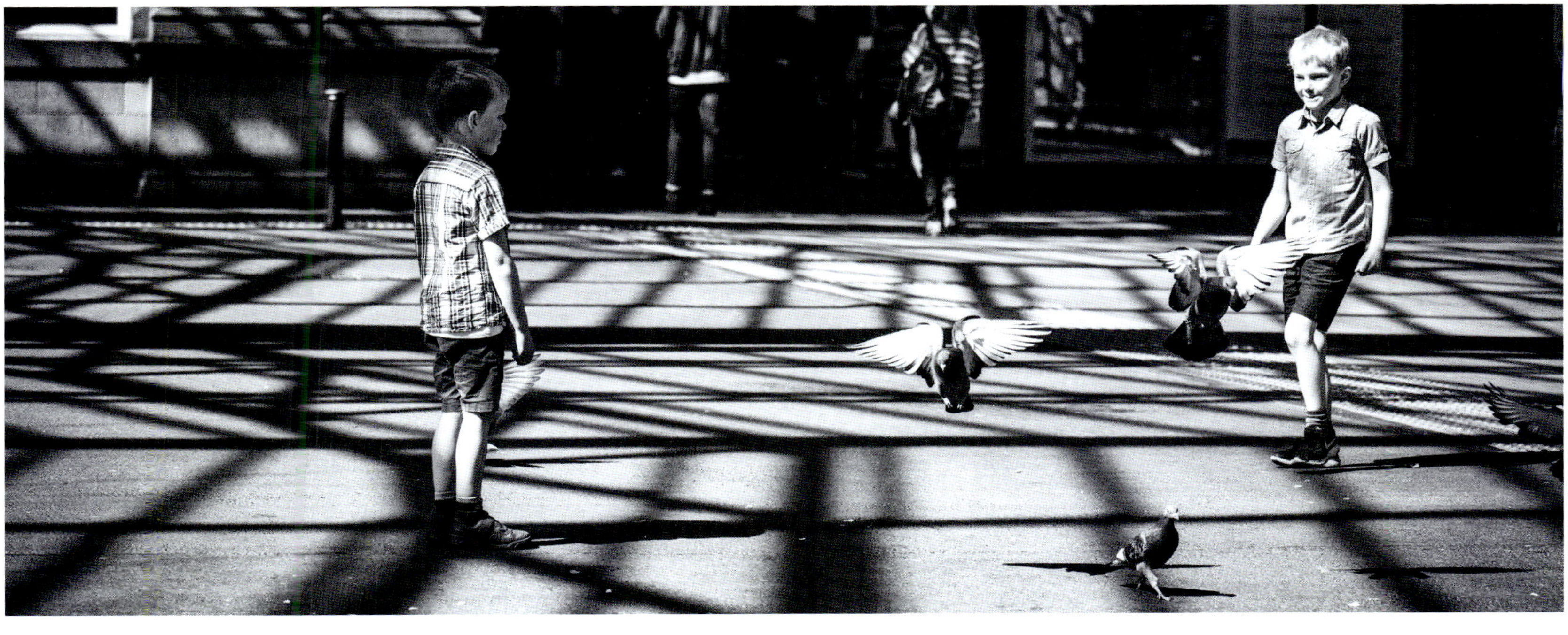

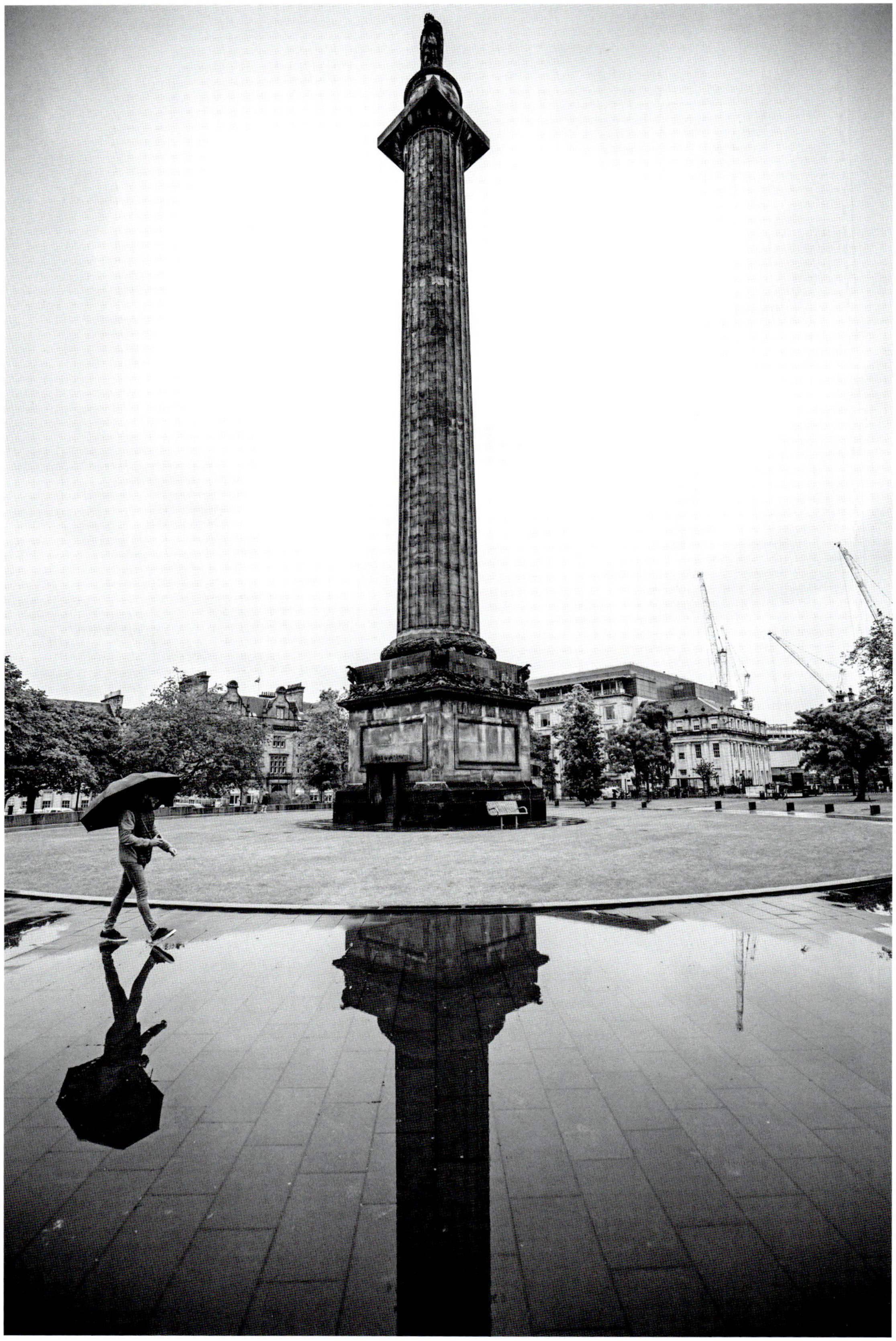

A MARCHING BAND

I saw a Marching Band, walking,
Walking across St Andrew Square,
Heads bowed into the North Sea wind,
Instruments sheathed and protected,
Drums dragged behind on reluctant wheels,
Save for the Sousaphone,
Which wrapped its vibrant coils around
A fat man with no hiding place;
Up front the conductor led the way,
His umbrella holding a high note,
Against the thrashing rain,
The bedraggled ensemble breaking into step,
Following his direction - if not his enthusiasm;
Yet strip off the dull jackets,
Release the brass and drums,
Let them join in lines of hope,
Break out the uniforms,
Keep time,
Share their music,
Let the trumpets call;
But meantime,
Just let them safely cross the road,
Without losing the fat man,
And his Sousaphone.

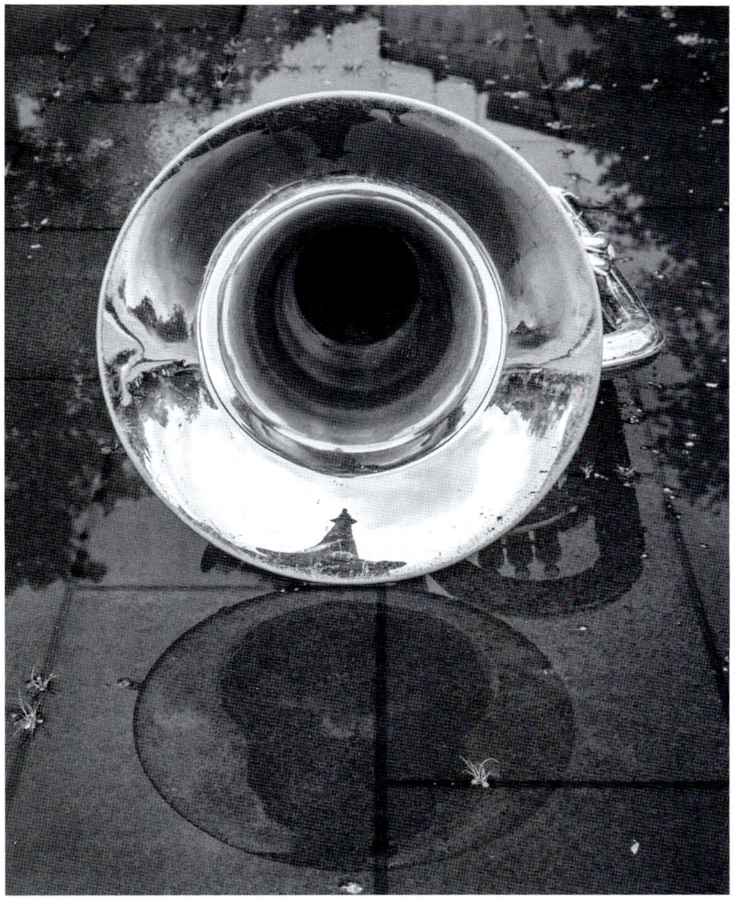

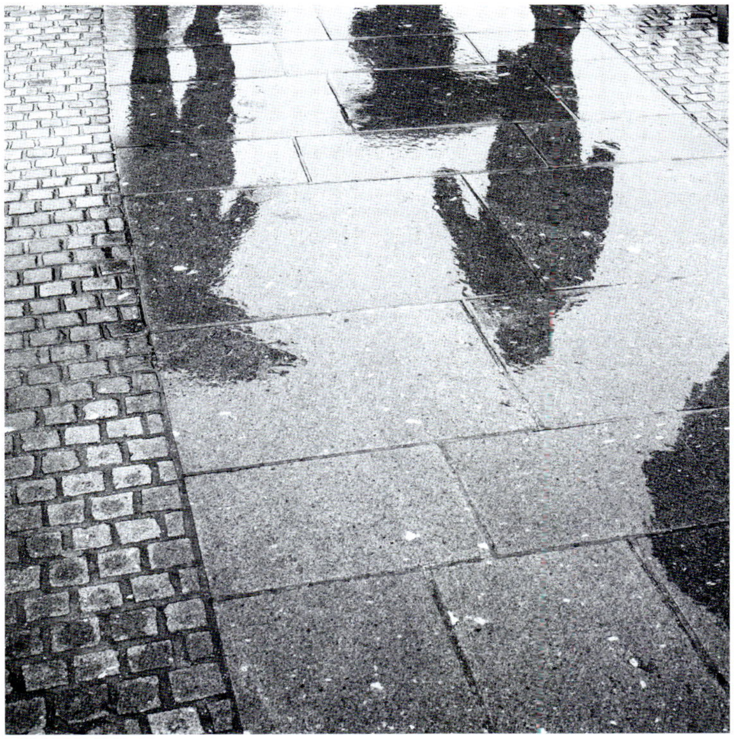

POEMS IN A HIGH WALLED GARDEN

She sips her lemon tea
Within a high walled garden,
Beneath a perfect square of sky,
Broken by erratic clouds,
And sliding gulls;
While all around,
In, peaceful riot,
The colours take their chance,
As shadows steal,
Across the grass,
Shrinking, squeezing,
Pressing out the flowers from her space;
And throughout,
Despite the darkness carving out the light,
She makes the most of every hue,
Of every scent, of every sense,
As single lines are drawn up,
From deep within a hidden well,
And linked together in endless chains,
To lift her far beyond this place;
She raises sonnets from a page,
Holding them gently in her hands,
Before releasing them,
To fly and soar beyond her sight;
These pictures grow and fill the void,
Her garden never dies,
Never falls to winter,
The high walled garden becomes her paradise,
A refuge, where her four score years and four
Give way to the reality of her mind,
Where roams a woman,
In the height of summer.

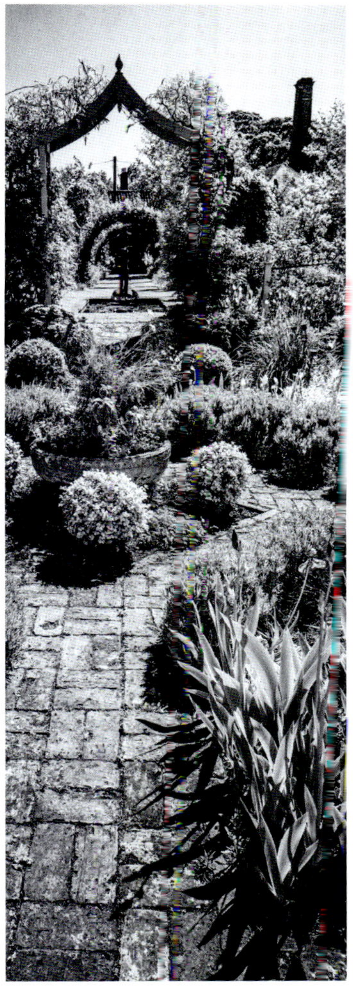

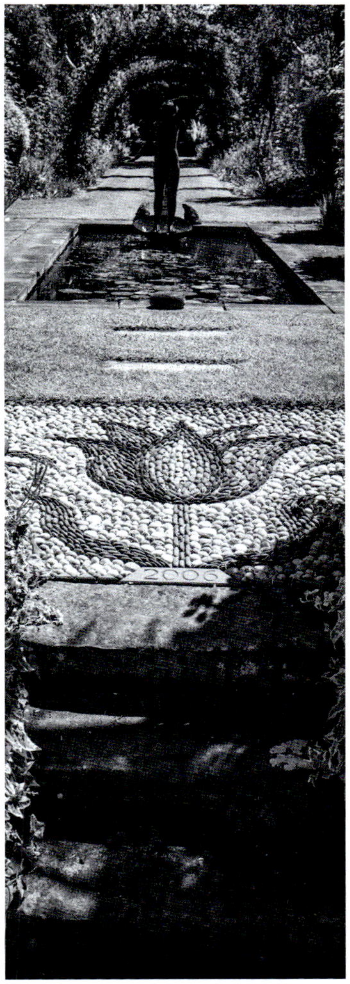

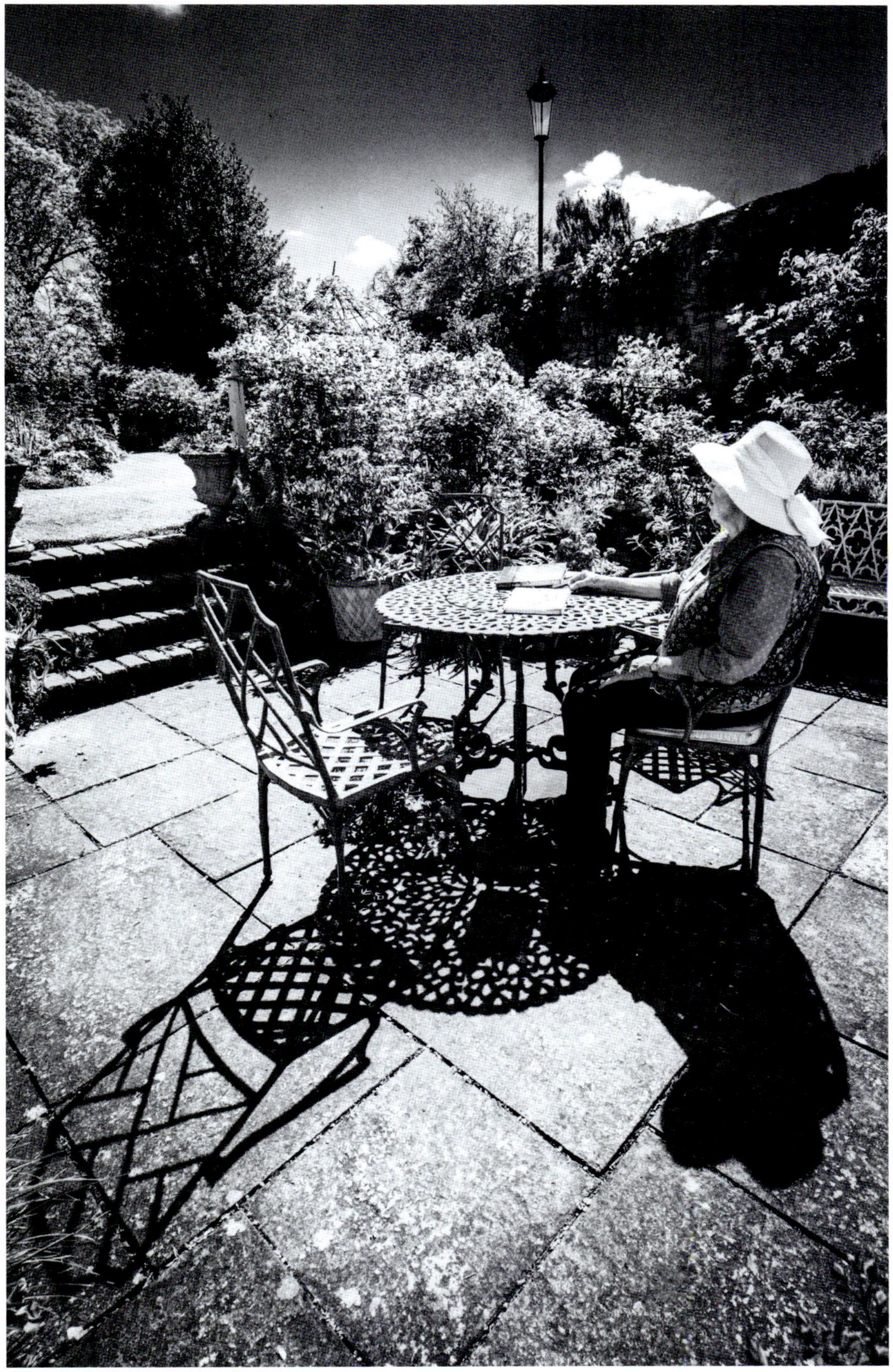

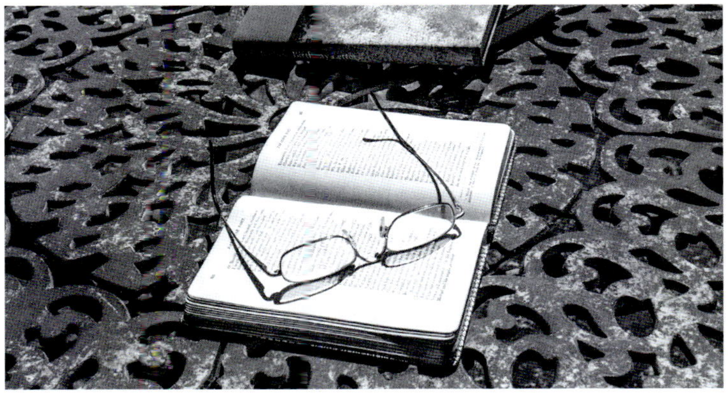

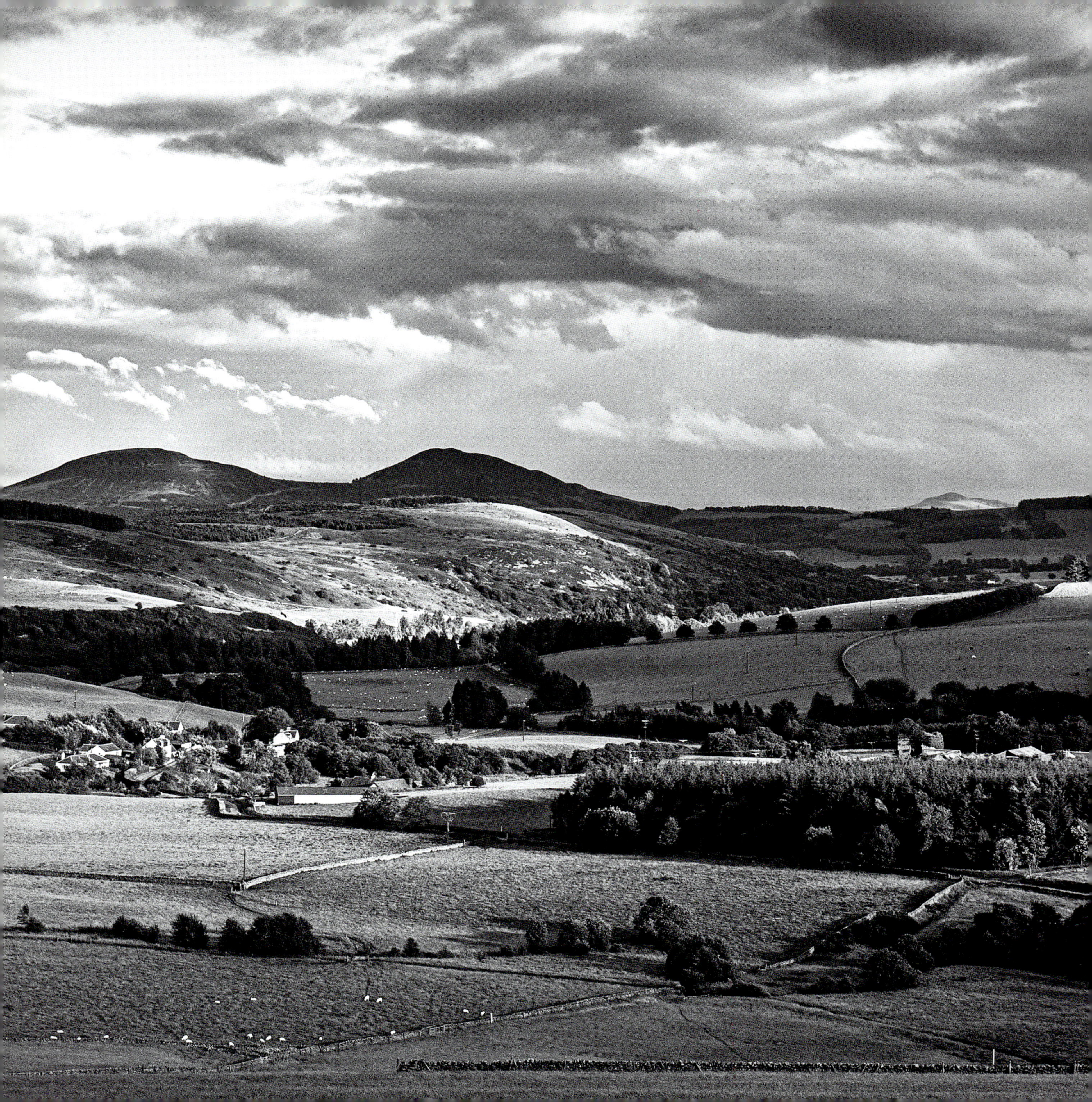

BORDERS INHERITANCE

In 2000, Gordon and Don put together their first exhibition of Picture-Poems entitled 'Borders Inheritance'.

The exhibition attempted to capture rural life in the Borders at the turn of the millennium, and was first displayed at Marmion's Restaurant, in Melrose. Its favourable reception greatly exceeded the pair's expectations, and they were then invited by the City of Edinburgh Council to exhibit at the prestigious Writers' Museum Gallery. This is situated in Lady Stair's House, built in the 17th century, and is dedicated to the lives and work of Scotland's great literary figures, in particular Robert Burns, Sir Walter Scott and Robert Louis Stevenson.

As things turned out, Scotland's rural heritage came under a much more immediate threat following an outbreak of foot and mouth disease in February, 2001. It was decided to put the entire exhibition up for auction, allowing a significant donation to be made to the Royal Agricultural Benevolent Institution, a body offering financial support to farming folk in hardship of all ages.

Gordon and Don had intended to produce a book to go with the Borders Inheritance project but were distracted by life. Here is a sample of that earlier work.

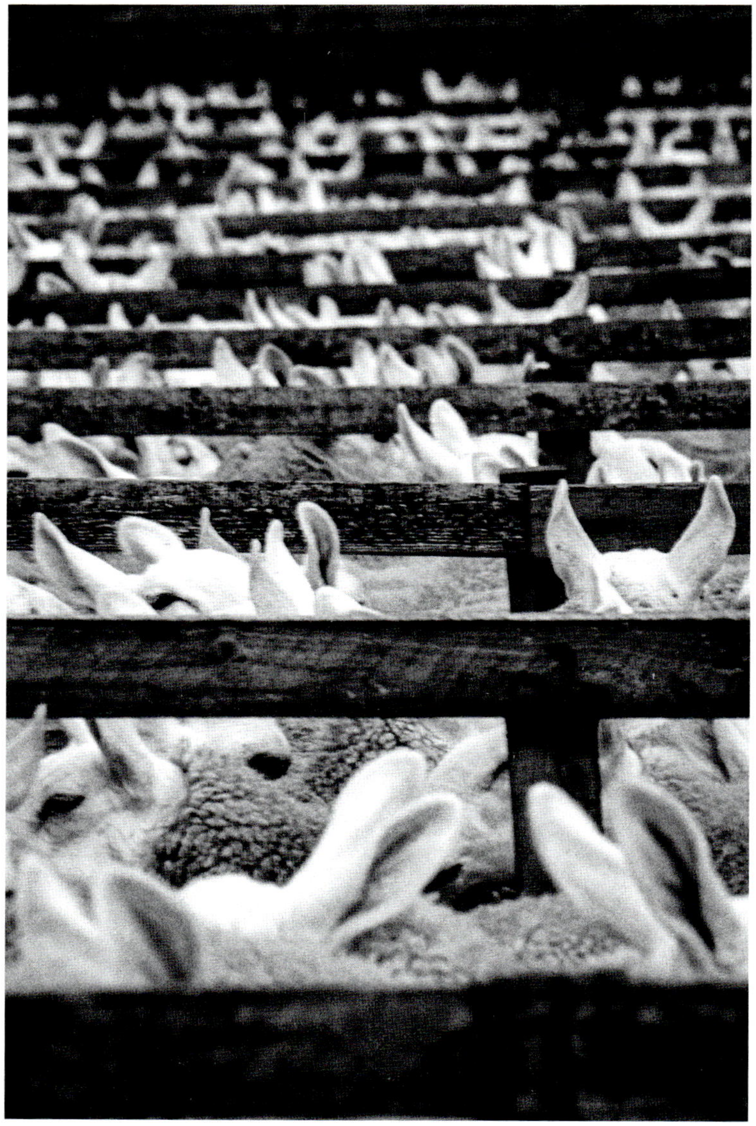

LUCK

Turn a mirror on itself
And draw your focus to a point.
A soundless endless echo
Which vanishes from sight.

And so we lift them from their hills
And pack them in their pen
These living single summers
Single summers without end.

See the noble and the haughty
Amongst the rabble and the dregs
The blue blood of the princess
Beside the bent and bowdy legged.

So will you take my luck sir?
I have a polished penny here
Polished by our lifetimes
Polished by our fear.

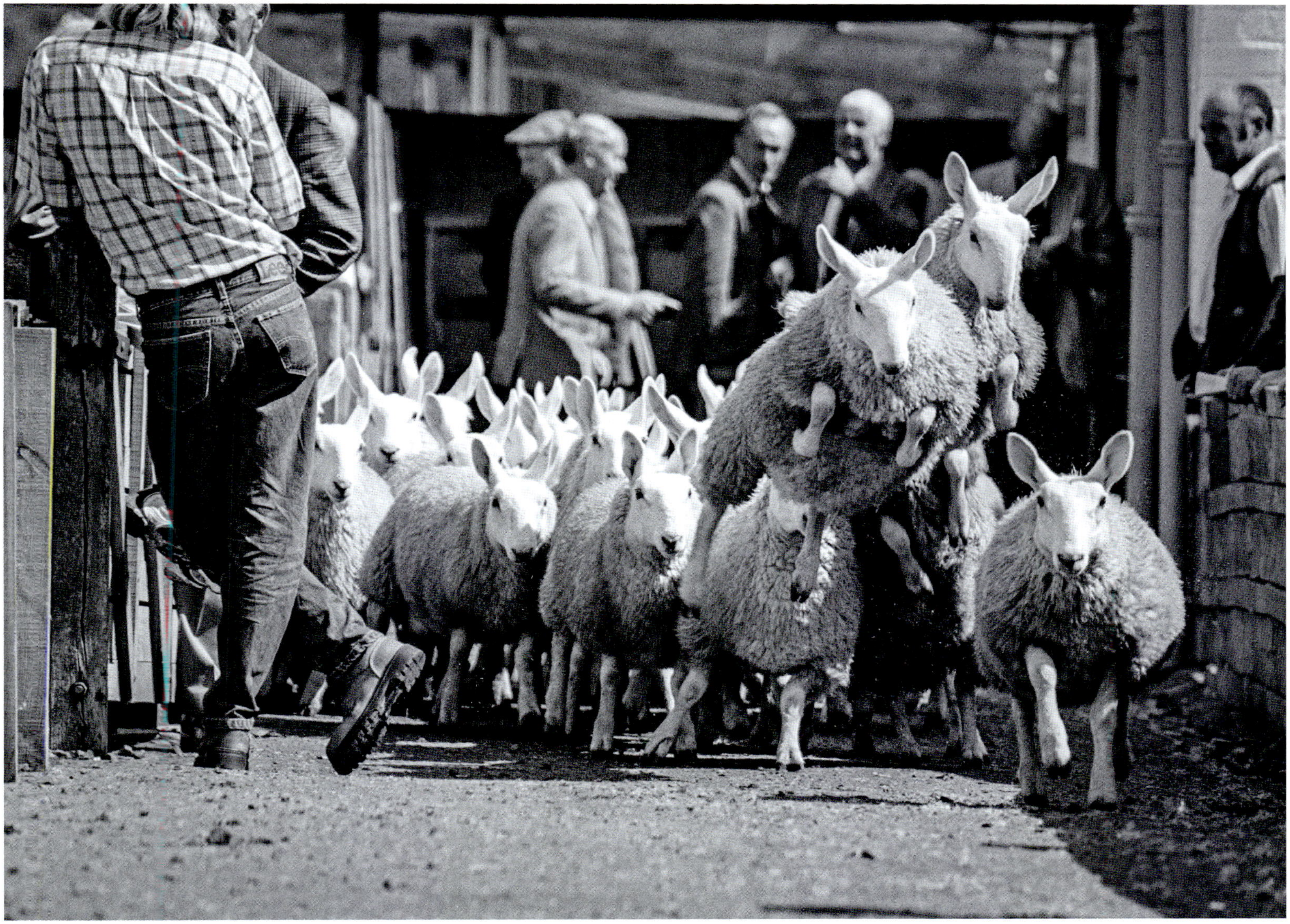

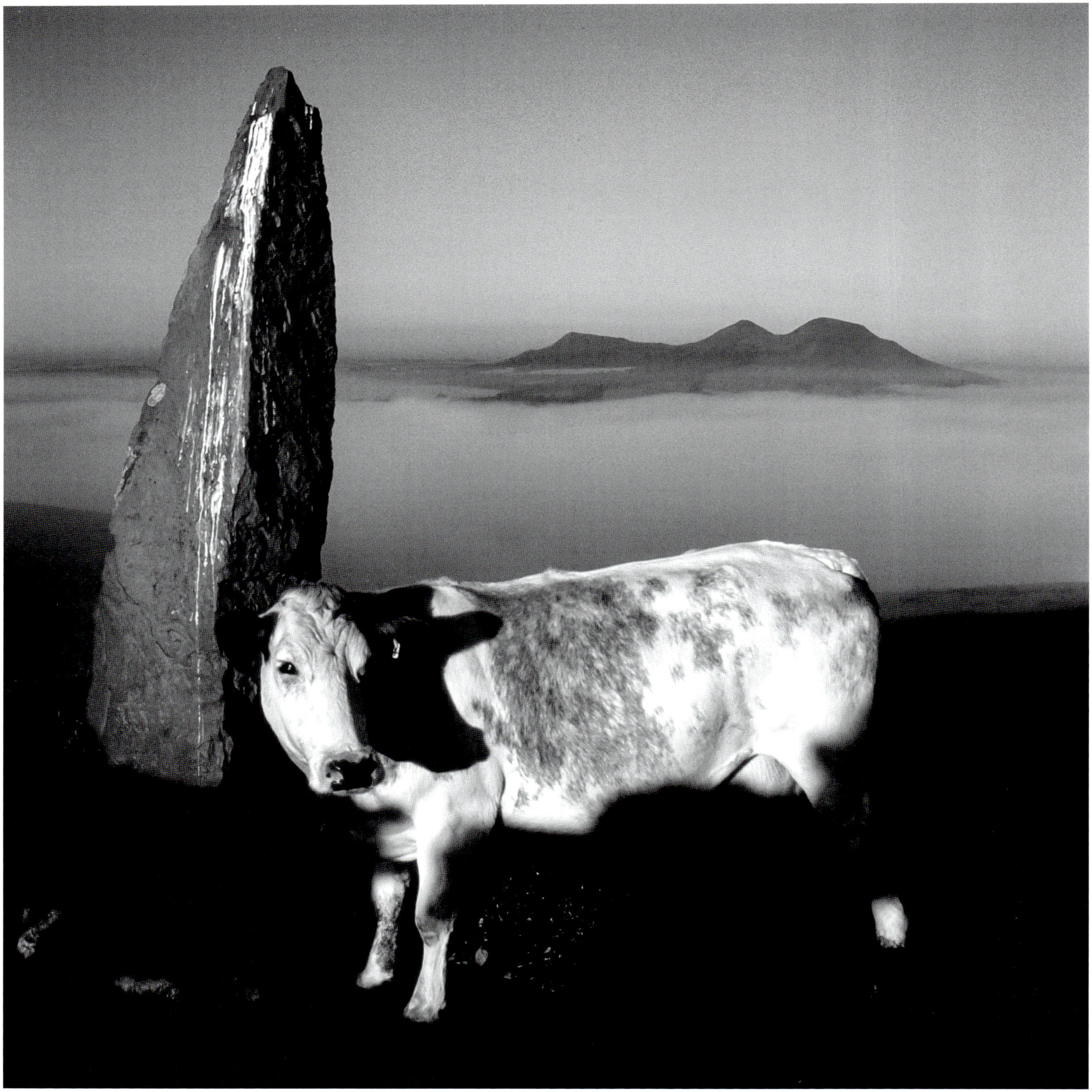

THE COW AND THE PHOTOGRAPHER

Beddit in ma comfy grund
Chowin' on ma dreams
I spied ye wi ma half shut ee
An' heard yer pechs and groans.
As on ye struggl't up ma hill
An' heft up oan yer back
A monster wi three legs or mair
Came climbin' oot yer sack.
A many splindered whirligig
It danced upon the rocks
Until ye got the better o' it
An' tied it doon wi blocks
The horny-goloch wisnae beat
Its legs it push'd an' sprouted
An' afore I even kent ma'sel
I had hupped and shouted.
But as the sun began to rise
It clutched ye tae its breest
Despite ma warnings and ma cries
It wis aboot tae feast.
So up I stotted tae yer aid
I couldnae tak nae mair
An' looked the beastie in the eye
An' gied ma cauldest stare.
But whit a stramash did ye stir
Ye shouted, screamed and cried
An' then ye picked a muckle stane
An' at ma heid ye shied.
Weel patience din I charged ye baith
It folded wi' a shunt
An' you ye graceless donnert man
Went fleein' wi a dunt.
An' galloped aff wi scittered shanks
Yer breek arse at yer ankles
Wi'oot a single word o' thanks
As the monster lay in fankles.

TWEED MIST

The distant tower,
Becalmed on a silent sea,
That gently ebbs,
Unveiling an army
On the march,
That captures the
Repeating ridges,
Soundlessly spilling,
Between standing hills,
A morning's inversion,
Beating its retreat,
Escaping down
Ancient valleys,
Running now,
For cover,
Saving its force,
For another day;
And in a moment
The morning shines,
And beckons,
"Hail smiling morn",
The trooper
Cries.

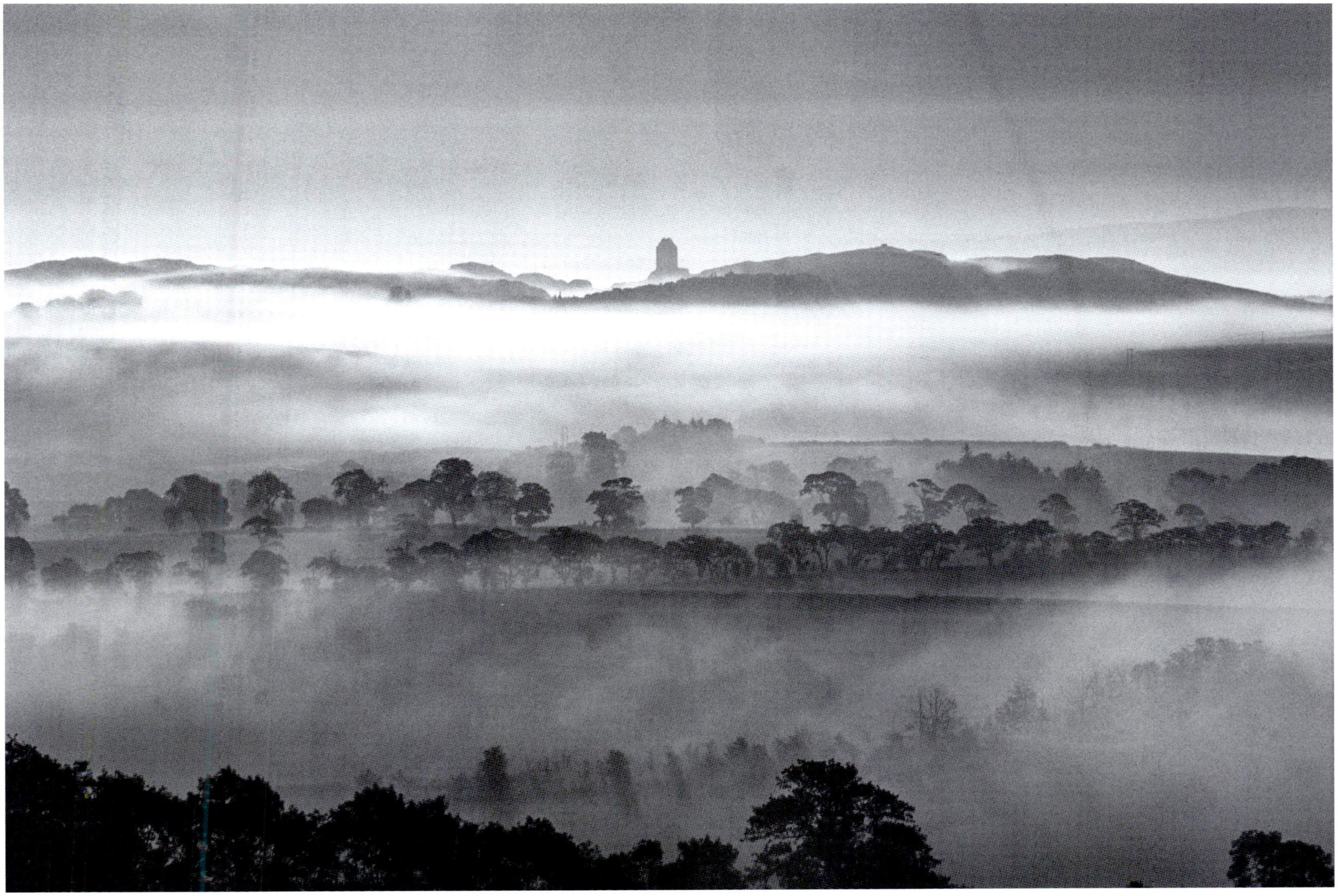

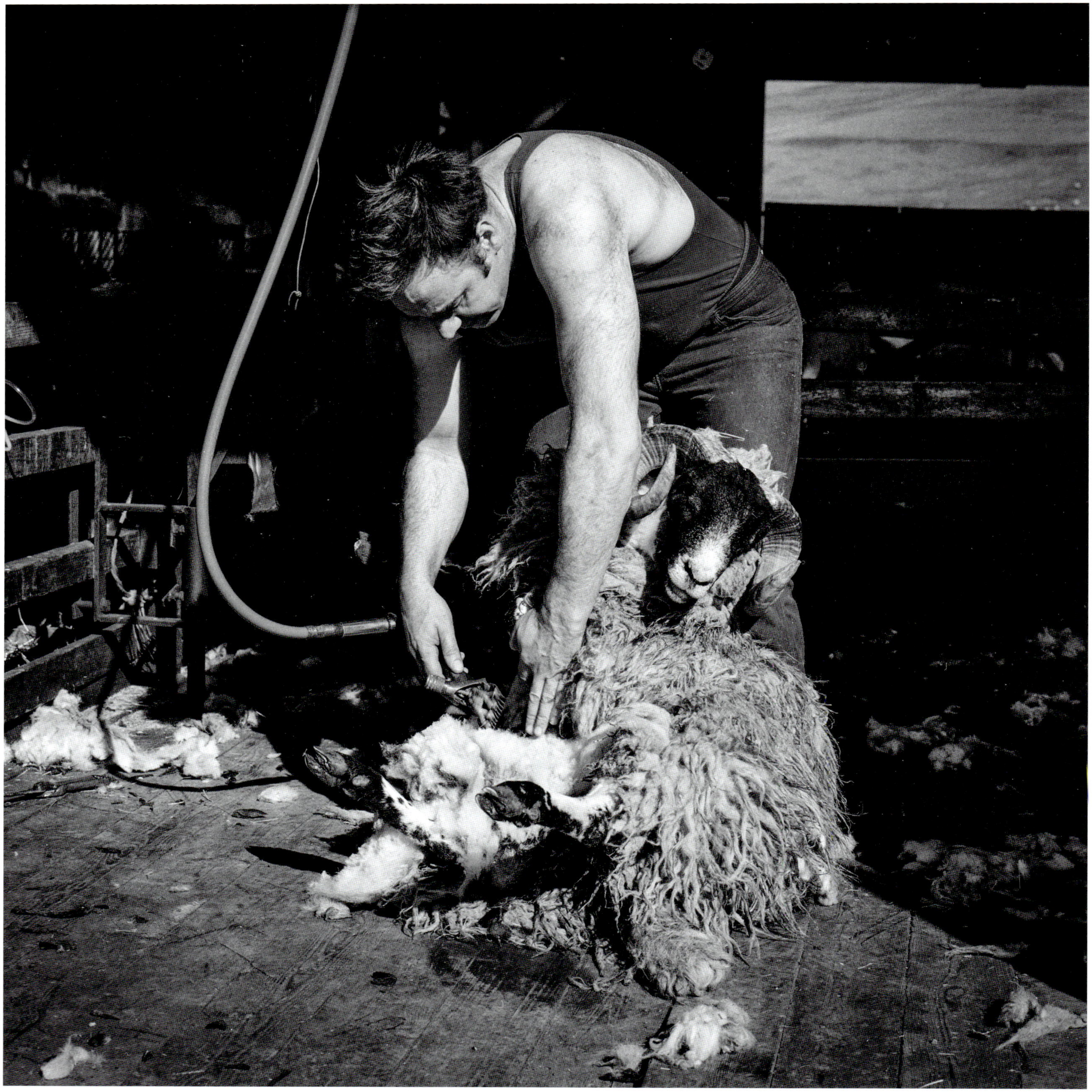

THE CLIPPING

Surrounded by the Cheviots
A soaring sun and diving Peewits
The clipper rigged his gear with a master's expert eye;
Blades sharpened with affection
Each caught a bright reflection
As perfect and as pure as a Curlew's melancholy cry.

The pace was tight and measured
As if each moment treasured
By a man who took his comfort from the magic in his hands;
His skills were years in making
Ten thousand hours back breaking
As a passion grew inside him that no layman understands.

No tricks, no ostentation
No frills, no decoration
Yet the veins upon his trunk-like arms were all but fit to burst;
Shirt soaked with perspiration
Eyes fixed with concentration
As if imprisoned by the talent with which he had been cursed.

He cast each fleece upon the ground
Amidst the unrelenting sound
Of dogs and sheep and buzzing shears, a noise that never left the ears;
His arm found a rhythmic groove
Hypnotic ease to every move
As seconds passed and minutes passed from hours into years.

The day was almost finished
Yet his art was not diminished
By the knowledge that his labours were nearly at an end;
For pride imbued his every action
He could not slacken by a fraction
Addicted to a lifestyle to which there is no mend.

DECEMBER MILKING

Shackled to his rock
He orbits round his chosen hours,
Yet it chose him,
Picked him from the crib
And left him here
Without a place to go.
Yet his ladies wait their turn
And heave their heavy bags
Between their spindled legs,
Suspending from a scaffold frame
Their precious loads,
Which bulge against their swing.
Escaping from the gloom,
Their well-chewed breaths
Rise above the biting cold,
And white trickles from a teat
Tracing lazy lines and circles
Amongst the shit-slapped floor.
He locks into his ritual
And readies for the dance,
Pacing round his pulpit,
Gently laying hands
And tracing daughters back
Some thirty years.
A meeting of machines,
One bred, one made,
Each built to fit the other,
Turning green to white.
As pulsing beat of stainless steel
Sucks its greedy fill.
He takes his pride from here,
Measuring against the past,
Driven on by need
To prove himself,
Against himself,
To make his mark upon the land.
And yet, not far from here
It lies in sterile lines,
Loss leader for the giants,
Who squeeze pennies from the tit,
And slowly close their careless fingers
Around a way of life.

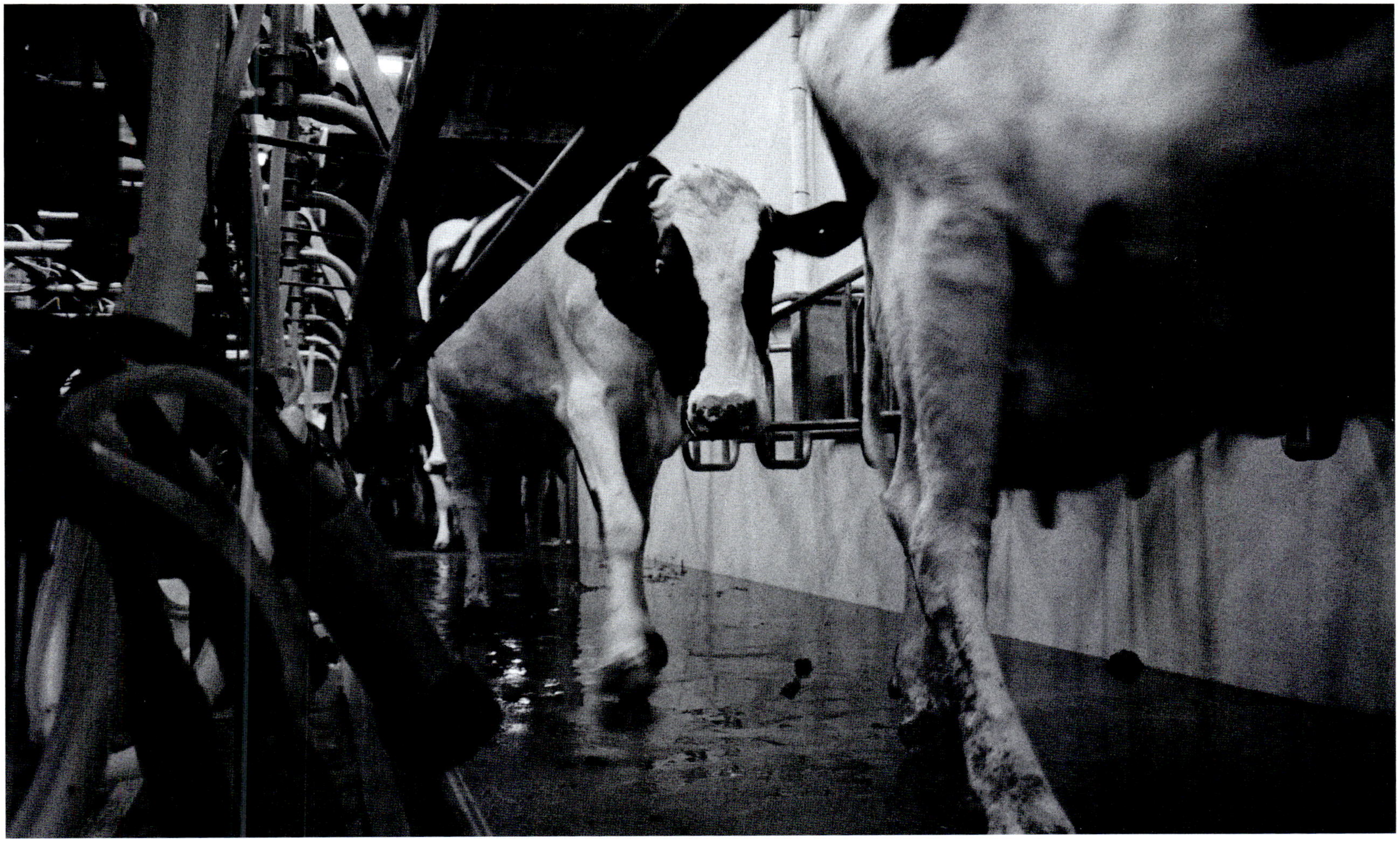

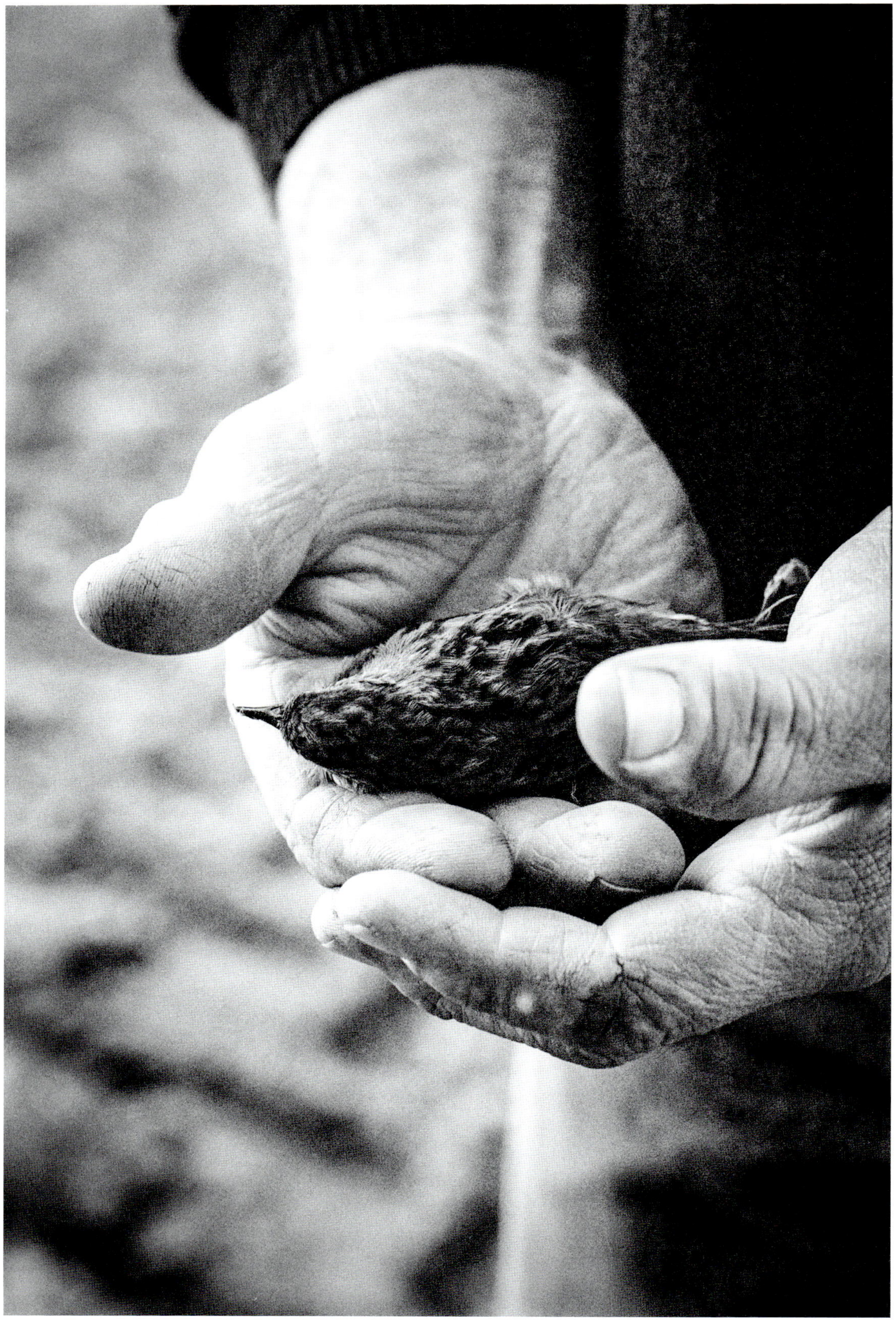

A FARMER'S HANDS

I stumbled back nearly fifty years.
As the heady mix of engine oil and leather
Threw me back into the benchseat
Alongside the old farmer.

A giant of a man
As dour as he was big
Who gripped the wheel with massive fists.
And stared out far beyond his field of view.

I knew better than disturb his practised silence
And craned my neck to see over the polished bonnet
Lining up the silver emblem
As my Spitfire's gunsight.

My game and his peace
Were broken by a sickly crack
And in the instant that it hit the glass
I caught its screaming eye.

The old man said nothing
As we rolled to a clumsy halt
And pulled himself stiffly from his seat.
The late evening sun cast his shadow forty feet.

He stooped and lifted the tiny form
Lost in his callused hands
And a fragile tear splashed
Silently on the dusty road.

FREEDOM

Ma body shaks wi' unseen tremmles,
Fixed een stare wi'oot relief,
Dinna stand here ony longer
Let's be aff awa' frae here,
Ower gress and weed and thistle
Stretch and coil, stretch and coil,
Whit a feelin, freedom, life.

"Keep weel wide!"
I'm mindin' fine
Steady lass, I ken the way.
Doon.
There, here nae bother.
Proddin for'ards, gently does it
Lifted weel and athegither,
Nancy Hunter, ye'll be pleased as hell.

Help me noo, I canna see
The straightest path frae here to there.
A course old yin turns, thinks better o' it
And pushes back tae find the front.
Steady pace, it's as ye taught me,
Working yin side then the ither.
Yir silent words ring in ma heid.

We reach the circle wi'oot mishap
You stand.
I wait.
They graze.
Bide my time,
Slowly, slowly
A gap appears, it's a' we need.
I'm in it nivver had a chance.

Push on noo towards the finish.
Why dis it a'ways have tae end?
Dae yir part noo, a final flourish,
Just be canny wi' yon stick!
But they are broken, howked and hummled
And any sowl could close a gate.

We've won, or so ye tell me,
I'm nivver just sure what that means,
Ye reach doon and stroke centuries o' preparation.
But let's be aff awa' frae here,
Ower gress and weed and thistle,
Stretch and coil, stretch and coil
What a feeling, freedom, life.

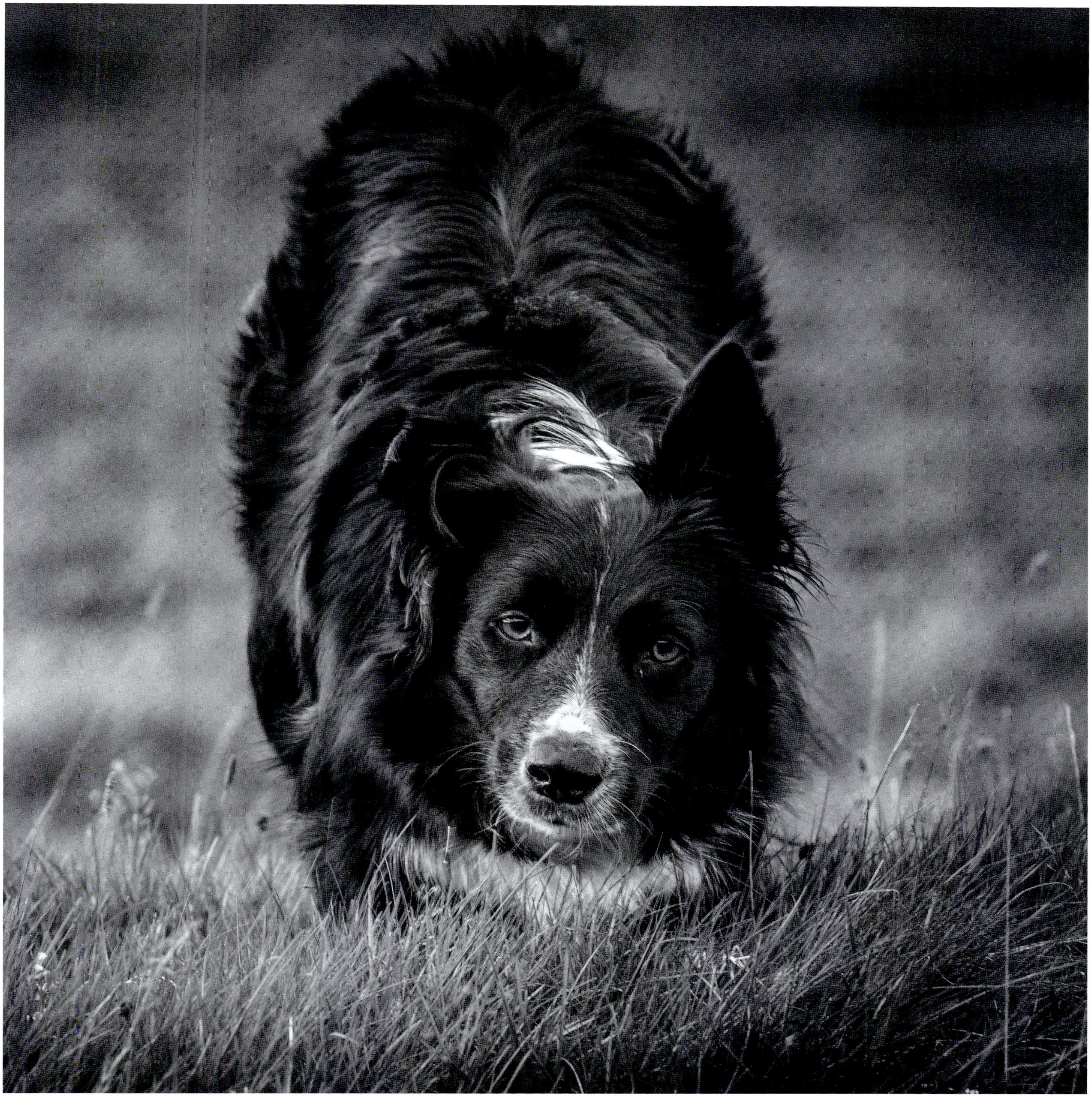

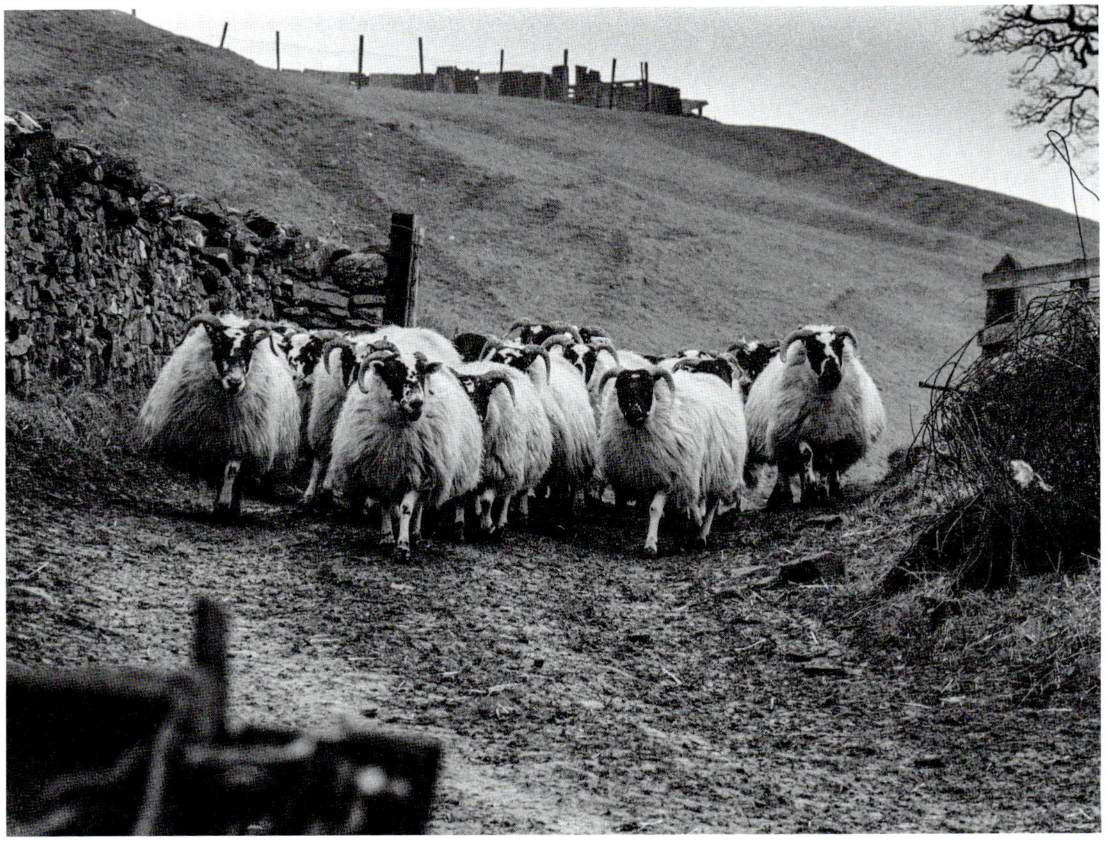

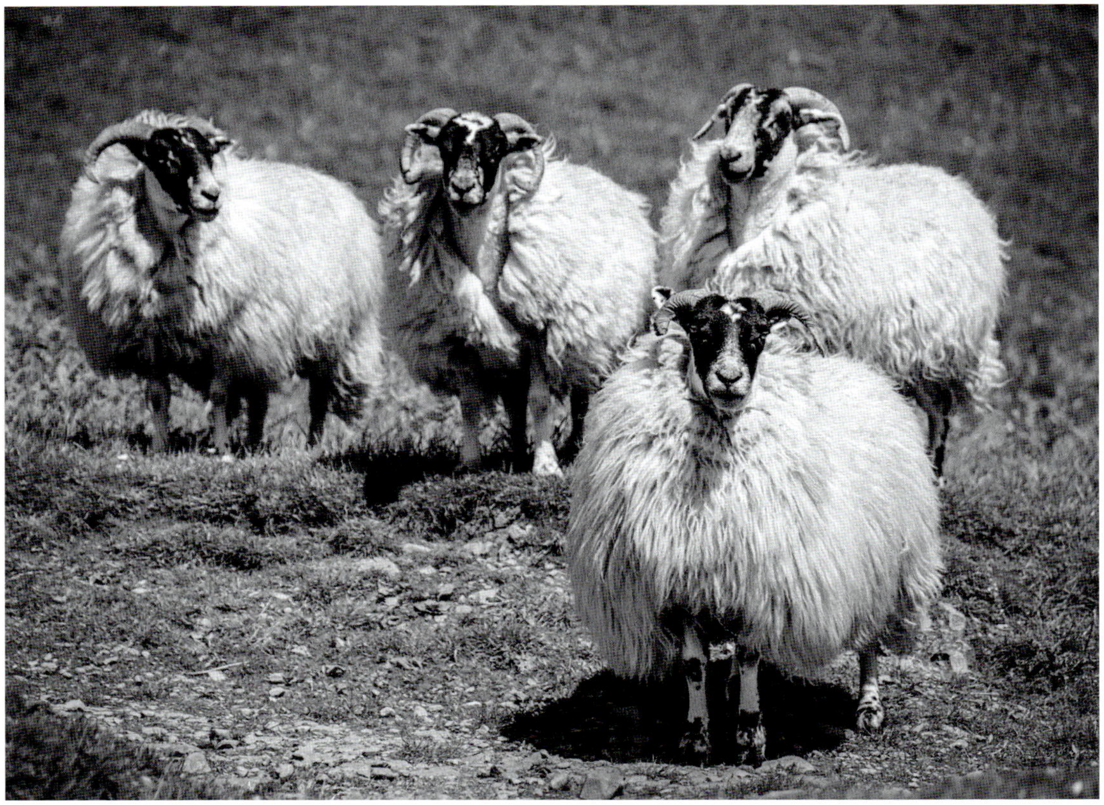

LAST OF THE BLACKIES

Gently tilt a hillside,
And pour its vintage at our feet.
Shake free the stubborn drops,
Which try to hold their place
Amongst their own,
But gather speed
And bunch and rush
The narrowed neck,
To spill upon the floor,
Leaving us to smash
The empty bottle
On stony ground.

LEADERFOOT LADY

She holds the eye
Her straight lines and perfect curves
Entwine with nature's random pattern.
Lifting her skirt well clear
She dips her toes
In the cool black water
Her amber stones softening in the sun
Like tears in an empty wine glass
And melt into their reflection
Leaving her pathway in the sky
To wither on the vine
A monument to Beeching's folly

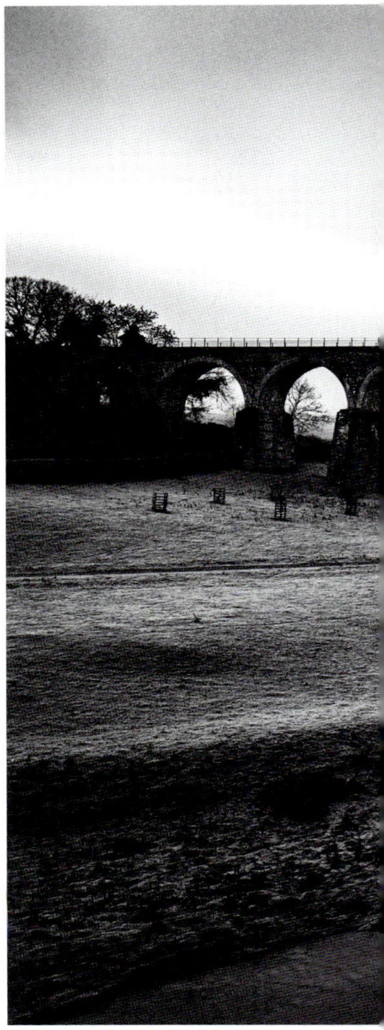

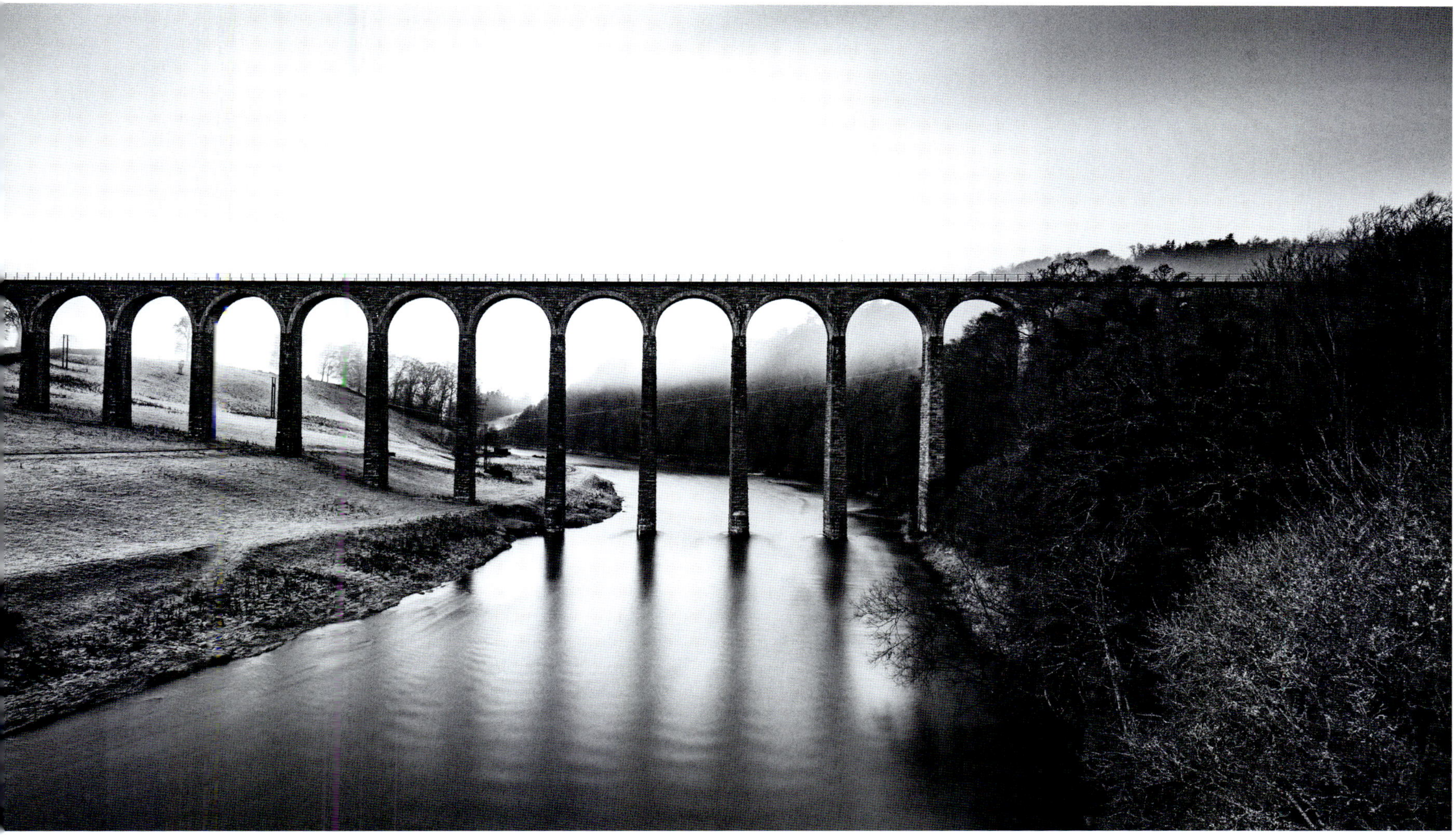

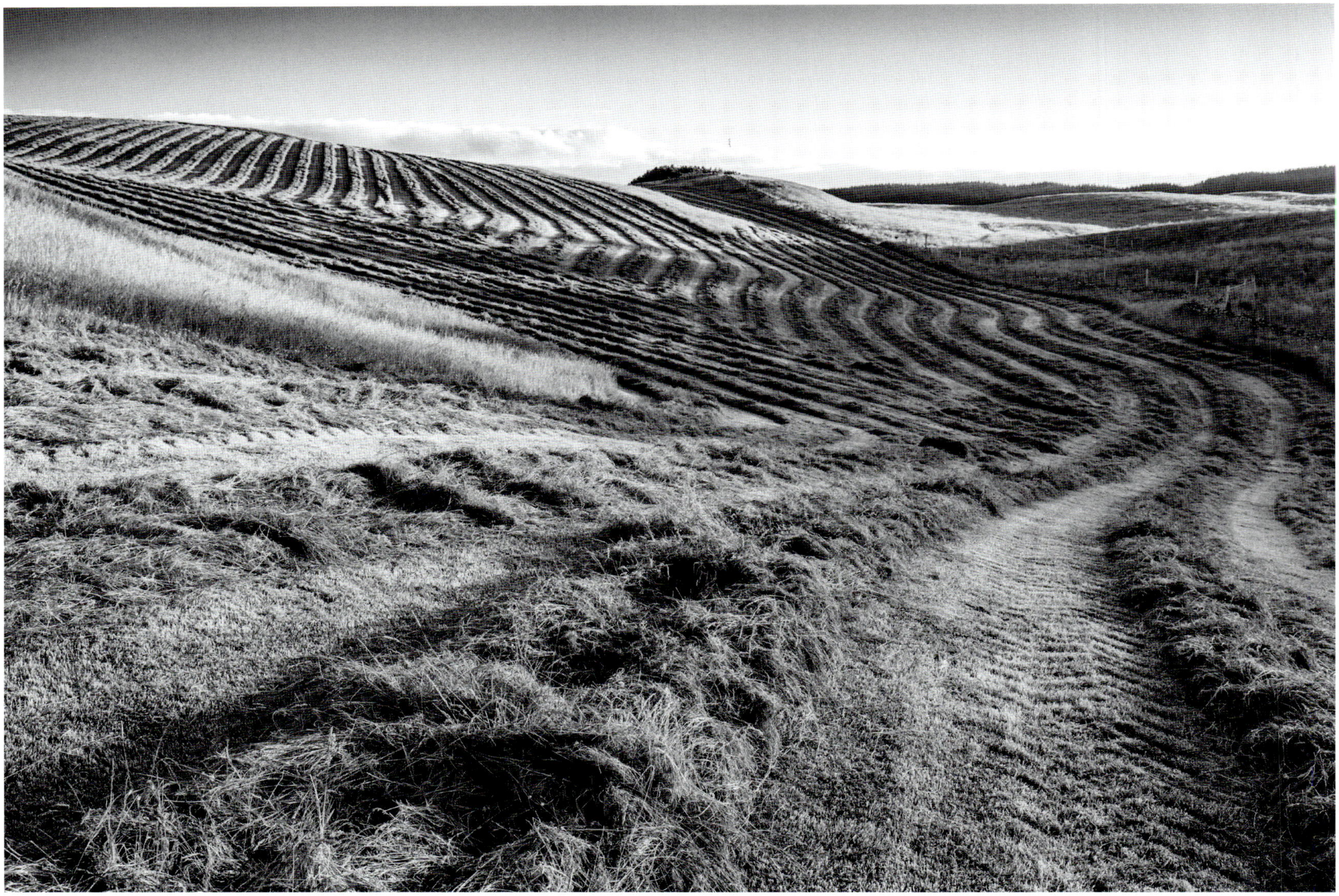

CONTOURS

I found a map,
A map where
Rivers never run,
Where tides will never turn;
A map where
Mountains never rise,
Where valleys never fall,
Or cities sprawl;
A map where
Trees will never grow,
Where streams
Will never flow;
But where,
For seven days,
Green waves,
Will break upon a yellow sun.

THE STARLING SYMPHONY

Unbidden, they arrive,
Iridescent crotchets,
Black minims,
Garrulous quavers,
Eight birds to a bar;
The five-line stave sags heavy
With their weight,
Three semitones and an A sharp,
Change places,
Gathering themselves,
Before melody takes off into
Flights of
Pandemonium,
Sweeping across
An evening sky;
The unseen hand
Guiding their course
From chaos to control,
The pulsing rhythms,
The changing tempo,
Hypnotise the mind,
Each movement builds
Upon the last,
Leading us towards the end,
A final rhapsody,
"For joy, for joy" they cry,
And then, within an instant,
They disappear, as one,
Beyond the stars.

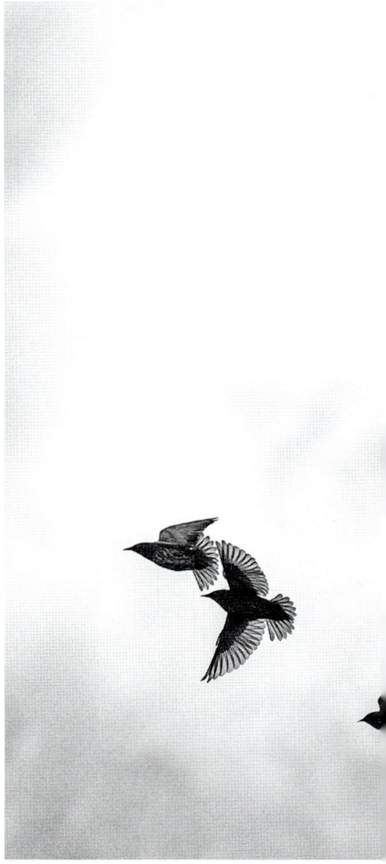

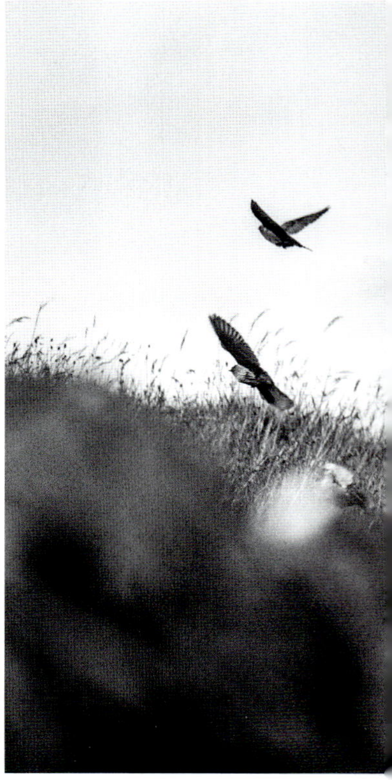

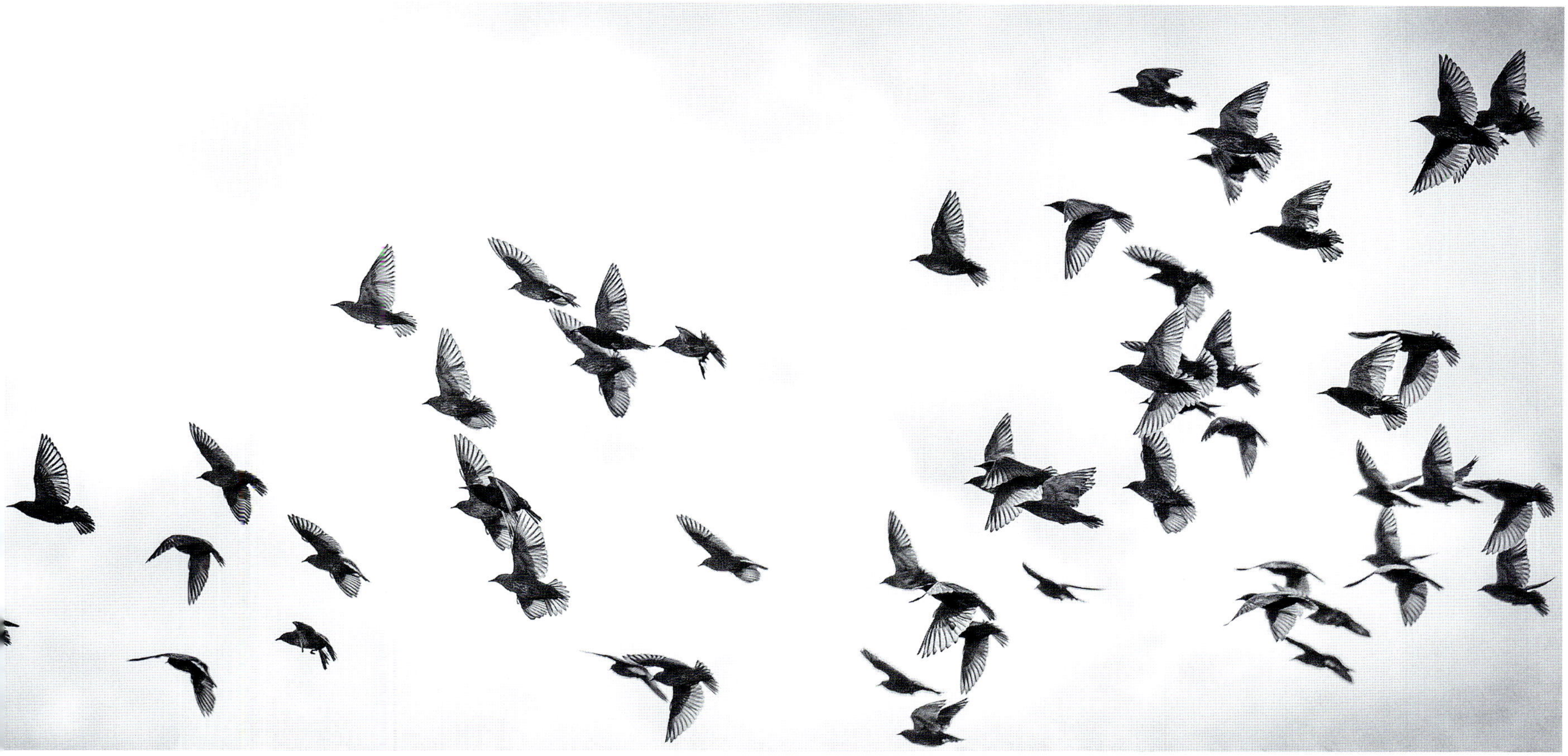

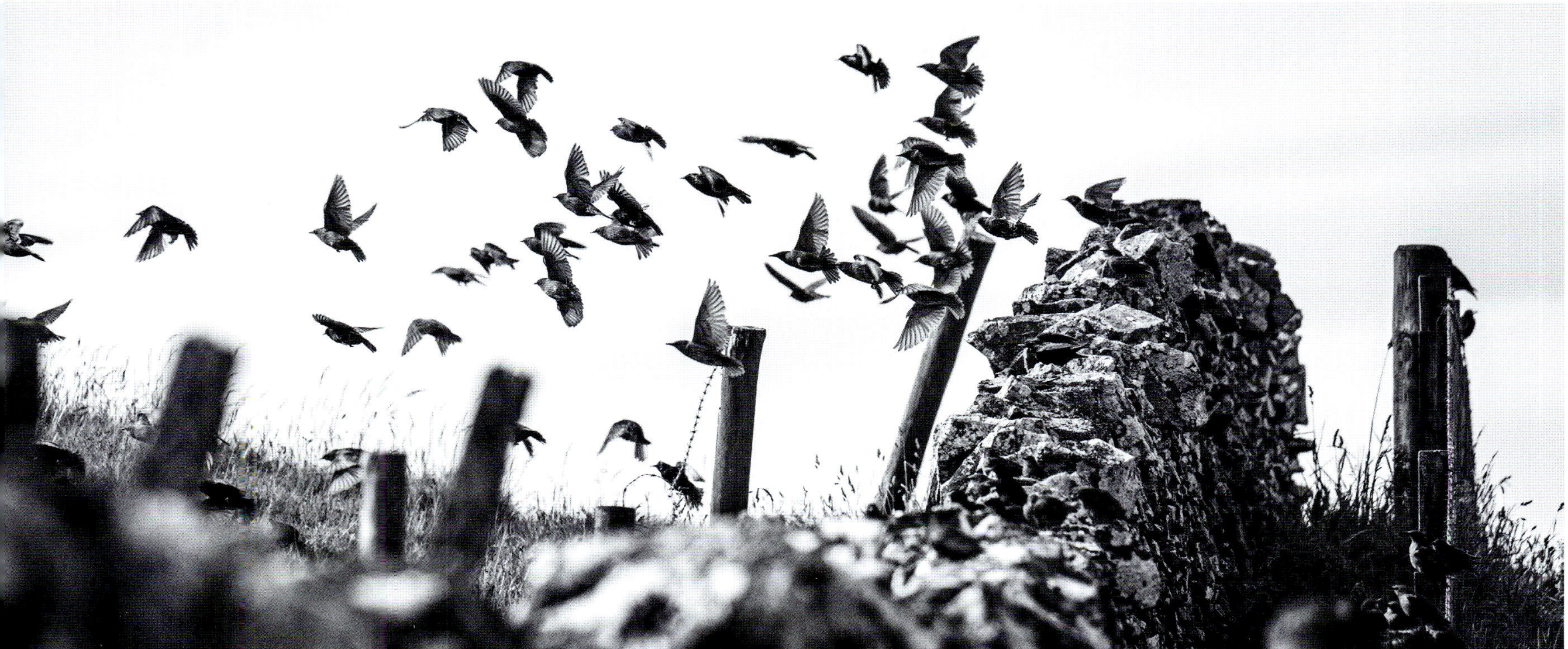

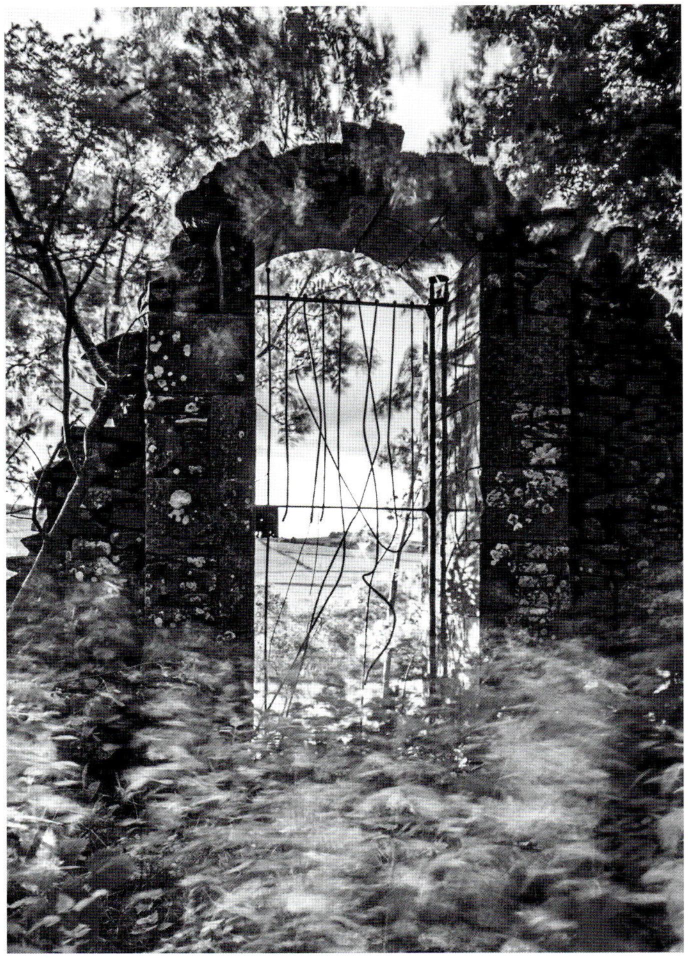

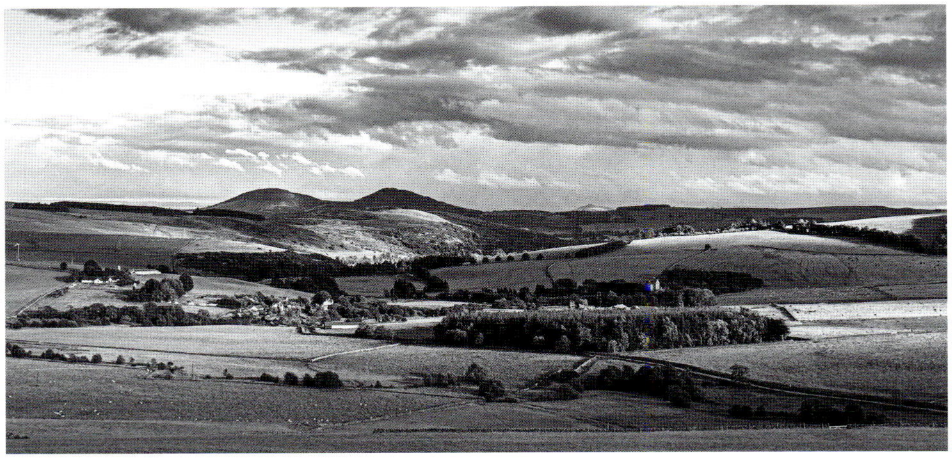

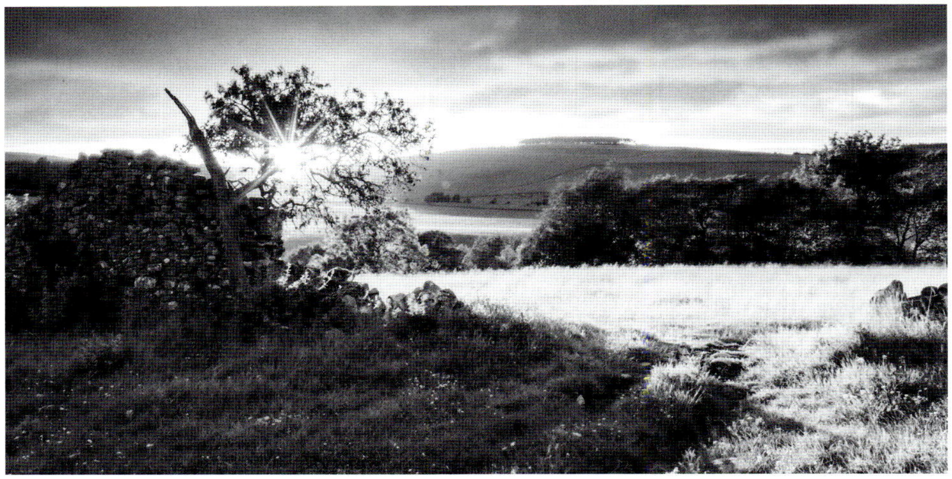

LANGSHAW ECHOES

If you go up the Ellwyn
Two miles from the Fairydean
You'll come on an enchanted place
The best I've ever seen;
Now stand outside the Smithy House
And close your eyes and listen
You'll hear the echoes of the past
And all that we've been missing.

You'll hear the water on the wheel
That drove the old sawmill
You'll hear the echoes of the past
I wouldn't bear them ill;
Now hear the children in the school
All chanting out their tables
And hear the clanking of the team
Returning to their stables.

Now hush you now and hold your peace
What's that I hear a ringing?
Why it's the smith at work again
He's seeing to a shoeing;
And hear the cackle from the fields
Sheaves gathered in the sun
The sound of over twenty folk
When now there's only one.

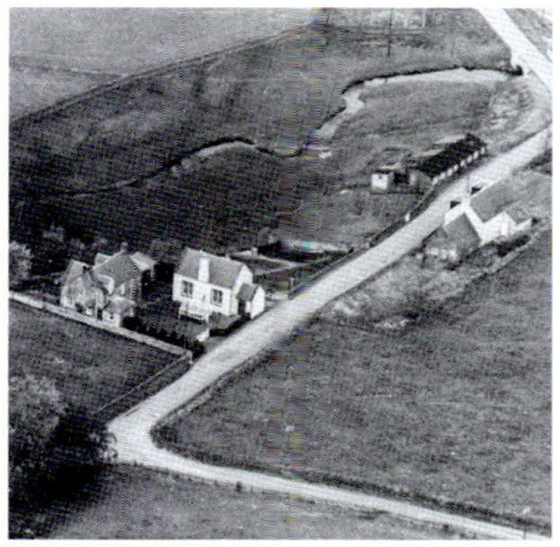

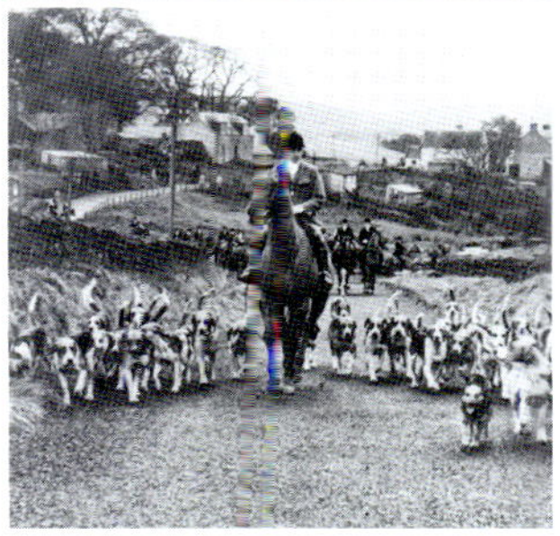

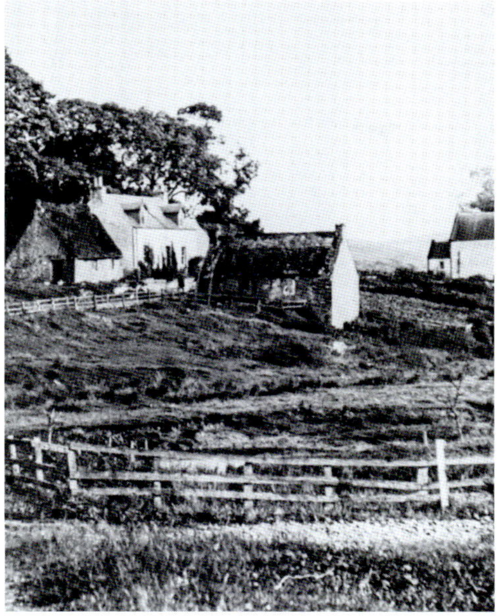

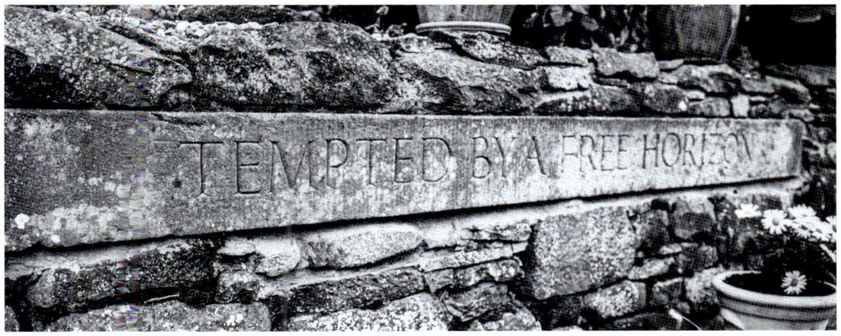

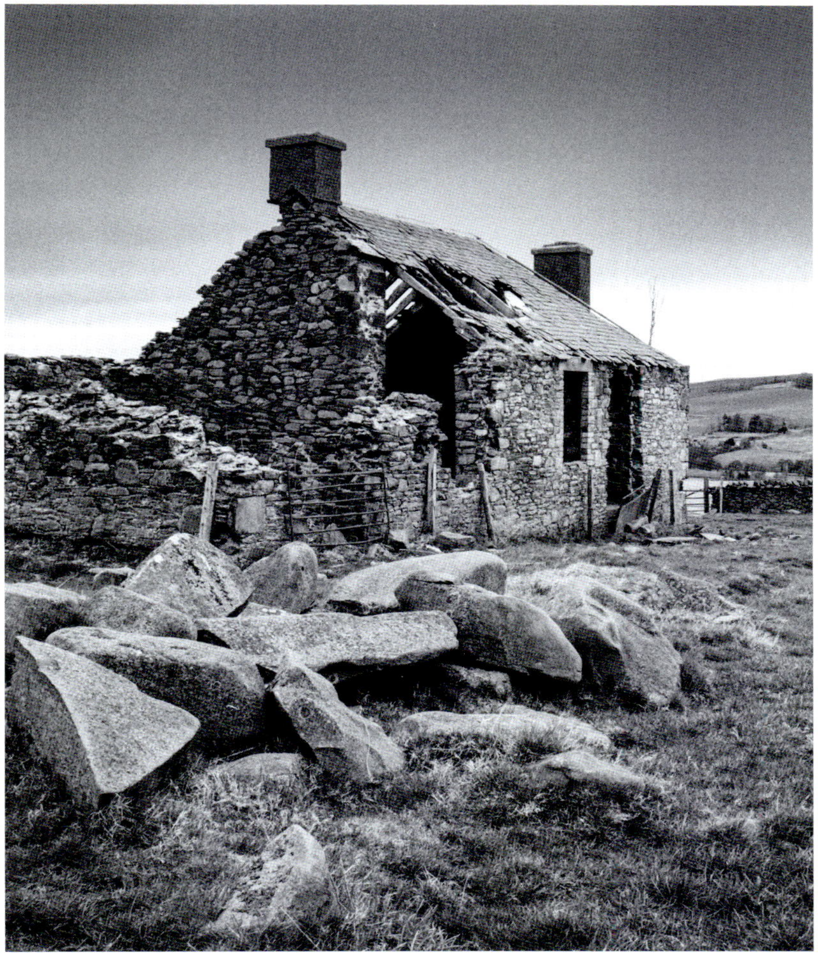

Now listen to the squeezebox
To the shouts and awful squeals
The village hall is shaking
To the rhythm of the reels;
And late at night you hear them
As they make their way back home
To Colmslie and Glendearg they trail
Not scared to walk alone

Now hear the echoes further back
The Reivers and their men
Returning from a battle
They've done their part again;
The building of the towers
Rings out across the land
Each blessed stone they put in place
Was lifted up by hand.

There are some who say that echoes
Are really best forgot
That life is for the here and now
And to settle for your lot;
But I would just remind us
Not to live our lives so fast
For the noise we make today
Will join the echoes of the past.

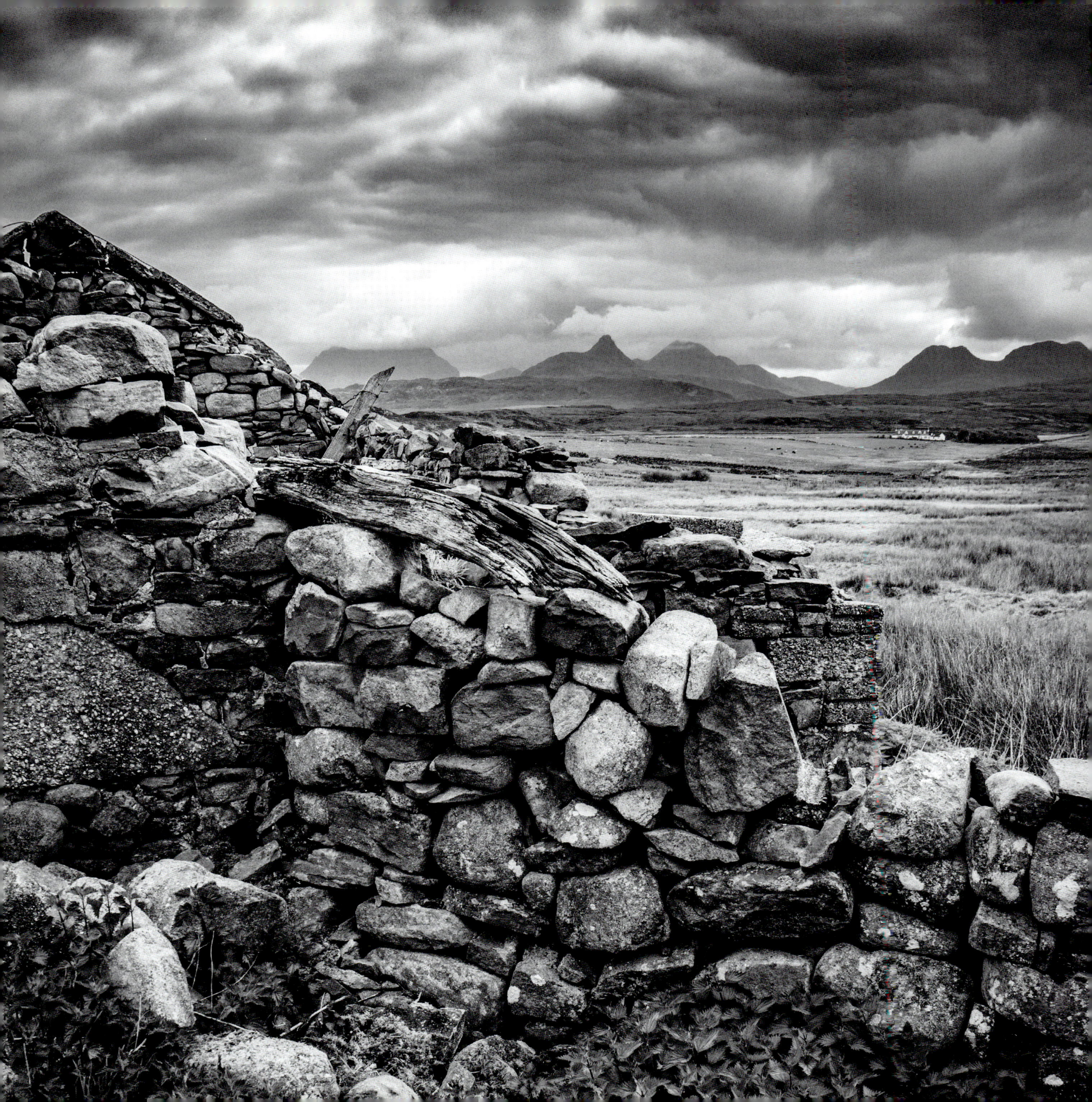

SCOTTISH INHERITANCE

A recurring question from people who've had an early glimpse of *Edinburgh Revisited* has been to ask why Gordon and Don limited themselves to Edinburgh, when Scotland would provide a much more far-reaching subject. As their work has progressed in this collection, they have come to recognise that Picture-Poems would be an excellent way to capture the essence of Scotland's people, its life, history, geography, industry and future.

The following are two examples of what will feature in a new collection, to be called *Scottish Inheritance*. Gordon and Don hope such a work would be of interest to all those people who belong to, came from, have an affinity for, have visited, or simply want to find out more about this incredible country. No date has been set for its publication, but rest assured the pair will enjoy both the process of identifying topics for the collection, as well as the artistic challenge of completing the work.

SWILCAN BRIDGE

Where Old Tom Morris stood and took a line of sight
Towards an unimagined time, stands a bridge
Which spans the years and dreams of man.

Its keystone bears the weight of echoes
And binds them to the stones,
Which gently rise above the tended calm.

Until it comes once more to life.
And takes its rightful place
As a passage from mortality,

Lifting those who float across its sweep,
In joyful pandemonium,
To taste fame's momentary nectar.

Or those, like Nicklaus, the Golden Bear,
Who blessed it with his presence
And turned granite into gold.

Or Spain's magician,
A sorcerer who touched our lives
And conjured victories from an empty hand.

Or see a place where Tiger prowls
His power launched in peerless grace
Before he crushes breath from man and links alike

Yet for some a set of scaffold steps.
A gangplank which drops them from the dizzy heights
In painful public execution.

But all build memories for generations,
Scratching marks upon life's fleeting walls
But losing to a simple stone- built arch,

Which takes its comfort that its gateway
Between two different worlds,
Lies beyond the wealth of man.

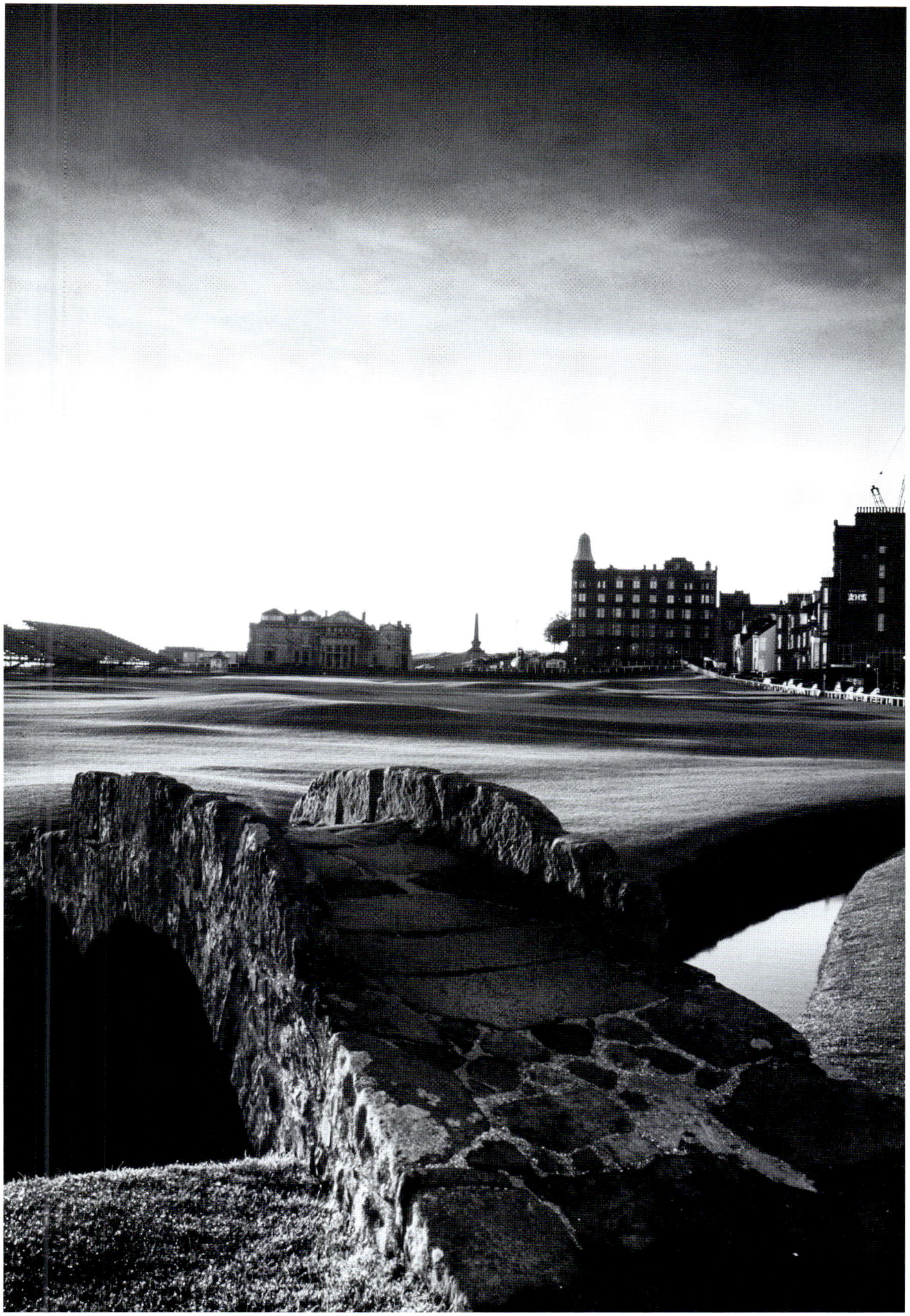

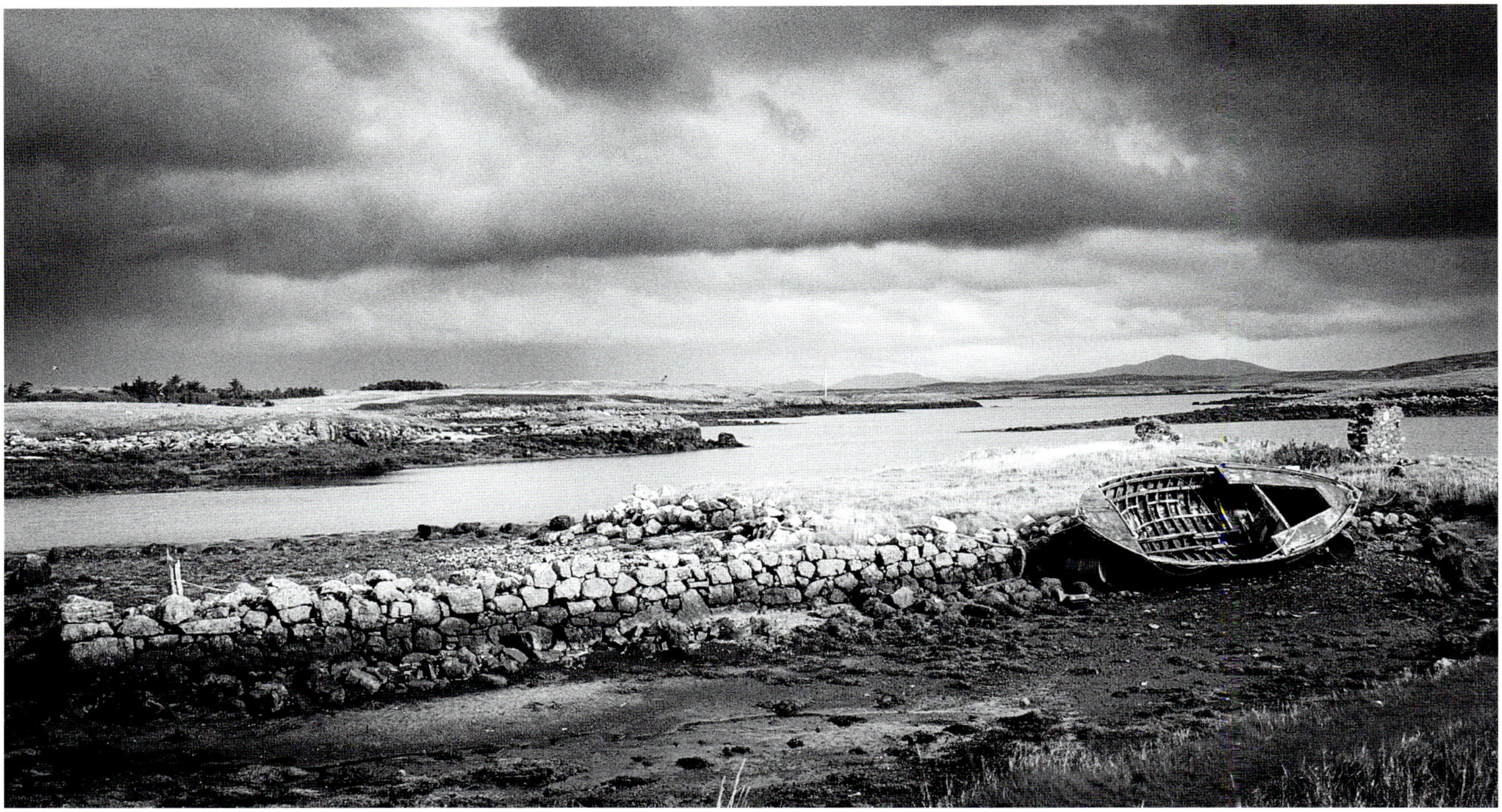

ABANDONED BOAT

Somewhere,
In her darkening mind,
Lies an abandoned boat,
With broken breast
And out-turned ribs,
A bleaching
Skeleton of dreams,
That ferried memories,
Across a lifetime's course,
Holding them safe
Against the heaving waves,
Charting a passage,
Beyond the Minches
And the Sounds,
Anchoring,
Her being,
Her sense of self,
Until it ran ashore,
Forsaken by
The fleeing tide,
Leaving her aground,
An empty vessel,
Becalmed,
With nowhere
To go.

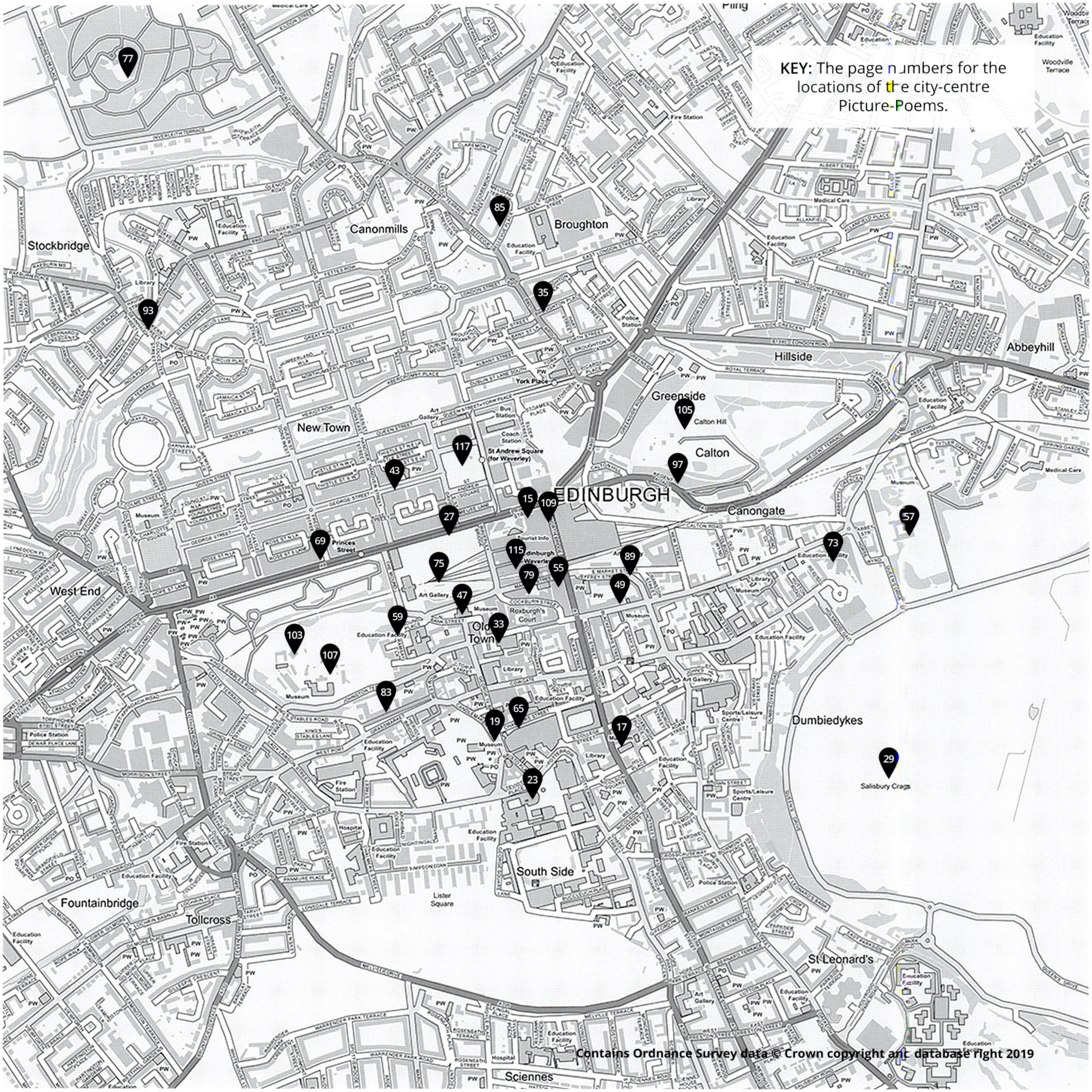

KEY: The page numbers for the locations of the city-centre Picture-Poems.
Stockbridge
Canonmills
Broughton
Hillside
Abbeyhill
Greenside
Calton
New Town
EDINBURGH
Canongate
West End
Old Town
Dumbiedykes
Salisbury Crags
South Side
Fountainbridge
Tollcross
St Leonard's
Sciennes
77
85
35
93
105
117
43
97
15
109
27
69
57
115
73
89
75
79
55
49
47
59
33
103
107
83
65
19
17
29
23
Contains Ordnance Survey data © Crown copyright and database right 2019

BEHIND THE PICTURE-POEMS

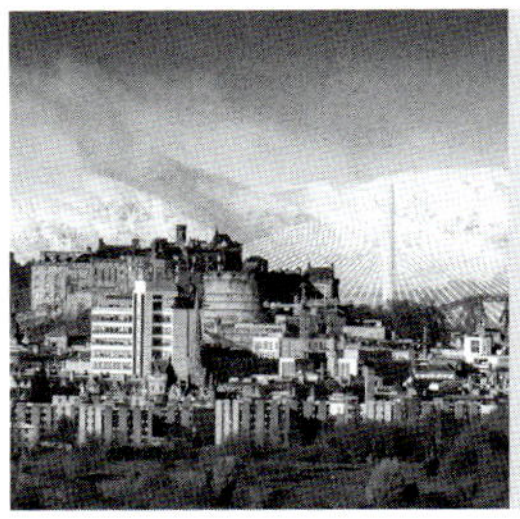

HINTERLAND

- Page 13 -

This photograph has not been doctored in Photoshop. It is a single image taken on a 'long' lens from afar. Hence the compression. The view only appears on a few clear days every year, but if you stand in the right place (a closely guarded secret!), you can see the snow-capped Ochil and Perthshire Hills looming up behind Edinburgh.

The photograph perfectly captures the idea of a Hinterland - which each and every one of us carries around, but is only occasionally brought into full view.

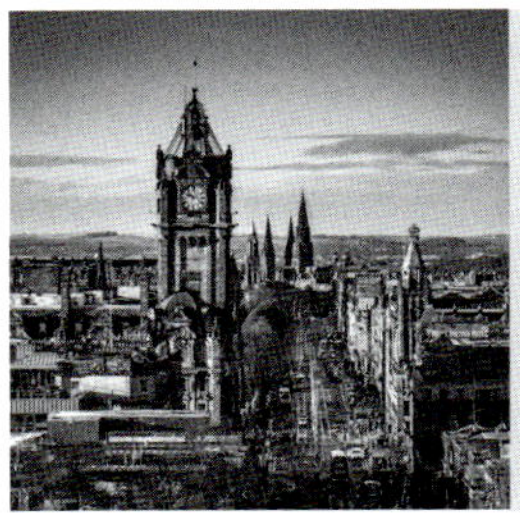

THE BALMORAL CLOCK

- Page 15 -

Since 1902, the hotel's clock has been set three minutes fast to ensure that the people of Edinburgh wouldn't miss their trains. The only day that the clock runs on time is on 31 December (Hogmanay) for the city's New Year celebrations. The clock tower, at 190 feet (58m) high, forms a prominent landmark in Edinburgh's city centre.

Resulting from a competition in 1895, the hotel originally opened on October 15, 1902. The building's architecture is Victorian, influenced by the traditional Scottish baronial style. It was designed by architect William Hamilton Beattie, and for most of the 20th century was known as the North British Hotel, or simply the 'NB', a traditional railway hotel built for the North British Railway Company adjacent to their newly rebuilt Waverley Station.

Spot the workmen on the building!

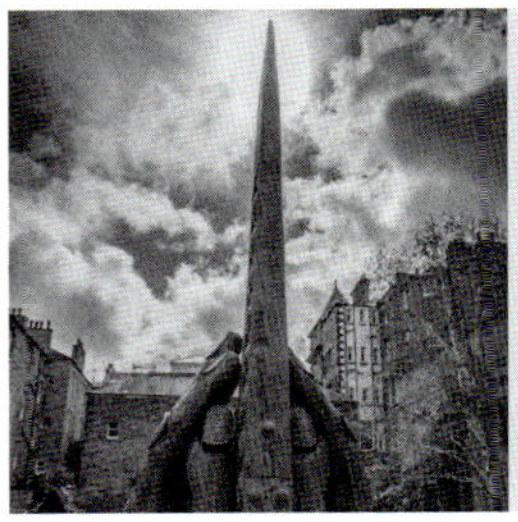

THE SURGEON'S KNIFE

- Page 17 -

A few years ago Gordon introduced Don to Gavin Bowyer, a surgeon, who explained his passion for surgery. The poem attempts to capture the essence of surgery. The main photograph was taken outside the Royal College of Surgeons of Edinburgh, and shows the remarkable sculpture by Denys Mitchell, 1994. The sculpture is entitled "Hinc Sanitas" (From Here, Health)

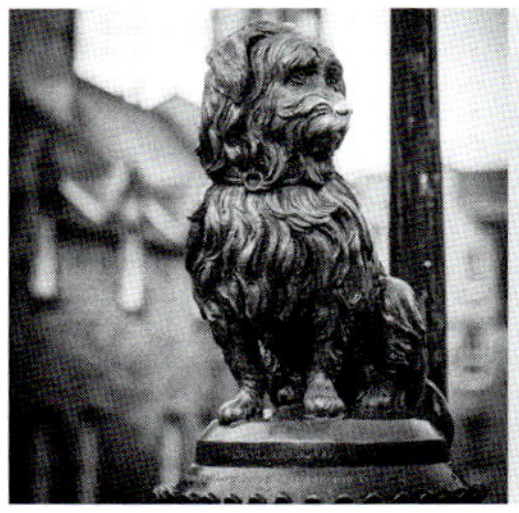

FRIENDSHIP

- Page 19 -

Greyfriars Bobby (May 4, 1855 – January 14, 1872) was a Skye Terrier who became famous for spending 14 years guarding the grave of his owner, Edinburgh policeman John Gray, until he himself died. Bobby's statue sits at the corner of Edinburgh's Candlemaker Row and George IV Bridge.

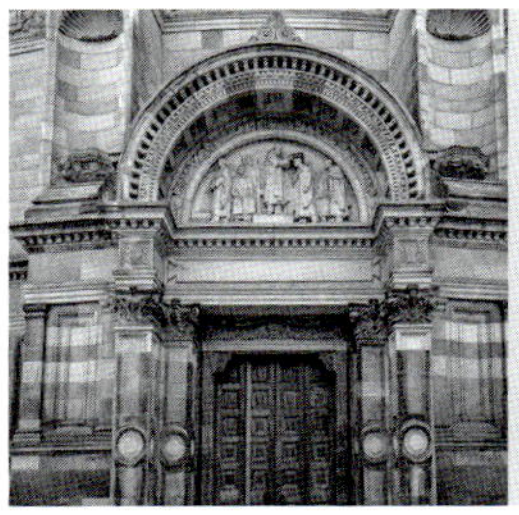

McEWAN HALL

- Page 23 -

The McEwan Hall is the graduation hall of the University of Edinburgh, presented to the university in 1897 by William McEwan, brewer and politician, at a cost of £115,000. Its architect was Sir Robert Rowand Anderson. A Category A listed building, the exterior of the D-shaped hall was completed in 1894. The hall's most striking feature is its large dome, on the inside of which appears a biblical inscription: "Wisdom is the principal thing, therefore get wisdom, and with all thy getting, get understanding. Exalt her and she shall bring thee to honour" (Proverbs 4:7). In 2015 the hall, as well as Bristo Square, closed for major refurbishment works, reopening in time for the 2017 graduations at a cost of £35M. As part of the graduation ceremony, each and every one of the 10,000 graduating students is 'capped' - a centuries-old ritual whereby those taking a degree are lightly tapped on the head with the cap by the university's vice-chancellor and principal. Legend has it that the cap was made from the breeches of sixteenth century religious reformer John Knox.

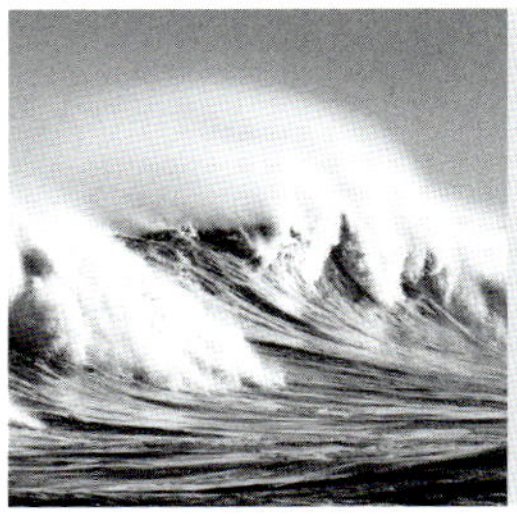

WAVES AGAINST THE WIND

- Page 25 -

This shot was taken facing out towards the Firth of Forth. In geological terms the Firth of Forth is a fjord, formed by the Forth Glacier in the last glacial period. The drainage basin for the firth covers a wide geographic area, including places as far from the shore as Ben Lomond, Cumbernauld, Harthill, Penicuik and the edges of Gleneagles golf course. The firth extends out until it meets the North Sea just beyond the Isle of May.

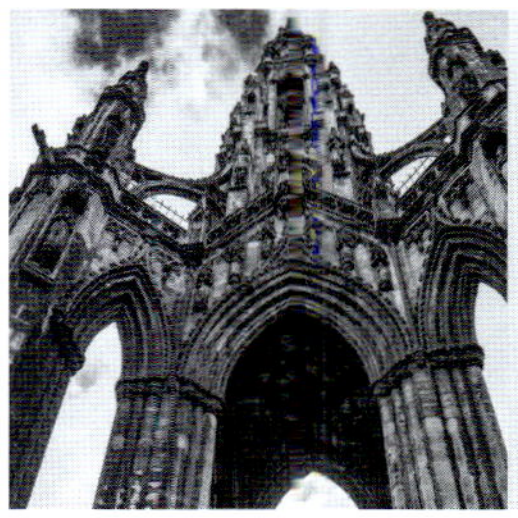

SCOTT MONUMENT

- Page 27 -

The Scott Monument is a Victorian Gothic monument commemorating celebrated Scottish author Sir Walter Scott. It is the second largest monument to a writer in the world (after the José Martí monument in Havana), and stands close by Edinburgh's Waverley Railway Station - named after Scott's Waverley novels. The tower is 200ft 6ins (61.11m) high, and has a series of viewing platforms reached by narrow spiral staircases. The highest platform is reached by a total of 288 steps, allowing panoramic views of central Edinburgh. Following Scott's death in 1832, a competition was held to design a monument in his honour. George Meikle Kemp was declared the contest's winner, while Sir John Steell was commissioned to create a statue of Scott to rest in the space between the tower's four columns. The statue, made from white Carrara marble, depicts Scott seated, quill in hand, with his dog Maida by his side.

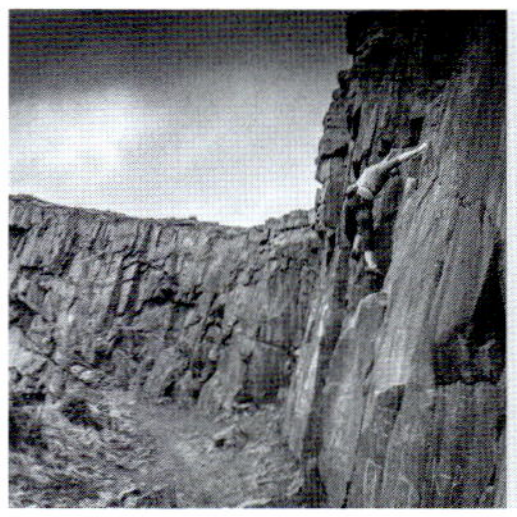

SALISBURY CRAGS

- Page 29 -

Salisbury Crags are a series of 46-metre (151ft) cliffs at the top of a spur of Arthur's Seat, rising on the west flank of Holyrood Park. At Hutton's Section, the Edinburgh geologist James Hutton (1726-97) recognised that the rock now forming the crags had been injected in a molten state, disproving the suggestion the rocks had crystallised from a supposed primordial sea. The hard dolerite which forms the crags was quarried to use as cobblestones in Edinburgh's streets from the mid-17th Century.

Salisbury Crags are part of a Scheduled Ancient Monument (SAM) and Site of Special Scientific Interest (SSSI). The steep face of hard rock would seem perfect for climbing, and 100 years ago the crags were a popular climbing and mountaineering location. However, more recently climbing was prohibited because of the risk to climbers and other park users from falling and broken rocks. In 1995 this restriction was relaxed to allow climbing in the South Quarry.

Harold Raeburn was brought up nearby and became the leading climber of the Scottish Mountaineering Club not long after joining the organisation in 1896.

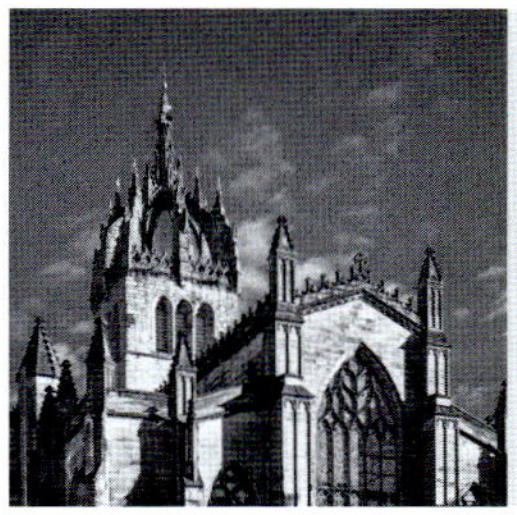

A CITY'S CROWN

- Page 33 -

St Giles' Cathedral, also known as the High Kirk of Edinburgh, is the principal place of worship of the Church of Scotland in Edinburgh. Its distinctive crown steeple is a prominent feature of the city skyline. The building is situated roughly one-third of the way down the Royal Mile (which runs from Edinburgh Castle to Holyrood Palace). The crown steeple (or crown spire) was built in 1495, and takes the form of a traditional church steeple, in which curved stone flying buttresses combine to replicate the open shape of a rounded crown.

The Scottish crown dates from 1540, having been made from Scottish gold melted down from a previous crown. It was first used when James V wore it for the coronation of his second Queen, Marie de Guise, the mother of Mary Queen of Scots. It is encrusted with 20 precious stones and 22 gemstones, along with Scottish freshwater pearls.

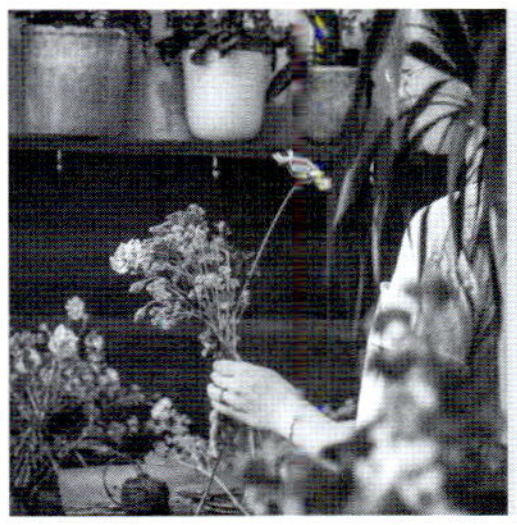

FLOWERSHOP

- Page 35 -

In their student days, Gordon and Don both drove fruit vans for Rankins, at the time one of Edinburgh's biggest grocers and florists. The addresses of the shops in 1976 were: 9 Baxter's Place; 37 Constitution Street; 21 Dalry Road; 35 Deanhaugh Street; 61 Earl Grey Street; 27 Easter Road; 15 Elm Row; 7 Great Junction Street; 50 Home Street; 18 Nicolson Street; 79 Nicolson Street; 164 Portobello High Street; 21 St Patrick Square; 19 South St Andrew Street; West End.

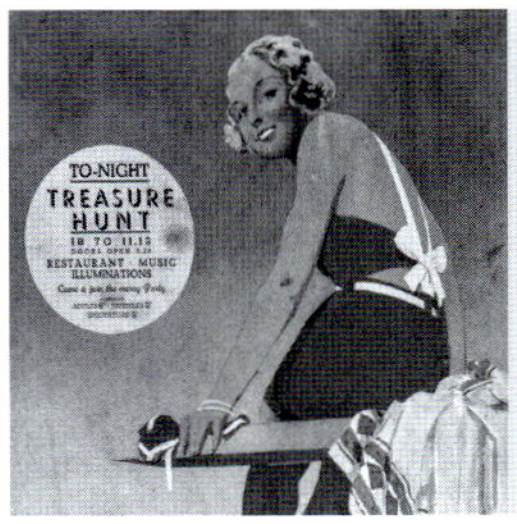

PORTOBELLO BATHER

- Page 37 -

Portobello Open Air Pool was opened in Portobello, Edinburgh, on May 30, 1936, at a cost of £90,000. In its heyday the pool could accommodate 1,300 bathers and 6,000 spectators. One of its principal attractions was the wave-making machine which, at a cost of £7,000, was the first to be installed in an outdoor pool in the UK, capable of generating waves up to three feet high. In its first season, 290,000 bathers and almost 500,000 spectators visited the pool. By the late 1970s the pool's popularity was on the wane. The advent of cheap package holidays abroad played a pivotal role in its decline, and its fortunes fell further in 1978 following the closure of Portobello power station (which had provided its hot water). What little heat the water had previously managed to garner had now disappeared altogether. The 1979 season turned out to be the pool's last, and demolition was approved in 1988.

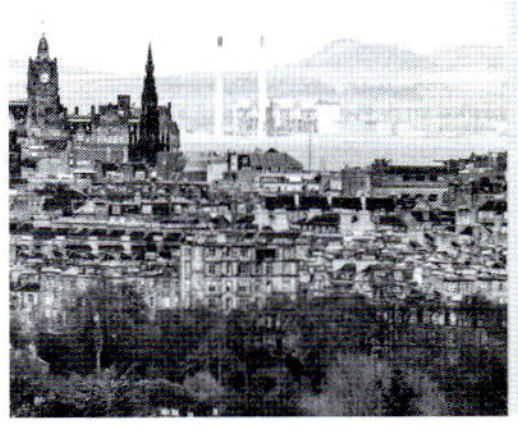

LOOKING EAST

- Page 39 -

Cockenzie power station was a coal-fired power station situated on the south shore of the Firth of Forth, near the town of Cockenzie and Port Seton, eight miles (13kms) east of Edinburgh. The station's distinctive twin chimneys dominated the local coastline from 1967 until the chimneys' demolition in 2015. Coal was originally supplied to the station directly from the deep mines of the neighbouring Midlothian coalfield, and subsequently from open-cast mines in the Lothians, Fife, Ayrshire and Lanarkshire, as well as from Russia.

The photograph was taken from Murrayfield golf course. The use of a 400mm lens results in the power station looking as though it is looming over the city centre.

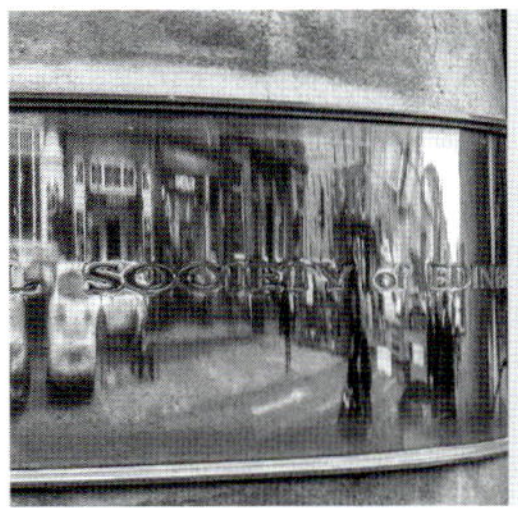

THE ROYAL SOCIETY OF EDINBURGH

- Page 43 -

The RSE was created in 1783 by Royal Charter for "the advancement of learning and useful knowledge". Its first meetings were held in the library wing of the principal building of Edinburgh University. In 1807 meetings moved to Physicians Hall, 14 George Street, Edinburgh, and in 1810 the RSE acquired 40–42 George Street. Here it remained until 1826, when space restrictions led the organisation to move to rooms in the new Royal Institution on the Mound, where it shared accommodation with the Society of Antiquaries. In 1909 the RSE transferred to its current premises at 22–24 George Street. Its first meeting was held here on March 1, 1909. Some of the greatest minds in Scotland have been Fellows of the RSE.

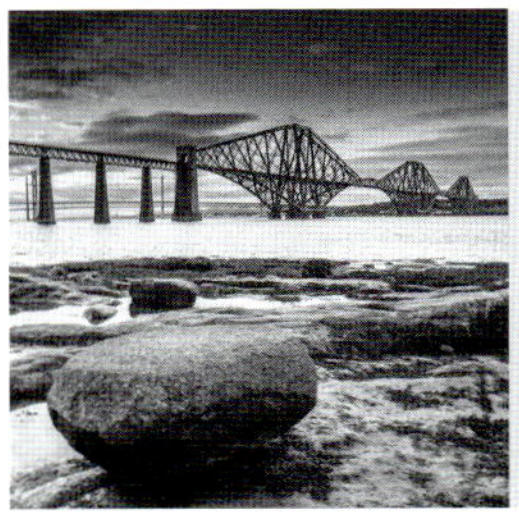

THE FORTH BRIDGE

- Page 45 -

Construction of the bridge began in 1882 and the structure was opened on March 4, 1890, by the Duke of Rothesay, the future Edward VII. Prior to the bridge's construction, ferries had to be used to cross the Firth. The bridge spans the Forth between the villages of South Queensferry and North Queensferry, and has a total length of 8,094 feet (2,467m). At the time of its opening, it could boast the longest single cantilever bridge span in the world (a record that lasted until Canada's Quebec Bridge was completed in 1919). Forth Bridge is still the world's second-longest single cantilever structure, with a span of 1,709 feet (521m). It is sometimes referred to as the Forth Rail Bridge (to distinguish it from the adjacent Forth Road Bridge), although this has never been its official name.

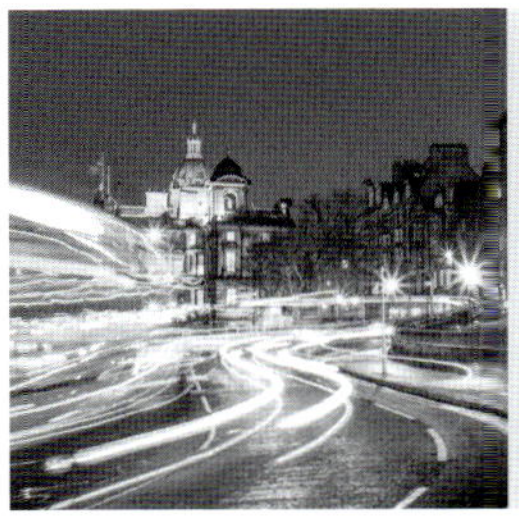

THE BANK

- Page 47 -

The Bank of Scotland was the third bank in the world to issue bank notes. The bank was founded on July 17, 1695, through an Act of the Scottish Parliament. The Bank of Scotland began by issuing notes and making loans (notes were issued in £100, £50, £10 and £5 denominations). A 20 shillings (one pound) note was introduced in 1704. The new notes proved a convenient and attractive means of payment, being easier to handle than coins. They were also more dependable, since their value was clearly stated and guaranteed by the Bank. Scotland became one of the first countries in the world to use paper currency from choice. The Bank's former headquarters are situated at the top of the Mound.

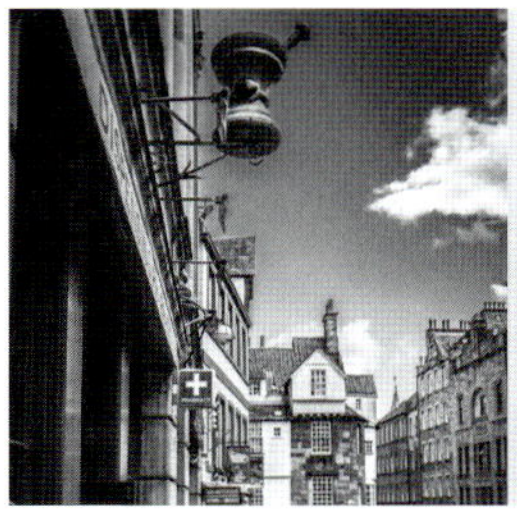

ROYAL MILE PHARMACY

- Page 49 -

The Royal Mile Pharmacy is situated on one of Edinburgh's most famous streets, not far from Protestant reformer John Knox's House.

Don was sitting opposite the pharmacy one morning prior to attending a meeting, and watched as a group gathered outside the chemist for their daily dose of methadone.

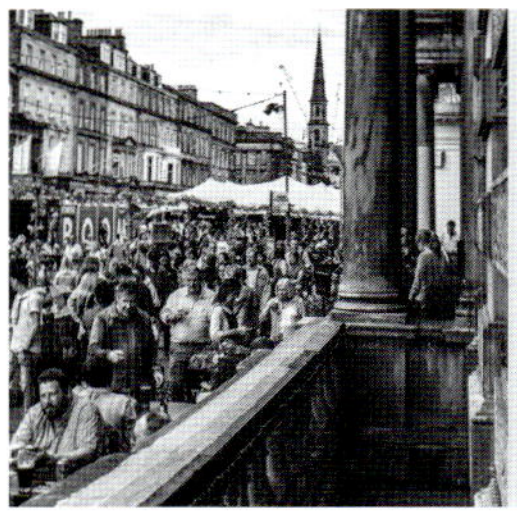

THE 'BLOODY' FRINGE

- Page 53 -

The Edinburgh Festival Fringe (universally known as simply 'the Fringe') is recognised as the world's largest arts festival, on average lasting 25 days and often featuring well over 50,000 performances. In 2018, a total of 3,548 separate shows took place at 317 venues across the city. Established in 1947 as an alternative to the Edinburgh International Festival, the Fringe takes place annually during the month of August. It has variously been described as the 'most famous celebration of the arts and entertainment in the world', and an event that 'has done more to place Edinburgh in the forefront of world cities than anything else'. Between 1976 and 1981, under the direction of Alistair Moffat, the number of companies performing rose from 182 to 494, securing its reputation on the global stage.

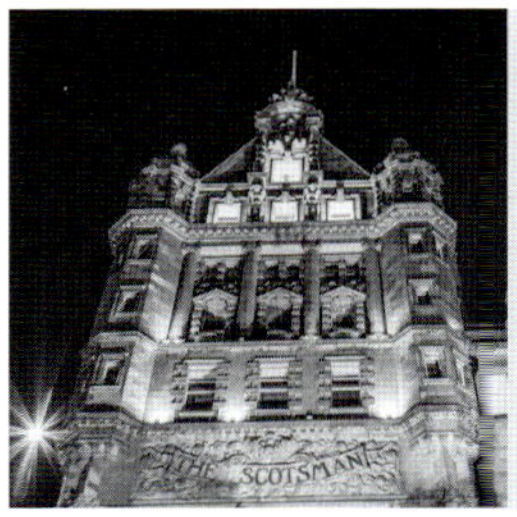

THE SCOTSMAN BUILDING

- Page 55 -

On December 19, 1904, "The Scotsman" newspaper moved to grand new offices, designed by Dunn & Findlay, facing on to North Bridge. The striking building took three years to build, and had access to printworks on Market Street (now the City Art Centre). The paper's printing press area in turn connected directly with Waverley station, below road level, to complete a highly efficient production line. "The Scotsman" ceased to operate from this building in 1994.

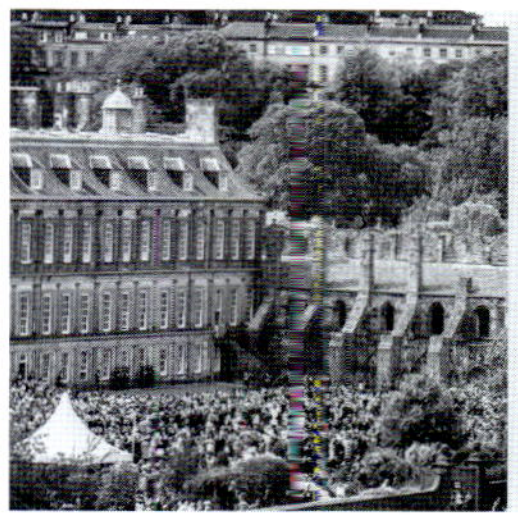

HOLYROOD GARDEN PARTY

- Page 57 -

A Garden Party is held in Holyrood Palace where the Queen welcomes around 8,000 people from all walks of Scottish life to spend a relaxed afternoon with her in the beautiful grounds of the palace. The Queen and the Duke of Edinburgh proceed down avenues, speaking to a random selection of guests. Music is provided by regimental bands and the Royal Scottish Pipers Society.

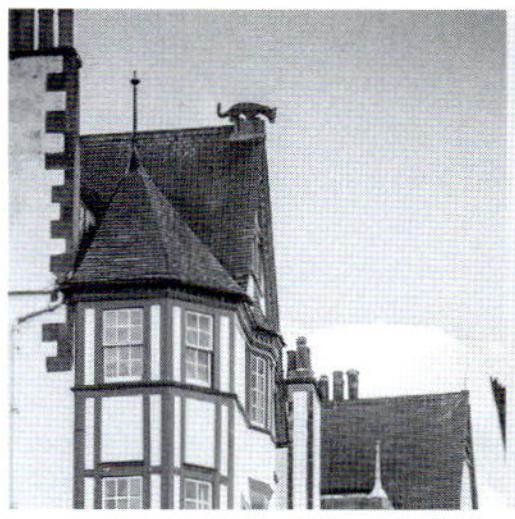

RAMSAY GARDEN CAT

- Page 59 -

Overlooking Princes Street, Ramsay Garden was developed into its current form between 1890 and 1893 by the biologist, botanist and urban planner Patrick Geddes. It began life as Ramsay Lodge, an octagonal house built in 1733 by the poet and wig-maker Allan Ramsay the Elder.

As well as housing wealthy families in private residences, Ramsay Garden was also home to many students.

The 'cat' is not in fact a cat at all. In its original form it possessed a barbed tail and upstretched wings, representing the devil himself, before storms over the past 100 or so years stripped it of its demonic features.

Many Edinburgh residents remain unaware of its presence. However, once seen it is thereafter easy to spot from many viewpoints.

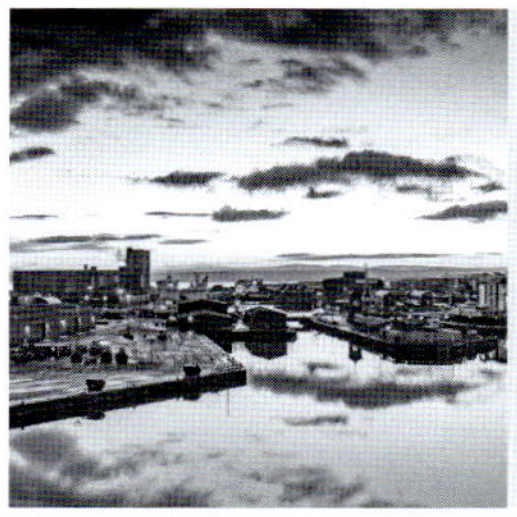

SUNSHINE ON LEITH

- Page 63 -

Leith is a port to the north of the city, situated at the mouth of the Water of Leith. The earliest surviving historical references appear in the royal charter authorising the construction of Holyrood Abbey in 1128. By 1833 the medieval settlements of Leith had grown into a burgh, and in 1920 the burgh finally amalgamated with Edinburgh.

Leith has a rich industrial heritage which includes whaling, sugar refining, ship-building, the wine and whisky trade, fishing, timber trading and rope-making.

In the 18th century ships used to leave Leith bound for West Africa, from where they would sail to the Caribbean. They would return to Leith laden with tobacco and sugar.

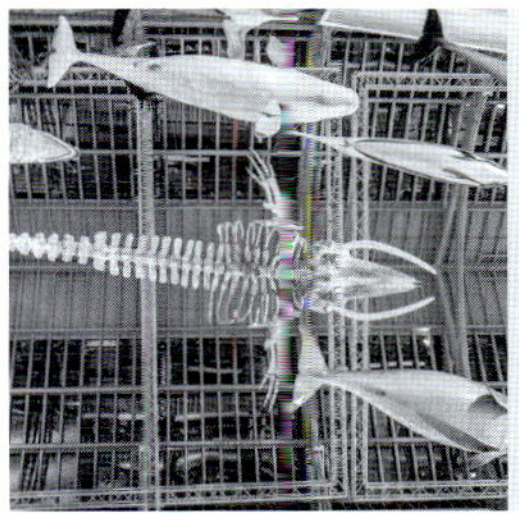

BLUE PLANET

- Page 65 -

The National Museum of Scotland was formed in 2006, following the merger of the new Museum of Scotland (focused on Scottish antiquities, culture and history) and the adjacent Royal Museum (whose collections covered science & technology, natural history and world cultures). The two connected buildings stand beside each other on Chambers Street, close by its intersection with George IV Bridge.

In the early 1970s the National Museum of Scotland displayed a piece of moonrock from the Apollo moon landings. It generated huge interest, with long queues of people lining up to see it.

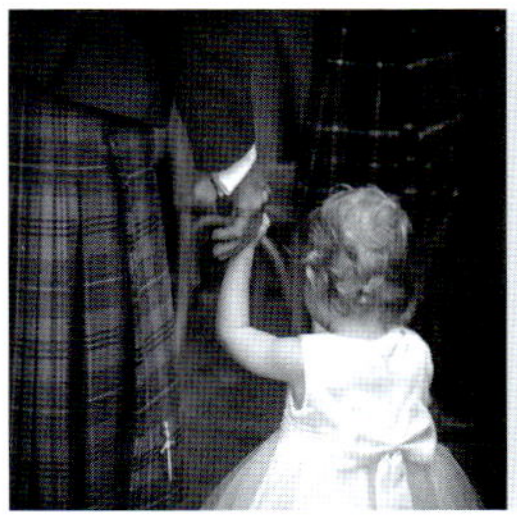

A CHILD'S HAND

- Page 67 -

Don wrote this poem before his sons were old enough to refuse his hand any more. Don recently came across this saying from Goethe, which has much the same meaning: "Children only need two things from their parents - roots and wings." The photograph shows John Rutherford, one of Scotland's most celebrated rugby players, holding the hand of one of his granddaughters.

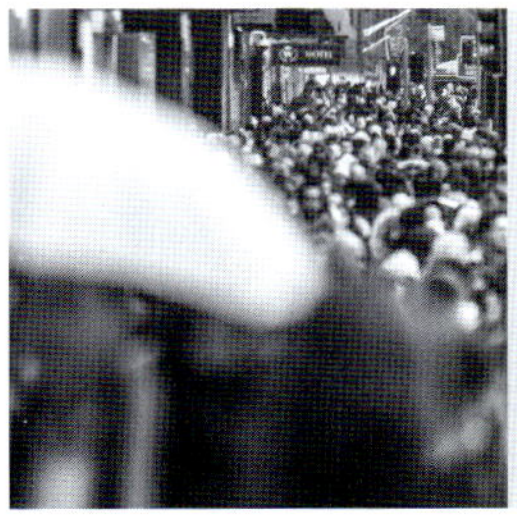

PRINCES STREET CONVERSATIONS

- Page 69 -

Princes Street is one of the major thoroughfares in central Edinburgh, and the main shopping street in the capital. As the southernmost street of Edinburgh's New Town, it stretches roughly one mile from Lothian Road in the west, to Leith Street in the east. Princes Street has virtually no buildings on its south side, allowing unbroken views of the Old Town and Edinburgh Castle. Although it remains popular with shoppers and tourists, it has relinquished its status as Britain's most expensive place to rent shop space outside London. Princes Street could well be one of the few streets in the UK subject to an order of Parliament restricting any building on its south side.

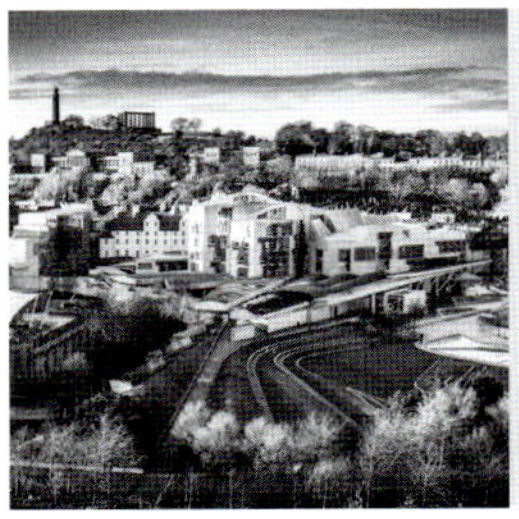

SCOTTISH PARLIAMENT

- Page 73 -

The Scottish Parliament building is the home of the Scottish Parliament at Holyrood, within the UNESCO World Heritage Site in central Edinburgh. Construction of the building began in June, 1999, with Members of the Scottish Parliament (MSPs) holding their first debate in the new building on September 7, 2004. The formal opening by Queen Elizabeth II took place on October 9, 2004. Enric Miralles, the Spanish architect who designed the building, died before its completion.

"We don't want to forget that the Scottish Parliament will be in Edinburgh, but will belong to Scotland, to the Scottish land. The Parliament should be able to reflect the land it represents. The building should arise from the sloping base of Arthur's Seat and arrive into the city almost surging out of the rock." — Enric Miralles, 1999.

From the outset, the building and its construction proved controversial. The choice of location, architect, design and even construction company drew criticism from, among others, politicians, the media and the Scottish public. Scheduled to open in 2001, it finally did so in 2004 - more than three years late and with an estimated final cost of £414M (well over 10 times higher than initial estimates of between £10M-£40M).

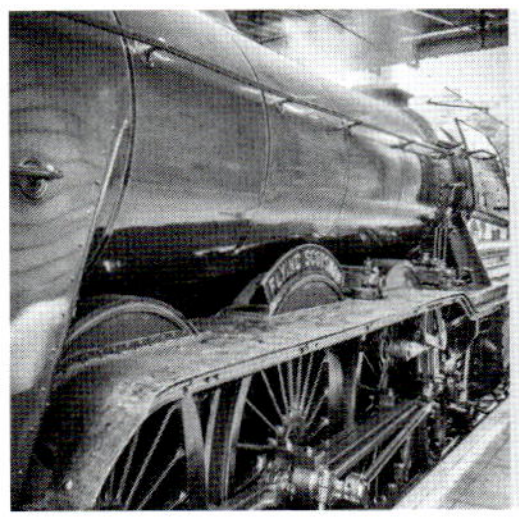

THE FLYING SCOTSMAN

- Page 75 -

The locomotive was built in Doncaster in 1923, becoming the first locomotive of the newly formed London and North Eastern Railway (LNER). It left the works on February 24, 1923, with the number 1472. It was designed by Sir Nigel Gresley as part of the A1 class – the most powerful locomotives used by LNER at that time.

By 1924, when it had been selected to appear at the British Empire Exhibition in London, the loco had been renumbered 4472, being given the name 'Flying Scotsman' after the London to Edinburgh rail service which started daily at 10am in 1862.

In 1934, the train was clocked at 100mph on a special test run – officially the first locomotive in the UK to have reached this speed.

Both Gordon and Don used to watch the Flying Scotsman pass through Portobello when they were five years old. The engine was retired from regular service in 1963 after covering 2.08 million miles. The memories live on.

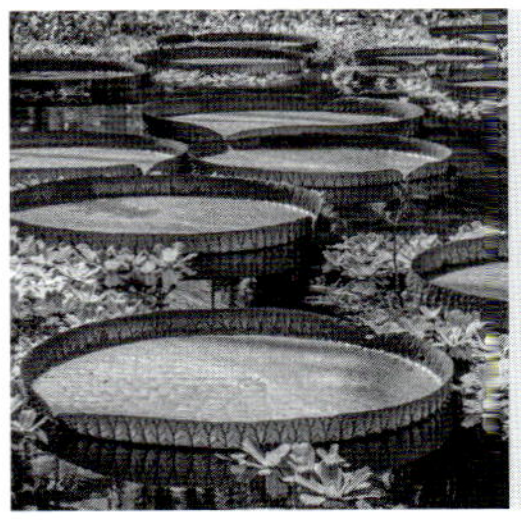

RETURN FROM SINGAPORE

- Page 77 -

The Royal Botanic Garden Edinburgh is set in over 70 acres of beautiful landscape just one mile north of the city centre. The garden offers superb panoramic views of the city skyline. 'The Botanics', as the garden is affectionately known, is breath-taking at any time of year.

This poem describes a true event. Don's grandparents lived in Malaya, where his grandfather managed a rubber plantation. As they waited at the quayside for the last boat to leave Singapore before it fell to the Japanese, Don's grandfather spotted an acquaintance behind the barrier. Without hesitation he offered her his ticket. He spent the rest of the war in Changi Prison. The story doesn't end there, however, as the boat was torpedoed and sunk by a submarine – fortunately Don's grannie had disembarked in Bombay as the vessel was overloaded. Neither knew the other was alive for over 18 months.

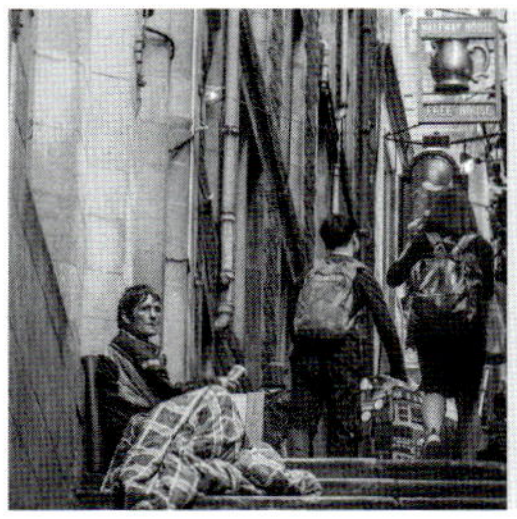

GRAVITY

- Page 79 -

If you are a homeless rough sleeper:

- Your life expectancy is 47 years. If you're a woman, this decreases to 43 years. (The average life expectancy in Scotland is 86.6 years).
- You are 13 times more likely to experience violence and 47 times more likely to be a victim of theft.
- You are three times more likely to die in a road traffic accident.
- You have a 50/50 chance of having a long-term mental illness, and are nine times more likely to commit suicide.

It is estimated that there are 3,500 homeless people in Edinburgh.

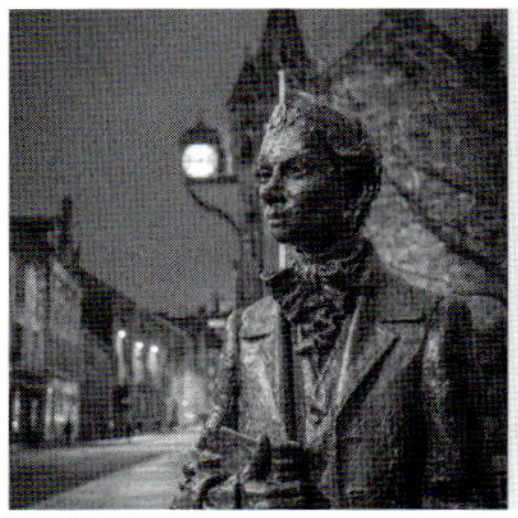

EDINBURGH'S MONUMENTAL NIGHT OUT

- Page 83 -

At the last count there were 53 statues in Central Edinburgh, of which 51 were of celebrated men. The only two statues of named women are those of Queen Victoria (at the foot of Leith Walk); and a South African woman and her child opposite the Usher Hall (celebrating Edinburgh's stand against apartheid).

The White Hart Inn opened in 1516, and is Central Edinburg's oldest public house.

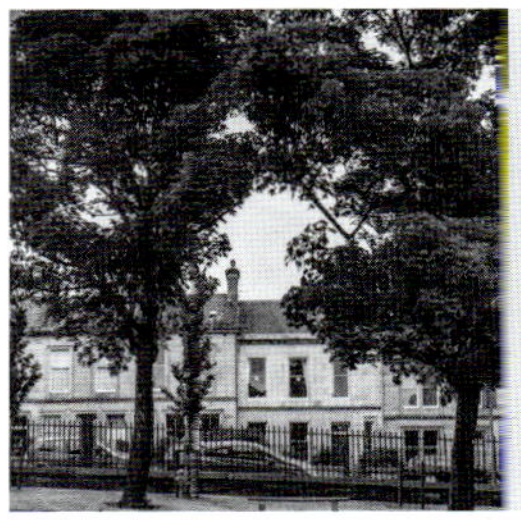

19 BELLEVUE PLACE

- Page 85 -

Don lived at 19 Bellevue Place from 1970–1976. He walked past the door of the house 40 years to the day he left his home to go to school for the very last time.

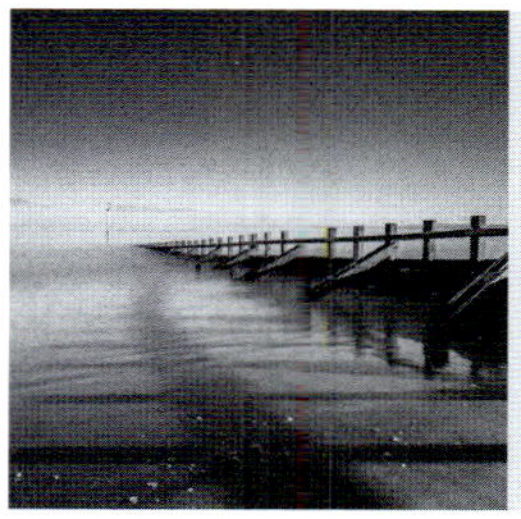

HIGH TIDE

- Page 87 -

Portobello is a coastal suburb of Edinburgh with a long history as a seaside resort. An advertisement for bathing machines for hire on Portobello beach appeared in the "Edinburgh Evening Courant" of June 11, 1795. Between 1846 and 1964 a railway station provided ready access for visitors. Portobello's peak period as a resort came in the late 19th century, after which it went into a slow decline. While visitors were primarily drawn from the inhabitants of Edinburgh, it was also once popular with Glaswegians, particularly during the fortnight-long Glasgow Fair 'trade holiday'. By the 1960s, amusement arcades and permanent funfair attractions had sprung up in Portobello. However, from the 1980s onwards these gradually disappeared, so that by the end of the 20th century Portobello's promenade had almost no attractions left specific to its seaside location.

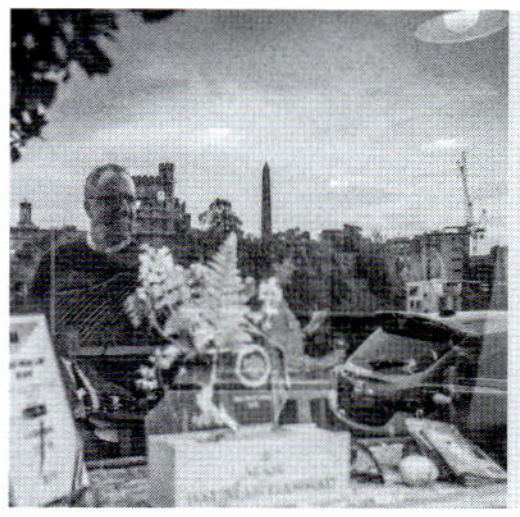

UNEXPECTED MOMENT

- Page 89 -

La Garrigue restaurant is situated on Jeffrey Street and opened in 2001. Largely inspired by Jean-Michel Gauffre's rural upbringing in Languedoc, La Garrigue offers rustic family style cooking, complimented by a large selection of fine wines from this area of France commonly known as 'Le Midi'. It features rustic, hand-crafted Tim Stead tables and chairs, as well as original paintings by Andrew Walker from Jean-Michel's home town Bedarieux and his village Combret. The restaurant is themed around the food and wines of Languedoc, and is a cross between an upmarket restaurant and a bistro. The poem recounts an occasion when Don was passing the restaurant and unexpectedly saw his wife, Gill, standing at the counter.

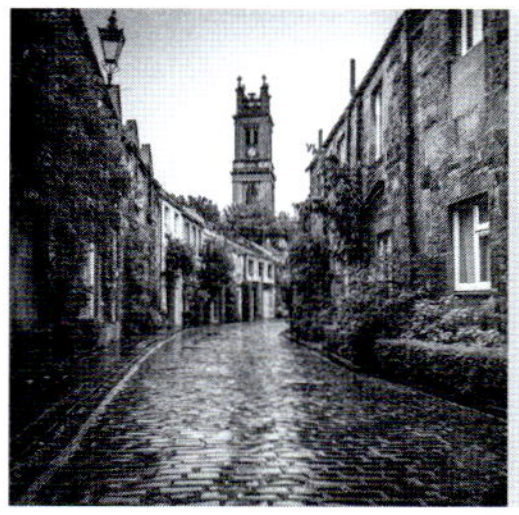

STOCKBRIDGE LOVERS

- Page 93 -

This picture-poem is the catalyst for *Edinburgh Revisited*, and was a wedding present for Don's son Doug, who married Sarah in Sydney in July, 2017. Doug and Sarah lived in Stockbridge before moving to Australia. Doug had proposed to Sarah in Leo's Beanery, situated on Howe Street, which runs north towards Stockbridge as an extension of Frederick Street. One evening Don and Gordon retraced the route from George Street to Stockbridge, resulting in the first contribution to *Edinburgh Revisited*.

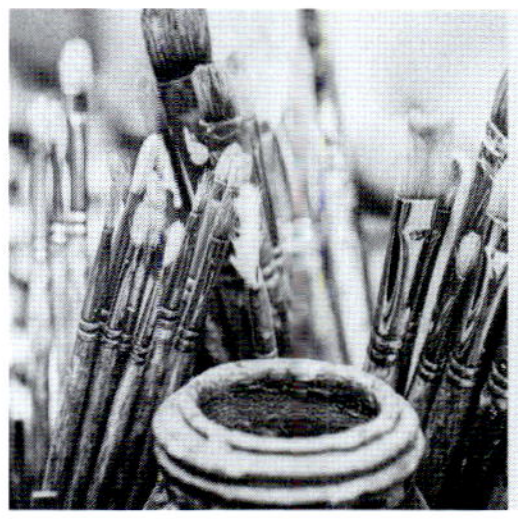

PORTRAIT OF A PRESIDENT

- Page 95 -

Gordon and Don were visiting the Royal College of Surgeons of Edinburgh to take a photograph for their Picture-Poem 'A Surgeon's Knife', when they were given a tour of the college by past vice-president Donald Macleod. They were struck by the portraits of previous Presidents hanging on the walls. The first President of the college (or Deacon, as they were known then) was Lancelot Barbour (1535-36). During their tour they met the current President, Michael Lavelle-Jones, who by coincidence was that very day, having a first sitting for his own portrait.

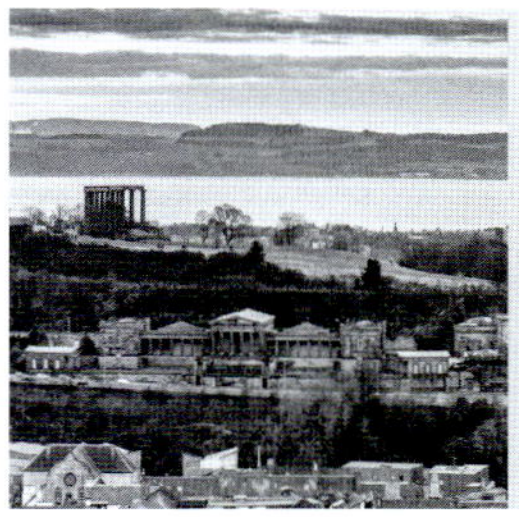

THE OLD ROYAL HIGH SCHOOL

- Page 97 -

This A-listed building was erected for the Royal High School between 1826 and 1829 on the south face of Calton Hill, part of Edinburgh's Acropolis, at a cost to the Town Council of £34,000. Of this, £500 had been given by King George IV as a token of royal favour towards a school which, as a royal foundation, had 'long conferred incalculable benefits on the community'. It was designed in a neo-classical Greek Doric style by Thomas Hamilton, and has been praised both as the architect's 'supreme masterpiece' and the 'finest monument of the Greek revival in Scotland'. After the Royal High School was relocated in 1968, the building became available for alternative uses and was refurbished ready to accommodate a new devolved legislature for Scotland. However, the 1979 devolution referendum failed to provide sufficient backing for a devolved assembly.

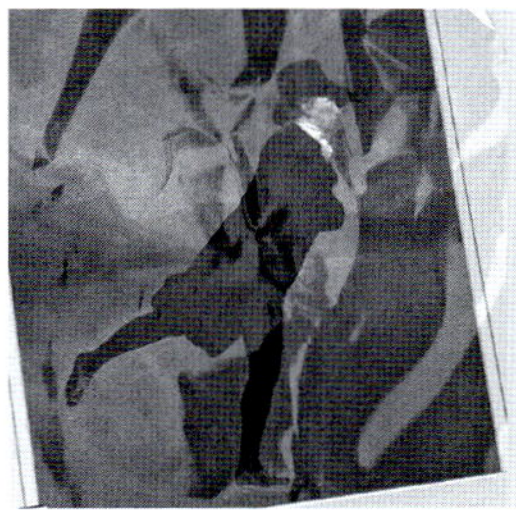

DUDDINGSTON SKATER

- Page 99 -

Duddingston Loch is located in Holyrood Park below Arthur's Seat. It is part of a nature reserve, much visited by wildfowl, herons and the great crested grebe, along with swans and ducks. It is the only natural loch in Edinburgh, and the largest in Holyrood Park. The loch is the setting for Henry Raeburn's famous painting 'The Reverend Robert Walker Skating on Duddingston Loch', better known as The Skating Minister. It remains a popular venue for skaters, and is a meeting place for Edinburgh Skating Club members. Nowadays, however, the loch rarely freezes over.

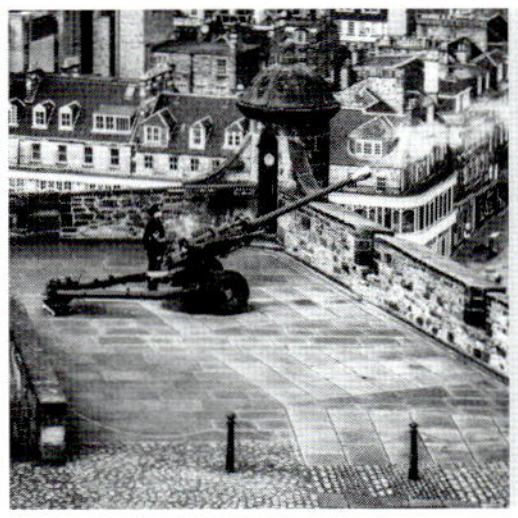

ONE O'CLOCK GUN

- Page 103 -

The One O'Clock Gun is a time signal fired each day from Edinburgh Castle at precisely one pm (except on Sundays, Good Friday and Christmas Day). The 'time gun' was established in 1861 as a signal for ships in the harbour of Leith and on the Firth of Forth. The original gun was an 18-pound muzzle-loading cannon (which required four men to operate it) fired from the castle's Half Moon Battery. It was replaced in 1913 by a 32-pound breech-loader, and then in 1952 by a 25-pound howitzer. The present One O'Clock Gun is an L118 light gun, brought into service in 2001. On Sunday, April 2, 1916, the One O'Clock Gun was fired in vain at a German zeppelin during an air raid. This was the gun's only known use in war.

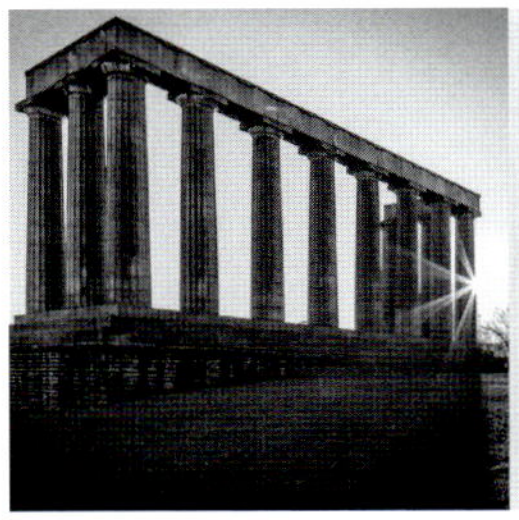

THE UNFINISHED MONUMENT

- Page 105 -

The National Monument of Scotland, situated atop Calton Hill to the east of Princes Street, is Scotland's national memorial to those soldiers and sailors who died fighting in the Napoleonic Wars. According to the inscription, it was intended to be 'A Memorial of the Past and Incentive to the Future Heroism of the Men of Scotland'. The monument was designed during the 1820s by Charles Robert Cockerell and William Henry Playfair. Modelled on the Parthenon in Athens, construction began in 1826 but, because of a lack of funds, was left unfinished in 1829. This gave rise to various nicknames such as 'Scotland's Folly', 'Edinburgh's Disgrace', 'Edinburgh's Folly' and the 'Pride and Poverty of Scotland'.

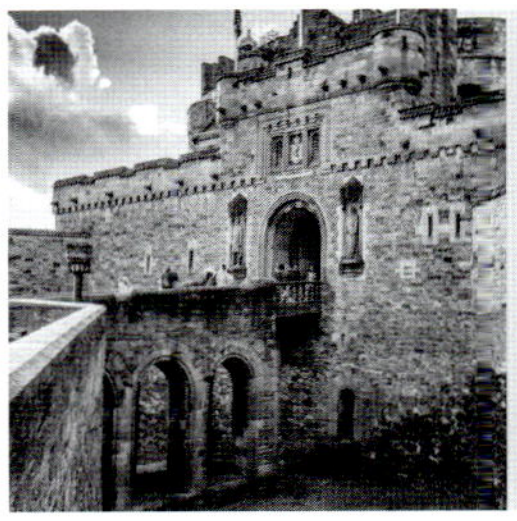

EDINBURGH CASTLE GUARDIANS

- Page 107 -

Sir William Wallace (the statue on the right) - famously depicted in the movie Braveheart - was among the first Scottish leaders to rebel against King Edward I of England. After winning the Battle of Stirling Bridge in 1297, he continued fighting against the English until his capture and execution in 1305. The following year Robert the Bruce (the statue on the left) declared himself King of Scots. Both statues were erected in 1929, and celebrated the 90th anniversary of standing guard over Edinburgh Castle on the May 28, 2019. Some of the jokes they tell each other to pass the time of day, were overheard on a visit to the castle by celebrated Scottish comedian Chic Murray.

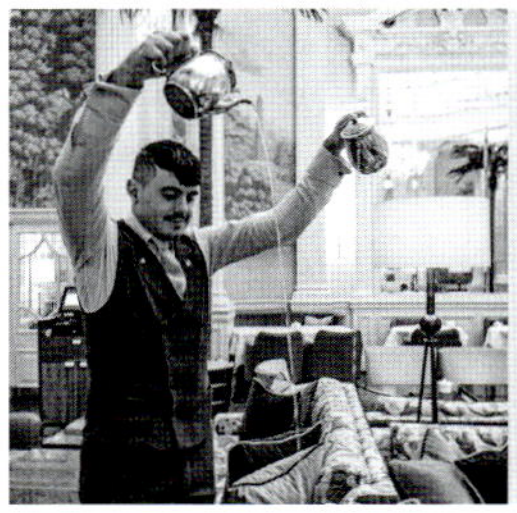

AFTERNOON TEA AT THE BALMORAL

- Page 109 -

Afternoon tea at the Palm Court has become a much-loved Edinburgh institution. Set within the heart of The Balmoral hotel, Palm Court boasts a glass dome as well as a Venetian chandelier, having been fully refurbished in 2013. Subtle local references can be spotted in the décor. The Palm Court's walls are decorated with specially commissioned hand-painted de Gournay wallpaper, with well-known follies of Edinburgh incorporated into the landscape. Throughout the afternoon a harpist plays on the balcony overlooking the Palm Court, while a much-loved feature of the tea ceremony is the 'high pour' - a feat taking consummate skill, but made to look effortless by staff.

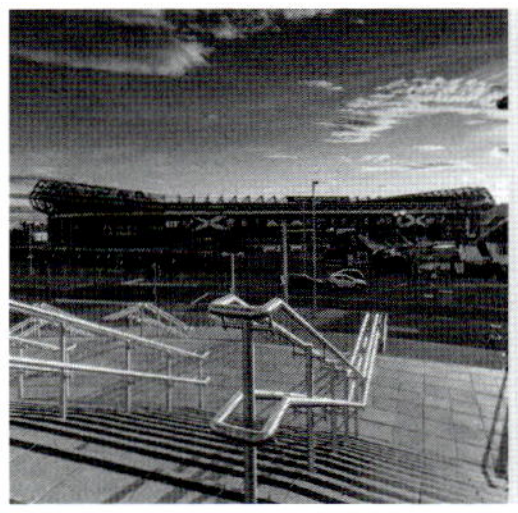

MURRAYFIELD DREAMS

- Page 113 -

Searching for a plot of land on which to build a national rugby ground, the Scottish Rugby Union identified 19 acres suitable for its requirements at Murrayfield. In 1922 it bought the land from Edinburgh Polo Club, financing the deal through a debenture issue. Over the next two years a stand and three embankments were constructed, and on March 21, 1925, England became the first international team to visit the new Murrayfield ground. A crowd of 70,000 watched Scotland defeat the 'Auld Enemy' to secure their first Five Nations Championship 'Grand Slam'. Murrayfield's record attendance stands at 104,000, which was set on March 1, 1975, when Scotland defeated Wales 12-10. This stood as a world record attendance for the next 24 years. Murrayfield was the setting for two further 'Grand Slam' triumphs by Scotland, in 1984 and 1990.

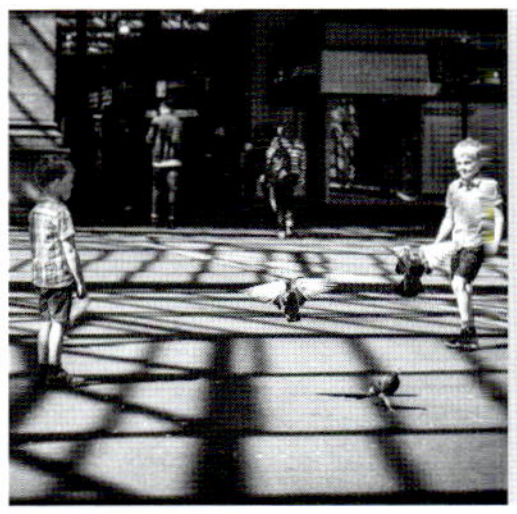

WAVERLEY STATION PIGEONS

- Page 115 -

Edinburgh Waverley railway station (also known simply as Waverley) is the principal station serving the city. It is the second busiest railway station in Scotland, after Glasgow Central. It is the northern terminus of the East Coast Main Line from London King's Cross, although some trains operated by London North Eastern Railway (LNER) continue to other Scottish destinations beyond Edinburgh. Don was walking through the station one morning when he observed two boys playing with the ubiquitous pigeons.

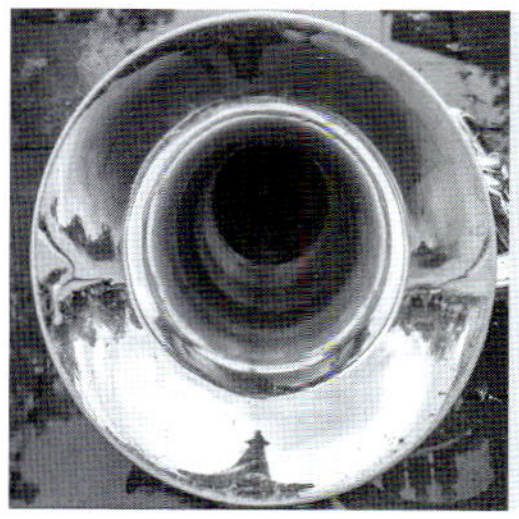

A MARCHING BAND

- Page 117 -

On a wet and windy Edinburgh summer morning, Don watched a group of musicians make their way across St Andrew Square, located at the east end of George Street. The construction of St Andrew Square began life in 1772 as the first part of the New Town, designed by James Craig. Within six years of its completion, St Andrew Square had become one of the city's most desirable and fashionable residential areas. As the 19th century drew to a close, St Andrew Square evolved into the commercial centre of the city.

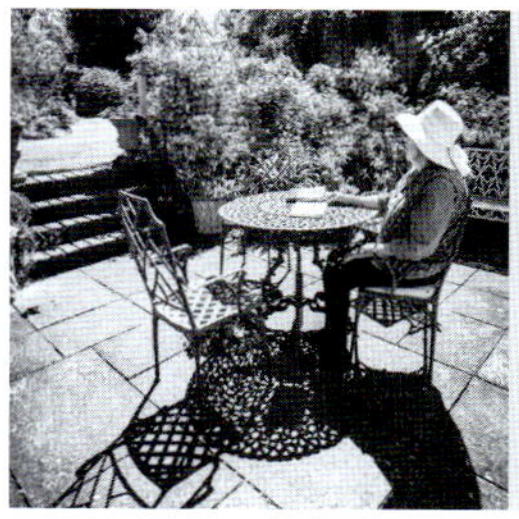

POEMS IN A HIGH WALLED GARDEN

- Page 119 -

This poem was originally written for Kathleen Noble, a close friend of Don's mother. The poem describes the first and only time he met Kathleen in his adult life. The photograph was taken in the garden of Shepherd House, Inveresk, the beautiful home of Sir Charles and Lady Ann Fraser. Ann is the model in the photograph. The garden opens to the public throughout the summer months.

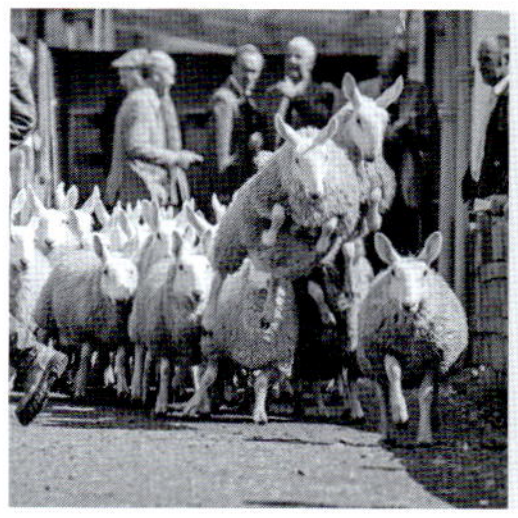

LUCK

- Page 123 -

There's an old tradition at farmers' auction markets where the seller gives the buyer a small amount of money 'for luck'. Overall trends in the sheep population showed its total decreasing by 800,000 (10.5 per cent) from 7.63 million in 2006 to 6.83 million in 2016.

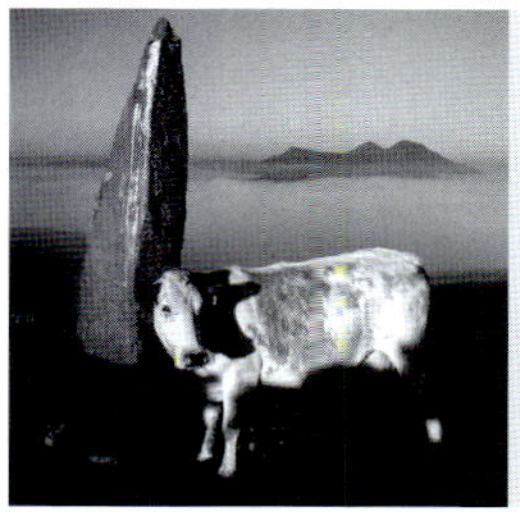

THE COW AND THE PHOTOGRAPHER

- Page 125 -

Gordon gave Don a photograph of an old cow, which he had taken one beautiful summer's morning using a tripod. This was Don's interpretation of the occasion from the cow's perspective. What one person thinks they are doing can often be misinterpreted by others.

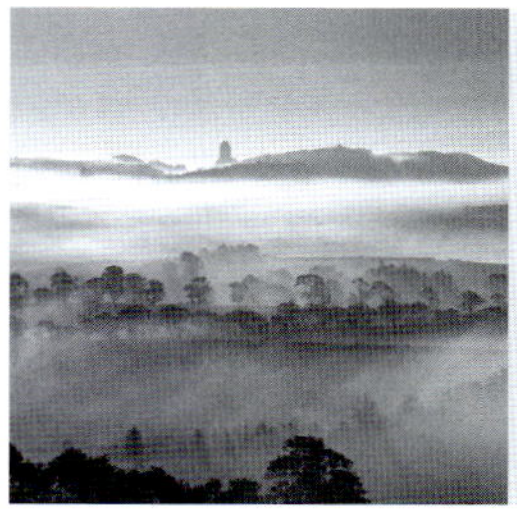

TWEED MIST

- Page 127 -

This photograph shows Smailholm Tower in the distance. Smailholm Tower is a peel tower around five miles (8kms) west of Kelso in the Scottish Borders. Its dramatic situation, atop a crag of Lady Hill, commands wide views over the surrounding countryside. It was originally built in the 15th century or early 16th century by the Pringle family. This family, originally spelt Hoppringle, who were followers of the Earl of Douglas, held the lands of Smailholm from the early 15th century, and managed part of Ettrick Forest for their feudal superior. The suffix 'holm' stands for little island; and "Smail" might be Smale, Smail, Smaile, Small, Smalles, Smalls or Smeal, derived from the Old English pre-7th Century 'Smael' meaning 'small, slender or thin', and was originally given as a nickname to someone of slight stature. It was the sight of Smailholm that fired Walter Scott's imagination when, as a young boy, he spent time with his grandparents at the nearby farm of Sandyknowe.

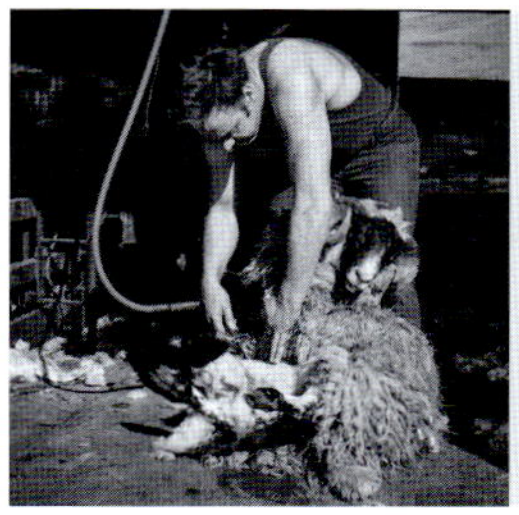

THE CLIPPING

- Page 129 -

Don spent a day with sheep shearers Angus Dickson and Geordie Bain (a former world champion) high up in the Cheviot Hills. Ten years later Angus was shearing sheep inside the Arctic Circle in Norway, when he came across a framed copy of the poem hanging on a wall! The Norwegian farmer refused to believe that the poem was actually about Angus. Gordon took this photograph of Angus clipping a Blackie tup (ram) at Plenderleith Farm in the Cheviot Hills.

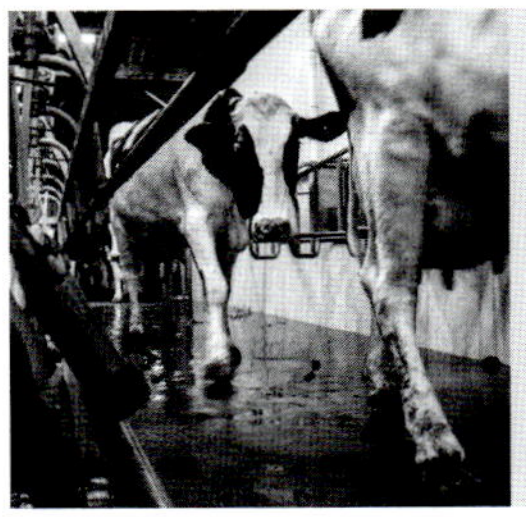

DECEMBER MILKING

- Page 131 -

This photograph was taken in 1999 and shows cattle making their way to the milking parlour. Twenty years on this system has been replaced by 'milking robots', allowing some cows to enter as many as four or five times a day, driven by the prospect of relieving the pressure of milk in their udders, as well as being able to eat while being milked.

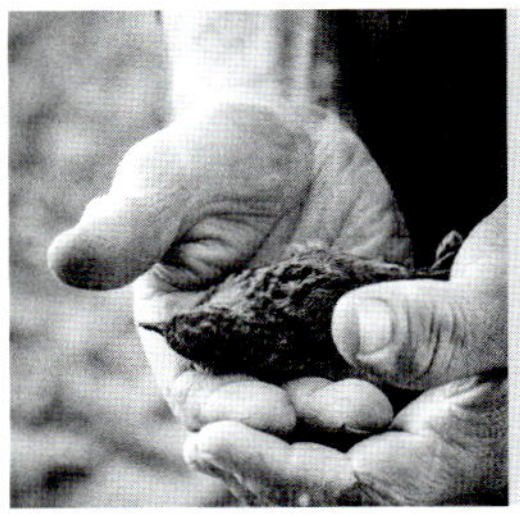

A FARMER'S HANDS

- Page 133 -

Don's father told him this story about a very dour, bad-tempered and, so it appeared, uncaring farmer who used to give him a lift back from school. One day they struck a bird with the car, and the farmer wept as he picked up the dead creature.

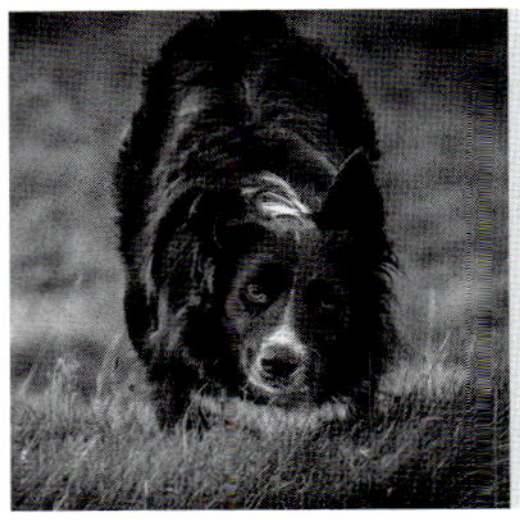

FREEDOM

- Page 135 -

This was the second poem Don wrote as an adult. Its subject was the British Sheep Dog Trial Championships. The poem was written from the dog's perspective and took first prize in the 1993 BP/Leopard Magazine national poetry competition: at that time the biggest prize for a single poem in Scotland.

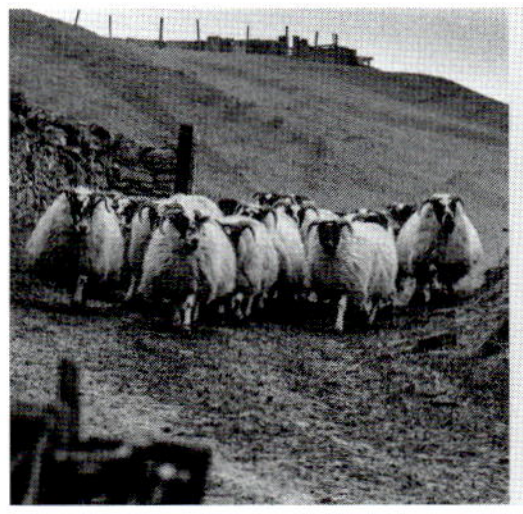

LAST OF THE BLACKIES

- Page137 -

All Blackfaces are horned, with black or black-and-white face and legs. The fleece should be free of black fibre and can vary from short, fine wool (used for carpets and tweeds), to strong coarse wool (sold mainly for the Italian mattress trade). There are several distinct types of animal within the breed. These have evolved over the years, influenced by climate, environment and grazing quality. This gives the breed the advantage of being able to produce species to suit every climatic condition. Monastery records of the 12th century tell of the Dun or Blackface breed of sheep. The monks used the wool for their clothes, and also exported large amounts to Europe. In the 16th century, King James IV of Scotland established an improved Blackface flock in Ettrick Forest, which was a remnant of the great Caledonian Forest, and comprised the county of Selkirk and parts of Peebles and Edinburgh. In 1455 it was annexed by the Crown, and became a royal hunting ground.

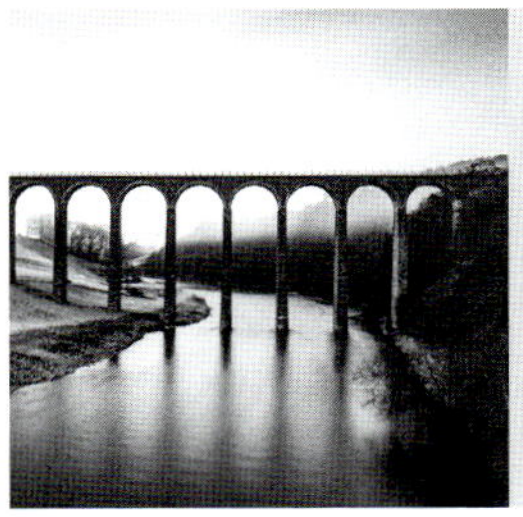

LEADERFOOT LADY

- Page 139 -

The Leaderfoot Viaduct was opened on November 16, 1863, to carry the Berwickshire railway connecting Reston with St Boswells, via Duns and Greenlaw. The railway engineers responsible were Charles Jopp and Wylie & Peddie. The viaduct stands 126 feet above the floor of the river valley. Each arch has a span of 43 feet and are constructed of brickwork. The abutments, piers and walls are rendered in rustic-faced red sandstone. In August, 1948, the railway was badly damaged by flooding, with no fewer than seven bridges being put out of commission. Although the line was closed to passenger traffic, freight trains continued to use the viaduct (as far as Greenlaw) until July, 1965. In 1981 the viaduct's poor condition resulted in the structure being scheduled for demolition. Its listed status was upgraded from Category B to Category A in 1986.

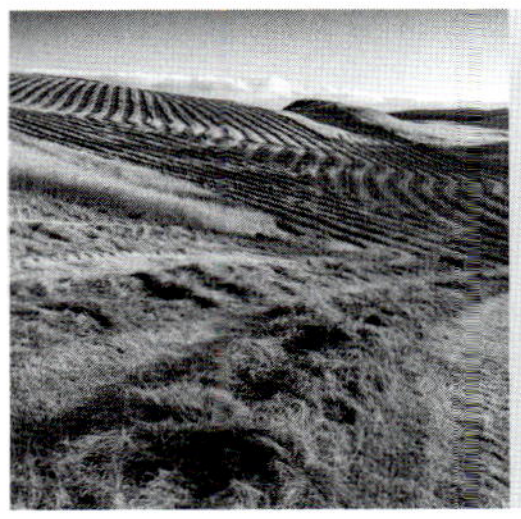

CONTOURS

- Page 141 -

Gordon took this photo of a hayfield and gave it to Don. Don saw the lines of cut grass as contours on a map.

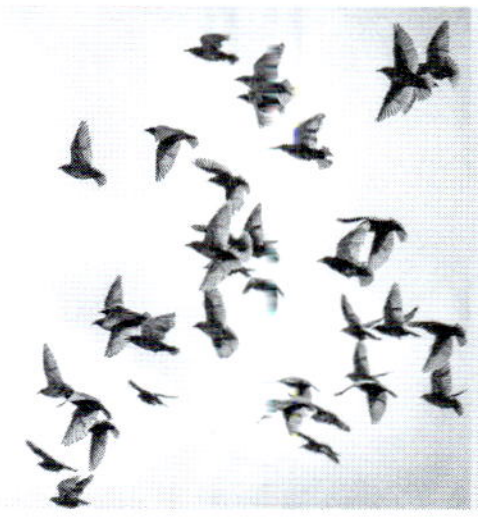

THE STARLING SYMPHONY

- Page 143 -

Smaller than a blackbird, with a short tail, pointed head and triangular wings the Common Starling (Sturnus Vulgaris) looks black at a distance but when seen close up is glossy with a sheen of purples and greens. Starlings are generally a highly social family, and a flock of starlings is called a murmuration. The cables of the Forth Road Bridge used to be black with starlings, while there was a great roost at Leith from the 1950s through to the 1970s; commuters heading home after a day's work would see thousands high above the city's crooked skyline, great flocks making for the docks.

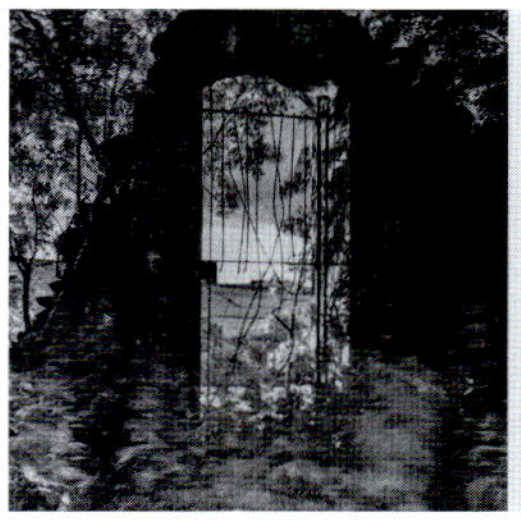

LANGSHAW ECHOES

- Page 145 -

Don has lived in Langshaw since 1984. The village lies three miles north of Galashiels. The word Langshaw means 'the long wood'. Don lives in Smithy House, formerly home to local blacksmiths, who would have operated from these premises for over 300 years. Right outside Don's home are traces of an old sawmill, as well as the flour mill that later replaced it. Across the road is the School House and next door is the Old Mill House. In days gone by the village's mill would have been powered by water drawn from the Ellwyn Burn. The burn runs all the way down to the River Tweed, flowing through what was described by Scottish laird (and reputed prophet) Thomas the Rhymer as 'Ellwyn's Fairy Dean'. Hillslap Tower, which features as Glendearg Tower in one of Sir Walter Scott's novels, lies in close proximity along with two other Border towers.

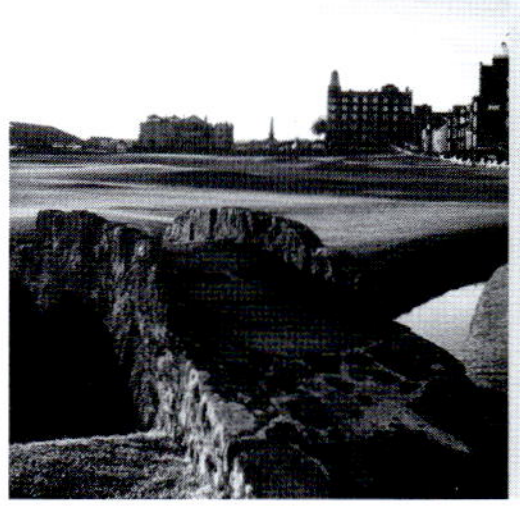

SWILCAN BRIDGE

- Page 149 -

The Swilcan Bridge, or Swilken Bridge, is a famous small stone bridge on the St Andrews Links golf course. The bridge spans the Swilcan Burn between the first and 18th fairways on the Old Course, and has itself become an important cultural icon in the sport of golf. The name Swilcan may derive from 'whirlpool, abyss in the sea', which comes from a root meaning 'to swallow'. It is tempting to see in this a reference, made either in humour or in anger, to what the burn did (and still does) to golf balls.

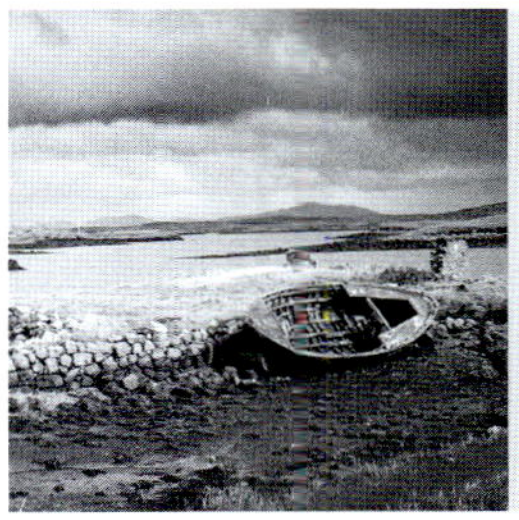

ABANDONED BOAT

- Page 151 -

Just 28ft long, the motorised open wooden boat was a lifeline for the few hardy souls who eked out a living on a remote island. For many years she plied the four miles to North Uist, carrying mail, cattle, coal and other supplies. Known by locals as Pacaid, (Gaelic for 'package') she was built more than 75 years ago for the MacDonalds, the last indigenous family to live on Heisgeir, or the Monach Islands. Her role ended in the 1940s when the islands were abandoned.

Alzheimer's disease, also referred to simply as Alzheimer's, is a chronic neurodegenerative disease that gradually worsens over time. It is the cause of 60-70 per cent of dementia cases. The most common early symptom is difficulty in remembering recent events. As the disease advances, symptoms can include problems with language, disorientation (including getting lost), mood swings, loss of motivation, not managing self-care, and behavioural issues. As a person's condition declines, they often withdraw from family and society. Gradually, bodily functions shut down, ultimately leading to death.

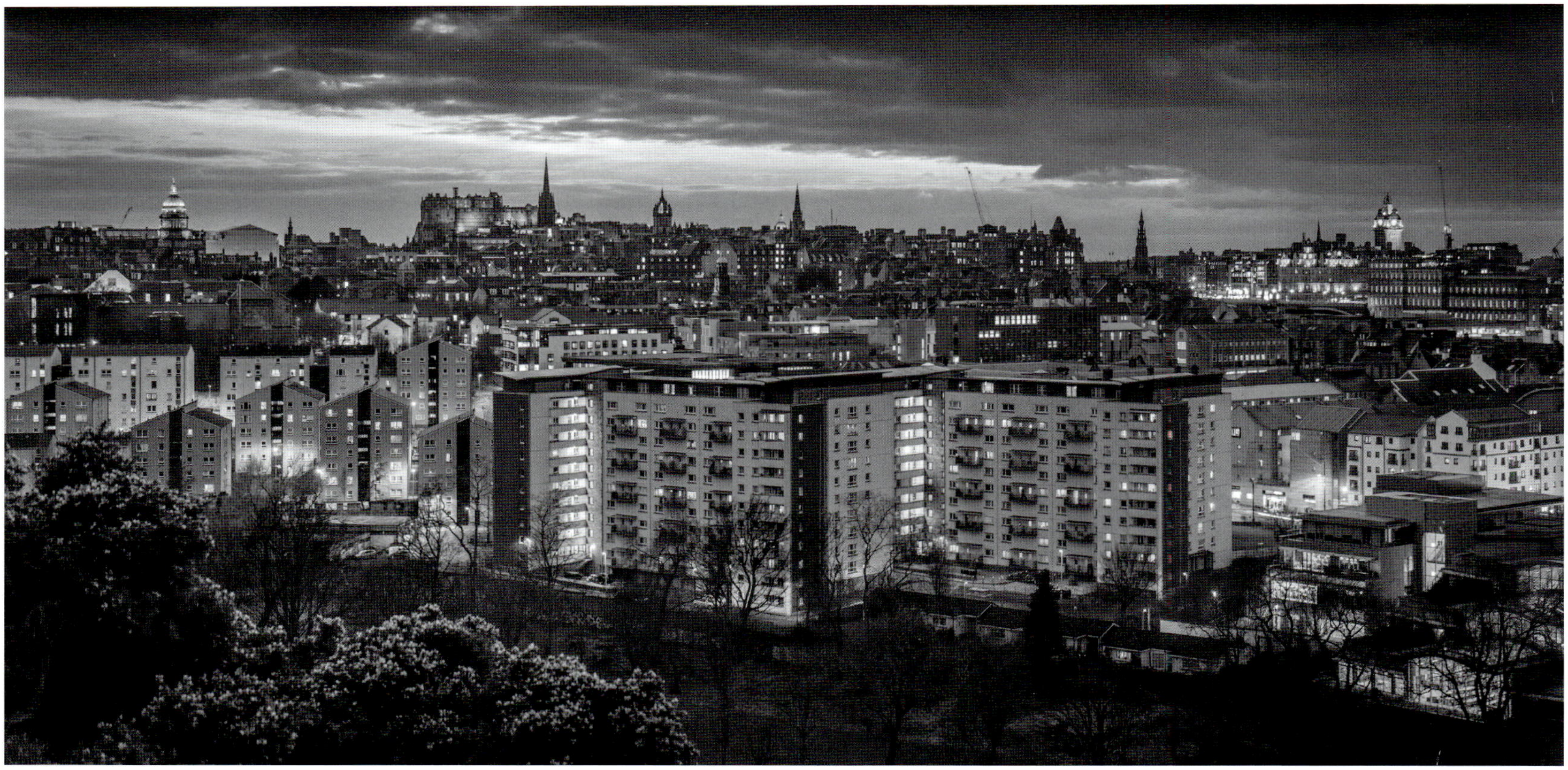

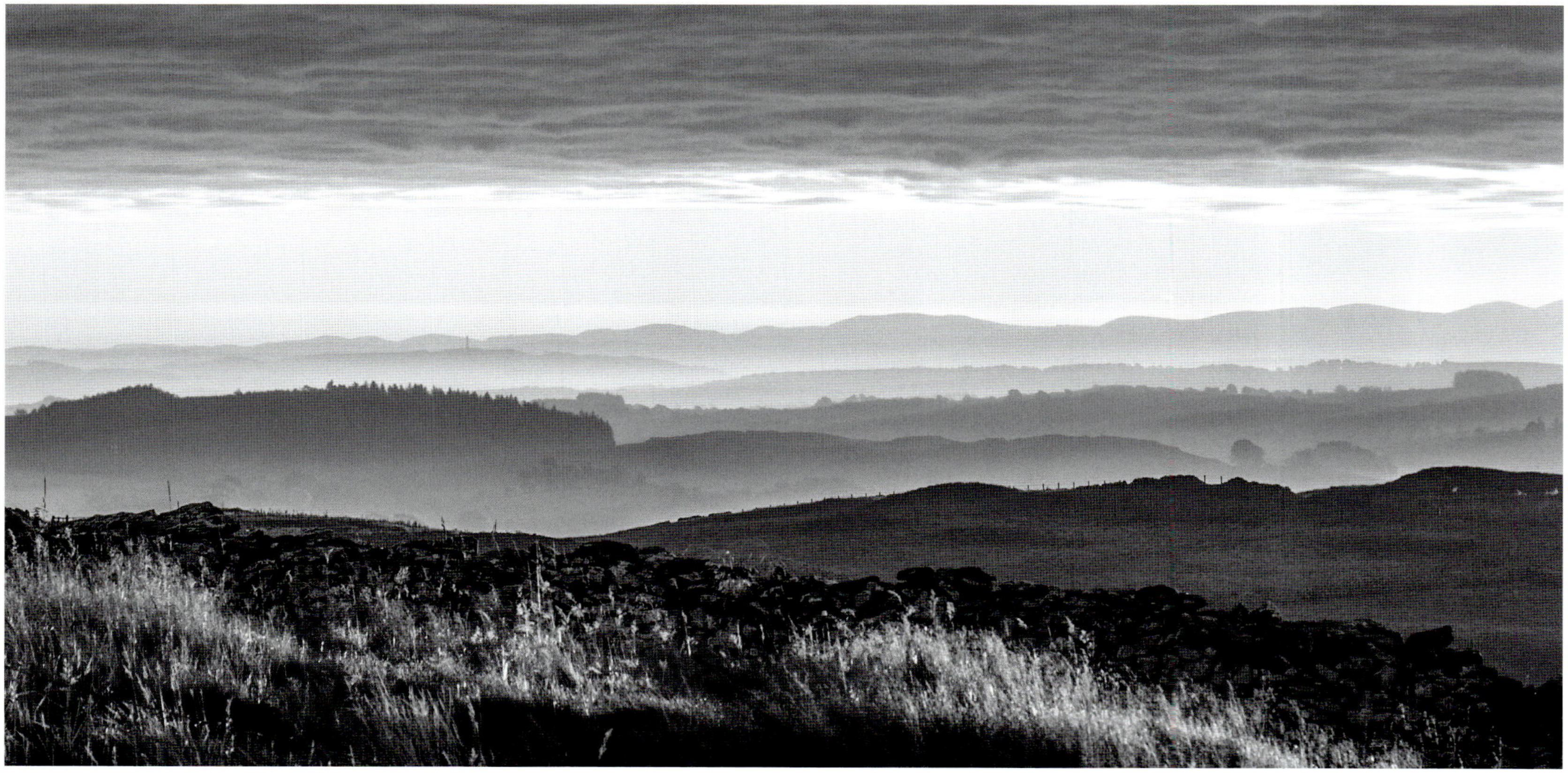

GORDON HUNTER

Gordon Hunter is a chartered surveyor who has operated in the UK commercial property market since qualifying from Edinburgh's Heriot-Watt University.

He is a founder of Ashkirk Properties, which advises corporate owners and occupiers, institutional investors, fund managers, property companies and banks. He served as managing director of Highcross Scotland, prior to which he headed up Ryden's property investment activities in the firm's Scottish, London and overseas offices. He was originally a member of Standard Life's property team.

Gordon has lectured at Aberdeen, Heriot-Watt and Napier Universities. He was a member of Scotland's Grand Slam winning rugby squad in 1984, and toured New Zealand, Australia and Romania with the national side.

His love of photography has grown over the past 20 years and he now possesses an extensive portfolio of images. Other activities include ski mountaineering and road/mountain biking. He is a member of the Empire Golf Society.

Gordon lives in the Scottish Borders with his wife Nancy, who farms. They have twins, Scott and Hayley.

DON LEDINGHAM

Don Ledingham is the founder and chief executive of Ceannas, the international leadership consultancy. A lifelong passion for education and leadership has led to his career as teacher, university lecturer, headteacher and executive director of education in two local authorities. He is the author of *A Small Step to Wise Leadership* (2017), and an honorary professor of leadership at Queen Margaret University, Edinburgh.

Don is married to Gill, and the couple have two sons, Doug and Lewis. He has lived in the Smithy House, Langshaw, in the Scottish Borders, for 35 years. Don's love of poetry stems from the moment his Primary 6 teacher, Miss Simpson, introduced him to the work of Norman MacCaig. Don's first published poem was about Edinburgh.

SINCE ONE

I can remember this fine city
When I was three,
and two,
But one......?
One, I can shake my head
And rack my brains,
And hop about on one whole leg,
But I don't know what this city was
When I was one,
and only one,
And now......?
and now I'm ten.

Donald Ledingham (Aged 10)

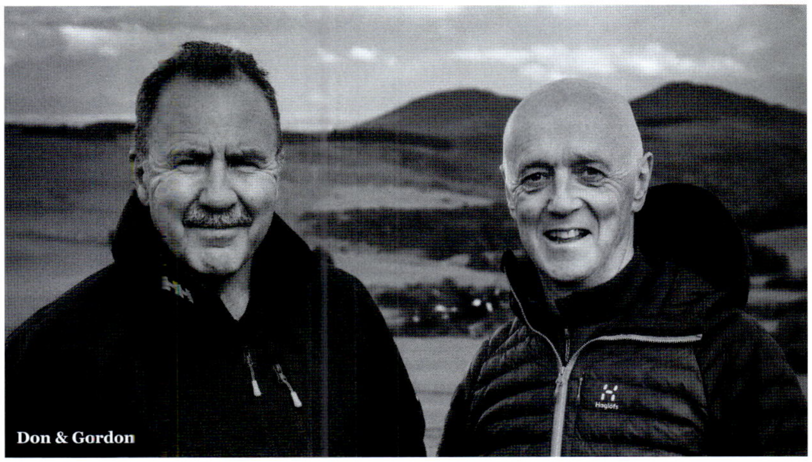
Don & Gordon

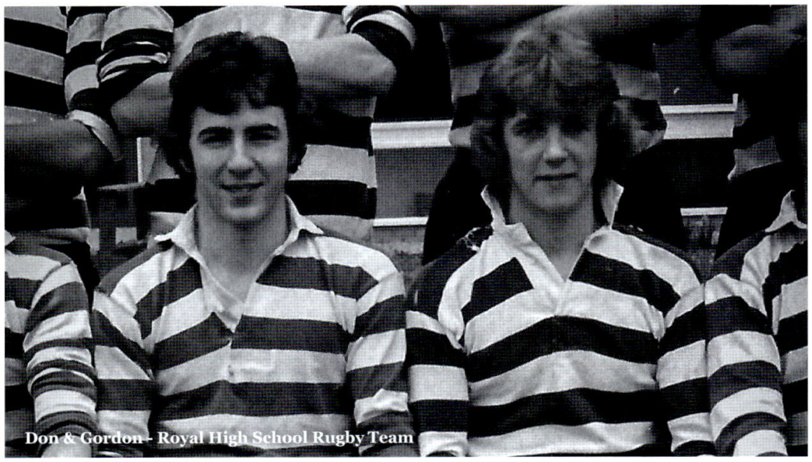
Don & Gordon - Royal High School Rugby Team

BEHIND THE PHOTOGRAPHS

My first 'real' camera was a Pentax K 1000 I bought in Hong Kong, while playing for the Scottish Co-optimists at the Hong Kong 7s in 1980 (for the record we beat New Zealand in the semi-final and were pipped by Fiji in the final – not a bad effort!). I used the Pentax to pretty poor effect for many years, not taking the time to understand the fundamentals of taking good snaps.

My interest in photography (with an emphasis on landscape) grew in the mid-90s when I invested in a Canon EOS 500, which I later upgraded to a Canon EOS 3. I began to realise the formula for how many cameras you should own is C+1 where 'C' is the current number of cameras you own! This also applies to guitars (G+1) and bikes (B+1) ... oh and skis (S+1)!

My technique improved as I read more magazines and books (no Google or YouTube in those days), and got to grips with the basics of exposure and composition. The quality of my images jumped with the acquisition of a tripod and shutter release cable. I still remember collecting my first pack of prints from Boots on Princes Street, Edinburgh, following my first 'proper attempt' at landscape photography in the beautiful Scottish Borders. I remember thinking: "Wow! Did I really take these photos?" as they were much better than I'd expected.

The well-known UK landscape photographer Charlie Waite was my hero, and I joined one of his courses in the Lake District. It inspired me to improve and to get out there during the golden daylight hours around sunrise and sunset. As one American golf course photographer said to me: "If you've not got your fly in the water you don't catch fish". In other words, you've got to get out early and late to improve your chances of catching some good light on your carefully selected subject. This, to my mind (together with good composition), creates great landscape photographs.

The use of Fuji Velvia for transparencies and Fuji Velvia for prints helped me create a series of vibrant shots.

I also met professional photographer Glyn Satterley, who came to the farm for a commission to photograph some fly fishers in a boat on Headshaw Loch enjoying a dram of whisky. We got chatting and he kindly cast an eye over some of my snaps. He gave me plenty of encouragement, telling me to stick at it and do something with my work. This was just the spur I needed to work harder on my hobby. Twenty years on and Glyn is a still a good friend who's always willing to share his wisdom.

Determined to take higher quality shots, and unaware of the imminent digital revolution, I invested in a medium format camera, a Bronica GS-1 6x7 (with 'GS' standing for Grand Shooting, which sounded good to me!).

This was the gear I used when Don and I put together our first picture-poem collection 'Borders Inheritance'. The exhibition gave me the chance, as Glyn had suggested, to 'do something with my work'.

DIGITAL

I then took a break from buying camera equipment, as the digital revolution was gathering pace ... much to the chagrin of traditionalists. However, to my way of thinking digital provided huge benefits, not least the ability to see images immediately, rather than waiting several days to get your shots back from the lab. This made learning and improving your technique a whole lot easier. My first digital SLR was a Canon EOS 20D, with a massive 8.2 megapixels!

During the *Edinburgh Revisited* project, I would typically shoot in aperture priority mode to control the depth of field. This means the camera automatically sets the shutter speed which, in turn, I vary with ISO adjustments. Long exposures are okay thanks to the tripod and shutter release cable, or in-built self-timer.

A good many of Don's poems demanded I use techniques outside my comfort zone (i.e. shooting people, interiors and street scenes). As Don sat at his desk writing poems, he was unaware of the challenges he was setting: "You need to photograph a murmuration of starlings" ... or ... "can you get some shots of the Flying Scotsman coming out of Waverley Station?" ... or ... "you need to capture the precise moment when the One O'Clock Gun is fired" (which I nearly missed due to a tourist asking me a question at three seconds to one!). However, I've really enjoyed the various challenges, and the viewer will no doubt judge the worth of my work. One day I'll be able to call myself a photographer.

COLOUR OR BLACK & WHITE?
We made an early decision to go for a black & white, fine art look for *Edinburgh Revisited*. To me there's something emotive and timeless about black and white images, and Edinburgh is certainly a timeless city.

Historically some photographers took the view that serious, documentary and fine art photography must be shot in black-and-white. Legendary photographer Henri Cartier-Bresson, known for his evocative monochrome shots, once quipped that 'colour is bullshit'.

In saying this we weren't trying to be arty, we simply felt that cityscapes photographed better in black & white. Don and I felt books mixing colour and black & white photos just don't work so well.

Our decision definitely influenced my various photo shoots. High contrast shots work in black and white, and where possible (and relevant to the poem) I tried to shoot images which emphasised form, contrast, and shapes. Everything was shot in colour but converted to black & white in post-production.

MY CURRENT GEAR:
Canon 5D MK IV – This is my main camera body following an upgrade from the 5D MK III, which now acts as my back-up. The big difference is the full-frame sensor increasing from 22.3 megapixels to 30.4 megapixels, allowing a lot more room to create very large, high-quality prints. It also has a touch screen, offering more versatility and creativity options.
Canon EF 24 – 105 f4L IS USM – My most used lens. It offers amazing image quality throughout the focal range, and is perfect for a wide variety of landscape situations. It has also proved useful for the non-landscape shoots I've undertaken on the Edinburgh Revisited project.
Canon EF 100 – 400mm f/4.5 – 5.6L IS II USM – This lens lets me get in close to distant subjects and take compression effect shots. These pick out distant details that demand a second look – Hinterland being a good example. The image stabiliser and high-quality optics deliver superb sharpness.
Canon EF 16 – 35mm f/2.8L III USM – This is my wide-angled lens and allows me to get in really close to the foreground interest. Again, it offers great sharpness through the zoom range. I have occasionally used 'focus stacking' to achieve front-to-back sharpness.
Kirk L-Bracket - Allows instant rotation of my camera 90° and prevents ball head slippage (one of those accessories I wish I'd bought years ago!).
GITZO GT 2532 Tripod – A lightweight and sturdy tripod, ideal when lugging heavy equipment up mountains or through the streets of Edinburgh. I use it in conjunction with a Sirui K-20X Ball Head with quick release plate.
Canon TC-80N3 Shutter Release - this ensures there is no camera shake when releasing the shutter, resulting in sharper images. The mirror lock-up facility on the 5D is a great help. It also acts as a timer during long exposures, which can often last several minutes.
LEE Filters – 100mm System - I use 6 stop and 10 stop Lee ND filters, graduated ND filters, and a polarising filter which causes minimal vignetting (light fall-off) even at 16mm. This is a simple and quick to use high quality filter system.
LEE Filters Pouch – Keeps all my filters together and safe.
Hoodman Outdoor HoodLoupe – This allows me to better view images on the camera's LCD screen, cutting out all sun glare.
Mindshift Backlight 26L – A really solid backpack style camera bag. Comfortable and with room for all my gear (plus room for a laptop, spare clothes, food etc.).

POST-PRODUCTION:
Adobe Lightroom – I use this amazing bit of software to edit and organise my library of RAW image files. The editing includes lens correction, cropping, adjustments to exposure, whites & blacks, highlights & shadows, contrast and clarity. In some images I introduce a slight vignette.
Adobe Photoshop – primarily used for dust spot removal, focus stacking and stitching panoramas.

PRINTING:
Canon ImagePROGRAF PRO-100 Printer – Produces fantastic prints up to A2 in size.
Papers – I use a number of fine art inkjet printing papers, depending on the image I'm printing and the target result. Is it colour or black & white? Does it demand a gloss, semi-gloss or matt finish? The papers include: Fotospeed Platinum Baryta 300gsm & Smooth Cotton 300gsm, Hahnemühle Photo Rag 300gsm and Bamboo 290gsm.

G.H.

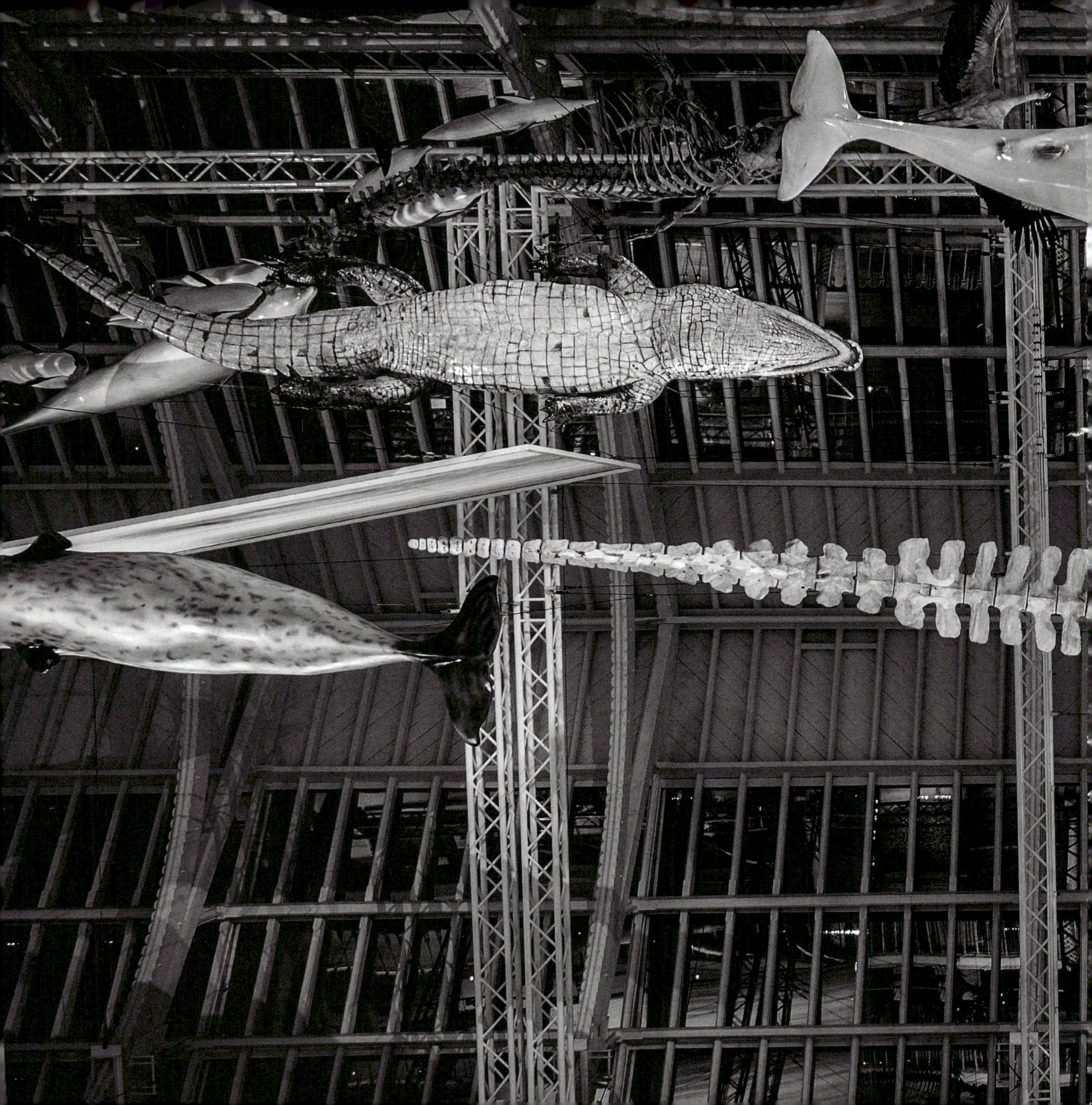